CONTEMPORARY ISSUES IN THEORY AND RESEARCH

Recent Titles in Contributions in Sociology
Series Editor: Don Martindale

CONTEMPORARY ISSUES IN THEORY AND RESEARCH

A Metasociological Perspective

Edited by
WILLIAM E. SNIZEK
ELLSWORTH R. FUHRMAN
MICHAEL K. MILLER

Contributions in Sociology, Number 33

GREENWOOD PRESS
Westport, Connecticut • London, England

Library of Congress Cataloging in Publication Data

Main entry under title:

Contemporary issues in theory and research.

    (Contributions in sociology; no. 33 ISSN 0084-9278)
    Bibliography: p.
    Includes Index.
    1. Sociology—Addresses, essays, lectures.
2. Sociological research—Addresses, essays, lectures.
I. Snizek, William E. II. Fuhrman, Ellsworth R.
III. Miller, Michael K.
HM24.C654   301   78-4024
ISBN 0-313-20409-8

Library of Congress Catalog Card Number: 78-4024
ISBN: 0-313-20409-8
ISSN: 0084-9278

First published in 1979

Greenwood Press, Inc.
51 Riverside Avenue, Westport, Connecticut 06880

Printed in the United States of America

10 9 8 7 6 5 4 3 2 1

CONTENTS

INTRODUCTION

"Metasociology," a term popularized by Paul Furfey in his book entitled *The Scope and Method of Sociology: A Metasociological Treatise*, refers to that branch of sociology concerned with investigating the assumptions and value judgments underlying the theories and methods employed by sociologists. Such assumptions and value judgments often begin with the assertion that sociology is a science and proceed to incorporate the various theoretical (ontological) and methodological (epistemological) choices made daily. Needless to say, such assumptive choices directly affect the very content of sociology, thereby making metasociology an enormously important and far-reaching area of inquiry.

In many ways, metasociology represents a mechanism for mapping the discipline of sociology. As such, it can illuminate the history of sociology, its present status, and future form. In addition, metasociology also contributes to make explicit the assumptions underlying sociological investigations prior to the act of substantive theorizing. In so doing, discussions concerning assumptions remain analytically distinct from those of substantive sociology. Finally, by making assumptive choices explicit, the field of metasociology augments communication among scholars. Much in the form of psychotherapeutic dialogue, metasociology enables misinterpretations, noninterpretations, and the uninterpreted to be illuminated and, hopefully, resolved.

Stated in succinct fashion, the potential contributions of metasociology, and to some extent of this volume, are to: (1) render order and parsimony to the various prior, present, and future events which have or will occur in the discipline of sociology, (2) examine, in some detail, various of the assumptive choices made by sociologists in the conduct of their theory and research, and (3) further communication on basic issues among scholars. It is in this spirit of self-reflection and open communication, then, that we the editors make explicit the major premise of this volume, namely, "that knowledge of one's assumptions is *mutatis mutandis* to know something about the world one wishes to study."

The essays in this volume are divided into four major groupings. Part I, comprised of essays by Martindale, Ritzer, and Wiley, is intended to give an overview of the various persons, schools of thought, and paradigms which comprise the discipline of sociology. The next two parts each address a major aspect of metasociological inquiry, those of ontology and epistemology, respectively. The former addresses questions having to do with *what* one studies (theory); the latter, questions of *how* one goes about studying what it is one studies (method). Although obviously intertwined, these two broad questions are analytically separated for purposes of presentation and discussion. Furthermore, an attempt is made in Parts II and III to have the respective essays in each section complement one another. Thus, while Bealer addresses the ontological issue of one's unit of analysis in Part II, Blau focuses on the epistemological counterpart to this same question, one's level of analysis, in Part III. Similarly, Coser in his essay both explicitly and implicitly outlines what for him is the "substance" of sociology, while Cicourel details what he considers to be a promising way of conducting research—given *his* particular definition of the substance of sociology. And, finally, Blalock and Leik explore the nature of "good" theory from a theoretical and applied prospectus, respectively. Part IV, comprised of essays by Snizek, Tiryakian, and Sjoberg and Vaughan, focuses on the overall need for a more critical awareness of the assumptions underlying the theoretical and methodological approaches employed, and for a more reflexive sociology in general.

This anthology is intended to be used in upper divisional undergraduate or graduate courses in the broad areas of sociological theory, research methods, or some combination of the two. This book is also well suited for courses in the sociology of sociology, sociology of knowledge, history of sociology, and courses in the principles and issues of sociology. With the exception of the essay by Coser, which is a slightly revised version of his 1975 presidential address to the ASA, later published in the *A.S.R.* (December 1975), all essays in this anthology are original works written specifically for this volume. Every attempt was made by the contributors, initially, and later by the editors, to make each essay as readible as possible. Owing to space limitations, contributors should not be held responsible by the reader for omissions of either depth or breadth.

Finally, every attempt has been made, in assembling this volume, to include as many and as varied approaches to the field of sociology as possible. For example, Coser's essay criticizing the use of both "sophisticated statistical procedures" and "ethnomethodology," is coupled with essays by Blalock and Leik defending the former, and Cicourel the latter. Although some students unfortunately may find the juxtaposing of differing orientations confusing or disquieting, it is our intent by this means to spark debate and further inquiry into various of the issues raised herein.

ACKNOWLEDGMENTS

We wish to express our sincere gratitude to all those scholars who graciously agreed to write an essay for this collection. Without their contributions this book would not have been possible. In addition, we particularly wish to acknowledge the continued help and encouragement given us throughout this entire project by Alex Simirenko and Robert Bealer, of the Pennsylvania State University, Don Martindale, of the University of Minnesota, and Robert K. Merton, of Columbia University. At a time when some would question the accessibility and responsiveness of leading figures in the profession, these individuals, along with all contributors to this book, could not have been more accessible and responsive, nor offered us more assistance. To all our sincere thanks.

We also wish to thank Randall White for his invaluable editorial suggestions and unyielding attention to detail in the proofreading of various essays. Similarly, we wish to thank Deborah Brooks for her assistance in preparing the manuscript, and Cindy Crawford and Brenda Creeley for their endless patience in typing and retyping various portions of this anthology. Finally, our thanks to Clifton D. Bryant, of the Virginia Polytechnic Institute and State University, and E. Walter Coward, Jr., of Cornell University. As department chairmen, both supplied important logistical support in the form of departmental resources. More importantly, as colleagues both offered enthusiastic support for and helpful advice on the task we had undertaken.

CONTEMPORARY ISSUES IN THEORY AND RESEARCH

PART I

SOCIOLOGICAL THEORIES, IDEOLOGIES, AND PARADIGMS

This part explores the metasociological choices made by the analyst-historian of sociological theory. The differences within the discipline over the appropriate unit of analysis and methods of study are likewise evident in the writings of the historians and analysts. This lack of agreement then concerning how to order the discipline means that whereas some focus on theories and theory groups, others prefer ideologies or paradigms as the starting point. Clearly, the metasociological choices which govern the ordering of sociology have ramifications for what one eventually discovers or explores. These differing metasociological choices and their attendant consequences clearly emerge in the following essays by Don Martindale, George Ritzer, and Norbert Wiley.

Don Martindale's essay "Ideologies, Paradigms, and Theories" addresses the issue of how to order the sociological enterprise. According to Martindale, the 1960s and 1970s saw many traditional sociological premises challenged. In brief, his essay focuses on the challenge of an ideologically commited sociology and the questionable status of ordering sociology by paradigms. He further argues that the only reliable guide for the ordering of sociology is through the study and exploration of theories and the schools which supported and institutionalized them.

In a provocative manner, Martindale states that ideologies are easily separable from scientific theories. Ideologies possess persuasive intent and orient themselves toward what the world ought to be like. Theories, however, are simple descriptions and explanations of some phenomena—what is. He suggests that even though ideological commitment energizes new areas of research, it should not be confused with scientific theory. In the social realm there are no major discoveries without passion; nevertheless, this should never be confused with the discovery of empirical regularities.

Paradigms, unlike theories, have been variously defined. Martindale traces the meaning of paradigm through its use in grammar, the work of Robert Merton, Thomas Kuhn and his critics, Robert Friedrichs and George Ritzer. The term "paradigm" has such an ambiguous meaning that very little is gained by explicating sociology as a science populated by multiple paradigms (Martindale suggests some potential problems if we choose to view sociology as having them). Ultimately, he argues that one sense of paradigm can be saved—its parallelness with the ideal type of Max Weber. Interestingly enough, ideal types are only heuristic devices and cannot serve as replacements for scientific theories.

The traditional approach for ordering sociology has been based on the ideas of scientific theory and methods. Martindale briefly reviews the development of sociological theory from the seventeenth century to the 1960s. His classification system is based on the methodological choice of positivism or nonpositivism, while the theory types are classified according to their elementaristic or holistic character. This fourfold schema is then utilized to discuss the emergence of sociological theories in the 1960s and 1970s.

George Ritzer's essay "Toward an Integrated Sociological Paradigm" sets a different problematic for the ordering of sociological theory. As Ritzer understands it, sociology consists of multiple paradigms even though there may be disagreement about the quantity and nature of them. Ritzer argues that sociology needs an integrated paradigm, which he outlines in this essay.

Ritzer begins his essay by reviewing the work of Thomas Kuhn, as well as describing the emergence of new paradigms, recounting a recent attack on ethnomethodology by Coser (see this volume), and reviewing his own work and a criticism of it by Snizek. This material sets the stage for his central task—paradigmatic integration. In previous works, Ritzer has argued that sociology is dominated by three paradigms: social factism, social definitionism, and social behaviorism. Each paradigm emphasizes only selected aspects of behavior: macro-objective, macro-subjective, micro-objective, micro-subjective. According to Ritzer, sociology needs a paradigm which can synthesize each of the aforementioned elements: the macro-subjective, macro-objective, micro-subjective, and micro-objective realms of social behavior. In reviewing the work of Marx, Weber, and Parsons, Ritzer attempts to demonstrate that the basis for an integrated paradigm, at the macro-level, exists in their writings. At the micro-level, the writings of Mead, Schutz, Berger and Luckmann, and Gerth and Mills are utilized for their contributions to micro-level analysis. Ritzer concludes his essay by positing an outline of an exemplar for an integrated paradigm which includes macro-objective (law, language, and bureaucracy), macro-subjective (norms, values, and culture), micro-objective (conflict, cooperation, and exchange), and micro-subjective (mind, self) elements. Contrary to what the reader might assume, the exemplar for this integrated paradigm is not intended to replace any of the existing paradigms. Finally, Ritzer makes a strong case for the idea that an integrated paradigm must be comparative, historical, and dialectical.

Norbert Wiley's essay "The Rise and Fall of Dominating Theories in American Sociology" orders the discipline in a manner different from either Martindale's or Ritzer's. Wiley's essay represents an analytic history of sociology in America. He examines the history of American sociology from three interrelated perspectives: ideas, theory groups, and control over the intellectual means of production. According to Wiley, a theory must be strong in all three regards if it is to achieve domination. He also explains that the history of sociology can be scrutinized as a history of "ins" versus "outs." Sociology, he further argues, has never been dominated by one theory; yet some have achieved relative hegemony.

Wiley divides his analytic history into four distinct periods: the evolutionary, the Chicago School, functionalism, and the contemporary interregnum. The evolutionary period was characterized by the establishment of sociology in American universities, the founding of the *American Journal of Sociology*, and the development of a professional association. From another perspective, the early history of American sociology can be seen as being ruled by four currents of thought: evolution, German Idealism, traditional economics, and ethical commitments. Eventually, these patterns of thought were discarded by the Chicago School, which was established and perpetrated by figures such as Albion Small, W. I. Thomas, Ernest W. Burgess, Ellsworth Faris, and Robert E. Park. Wiley argues that the Chicago School was dominated by a pre-Blumerian kind of symbolic interactionism. This perspective tended to utilize single case studies, awareness of processes, and a great interest in, and perception of, the gestalt qualities of social phenomena rather than in the discovery of social laws. Chicago lost its dominance at the 1935 ASS convention when the majority voted to establish a new journal as the official voice of sociology, thus ending the supreme reign of the *American Journal of Sociology*. The positivists, having founded the *American Sociological Review*, now held control over not only the journal but also the access to Washington money and domination of the ASS.

Functionalism emerged in the late forties or early fifties. The functionalist hold was not unequivocal because it was competing with both the Chicago School and the positivists. Wiley describes Parsons' intellectual legacy and the social conditions under which he and the functionalists achieved dominance. Nevertheless, he indicates that the positivists in spite of not possessing strong theoretical commitments maintained control over many of the intellectual means of production. Positivist control, then, was at least an equal to that of the functionalist school. The highly politicized decade of the sixties only helped to further the cause of the positivists. Yet this positivism was unlike that of Giddings and Lundberg in that it relied upon technological development—the computer.

By the mid-seventies (the contemporary interregnum) everything was up in the air, so to speak. Both theory and methods were inundated with variations of older themes: dialectics, ideal types, ethnomethodology, cognitive sociology. Wiley concludes his essay by arguing that contemporary theorists and theory groups may find a common ground if they return to the classical problem of social order and view their own solutions to this problem as partial ones.

Martindale, Ritzer, and Wiley, in seeking to bring order into the sociological enterprise, do so from differing metasociological perspectives. Martindale and Ritzer concern themselves mainly with ideational groupings. Yet they are not in agreement concerning the role of paradigms for ordering the discipline of sociology. Whereas Ritzer clearly finds paradigms useful, Martindale is convinced that they are ambiguous in meaning and leave no clear basis for distinguishing ideologies from theories. Wiley, on the other hand, stresses multiple levels of analysis—ideas, theory groups, and control over the intellectual means of production. His analysis suggests that the predominance of certain theories is not due to simply their explanatory power. If one is going to examine the dominance of certain theory groups, then we must also understand the control over the intellectual means of production. The essays in Part I further suggest that the ordering of sociology, as a discipline, is as multifaceted as the theories and theory groups which the writers purport to examine. In part, this is due to the metasociological choices made by the analyst-historian of sociology.

Don Martindale

IDEOLOGIES, PARADIGMS, AND THEORIES

The 1950s was a period of rare consensus in American society and American sociology. American society had emerged from World War II as the foremost power on earth militarily, politically, and economically. A generation whose aspirations had successively been frustrated and deferred by depression and war was anxious to transfer to the suburbs, settle down, raise families, and enjoy the hard-earned new affluence. The international cold war and domestic McCarthyism tended to shut off and suppress radical dissent. At the same time, structure functionalism, America's first endemic form of sociological holism, seemed about to swallow up the last traces of opposition.

However, the consensus both in the society and in sociology was to be short-lived. The minority movements, the rise and fall of the poverty program, the ugly course of the Indochina war, the Watergate scandals, and, finally, simultaneous inflation and unemployment would dampen the nationalistic euphoria and transform the sense of domestic well-being into alienation and dismay. In sociology, theories that had long been out of favor were reexamined; the hard-won tradition of objectivity was challenged; arguments were advanced for an ideologically committed social science; humanism and science were conceptualized as antithetical, and a rift appeared between an antipositivistic sociology and a hardened positivism which paraded under the names of "theory construction" and "mathematical sociology."

In response to the chaotic state of the discipline that resulted from all of the currents and cross-currents of the 1960s and 1970s, repeated calls have been issued to bring order to sociological thought. The editors of the present anthology have suggested ideologies or paradigms or even the more traditional types of theories and research traditions as a means of bringing order out of the contemporary sociological chaos. Since there are enough problems broached in the editor's proposal to require a dozen monographs, I shall confine myself in the short space available to me to a few observations on the nature and place of ideology, paradigms, and theories in our discipline.

IDEOLOGIES

Few topics are more important or more confused than the place of ideology in social science. Alvin Gouldner (1973) led a screaming pack of assorted radicals with his denunciation of Max Weber's (1946) plea for social science objectivity. This radical position has varied from the view (1) that all sociology, whatever its pretenses, is value committed; through the view (2) that what current sociology most needs is a sociology of relevance; to the view (3) that sociology can only be advanced by forthright partisanship. In response to the many-sided assault on the tradition of objectivity, sociologists of the positivistic tradition have, in turn, hardened their position with demands for rigorous theory construction. In the course of the ongoing debate the place of ideology in sociology has grown increasingly moot.

Superficially, it is not difficult to distinguish scientific theory from ideology. A scientific theory is a set of generalizations for explaining a body of phenomena; an ideology is a set of arguments advanced with persuasive intent. Scientific theory is oriented to description and explanation, to what "is"; ideology is oriented to action, to some person's view of what "ought to be." In composition a scientific theory is made up of hypotheses or laws which it forms into an explanation; an ideology is composed of values which it forms into an axiology. The criteria of scientific theory are truth and falsity, validity and invalidity; the criteria of an ideology are some person's notions of goodness and badness. These contrasts may be summarized as in Table 1.

Offhand it would appear that the differences between ideologies and social

Table 1.

IDEOLOGY VERSUS SCIENTIFIC THEORY

Characteristic	Ideology	Scientific Theory
Objective	Prescriptive	Explanatory Descriptive
Location of operation	The World of Action	The World of Thought
Component elements	Values formed into an axiology	Laws formed into an explanation
Criteria	Good and bad	True and false

science theories are sufficiently evident to preclude confusing them. However, ideologies and social science theories are both anchored in the requirements of human social life. All human life involves both the necessity to take factual account of situations (to describe and explain) and the necessity to make choices and to act (to allocate priorities). Elements of evaluative preference are involved when one chooses a scientific career over others. Once launched upon a career, a scientist must choose some problems for study and omit others. There is no good reason to restrict the concept of ideology, as is sometimes done, to the more elaborate and bizarre forms of organizing preferences into an axiology such as those represented by the ideologies of classes, special interest groups, parties, and institutional elites. In the strictest sense, there is no possible human situation that could see an end of ideology. At best, one could expect the disappearance of some kinds of axiological systems in favor of others. At the same time the attempt to appraise facts objectively and to account for them without distortion, whether apart from or within the scientific process, should be seen as the difficult task it is. However, when it is accomplished, action becomes more efficient.

To compound the problems for the social sciences, a significant segment of their subject matter is made up of the ideas, notions, evaluations, and strategies of their human subjects. In other words, the ideological dimensions of interpersonal actions form much of the content of sociological study. Moreover, since much of the time the social scientist has personal values which differ from those of the subjects, an ever-present danger is the introduction, consciously or unconsciously, of private biases into the research. Furthermore, the subjects of research may recognize differences between their own values and those of the investigator and distort the findings either by giving what they think the researcher wants or needs, or by concealing from the investigator what they think might be disapproved of. For example, when research by black and white investigators of black subjects is compared, considerable discrepancies in findings appear.

In view of the multiple sources of bias, from the side of both the researcher and the subjects, it might seem that the safest route to scientific objectivity is to limit scientific research to neutral individuals (i.e., those individuals without intense commitments). However, human affairs are never simple. When one seeks the best and fullest evidence in an area of human endeavor, one usually finds it necessary to consult the very persons who were drawn to the area by deep personal involvement. Much of the best evidence on Old Testament materials has been produced by Protestants who had been drawn to the study by their religious commitments. In a similar manner much of the best evidence on Jewish social history and Catholic social history has been produced by pious Jews and Catholics, respectively. Some of the most penetrating studies of blacks, Chicanos, and women are being currently produced by black, Chicano, and female sociologists.

Passionate interest in a particular outcome can create selective perception and distorted interpretation such that one sees only evidence and argument for his/her cause. But only a scoundrel will manufacture evidence. Moreover, the exposure of carelessness and bias may do serious damage not only to a researcher but to the area of interest. A case in point is the recent exposure of methodological carelessness, and perhaps even the outright fraudulent fabrication, of data by Cyril Burt, the late authority on identical-twin-based studies of the genetic foundations of intelligence. At the same time, it is often the person with no particular interest in an area who stops short of the full evidence or who permits himself to be persuaded by superficial interpretations. The principle stands: In human affairs there is no major achievement without passion.

The confusion over the place of ideology in sociology is compounded further by the argument advanced by nineteenth-century collectivists and occasionally repeated by their twentieth-century follers: All social science *is* ideology. Much of the appeal of collectivism in the nineteenth century was based on the failure of their rationalistic predecessors to construct a rational picture of the world in which logical, empirical, and evaluative types of knowledge had a consistent and unambiguous place. The system of knowledge appeared to be in crisis. Empirical knowledge appeared to lack the certainty of logical knowledge; moral knowledge seemed to require presuppositions about action, such as freedom, which were in apparent direct contradiction with presuppositions about action in a context of scientific explanation. The answer by the collectivists was twofold: (1) that these were apparent contradictions due to analyzing thought from a static frame of reference; and (2) that they arose from analyzing thought from the standpoint of the experience of the isolated individual rather than the spiritual (mental) development of the entire community over time. Thus the holists argued that in the collective experience of the community over time, logical, empirical, and moral knowledge were interdeveloped. No truth is eternal, but rather relative to some particular set of historical circumstances. Contradictions are not only temporary but are necessary for development and are resolved in action, or as some of the collectivists were and are fond of saying, *praxis*.

This argument unavoidably committed its proponents to the conviction of an inseparable relation between thought and the rest of collective man's social condition, a relationship expressed in a terminology of super-, sub-, and infrastructures. It also carried with it the assumption that value commitments (ideology) are inseparable in principle from theory.

One of the few persons to confront the problem of objectivity directly from a collectivistic point of view was Karl Mannheim (1949). He found himself faced with this question: If all social knowledge can only reflect a particular situation at a particular time, how is objective social science knowledge possible? He tried to solve the problem in two stages: (1) by drawing a distinction between relativism and relationism and (2) by counting on the intellectual to supply a transperspective perspective.

Relationism . . . states that every assertion can only be relationally formulated. It becomes relativism only when it is linked with the older static ideal of eternal, unperspectivistic truths independent of the subjective experience of the observer, and when it is judged by this alien ideal of absolute truth. (Mannheim, 1949:270)

However, it should be noted that this formulation does not help much. Although it makes truth relational, it makes objectivity relative. Mannheim seriously toyed with the idea of resolving the problem of a relative objectivity by appealing to the unique perspective of a socially unattached intelligentsia, a characterization he borrowed from Alfred Weber. This characterization posited that intellectuals tend to be recruited from all classes and hence tend to reflect all social positions within their own.

There are two courses of action which the unattached intellectuals have actually taken as ways out of this middle-of-the-road position: first, what amounts to a largely voluntary affiliation with one or other of the various antagonistic classes; second, scrutiny of their own social moorings and the quest for the fulfillment of their mission as the predestined advocate of the intellectual interests of the whole. (Mannheim, 1949:140)

This, however, is still not very satisfactory, for it is not made clear how an intellectual recruited from the laboring class will transcend his perspective by, say, also adding the perspective of the intellectual to it. Nor is it clear why he should agree with another intellectual who combines an upper-class perspective with that of the intellectual. If he considered at all the possibility of a calculus of perspectives, Mannheim rejected it as absurd. He suggested rather:

. . . when observers have different perspectives, "objectivity" is attainable only in a . . . round-about fashion. In such a case, what has been correctly but differently perceived by the two perspectives must be understood in the light of the differences in structure of these varied modes of perception. An effort must be made to find a formula for translating the results of one into those of the other and to discover a common denominator for these varying perspectivistic insights. (Mannheim, 1949:270)

Although the model for Mannheim's reasoning was provided by physical perception, it is clear that this was an analogy for dealing with differences in orientation between people when they possess varying value commitments. More important than his success in reconciling conflicts in a holistic position on man, society, culture, and social thought was the fact that in his effort to establish the possibility of the achievement of scientific objectivity, he was being forced, step by step, to reinstitute analytical distinctions between thought and action, value and fact.

In summary, it can be said that the place of values and ideology is moot. It is moot because of the difficulty of achieving objectivity when value decisions surround the scientific enterprise and its conduct, and appear among the basic properties of the human subjects of the social scientist. But it is also an issue because of the persistence of social science traditions which, in principle, seek to erase the distinction between ideology and social science theory. It is under these circumstances that Karl Mannheim's torments over the problem of objectivity in social science take on especial fascination. Starting with collectivistic suppositions, he reintroduced the distinctions among logical, empirical, and evaluative forms of knowledge.

In view of all of the violent forces against it, scientific objectivity, when it is in fact realized, may be seen to have many of the characteristics of the moment of calm at the eye of a hurricane.

PARADIGMS

In grammar, a paradigm is a set of all forms containing a particular element such as the set of all inflected forms of a single root, stem, or theme. It is also a display in fixed arrangement of such a set. Paradigm also has the secondary meaning of a pattern or example. By extension from the secondary meaning, paradigm has occasionally been employed as a euphemism for ideal type. An ideal type is a thought-model which combines ideas and evidence into an analytical construct. In Weber's words:

An ideal type is formed by the one-sided *accentuation* of one or more points of view and by the synthesis of a great many diffuse, discrete, more or less present and occasionally absent *concrete individual* phenomena, which are arranged according to those one-sidedly emphasized viewpoints into a unified *analytical construct*. (Weber, 1949:90)

Still other meanings of the term appear in the 1950s with Robert Merton's usages. In his introduction to the second edition of his essays, Merton argued:

As here construed, codification is the orderly and compact arrangement of systematized fruitful experience with procedures of inquiry and with the substantive findings which result from the use of these procedures. . . . At periodic points in the book, I use the device of the *analytical paradigm* for presenting codified materials. (Merton, 1957:13)

The first of his paradigms was an outline of concepts and problems thought to be important for functional analysis; the second was a typology of possible behaviors resulting from cross-tabulating the orientation of an individual to cultural goals as positive or negative, and dichotomizing his willingness to use the legitimate means for attaining them as positive or negative. The third of Merton's paradigms consisted of a set of questions and an outline of possible answers, each designed to make uniform the systematic evaluation of a number of different positions on the sociology of knowledge. In the context of Merton's work paradigm had acquired the meaning of "summary outlines" and "heuristic check lists."

Merton discovered no fewer than five sterling virtues in paradigms of this sort for increasing the precision of qualitative analysis in sociology: (1) they provide an economical arrangement of central concepts; (2) they tend to make presuppositions explicit; (3) they advance the cumulation of theoretical interpretation; (4) they suggest systematic cross-tabulation of central concepts; and (5) they codify qualitative analysis in a manner approximating the empirical rigor of quantitative analysis (Merton, 1957:13-17).

In 1962 the historian of science Thomas S. Kuhn gave the concept of paradigm new meaning and significance. In a manner that could not be without fascination to social scientists, Kuhn addressed himself to the endless disagreements that prevail in the "soft" sciences in contrast to the symphony of consensus that usually seems to prevail in the "hard" sciences. In view of the long-standing inferiority feeling of so many practitioners of the social sciences, it is small wonder that hearts leaped when Kuhn announced his discovery that the difference was not one of principle, but a condition of historical stage. The soft sciences are in the preparadigm, and the hard sciences are in the postparadigm, stage. In the first meaning he assigned paradigms as "universally recognized scientific achievements that for a time provide model problems and solutions to a community of practitioners" (Kuhn, 1962:x). A paradigm begins its life as an achievement sufficiently arresting to attract a company of devotees, but it is sufficiently ambiguous to leave all sorts of problems to be solved. Moreover, it would appear a paradigm contains a whole potential system of science within its scope.

> Achievements that share these two characteristics I shall henceforth refer to as "paradigms," a term that relates closely to "normal science." By choosing it, I mean to suggest that some accepted examples of actual scientific practice—examples which include law, theory, application, and instrumentation together—provide models from which spring particular coherent traditions of scientific research. (Kuhn, 1962:10)

The endless bickering of the soft sciences arises from the fact that they are still in the preparadigm stage. Having entered the paradigm stage, the hard sciences are privileged to engage in "normal" science, that is, the routine tasks laid down in the paradigm. "These three classes of problems—determination of significant fact, matching of facts with theory, and articulation of theory—exhaust, I think, the literature of normal science, both empirical and theoretical" (Kuhn, 1962:33).

Paradigm creation gives its creators an aura of charismatic genius; acceptance of a paradigm by a lay member of the scientific community is not so much a rational decision as a conversion, an act of faith; the paradigm provides the scientific community with a unified gestalt-like perspective. The ordinary conception of theory making is false: it is actually a form of puzzle solving. The ordinary conception of scientific method is false; it is actually a form of illustration. Science does not progress—at least not in a linear sense—but undergoes periodic convulsive revolutions as one noncomparable faith replaces another.

Few theses have enjoyed more instant popularity in the social sciences than Kuhn's 1962 study. The discovery was quickly made that in structure functionalism, sociology had entered its long-awaited paradigm stage. In fact, only the last mopping-up operations remained. However, at the very time Kuhn's theses were being diffused, the consensus developed in the name of structure functionalism was breaking up. Hence there was some uncertainty as to whether sociology was still in the preparadigm stage or was just passing through its first phase as a mature, paradigm-dominated science, and was about to undergo convulsive reorganization under a new paradigm. However, the structure functionalists largely refused to stampede, and after nearly ten years of erosion of the structure functionalist point of view, Alvin W. Gouldner could announce as a personal discovery, in 1970, that there was a *coming* crisis of Western sociology represented by the fact that structure functionalism was acquiring sociological rivals: "Functional theory and Academic Sociology more generally, are now in the early stages of a continuing crisis" (Gouldner, 1970:341). Hence some sociologists decided that either sociology was still in the preparadigm stage after all, or perhaps it was uniquely a multiple-paradigm science.

Friedrichs (1970) made one of the most imaginative and ambitious attempts to reconstruct sociology from this point of view. He argued that sociology was not only characterized by multiple paradigms, but that its paradigms were multilayered, rising in two stages (first and second order).

Kuhn finds that natural scientific revolutions hinge upon shifts in the fundamental image a discipline has of its *subject matter*. A social science may have to confront a more fundamental paradigmatic dimension if it is to comprehend or extrapolate radical changes in the former, a level that addresses itself to the grounding image the social scientist has of *himself as scientific agent*. The reason this may be necessary is quite simple. Social scientists interact with their subject matter in a much more intimate manner than do scientists dealing with biological and physical phenomena. . . . The paradigms that order a sociologist's conception of his subject matter . . . may themselves be a reflection or function, of a more fundamental image; the paradigm *in terms of which he sees himself*. (Friedrichs, 1970:55-56)

It should be noted that Kuhn (1962) did not rest scientific revolutions on shifts in the fundamental image of a discipline's subject matter.[1] There were other novelties in Friedrichs' procedure. In contrast to Kuhn's assumption that mature science is measured by the unification of the entire scientific community behind a single paradigm, Friedrichs is more than half persuaded that sociology is fundamentally pluralistic. He does, however, toy with the idea that two antithetically constructed paradigms contest for dominance in sociology: the systems paradigm and the conflict paradigm, but that they may undergo dialectical synthesis in the future. Furthermore, Friedrichs departed from the Kuhnian formula by introducing the argument from the neo-idealists, and some of their humanistic followers, that sociology is unique in having humans as subjects; the self-image of scientists combines with the definition of the subject matter to provide a sociological paradigm with its peculiar relevance. In the case of sociology, the self-image of the scientist as priest combines with the systems conception of subject matter uniquely to qualify structure functionalism for a pro-Establishment role; the self-image of the scientist as prophet combines with the conflict conception of subject matter uniquely to qualify Marxist sociology for an anti-Establishment mission, at least in non-Communist countries.

Another interesting feature of Friedrichs' paradigm analysis of contemporary sociology is the extent to which he has translated the major sociological paradigms into conservative and radical ideologies, respectively.

While sociologists were seeking to come to terms with Kuhn's yeasty, new concepts, those same concepts were arousing interest in philosophical circles as well. They were made subject of a discussion by a colloquium in the philosophy of science in 1965 at which various differences between Kuhn's formulations and those of Sir Karl Popper were brought into central focus. Papers worked up in connection with the colloquim were brought to completion sometime after the conference and the proceedings were finally published in 1970, some time after the appearance of the Friedrichs study. Among them a paper by Margaret Masterman (1970) brought the various meanings assigned by Kuhn (1962) to paradigms under critical review.

She observed that Kuhn's quasi-poetic style made the ascertainment of his meanings difficult. She counted no fewer than twenty-one different meanings assigned to the term "paradigm" in Kuhn's 1962 study. Among them were: a universally recognized scientific achievement; a myth; a philosophy or constellation of questions; a textbook or classic work; a standard illustration; an anomalous pack of cards; a set of political institutions; an organizing principle which can govern perception; a general epistemological viewpoint; a new way of seeing; and something which defines the broad sweep of reality (Masterman, 1970:61-65).

For herself, Masterman argued, the one meaning of Kuhn's paradigm that represents an original contribution to the philosophy of science is recognition of an element which complements hypothetico-deductive theory. At times in scientific practice an artifact, which is also a concrete "way of seeing," is isolated and utilized analogically. "The trick which . . . starts off every new science, is that a known construct, an artifact, becomes a 'research vehicle,' and at the same moment, if successful, it becomes a paradigm, by being used to apply to new material, and in a non-obvious way" (Masterman, 1970:77-78).

In applying the term "paradigm" to any and all of different situations which Masterman carefully documented in her 1962 work, the term was permitted by Kuhn to range freely from a total system of scientific practice imposed bindingly on a scientific community to any part thereof. The argument automatically became ambiguous and circular. In his reply to his critics, Kuhn (1970b) acknowledged Masterman's criticism:

All of the objects of commitment described in my book as paradigms, parts of paradigms or paradigmatic would find a place in the disciplinary matrix, but they would not be lumped together as paradigms, individually or collectively. Among them would be: shared symbolic generalizations . . . ; shared models whether metaphysical . . . or heuristic . . . ; shared values . . . ; and other elements of the sort. Among the latter I would particularly emphasize concrete problem solutions, the sorts of standard examples of solved problems which scientists encounter first in student laboratories, in the problems at the ends of chapters in science texts, and on examinations. If I could, I would call these problem-solutions paradigms, for they are what led me to the choice of the term in the first place. Having lost control of the word, however, I shall henceforth describe them as exemplars. (Kuhn, 1970b:271-72)

By the time George Ritzer (1975a) undertook the integration of sociology in a paradigm framework, he had at his disposal the published proceedings of the colloquium. Moreover, in 1970 Kuhn (1970a) brought out a second edition of his book, in which he also proposed restricting the meaning of paradigm to exemplar. Howsever, Ritzer chose not to follow Kuhn in his restriction of the meaning of paradigm to exemplar, but opted to continue the usage of the 1962 edition of *The Structure of Scientific Revolutions*.

Paradigms were interpreted to be matrices of normal science, or more specifically, to consist of metaphysical world views (an idea Ritzer mistakenly attributed to Masterman)[2] taken together with an associated system of scientific practice and including: definitions of reality, exemplars, theories, and methodological preferences.

Ritzer maintains that three paradigms divide and organize sociology: social factism, social definitionism, and behaviorism. Social factism is best exemplified in the work of Durkheim. It defines social reality as social fact. It is theoretically elaborated in both systems (structure functionalism and conflict theory).[3] Methodologically, it is purportedly characterized by a love of surveys and statistics. Social definitionism, which is said to be best exemplified in the work of Max Weber, is said to conceive social reality as primarily consisting of people's interpretations of definitions of situations. This paradigm is theoretically illustrated by social action theory, symbolic interactionism, existentialism, ethnomethodology and phenomenology. Social definitionism has a methodological preference for introspective procedures, participant observation, and for qualitative methodology generally. Behaviorism is exemplified in the work of B. F. Skinner. It defines social reality as social behavior. It is theoretically developed in behavioristic sociology and in the exchange theory of Peter Blau and George Homans. It is characterized by methodological preferences for laboratory experimentation.

Some selectivity was required to impose this formalism on the thought and practice of current sociology. It appears to overlook the fact that Weber and Durkheim are exemplars to persons of a variety of schools of sociology. Weber does not, as Ritzer himself notes, fit easily into the paradigm of social definitionism of which he is taken as an exemplar. There were other cases of poor fit. Also, no note was taken of the fact that while some problems lend themselves more easily to one kind of methodological procedure than others, there are no sound reasons why theorists of any persuasion should not exploit any or all of the discipline's methodological resources whenever they are suitable to the problem at hand. In any case, the tight gestalt-like unity which Kuhn postulated to hold through all phases of a paradigm-dominated discipline is lacking.

In general, there has been a failure by sociologists to consider the very different implications for a scientific community divided into a set of competing paradigms rather than domination by a single one. One could anticipate some of the differences that one finds between a church or ecclesia, on the one hand, and a set of denominations and sects on the other. A scientific matrix dominated by a single orthodoxy is one thing; a closely related set of competitive scientific matrices, each with its unique definition of reality, exemplars, theories and methods, is quite another. One could expect either fierce politicization or the mutual unmasking of ideological bias and a competition of truth.4 In any case, a novice initiated into the second type of scientific milieu would never be without alternatives.

The one meaning Masterman was willing to leave to Kuhn when she sheared away the others—that is, paradigm conceived as a concrete example or procedure which entails a *way of seeing*—bears considerable similarity to Weber's (1949) conception of ideal types as one-sided accentuations of one or more points of view taken together with a synthesis of discrete, concrete, individual phenomena. Both the limits and functions that Masterman assigned to paradigm in this special sense are similar to those Weber assigned to the ideal type. Weber observed:

This procedure can be indispensable for heuristic as well as expository purposes. The ideal typical concept will help to develop our skill in imputation in *research*: it is no "hypothesis" but it offers guidance to the construction of hypotheses. It is not a *description* of reality but it aims to give unambiguous means of expression to such a description. (Weber, 1949:90)

Weber assigned a critical role to ideal-type procedures in the rise of research traditions that superficially, at least, sound similar to those assigned by Masterman; he recognized heuristic roles played by ideal types in the transmission of scientific culture that sound similar to those assigned by Kuhn. However, Weber thought the essence of science was to be found in its theories, not in its ideal types.

THEORIES

The traditional approach to sociology was based on the notion that the essence of science was to be found in its ideas and its methods. As a result, the most appropriate way to characterize a discipline should be by way of a review of its theories and research traditions. Theory in science is any coherent group of general propositions used as explanatory principles for a class of phenomena. The body of adherents of a given theory is a school. A scientific method consists of the systematic procedures by which principles of explanation are applied to phenomena and their explanatory, predictive, and manipulatory power is ascertained.

Like all human enterprises, theory development has to start somewhere in the midst of ongoing activity. All sciences made their original departure from the context of everyday activity and commonsense thinking. To the extent that a science is more successful than common sense in explaining the world, it will begin the transformation of common sense into its own image. Moreover, new departures in theory increasingly take previous scientific practice as their point of departure.

New theories seem to originate as leaps of the mind to a new plane or as flashes of the imagination. At this stage they are often mythopoetic, frequently taking the form of surprising new metaphors or intuitive fusions of ideas and evidence which suggest relationships not previously suspected. Some students have described these creative theoretical departures as "transcendent hypotheses."

When first introduced a transcendent hypothesis may be extremely vague, provided only that it entails the laws which it is intended to explain. When Huyghens tried to explain the diffraction and the interference of light by means of his undulatory theory, he had no clear idea of the nature of the waves he supposed to occur, but the wave-motion seemed to render some laws of optics intelligible and there was no rival suggestion that could do as much. (Kneale, 1953:356)

It is quite evident that Masterman reinterpreted Kuhn's paradigms in such a way as to liken them to the notion of transcendent hypotheses. Paradigms were, she argued, a special class of analogies which involved both concrete examples of procedure and a new way of seeing. If one reserves the term "theory" for a worked-up, logically interrelated set of explanatory principles, a transcendent hypothesis (paradigm) is pretheoretical and, as both Kuhn and Masterman seem inclined to urge, can operate to institute the scientific process prior to the appearance of theory. If, however, one treats a transcendent hypothesis (paradigm) as the first crude form of theory and as a new way of organizing evidence, it should not be located outside theory, but rather is a most integral part of that theory. With considerable frequency, as a theory and its associated research tradition develop, an idealized version of the original way of looking at and handling evidence is utilized as a model (heuristic paradigm) for teaching purposes. Kuhn seems to have been most enamored of exemplars (heuristic paradigms) and models employed for socialization and the teaching purposes of a scientific tradition. Masterman is most interested in transcendent hypotheses, paradigms functioning in a context of discovery. Reichenbach's (1953) observations are pertinent to the kinds of paradigms that excited Masterman:

> The act of discovery escapes logical analysis; there are no logical rules in terms of which a "discovery machine" could be constructed that would take over the creative function of the genius. But it is not the logician's task to account for scientific discoveries; all he can do is to analyze the relation between given facts and a theory presented to him with the claim that it explains these facts. In other words, logic is concerned only with the context of justification. (Reichenbach, 1953:231)

A curious thing has happened in the course of the recent discussion of the role of paradigms in science. A tendency has been present to separate the creative aspects of science from its routine hard work. This transforms the scientific process into flashes of genius (which are conceived as prescientific or extrascientific) and the formation of cults and rituals of compulsively neurotic puzzle solving. The result is a caricature of the scientific process. Still the most satisfactory way of appraising the status of sociology, or of any science, is in terms of an inventory of its theories. Moreover, the fuller one's picture of the development of theory and its associated research traditions, from its foundation often in a powerful metaphor to the establishment of its principles of explanation through the translation of its laws into mathematical formulas, the better one's understanding of the nature and limits of the discipline's explanatory power. This may be illustrated by a few brief notes on the rise of sociological theory and a sketch of the current theoretical landscape of sociology.

The naturalization of social life in the seventeenth and eighteenth centuries which laid the foundation for the rise of the social sciences in the nineteenth century was immeasurably speeded by a favorite metaphor of the rationalistic social philosophers: the social contract. This suggested radical reappraisal of the relations between an individual and his associates in social groupings of most diverse sorts. It thrust the rational quid pro quo into central position regarding the estimation of social situations. Social relationships which had previously been left unexplored because of traditionalistic or religious reasons were examined, and sometimes surprising discoveries were made about them. In the process social life tended to lose dimensions of mystery and awe and were thus made open and down to earth. The conclusions became inescapable: Much could be learned by applying to human social life the methods that had proved their worth in the study of the physical world.

In the nineteenth century, if one takes the conventional position which traces the rise of sociology to the influence of Saint-Simon and Comte, the metaphor of society as an organism presided over the birth of sociology proper. Organismic analogies of society were by no means new. However, the proposal to study simultaneously the social organism while employing the positivistic methodology of science was an interesting realignment of previously discrete and to some extent opposed traditions. The new science is accurately described in terms of its basic conception of social reality and its presuppositions as to how this is best studied as positivistic organicism. The conceptual resources of the new theory received their first elaboration in the works of pioneering figures such as Comte, Spencer, J. S. Mill, and Lester Ward. They constituted sociology's first school. Positivistic organicism was further elaborated and partially biologized under the influence of Darwinian biology. The theory was brought to its classic formulation in the work of persons such as Ferdinand Tönnies and Emile Durkheim.

There will always be a question as to when innovations in an emerging body of theory are so basic as to warrant the establishment of a new theory. Accident and personality variables, such as intransigence, ambition, and the like, often play a role. Sometimes traditions split off from the main body only to rejoin it at a later stage of their mutual development. Somewhat parallel to the manner in which the Marxians split off from the Hegelians, the conflict theorists in sociology split off from the positivistic organicists. The conflict theorists appealed to a wide spectrum of historical authorities, e.g., Hobbes, Machiavelli, Polybius in Antiquity, and Ibn Kahldun in the Islamic Middle Ages, who were almost completely ignored by the positivistic organicists. They were the first sociologists to take Marx seriously, and when Marxism was eventually seen as a type of sociological theory, it was classified as a form of conflict theory. The conflict theorists virtually founded a series of new subdisciplines such as the sociology of power, the sociology of law, the sociology of stratification. The conflict theorists came to see themselves as a separate school of sociology. However, some of their heirs in the twentieth century seem prepared to join ranks with the twentieth-century heirs of positivistic organicism.

Toward the end of the nineteenth century and in the opening decades of the twentieth century, sparked in some measure by problems in Western society, a series of revolts was staged in the ranks of sociologists against both positivistic organicism and conflict theory. The revolt was directed against the holistic concept of social reality held by the first two schools of theory. Previously, society was considered analogous to an organism by the positivistic organicists and analogous to battlefield warfare by the conflict theorists. Social reality was now reconceptualized as interindividual activity or as the interactive process.

Analysis was carried out either on the basis of a micro-analysis (neo-Kantian and phenomenological sociology), or on the basis of the individual and his behavior (pluralistic behaviorism, social action theory, and symbolic interactionism). At the same time, these elementaristic approaches to social life, in contrast to the holistic approaches of positivistic organicism and conflict theory, employed either nonpositivistic or modified positivistic methods depending upon the subject matter of their inquiry.

Finally, in the period after World War II, some structure functionalist sociologists (or systems theorists, as they are sometimes called) returned to a type of holistic social theory having many similarities to positivistic organicism. Durkheim was the particular patron saint of this theory. It dominated, for a time, many of the most prestigious universities in America and included among its ranks some of America's most eminent sociologists. By cross-tabulating the major methodological preferences of various schools of sociology with the primary conceptualizations about the social realities they study, it is possible to outline, as is done in Table 2, the major typological differences between the major theories.

The 1960s and 1970s brought accelerated transformations as the adherents of some older positions died off and left no direct heirs. Such was the fate of

Table 2.

MAJOR SOCIOLOGICAL THEORIES TO 1960: CONCEPTION
OF SUBJECT MATTER AND METHODOLOGICAL PREFERENCE

Methodological Preference	TheoryType	
	Elementaristic	*Holistic*
Non-positivistic	Neo-Kantian formalism	
	Phenomenological sociology	
Positivistic	Pluralistic behaviorism	Positivistic organicism
	Social action theory	Conflict theory
	Symbolic interactionism	Structure functionalism

Source: This is the basic typology developed in Don Martindale, *The Nature and Types of Sociological Theory* (Boston: Houghton Mifflin, 1960).

pluralistic behaviorism, neo-Kantian formalism, and positivistic organicism; for example, Lundberg died and Sorokin changed his position to what he described as integral social theory. Meanwhile, with the decline in the stridency of the cold war and the fading of McCarthyism, conflict theory, particularly in its Marxist versions, was revitalized. On the other hand, as inroads were made into structure functionalism and attention was called to the fact that conflict theory and structure functionalism were both holistic, the suggestion was made repeatedly that perhaps some day the two positions would amalgamate. Also during this period, pressures toward merging theory and ideology in the name of a relevant and critical social science led to increased attention in the Frankfort School of critical theory which, from the 1920s through World War II, had been making the theoretical trek from Marx back to Hegel. Moreover, disillusionment with both society and with all forms of holistic theory was a component in the rapid development of a number of elementaristic positions: phenomenology, ethnomethodology, existentialism, and symbolic interactionism.

Disillusionment, with positivistic methods, manifest in both holistic and elementaristic circles, led to a strengthening of antipositivistic methodologies, manifest among the phenomenologists, existentialists, ethnomethodologists, some symbolic interactionists, integralists, and critical theorists. The counter-insurgency of positivism became manifest through increasing interest in theory construction and mathematical sociology. This was embraced with particular enthusiasm by behavioristic sociologists, including Blau and Homans, who occupied the spot vacated by the disappearance of pluralistic behaviorism. It is still useful to type the various sociological theories by methodological preference and by theory, as shown in Table 3.

CONCLUDING NOTE

Even from a brief review, it quickly becomes clear that the attempts to order sociology by ideology and by paradigm compound its confusions.

There is no effective action without passion, and the value commitments of individual scientists will forever motor their fields of study. Also, in the case of social scientists, the value choices and ideologies of their subjects will tend to combine or conflict in various ways with personal commitments, tending to lure them from the chaste path of objectivity. However, the pathos of science is contained in the disciplined acceptance of findings, however inconvenient, awkward, embarrassing, or dismaying they may be. It would needlessly emasculate science to insist that values and ideologies play no role in the choice of problems. In the case of sociology, most new departures have had strong ideological commitments at the start. But science is an institutionalized reality principle which seeks to purge understanding of distortion from both the en-

Table 3.
THE LANDSCAPE OF SOCIAL THEORY IN THE 1970s

Methodological Preference	General Theory Type	
	Elementarism	*Holism*
Acceptance of nonpositivist or modified positivist methods	Phenomenology Existentialism Ethnomethodology	Integral sociology (Sorokin) Radical Romanticism (C. W. Mills and some neo-Marxists) Critical sociology; reflexive sociology
Relatively strict positivists	Symbolic interactionism Social action theory Behavioristic sociology (including the exchange theory of Blau and Homans)	Structure functionalism (or systems theory) Conflict theory (especially the more orthodox forms of Marxism)

Source: This is the typology put forth in Don Martindale, *Sociological Theory and the Problem of Values* (Columbus, Ohio: Charles E. Merrill, 1974).

chanting dreams and drunken passions of action. To order sociology by ideology is to blur the entire significance of a sociological science. Still, from time to time, it makes sense to distinguish an Establishment sociology from an anti-Establishment sociology, or a radical sociology, and to recognize that in the early stages of special applications of sociological principles to sensitive social areas such as black sociology, women's sociology, Chicano sociology, and American Indian sociology, ideological commitments may be present.

Paradigms have proved to be a family of conceptions with too many contradictory meanings to be a trustworthy guide for the ordering of sociology. Moreover, the only senses of the term which Kuhn and his philosophic critics seem prepared to accept, after nearly a decade of wrangling, will not perform the functions Kuhn originally assigned to them, and which so powerfully attracted some social scientists. It would not be unfair to say that Kuhn took the idealized scientific experiment traditionally employed for heuristic teaching purposes and transformed it into the paradigm of normal science. The chief result of this was to dramatize the extent to which social factors intrude upon the content of scientific study. However, the charismatic genius and the circle of converts whose activities tend to transform theorizing into puzzle solving, and verification into illustration, merely represent one possible ideal-typical presentation of the nature of scientific change, as Max Weber would undoubtedly have said. It is hardly a proper foundation for classifying and accounting for the events that transpire within scientific disciplines, though it does focus attention on a particularly interesting set.

It remains that the most trustworthy procedure for taking account of the ideas and procedures which constitute a science, including sociology, is the traditional practice of examining its theories and their development in the schools that promote them and institutionalize them, and finally, critically exploring the research traditions which emerged in their name.

NOTES

1. Differences in basic conception of the discipline's subject matter was, incidentally, one of the foundations of the typology of sociological theories developed in Don Martindale, *The Nature and Types of Sociological Theory* (Boston: Houghton Mifflin, 1960).

2. Masterman had observed "they," various persons who have been interested in Kuhn's paradigms, "assume without question that paradigm is a 'basic theory' or that it is a 'general metaphysical viewpoint'; whereas I think it is in fact quite easy to show that, in its primary sense, it cannot be either of these" (Masterman, 1970:61).

3. Various arguments have been advanced ranging from the observation that systems theory and conflict theory are both forms of holism, to the argument that various combinations of the positions are possible. In general, the radical is inclined to insist that any fusion of the two positions is out of the question. As noted previously, Friedrichs (1970) treated the two positions as conflicting opposites.

4. Masterman (1970) devoted some attention to what she considered to be the primary differences between a preparadigm science, multiple paradigm science, paradigm science, and a dual paradigm science (see Masterman, 1970:73-75).

George Ritzer

TOWARD AN INTEGRATED SOCIOLOGICAL PARADIGM

Thomas Kuhn's (1962, 1970a) work on the structure of scientific revolutions has sparked reflexive activity in a variety of disciplines (e.g., Stanfield, 1974, in economics), including a growing body of work in sociology (e.g., Friedrichs, 1970; Effrat, 1972; and to a lesser extent Eisenstadt and Curelaru, 1976). In addition, there is my own work (Ritzer, 1975a, 1975b), in which I concluded that sociology is a multiple paradigm science. Most analysts of the state of sociology agree with this conclusion, although there is considerable disagreement on the nature of sociology's multiple paradigms. In the first part of this essay I shall briefly review my previous efforts to analyze the paradigmatic status of sociology. The heart of the paper lies in the second section, in which the case is made for still another sociological paradigm that deals in a more integrated fashion with social reality than any of the extant paradigms. Such a paradigm would not replace existing paradigms, but rather is designed to supplement them by dealing with issues that are beyond their scope. In my view, existing sociological paradigms seem best able to cope with specific "levels" of social reality and what is needed is an integrated paradigm that deals with the interrelationship among various levels.

REFLECTIONS ON EARLIER WORK ON THE PARADIGMATIC STATUS OF SOCIOLOGY[1]

Kuhn sees a science at any given point in time as dominated by a specific paradigm (defined for the moment as a fundamental image of a science's subject matter). Normal science is a period of accumulation of knowledge in which scientists work on, and expand, the reigning paradigm. Inevitably, however, such work spawns anomalies or things that cannot be explained within the existing paradigm. If these anomalies mount, a crisis stage is reached, which ultimately may end in a revolution in which the reigning paradigm is overthrown and a new one takes its place at the center of science. Thus a new dominant paradigm is born and the stage is set for the cycle to repeat itself.

The key term in Kuhn's work, as well as in its application to sociology, is the paradigm concept. Unfortunately, Kuhn initially defined the concept in a number of different ways (Masterman, 1970), and his later effort to cope with this ambiguity resulted in what is in my opinion an overly narrow conception of a paradigm as an exemplar, or concrete puzzle solution that serves as a model for later scientists. Kuhn came to this definition because of criticism that the thrust of his earlier work was to characterize science as highly subjective and irrational. Since I believe that science has these characteristics (on this see Watson, 1968; Mitroff, 1974), I feel the following definition of a paradigm is true to the thrust of Kuhn's earlier work:

A paradigm is a fundamental image of the subject matter within a science. It serves to define what should be studied, what questions should be asked, how they should be asked, and what rules should be followed in interpreting the answers obtained. The paradigm is the broadest unit of consensus within a science and serves to differentiate one scientific community (or sub-community) from another. It subsumes, defines and inter-relates the exemplars, theories, methods, and instruments that exist within it. (Ritzer, 1975a:7)

Employing this definition of a paradigm, I argued that sociology was dominated by three paradigms which I labeled the social facts, social definition, and social behavior paradigms. Briefly, those sociologists who work within the social facts paradigm focus or macro-structures, look to the work of Emile Durkheim as their exemplar, use structural-functional and conflict theory, and tend more often to employ the interview/questionnaire and historical/comparative methods. Those who accept the social definition paradigm focus on the action and interaction that result from the minding (i.e., creative mental) process, accept Max Weber's work on social action as the exemplar, employ various theories including action theory, symbolic interactionism, and phenomenology-ethnomethodology, and are more prone in their research to use the observational method. Finally, those who accept the social behavior paradigm focus on behavior and contingencies of reinforcement, view B. F. Skinner's work as their exemplar, operate from behavioral or exchange theory, and tend to prefer the experimental method.

In my earliest work I contended that sociobiology and critical sociology were showing signs of achieving paradigmatic status within the discipline.[2] If anything, these perspectives show even more vitality today than they did a few years ago. The strength of sociobiology is reflected in the enormous amount of publicity devoted to Edward Wilson's *Sociobiology* (1975), which has been the subject of great attention in the major sociological journals. Although this may simply be another cycle in sociology's long-standing love-hate relationship with the issue of how much social behavior can be explained biologically, it could also be that sociologists will finally overcome their historical insecurity about biology and begin an era in which a number of them make this the focus of their work. Already people like Pierre van den Berghe (1975), Allan Mazur and Leon Robertson (1972) are identified with this approach. Similarly, critical theory, which is already strong in Europe, is of growing significance in the United States. It seems to be the true inheritor of the neo-Marxism which has been latent in sociology until recent years as well as the now moribund radical sociology of the late 1960s. Reflective of this growth is the increasing familiarity in America with the school in general (Jay, 1973; Connerton, 1976) and in particular with the work of its most important modern exponent, Jurgen Habermas (1968).

Although I did not mention it in my earlier work, it seems clear now that structuralism also has the *potential* of emerging as a new sociological paradigm. At the moment it remains largely on the periphery of sociology, with the most notable inputs stemming from linguistics and anthropology, particularly in the work of Lévi-Strauss (1969). Sociology now has its own practitioners (Cicourel, 1974) and defenders (Carpenter, 1976) of structuralism, and we can anticipate greater interest in the future. However, it is also easy to forecast heightened political attacks. In fact, we have already seen Goddard (1976) unleash an attack on this potential paradigm. In Goddard's view, should sociology accept the structural approach, it would "compromise absolutely what is perhaps its own fundamental premise . . . that ideas and symbols are formed in their material context of given social milieux . . . the idea of a sociological materialism which inaugurated sociology as a special discipline would have to be completely abandoned" (Goddard, 1976:132). If structuralism was not a serious contender for paradigmatic status, it would not have been singled out for such a harsh attack.

The attack on structuralism brings us back to a general theme in my earlier work—the pervasiveness of political conflict in sociology. Although some competition and conflict between paradigms are certainly useful, it is clear that these conflicts have frequently had negative consequences for the discipline as a whole. All too often, sociologists have exaggerated the capabilities of their approach while viciously attacking the utility of the others. The noise of this political conflict has made it difficult to see the intellectual affinity between the various paradigms. Lest we think that this kind of political attack is a thing of the past, we need only turn to Lewis Coser's (1975) presidential address to the American Sociological Association.

Coser's attack on ethnomethodology is an extreme example of interparadigmatic conflict. In his address, and in much of his work, Coser is an exponent of the social facts paradigm. As such, he can be seen as engaging in a politically motivated attack on a theoretical component of the social definition paradigm. True to the general character of such attacks, Coser sees few redeeming qualities in ethnomethodology and subjects it to a brutal attack. As is typical of such political attacks, Coser engages in a great deal of name-calling in labeling ethnomethodology "trival," "a massive cop-out," "an orgy of subjectivism," and a "self indulgent enterprise." The motivation behind this viciousness lies in the fact that social definitionism has long been a competitor with Coser's social factism for predominance within sociology. This is just the latest of a long history of attacks by proponents of each of these paradigms on the other. To be fair, the ethnomethodologists in their reply to Coser show far more sensitivity to the dangers of political conflict in calling for an integrated study of social facts and social definitions (Mehan and Wood, 1976).

Within the three paradigms discussed earlier one can anticipate changes among their theoretical components in the future. Structural functionalism seems likely to decline in importance as does the conflict theory that is little more than a mirror image of structural functionalism (e.g., Dahrendorf, 1959). On the other hand, a conflict theory that returns to its original Marxian structural roots (e.g., Bottomore, 1975) unadulterated by the Marxists (Bender, 1975) is showing signs of life. We are likely to continue to see efforts to reconcile structural functionalism with various forms of conflict theory (e.g., Lipset, 1975). Action theory seems of little more than historical interest, and symbolic interactionism, despite a few hopeful signs (e.g., a new journal bearing its name), seems to be following action theory into the sociological history books. Among social definitionists, there is a dramatic shift in the direction of phenomenology/ethnomethodology as well as the related perspective of existentialism (Manning, 1973), particularly the relevance of Sartre (Craib, 1976) to sociology. The theories associated with social behaviorism (behavioral sociology, exchange theory) should continue to be attractive to a relatively small, but significant, number of sociologists. Although many are put off by their reductionism, others are attracted by the potential of a technology for ameliorating social ills (Tarter, 1973). Still others might find recent efforts (e.g., Staats, 1976) to reintegrate mental process into behaviorism attractive.

I also have some additional thoughts on the methodological components of the sociological paradigms. I castigated social factists for not doing more historical/comparative research, and I still believe that this is an underutilized method. However, in recent years we have seen a resurgence of this method in important studies by Wallerstein (1974), Paige (1975), and Chirot (1976). I also now think that the use of census-type data as well as historical documents (Goudsblom, 1977) should be included as important tools of the social factists.

The most general methodological point of my earlier work was the linkage between paradigm and method. I argued that social factists are more likely to use interviews, questionnaires, and the historical/comparative method; social definitionists tend to prefer observational methods; and social behaviorists seem to prefer experiments. These assertions were tested by Snizek (1976), who concluded that the linkages are not as I assert and that the dominant method in all three paradigms is the interview/questionnaire. Although one must laud Snizek's effort to test my assertions, there are a variety of problems in Snizek's research that make his conclusions problematic (Ritzer, 1977a). Nevertheless, additional research may well prove that the cheap and efficient interview/questionnaire is dominant within all paradigms. If this proves to be so, I would argue that it stems from the expediency of sociologists of all persuasions and not from an intellectual affinity between this method and all the paradigms. *If* interviews and questionnaires are shown to be preferred universally, I would then contend that the experimental method is used *more often* by social behaviorists than social factists or social definitionists; the observational method is used *more* by social definitionists than adherents of the other paradigms, and the interview/questionnaire is used *more* by social factists than the supporters of the other paradigms. A true test of all of this awaits further research.

Toward Paradigmatic Integration

Because of the one-sidedness of extant sociological paradigms, I perceive a growing interest in, and awareness of, the need for an integrated approach among a wide range of sociologists. Among those identified with structural functionalism we find Robert Merton (1975:30) arguing that structural analysis "connects with other sociological paradigms, which, the polemics not withstanding, are anything but contradictory in much of what they suppose or assert . . . recent work in structural analysis leads me to spheres of agreement and of complementarity rather than to the alleged basic contradictions between various sociological paradigms." More specifically, Merton (1975:31) later says: "Many ideas in structural analysis and symbolic interactionism, for example, are opposed to one another in about the same sense as ham is opposed to eggs: They are perceptively different but mutually enriching." Among the social definitionists, Mehan and Wood (1975:180) say that ethnomethodology "begins by accepting the reality of an external and constraining world. To this assumption is added an acceptance of the facticity of ceaseless reality work. The problem of a general theory of social order is thus determining the properties that relate structural activities to structural 'facts.'" Among social behaviorists we find people like Staats (1976) returning to the original Meadian project of integrating the minding (i.e., creative mental) process with traditional behaviorism. Even the new sociobiologists are able to see the reconcilability of their approach with other sociological orientations. For example, Edward O. Wilson (in Barash, 1977:xiv) admits: "Human behavior is dominated by culture in the sense that the greater part, perhaps all, of the variation between societies is based on differences in cultural experience. But this is not to say that human beings are infinitely plastic."

Despite a lengthy list of thinkers who recognize the need for theoretical integration, we continue to see the tendency to emphasize, and often overemphasize, the importance of a particular set of variables. Thus for many social factists individuals are seen to be determined largely by macro-structures, whereas for a large proportion of social definitionists it is individuals who determine social structures. Similar claims are made by the supporters of the other paradigms or would-be paradigms. The weaknesses of these efforts underscore the need for an integrated paradigm, and I would like to turn now to a discussion of a preliminary effort in that direction.

An Exemplar for an Integrated Sociological Paradigm [3]

I intend to cope with some of the problems in extant paradigms by trying to "create" an exemplar for a new integrated paradigm.[4] That is, I want to outline a model that I hope will prove attractive to a number of sociologists who are dissatisfied with the available sociological paradigms. I hasten to add, and shall show, that this paradigm has existed in sociology since its inception as a distinctive discipline. I simply wish to call attention to an alternative that has always existed, albeit implicitly, in sociology.

The key here is the notion of "levels" of social reality.[5] I do not mean to imply that social reality is really divided into levels. In fact, social reality is best viewed as a wide range of social entities that is in constant flux. In order to deal with this, given its enormous complexity, sociologists have abstracted out various levels for sociological analysis. Thus the levels are sociological constructs rather than really existing in the social world.

For our purposes the major levels of social reality can be derived from the interrelation of two basic social continua—the macroscopic-microscopic and objective-subjective. The macroscopic-microscopic dimension relates to the magnitude of social phenomena ranging from whole societies to social acts, whereas the objective-subjective refers to whether the phenomenon has a real, material existence (e.g., bureaucracy, patterns of interaction) or exists only in the realm of ideas and knowledge (e.g., norms and values). Figure 1 is a schematic representation of the intersection of these two continua and the four major levels of social reality that are derived from it.

It is my contention that a new sociological paradigm must deal in an integrated fashion with the four basic levels of social reality identified in the figure. An integrated sociological paradigm must deal with macroscopic objective entities like bureaucracy, macro-subjective structures like culture, micro-objective phenomena like patterns of interaction, and micro-subjective facts like the process of reality construction. Remember that in the real world all of these gradually blend into the others as part of the larger social continuum, but we have made some artificial and rather arbitrary differentions in order to be able to deal with social reality. These four levels of social reality are posited

Figure 1. Major Levels of Social Reality

MACROSCOPIC

I. Macro-objective	*II. Macro-subjective*
Examples include society, law, bureaucracy, architecture, technology, and language.	Examples include culture, norms and values.

OBJECTIVE ─────────────────────────── *SUBJECTIVE*

III. Micro-objective	*IV. Micro-subjective*
Examples include patterns of behavior, action, and interaction.	Examples include the various facets of the social construction of reality.

MICROSCOPIC

for heuristic purposes and are not meant to be an accurate depiction of the social world.

An obvious question is how these four levels relate to the three paradigms outlined in my earlier work as well as the integrated paradigm being developed here. Figure 2 relates the four levels to the four paradigms.

Figure 2. Levels of Social Reality and the Major Sociological Paradigms

Levels of
Social
Reality   *SOCIOLOGICAL PARADIGMS*

Levels of Social Reality	Paradigm	Proposed Integrated Paradigm
Macro-subjective	Social Facts	Proposed Integrated Paradigm
Macro-objective		
Micro-subjective	Social Definition	
Micro-objective	Social behavior	

The social facts paradigm focuses primarily on the macro-objective and macro-subjective levels, the social definition paradigm is largely concerned with the micro-subjective as well as that part of the micro-objective world that depends on mental processes (action), and the social behavior paradigm deals with that part of the micro-objective world that does not involve the minding process (behavior). Whereas the three extant paradigms cut across the levels of social reality horizontally, the new integrated paradigm cuts across vertically. This depiction makes it clear why the proposed paradigm does not supersede the others. Although each of the three existing paradigms deals with a given level or levels in great detail, the proposed integrated paradigm deals with all levels, but does not examine any given level in anything like the degree of intensity of the other paradigms. Thus the choice of a paradigm depends on the kind of question being asked. Not all sociological issues require an integrated approach, but it is certain that at least some do.

Given this background, let me now turn to the heart of this paper—the development of an exemplar for an integrated sociological paradigm. I want to do this in two stages. First, I want to show that embedded in many of the seemingly one-sided approaches in sociology are the rudiments of the kind of integrated approach being discussed here. Secondly, I shall turn to a discussion of the basic elements of an integrated sociological paradigm.

IMPLICIT INTEGRATIVE APPROACHES TO SOCIAL REALITY

In this section I shall focus on the integrative efforts of those sociologists previously identified with the social facts and social definition paradigms; omitted to keep the discussion within reasonable bounds will be a discussion of similar possibilities among social behaviorists even though they do exist. For example, Homans' (1974) concept of distributive justice clearly implies that people engage in mental processes prior to emitting behavior.

Let me begin by discussing the four theorists (Durkheim, Marx, Weber, and Parsons) who clearly focused on macro-objective and macro-subjective social phenomena. Despite their focus, all of them had at least some useful conception of a perspective that deals integratively with all of the major levels of social reality.

Durkheim is the weakest of these four theorists in terms of our integrative goal. His differentiation between material (e.g., law, architecture) and nonmaterial (e.g., social currents and collective conscience) social facts is useful for our purposes, since they parallel the macro-objective and macro-subjective categories, but he offers us little on the relationship between these two types of macroscopic entities. However, Durkheim's greatest problem lies in the fact that he did not delineate in any detail the relationship between these macroscopic units and microscopic social reality. Helpful here is Durkheim's notion of "social currents" as a type of macro-subjective social reality. Social currents such as "great movements of enthusiasm, indignation, and pity *do not* originate in any one of the particular individual consciousnesses. They come to each of us from without and can carry us away in spite of ourselves" (Durkheim, 1964:4). A specific example, from his study of suicide, is the social current of anomie, which when increased in strength as in times of social disruption can lead to increases in the rate of anomic suicide. But these social currents cannot exist outside of individuals; they must have an intra- and intersubjective existence. That they are shared intersubjectively and exist intrasubjectively renders these currents micro-subjective. It is this sort of analysis in Durkheim's work that leads Nisbet (1974) to argue that there is not one iota of difference between Mead and Durkheim, who, while both giving priority to the social, understand the importance of micro-subjectivity. When these currents have an impact on action such as the case given by Durkheim of an increasing propensity to commit suicide, they also have a micro-objective existence. Thus we can see that Durkheim did have at least a rudimentary conception of an integrated approach despite his emphasis on macroscopic phenomena.

However, Durkheim's perspective has serious problems as a potential exemplar for an integrated paradigm. For one thing the linkages between the various levels are not spelled out and that must be a major concern of such a paradigm. Even Nisbet (1974:115), who is a sympathetic observer, recognizes this problem: "Admittedly one might wish that Durkheim had given more attention to the specific mechanisms by which collective representation(s) in society are translated, in distinctively individual and other creative ways, into the individual representations that reflect man's relationships to society." For another, Durkheim offers us basically only a one-way causal model. We can clearly see how macroscopic structures (e.g., social currents or, more importantly, the collective conscience) constrain micro-objectivity and micro-subjectivity. What we cannot see is how the macro-structures are created and continually shaped by micro-processes. That is, actors are affected by the larger society, but there is no discussion of how the actors contruct and daily reconstruct that society. Durkheim's actors are basically, to use Garfinkel's phrase, "judgmental dopes" who are largely lacking in the ability to create social reality. This is reflected in Durkheim's rather curious notion of freedom in which individuals are free when they are constrained by larger social forces that allow them to control the passions that would otherwise enslave them. Freedom comes from the constraints of macro-structures. A more useful integrative approach must accord less power to society and more to the creative abilities of actors.

I believe that Marx comes closer to an adequate integrated conception despite the fact that he too ultimately accords too much significance to macro-structures. Marx begins with an active, creative, voluntaristic conception of people. He sees people as inherently social, engaging in interaction with others in collective efforts to appropriate nature. Marx believes that people are endowed with active, creative minds that play a crucial role in social development: "What distinguishes the worst architect from the best of bees is this, that the architect raises his structure in imagination before he erects it in reality" (Marx, in Bender, 1970:360). But after people erect these structures in their minds, they often proceed to construct them in the real world. Thus over the course of history a series of structures comes to exist in society; out of micro-subjective and micro-objective processes emerge society's macro-structures. Implied here, at least theoretically, is a dialectical relationship between the micro- and macro-levels. People construct social reality and that reality comes, in turn, to play a role in the social creation of people. However, Marx's theoretical model is subverted by the actual events of history, particularly the development of capitalism. The social structures that our ancestors have created historically came to have an existence of their own, an existence that is, at least for the historical moment, beyond the control of people who created them in the first place. We are constrained, if not controlled, by these macro-structures. People continue to engage in micro-subjective and micro-objective processes, but these have less and less impact on macro-structures. This is the meaning of Marx's famous idea that people create history, but they do not create it as they wish. Our contemporary creations are constrained, if not subverted, by larger macro-structures.

The preceding discussion of the reality of macro-structures is, as Lukacs (1968) has pointed out, only one of the double meanings of the central Marxian concept of reification. Reification not only implies the reality of macro-structures, it also relates to the micro-subjective level. That is, people at the level of consciousness tend to "forget" that they, or their ancestors, created macro-structures and since they created them, they have the power to change them. People come to believe that macro-structures have a life of their own, a life that is beyond the ability of the actor to understand or to change. Obviously, reification at the micro- and macro-levels is interrelated; each supports the other in serving to enable the macro-structures of capitalist society to exist beyond the control of most actors.

As a result of these processes, the dialectic between the macro- and micro-levels is destroyed in capitalism. People no longer have the ability, as long as they continue to act normally, to affect or alter macro-structures. They continue to engage in micro-subjective and micro-objective processes, but these have little impact on the larger structures. This is reflected in the fact that the liberating potential of class consciousness is subverted by false consciousness. As a result, individual action and consciousness either reinforce capitalist society or are reduced to insignificance in shaping the larger society. It is this that leads Marx to focus progressively on macro-structures and virtually to ignore the micro-level. What was going on at the micro-level was insignificant, and in order to make it significant again, Marx felt he had to engage in a critique of macro-structures in order to help bring them down and thereby rein-state the significance of microscopic processes.

I want to make it clear that Marx's structural determinism is restricted to capitalist society. In his image of human nature people are endowed with self-consciousness and the ability to act significantly. Furthermore, the importance of self-consciousness and action would be reasserted once the structures of capitalist society had been destroyed. When people develop a true class con-sciousness, they will act to overthrow the system that has been reducing to in-significance what they say and do.

From the point of view of this paper, the problem with Marx's work stems from his political beliefs and not his theoretical system. His theoretical system is based on a dialectical relationship between all four of the levels of reality identified previously. However, his political sympathies led him to focus on macro-structures and largely to ignore micro-structures. Although the signifi-cance and operation of these micro-structures are alluded to in his work, they are overwhelmed by his concern with macro-structures. Marx's dialectical model of the relationship between the various levels of social reality is of great help to us, but it is clear that we must look elsewhere for a more profound understanding of micro-subjectivity and micro-objectivity.

Interestingly, Weber presents us with some of the same problems. Like Marx, it can be argued that Weber was engaged in a sociology of reification (Mitzman, 1969). Weber, too, saw the modern world as one in which reified social structures were progressively eliminating the significance of individual thought and action. But unlike Marx, Weber saw the problem lying in the pro-gressive rationalization and bureaucratization of the world, particularly the Occident, and not in capitalism, which was but one manifestation of this broader development. Also, unlike Marx, Weber saw no way out and forecast increasing rationalization, the development of the "iron cage." From our point of view, the problem in Weber's thought, like that in Marx's system, is the fact that despite a dual concern with macroscopic and microscopic processes, he accorded far too much attention to the macro-level of analysis.

Nevertheless, Weber does have a conception of the multiple levels of reality and the relationship between them. At the macroscopic level, his interest in rationalization can be seen as a concern with macro-subjective factors, the norms and values of rationalization. His interest in macro-objective factors is epitomized by his interest in bureaucratic structures. Furthermore, Weber was attuned to the relationship between these two macroscopic levels. The progres-sive rationalization of the Western world had created bureaucratic structures, and these macro-objective structures were, in turn, furthering the macro-sub-jective rationalization of the world. Although Weber clearly focused on the macro-level, he also had a clear conception of the two micro-levels. He under-stood that people have minds and that what people think makes a difference.

Furthermore, he understood that people engaged in action and interaction and they, too, were important. He also traced out how patterns of action and interaction evolved into more and more macroscopic objective structures. Weber is clearly, from our point of view, on the right track in this analysis of the multiple levels of society.

However, Weber, like Marx, is ultimately subverted theoretically by his political beliefs. Weber was clearly appalled by the progressive rationalization and bureaucratization of society. He felt that these developments were largely eliminating the importance of individual thought and action. Thus, despite some attention to the hope of individual actions to control these systems, Weber focused his considerable theoretical powers on macro-structures. Even charisma, which would seem to imply the significance of the microscopic level, does not help us much. In fact, Weber is primarily interested in how charisma becomes institutionalized, rather than the potentially revolutionary impact of individual action. Most depressing, in this regard, is Weber's idea of unanticipated consequences. This implies that even when individual action has an impact, it is often different from that intended by the actor. Thus individual Calvinists acting to carry out the logic of their religion helped produce an economic system that they did not anticipate and that would ultimately play a role in subverting their religion, as well as religion in general.

Despite his focus on social facts, Parsons always had a deep concern with the relationship between the multiple levels of social reality. This is clear in Parsons' four systems of action—cultural, social, personality, and biological. The cultural and social systems clearly parallel what we have been calling the macro-subjective and macro-objective. Although Parsons' biological organism does not bear on the issues being discussed here (although it does anticipate the current rebirth of interest in biosociology, cf. Barash, 1977), his personality system is at least partially coterminous with the micro-subjective realm. All that is omitted is a concern for the micro-objective which Parsons might see as included in the social system. Furthermore, Parsons clearly enunciated the belief that it was the integration of the macro- and micro-levels of social reality that lay at the heart of sociology: "The integration of a set of common value patterns with the internalized need-disposition structure of the constituent personalities is the core phenomenon of the dynamics of social systems. That the stability of any social system except the most evanescent interaction process is dependent on a degree of such integration may be said to be *the fundamental dynamic theorem of sociology*" (Parsons, 1951:42; my italics). Parsons' concern with this relationship is clearly in line with our interest in developing an integrated approach to social reality.

Despite his promise of providing an integrated theory, the weight of Parsons' argument is on the side of macro-structures, on the impact of the social and cultural system on the personality. The personality either is externally constrained or constrains itself as a result of the internalization of the societal value system. The ability of the personality system to affect or alter macro-systems is minimal or nonexistent. The personality system provides resources to the larger systems, and it is, in turn, constrained by them. Thus although Parsons is concerned with the relationship between the personality and the social system, it is clearly not an equal partnership; the personality is reduced to a subordinate system. The power of these larger systems is reflected in the oft-noted disappearance of voluntarism from Parsons' later work.

In addition to sharing a weakness at the microscopic level with Marx, Weber, and Durkheim, Parsons also has the additional problem of offering an abstract system that lacks a sense of the real world and of the historical development of that world. An adequate theory of the multiple levels of social reality requires that the theorist be embedded in the real world and the historical changes that characterize that world. Although Parsons (1966, 1971) tried in his fashion to deal with social change in his later work, his basic theoretical system lacks a historical component.

Turning now to theorists who focused primarily on the microscopic levels, we find that despite this focus Mead also has at least a sense of the relationship between macroscopic and microscopic phenomenon. Indeed, his conception comes closer than Parsons' to the imagery suggested by Marx's theory, if not his praxis, of the dialectical relationship between the multiple levels of social reality. In the introduction to *Mind, Self and Society*, Mead says that the individual "constitutes society as genuinely as society constitutes the individual" (Mead, 1934:xxv). Later he says: "The 'I' is the response of the individual to the attitude of the community as this appears in his own experience. His response to that organized attitude in turn changes it" (Mead, 1934:196). Thus there are clearly indications that Mead had a sense of an integrated approach to social reality.

Nevertheless, Mead does not offer such an integrated approach. In fact, his problems can be seen as almost the mirror image of the problems of Parsonsian theory. Whereas Parsons devoted most of his attention to culture, Mead focused on consciousness. Parsons, as we have seen, tended to lose sight of voluntarism while it is a crucial aspect of Mead's analysis: "For it is their possession of minds or powers of thinking which enables human individuals to turn back critically, as it were, upon the organized social structure of the society to which they belong (and from their relations to which their minds are in the first instance derived), and to reorganize or reconstruct or modify that social structure to a greater or lesser degree . . ." (Mead, 1934:308). At the same time that we are offered a rich conception of micro-subjectivity, we are given little sense of macro-structures and the way they constrain and coerce individuals. Take, for example, Mead's (1934:270) argument that a society "represents an organized set of responses to certain situations in which the individual is involved."

Such an image of society clearly fails to describe the macro-objective and macro-subjective structures that make up society and the way these operate on the micro-levels of thought and action.

Although he is embedded in the phenomenological approach, Schutz offers a particularly useful analysis of micro- and macro-subjectivity as well as some insight into micro-objectivity. This means, given the four levels of reality of concern here, that Schutz's obvious weakness lies in the omission of any serious discussion of macro-objectivity. In his most important work, Schutz (1967) begins with a discussion and critical analysis of Weber's microscopic sociology, particularly his interest in the actor's subjective meaning context. But Schutz is dissatisfied with Weber, a dissatisfaction that comes as little surprise to Weberian scholars who recognize that the bulk of Weber's contribution lies at the macroscopic, not the microscopic, levels. Schutz then turns to the philosophers Husserl and Bergson for greater insight into the minding process. These influences lead Schutz to pay a great deal of attention to consciousness and such intrapsychic processes as the stream of consciousness, meaning, and the in-order-to and because motives. It is interesting that Schutz must ultimately turn to philosophers for insight into micro-subjectivity. It became clear to Schutz, as it has to many sociologists, that it is difficult (to put it mildly) to study consciousness scientifically. Thus Schutz came to the highly questionable assertion, perhaps because he was deeply concerned with developing a *scientific* conception, that the study of consciousness is *not* part of sociology.

Schutz moves next to the we relationship, or the face-to-face interpersonal relationships that make up the micro-objective world. But Schutz, despite some excellent insights into this process, also rules it out of sociology because such relationships are, in his view, unique and would involve trying to gain an understanding of consciousness intersubjectively. Aware of this level of social reality, Schutz leaves it behind as he moves to what he considers the proper domain of sociology, the *mitwelt* or the world of contemporaries. This is the world of not directly perceived or encountered contemporaries, and it is deemed by him to be "the sole subject of the social sciences" (Schutz, 1967:15).

The heart of Schutz's analysis lies in his discussion of the world of contemporaries. In this world, we engage in what Schutz calls "they relationships" rather than we relationships. This means that we do not relate to contemporaries personally or subjectively, but rather as anonymous processes. There is a wide range of anonymity in the *mitwelt*, ranging toward people once encountered face to face and whom one could meet again, to macroscopic entities like the state. We deal with consociates in the we relationship micro-subjectively, but can only grasp contemporaries macro-subjectively. In Schutz's terms: "The subjective meaning-context has been abandoned as a tool of interpretation. It has been replaced by a series of highly complex and systematically interrelated objective meaning-contexts" (Schutz, 1967:184). Thus Schutz focuses on the macro-subjective level, the same level that occupied the attention of most of his predecessors in the German historicist tradition—Dilthey, Rickert, Weber, and others. This leads Schutz, as it did Weber, to focus on the scientific study of first-order typifications (of either people or courses of action) that are used in our relationships with contemporaries rather than the more personalized relationships of those with consociates. These objective types can be studied scientifically, whereas micro-interaction and consciousness cannot.

In addition to lacking a strong conception of the macro-objective, the problem with Schutz's work lies in the fact that he rules out of sociology the micro-objective and micro-subjective realms despite his rich insights into them. As a result, he lacks an analysis of the relationship between his focal concern, the macro-subjective, and these other levels of social reality. In order to be useful, the microscopic levels must be integrated with Schutz's macro-subjective focus and combined with a much stronger conception of the macro-objective.

Even though there are certainly other thinkers, both classic and contemporary, who have had something to say about the relationship between the four levels of social reality identified in this paper, I would like to close this section by discussing a few specific works that focus directly on the issues raised here.

We can begin with Berger and Luckmann's *The Social Construction of Reality* (1967), since it relies heavily on the work of Alfred Schutz, which we have just discussed, and because it seems to be the best lead available in our effort to find an integrated approach. Berger and Luckmann begin with a self-conscious interest in developing an integrated paradigm by seeking to relate Max Weber's microscopic work on social action to Emile Durkheim's analysis of social facts. In so doing, and integrating those perspectives with Schutz's ideas, they develop a version of Marx's dictum of the relationship between people and history that is the most succinct statement extant on the integrative concern in this paper: "Society is a human product. Society is an objective reality. Man is a social product" (Berger and Luckmann, 1967:61). There are a number of useful implications to be derived from this statement. First, we should study the way in which people historically produce society and its social structures and social institutions. Second, as a result of this process, we should be concerned with the way in which society becomes an objective reality. Finally, we should examine the way in which society, once it has achieved objective facticity, produces people through socialization and other ways.

Although Berger and Luckmann offer a provocative lead toward a theory of multiple realities of social life, their approach has a fatal flaw owing to its linkage to the phenomenological tradition. That flaw lies in their focus on subjectivity at all levels and their almost total omission of any consideration of micro- and macro-objectivity. Perhaps most disastrous, and most inexplicable given their initial orientation, is the omission of any serious consideration of the kind of macro-objective factors that so concerned people like Marx. The only thing approaching an objective structure in their work is language, and even it is treated more subjectively than objectively. This failure is exemplified by the way in which they define social structure: "The sum total of these typifications and of the recurrent patterns of interaction established by them" (Berger and Luckmann, 1967:33).

To be fair, however, we should point out that despite these failures, Berger and Luckmann are stronger on the micro-subjective level than Schutz. Whereas Schutz defines this out of sociology, Berger and Luckmann make it integral to their theory. More importantly, they have a clear conception of the relationship between micro- and macro-subjectivity, that is, the way macro-subjective factors emerge out of the micro-subjective realm. This is a major advance over Schutz's work, in which the two are rather separate. But this strength is simultaneously a problem, for it reduces all of sociology to the subjective realm, an obviously indefensible position. I believe that Berger and Luckmann were conscious of this problem by defining their work as a sociology of knowledge and not as a sociological theory. If we accept their limitation, it is clear that a more adequate conception must deal with more than the subjective realm.

Written almost fifteen years earlier, Gerth and Mills' *Character and Social Structure* (1953) charts a similar course for sociology. The authors seek to integrate character (or the micro-subjective) theories of Freud and Mead with the macro-objective and macro-subjective theories of Marx and Weber. They also have a conception of action and interaction which means that they do deal with all of the levels of concern in this paper. Their stated goal is "to link the private and the public, the innermost acts of the individual with the widest kinds of social historical phenomena" (Gerth and Mills, 1953:xvi). This integrative concern reflects a profound interest in history, probably stemming from the authors' interest in the work of Marx and Weber. This is an important component of any integrative theory, one that is lacking in a number of approaches, most notably as we have seen in Parsons'.

The link between social levels for Gerth and Mills is the concept of role: "the key term in our definition of the person is also the key term in the definition of institution . . . the major link of character and social structure" (Gerth and Mills, 1953:22-23). Although offering a widely accepted conception here, I believe that their effort is hurt at this point because lost in the process is any real conception of actors and their thoughts and actions. This loss of micro-processes is compounded when the authors declare that their general aim is to "display, analyze, and understand *types* of persons in terms of their roles within institutions in given orders and social structures within various historical eras; and we want to do this for each institutional order" (Gerth and Mills, 1953:34; my italics). This constitutes a perversion of the Weberian use of ideal types. For Weber, ideal types were not the subject matter of sociology, but methodological tools to get at the subject matter—real actors in history. For Gerth and Mills, ideal types become *the* subject matter, with the result that real actors and actions drop out of their perspective. Also omitted are what they call the "ephemeral modes of social interaction" (Gerth and Mills,

1953:20). As a result, the kinds of actions and interactions that are of concern to people like the ethnomethodologists are omitted.

Although the focus is on types, roles, and institutions, Gerth and Mills adhere to the belief that actors have self-consciousness, self-awareness, and at least "some autonomy." Yet it is clear, and even as partisan a supporter of Mills as Scimecca (1976) agrees, that the macroscopic elements of this approach are paramount. Furthermore, Scimecca (1976:85) sees Mills moving progressively toward such a macro-orientation in his later works: "Mills, in his subsequent works, would concentrate more on objective factors, what he referred to as 'the main drift' of these historical and structural forces that were often impersonal and unrecognized by those who suffered their 'impact.'" Despite this trend in Mills' work, and the obvious macroscopic bias in *Character and Social Structure*, it does offer a number of the elements needed for an integrated approach to the multiple levels of social reality.

I can close this section by saying that we have certainly had a number of leads toward an integrated sociological paradigm. In fact, there are many others. Among the ethnomethodologists we can see that Mehan and Wood's (1976) call for an interrelated approach to social structure *and* structuring is also of this genre. Similarly, Ian Craib (1976) has discussed the relevance of the ideas of Jean-Paul Sartre to sociology and concluded that what he has to offer is "a very sophisticated Weberian position which can be used as an underpinning for a Marxist structural analysis, attempting to combine methodological individualism and a methodological holism in a unified theory" (Craib, 1976:12). The phenomenologist George Psathas offers a similarly integrative perspective: "When social science recognizes that the objective reality of society, groups, community, and formal organization is subjectively experienced by the individual and that these subjective experiences are intimately related to the subsequent externalization and objectication procedures in which humans engage as they think and act in the social world, then a more informed and reality-based social science will result" (Psathas, 1973:13). Later, Psathas, who bases his analysis at the micro-subjective level, makes the case for relating these to various kinds of macro-structures: "... it is also appropriate for me to examine the language system and how it structures experience, the organizational and social structures in which persons live, and the cultural system with its systems of belief, value, and knowledge, all of which provide meaningful structures for those humans who share and live within them" (Psathas, 1973:16). I could go on, but it is clear that many people have had a great deal to say about the need for, and possibilities of, an integrated sociological paradigm. It is time now to turn to the lesson of all of this, the nature of such a paradigm, at least in schematic form.

An Exemplar for an Integrated Paradigm

The preceding section constitutes the background for the effort in this section to sketch out an exemplar for a sociological paradigm that deals in an interrelated fashion with the basic levels of social reality detailed earlier. The following enumeration, drawing on the analysis of sociological theorists offered earlier in this paper, is intended as a first approximation of an integrated paradigm. It will undoubtedly undergo changes as additional thought and research point up problems in it as well as additional ideas that need to be added.

First, the paradigm being outlined here is not intended to replace any extant sociological paradigm. The already existing paradigms *are* useful for analyzing given levels of social reality. The social facts paradigm is most useful for the study of macro-objective and macro-subjective social phenomena. The social definition paradigm works best at the levels of micro-subjective and micro-objective social reality. The social behavior paradigm has the greatest applicability to the micro-objective world. As long as the adherents of each of these approaches refrain from claiming to explain all of social reality, their paradigms can be of great utility to sociology. Although attempting to explain all social phenomena is a laudable goal, it cannot be done with a paradigm which is inherently based on one, or at best two, levels of social reality.

Second, the essence of the new, integrated sociological paradigm lies in the interrelationship of the four basic levels of social reality: (1) the macro-objective; examples include law, language, and bureaucracy; (2) the macro-subjective; examples include norms, values, and culture; (3) the micro-objective; examples include forms of social interaction like conflict, cooperation, and exchange; and (4) the micro-subjective; examples include mind, self, and the social construction of reality. The essential point is that these various levels must, within the paradigm being proposed here, be dealt with integratively. That is, any specific subject of study must be examined from an integrated point of view. For example, the coming of the so-called postindustrial society (Bell, 1973) must be examined as an interrelated process involving changes in diverse social entities such as bureaucracies, norms, patterns of interaction, and consciousness. It may be that in such a case macroscopic variables are most important, but that should not permit us to ignore the other levels. Conversely, on other issues microscopic factors may be of greatest explanatory power, but that does not mean that macroscopic variables are of no significance. Many questions require an integrative approach, although the significance of any given level will vary from situation to situation.

Third, I think it likely that even with an integrated paradigm, the greatest attention in contemporary sociology is likely to be focused on macroscopic levels of social reality. This will occur for the same reason that people like Marx and Weber were led to focus on this level: that is, the nature of large-scale modern society tends to overwhelm the microscopic level. Despite this, I believe we must never lose sight of the existence and significance of both the micro-objective and micro-subjective realms. People act, interact, and create social reality in even the most reified societies, and those actions do at some time and to at least some degree have an impact on the larger society. Real people act in behalf of, or are acted on by, macro-structures, and sociology *must never lose sight of this fact*. When we do, we tend to create arid intellectual systems that do little more than further support an already reified social structure. In addition, sociologists must not omit the more ephemeral modes of social action and interaction in their focus on macro-objective and subjective entitites. Some of the noninstitutionalized realms of social reality may someday alter institutionalized realms or themselves become the accepted way of doing things.

Fourth, despite the fact that we have identified four basic levels of social reality, we should bear in mind that the social world is a world in flux and is not neatly divided into four levels. Thus the various microscopic phenomena are at some point rather arbitrarily transformed into the macroscopic level. The four-level schema does violence to the real world, and we must never forget that. However, all such schema have this problem, but they must be created in order to be able to handle the complexities of the social world. We must be careful not to reify this, or any other, conceptual schema. It is the real world, and not the schema, that is the subject matter of sociology.

Fifth, the paradigm being espoused here must inherently be comparative either over time or cross-societally. The interrelated character of this approach allows us to collect data by any or all methods (questionnaire, interview, experiment, observation, etc.), but if we are truly interested in understanding the dynamics of the interrelationships among various levels of social reality, we must be able to compare different societies in order to get a sense of the differences (and similarities) in the way in which the various levels work with, or against, each other. I believe that most of the truly great sociologists like Marx, Weber, and Durkheim utilized comparative methodology and they, of course, also had an implicit integrated paradigm.

Sixth, an integrated paradigm must be historical; it must eschew the idea that a single abstract theory can be developed that can explain all of social reality in all societies throughout history. Although all levels can be found in all societies, the weight of each and the relationship among them will vary from one society to another. This paradigm must also be oriented to the study of the changing nature of social reality over time. Although we might be interested in the study of contemporary reality, it must always be seen in the context of the changing nature of society.

Seventh, the integrated paradigm being proposed here has much to gain from dialectical logic, although the wholehearted adoption of the dialectic would seem to be prohibited by the political ideologies associated with, and sometimes infused in, it. I am not the first to propose the resurrection of the mode of thought associated with Hegel and Marx. Friedrichs (1972) made a similar effort a few years ago although his major goal seemed to be bridging the differences between system and conflict theory and not the broader objective undertaken here. The dialectic is notoriously difficult to deal with, in part because it is hard to capture in static words and sentences. Furthermore, the dialectic carries with it certain radical political implications that has made it anathema to many sociologists. Nevertheless, there are a number of aspects of the dialectic that are useful to sociology, particularly to the kind of integrated analysis being proposed here.

The dialectic is rooted in the real world of individual thought and action. It sees people producing larger social structures and those structures coming, in turn, to constrain and coerce actors. It therefore has a very clear image of the interrelationship between the microscopic and macroscopic realms. Yet it does not give primacy to one or the other; they are seen as dialectically related.

The dialectic begins with the epistemological assumption that in the real world "everything is interconnected and forever in flux" (Ollman, 1971:54). There are therefore no hard-and-fast dividing lines between social phenomena. This sort of imagery is clearly in line with the one behind the integrated approach being offered here. Despite this image, dialecticians realize that in order to be able to deal with this world in flux, they must develop conceptual schema. A schema clearly implied by the dialectic is one that carves the real world up into various levels. This, of course, is the schema employed here, although innumerable other schema are possible, even desirable, in order to gain greater insight into the complexities of the modern world.

Whatever schema one adopts, the dialectic attunes us to look for the interrelationships among the various components. We should not be satisfied with merely dividing up social reality and then categorizing bits and pieces of social life. Rather, we must always be attuned to the manifold ways in which each of the entities is related to all of the others.

Not only does the dialectic lead us to look for levels, or other components, of social reality, but it also attunes us to the likelihood of contradictions within and between the various levels. The existence of such contradictions is a basic finding of virtually every major sociologist. Marx, of course, focused on the contradictions that exist within capitalist society, but insights into contradictions also exist in the work of Weber (rationalization versus individual freedom), Simmel (subjective versus objective culture), and many others. The study of such contradictions lies at the heart of a dialectical approach to social reality.

The dialectic also leads the sociologist to look beyond the appearance of social reality to its essence. To use Peter Berger's term, this means that sociology is engaged in the business of "debunking" (1963). We must never be content with individual rationalizations or group ideologies, but must look instead for the "real" nature of social reality.

In sum, the dialectic focuses on the real world and the relationship between the microscopic and macroscopic levels of social reality, sees the world as forever in flux, thereby necessitating the creation of conceptual schema to deal with it, looks to the relationship between the various levels of society (as long as we keep in mind that there are no hard-and-fast dividing lines in the real world), attunes us to the likelihood of contradictions between levels, and urges the sociologist to look beyond appearances to the essence of social reality.

The dialectical mode of logic has much to offer to the integrated paradigm being espoused here. We may prefer less ideologically loaded terms like "relational" or "multicausal" to describe the approach taken here, but we should not lose sight of the fact that we shall be borrowing a good number of our insights from the dialectic.

SUMMARY AND CONCLUSION

Sociology is a multiple paradigm science. In this paper I have reviewed my image of that status and extended some of the ideas offered in my earlier work. My major goal, however, has been to make the case for a new, more integrated paradigm. To that end I reviewed the work of major sociologists who have offered useful leads in that direction. Although none of these is totally adequate, many sociologists have had a sense of such an integrated approach. Based on these works, I offered an outline of an exemplar for an integrated paradigm. Such a paradigm would not replace, but would supplement, extant sociological paradigms. It would deal in an integrated fashion with the four major levels of social reality—macro-objective, macro-subjective, micro-objective, micro-subjective. Despite this range of interest, sociologists who operate within this paradigm are likely to focus on macro-structures because of the reified nature of modern society. Although the focus is on levels of social reality, we would not lose sight of the fact that levels are simply sociological constructs and that the real world is a vast continuum in constant flux. Such a paradigm demands a comparative methodology either cross-culturally or over time. It must also have a sense of history oriented to the study of change and eschewing a single, abstract, ahistorical theory. Finally, such an integrated paradigm has much to gain from the dialectic which attunes us, among other things, to the manifold relations among the various levels of social reality.

I have only been able to present an outline of an integrated sociological paradigm in this paper. There is clearly much to be done with it, but as Kuhn points out, one of the things that makes a paradigm attractive is the fact that it does not answer all of the questions and leaves much to be done by others. It is hoped that the need to fill in the bare bones will make this integrated paradigm attractive to some sociologists who are dissatisfied with the existing ways of dealing with social reality and see some utility in a more integrated approach.

NOTES

1. Much of this section is derived from George Ritzer, "Sociology: A Multiple Paradigm Science," *American Sociologist* 10 (1975):156-67.

2. This section is based on George Ritzer, "Reflections on the Paradigmatic Status of Sociology," presented at the Alpha Kappa Delta Meetings, Richmond, Virginia, 1977.

3. What follows is based on George Ritzer, "An Exemplar for an Integrated Sociological Paradigm," presented at the Plenary Session of the Midwest Sociological Society Meetings, 1977.

4. Thomas Kuhn, especially in his later work, would clearly be uncomfortable with the idea of creating an exemplar. However, Kuhn, at least in his later work, thinks of exemplars as concrete puzzle solutions. There are few, if any, of these in sociology. Our major exemplars are program statements like Durkheim's case for social facts as the subject matter of sociology. This paper is an attempt to create an exemplar in the Durkheimian tradition.

5. This paper has much in common with the work of Georges Gurvitch (Bosserman, 1968). Gurvitch uses the idea of levels of social reality, although he employs more levels and they are developed on different bases than the levels employed here. Gurvitch employs the idea of the dialectic, which is also utilized later in this paper. However, this paper does not flow from Gurvitch's work, but rather from the effort to analyze the paradigmatic status of sociology and to propose a new paradigm that deals in an integrated fashion with the various levels of social reality. Although there are parallels between Gurvitch's work and this paper, Gurvitch's orientation has not had a profound influence on this work.

Norbert Wiley

THE RISE AND FALL
OF DOMINATING
THEORIES IN
AMERICAN
SOCIOLOGY

The history of American sociology falls into certain patterns that are more interesting than the sum of their parts. Theory changes discontinuously every decade or two, and the pattern of change is noticeably conditioned by larger social change, competing theory groups, and social processes that relate groups to ideas. The examination of these patterns can shed light on the theory of any given period, including the present. It also suggests that much of sociology's capital lies in its history—a series of successive insights—often lost and forgotten but available to the language that can name them all. Such a language cannot be constructed overnight, but I shall suggest a few ideas in that direction, drawing from them a brief analytic history of American sociology.

One way the contours of American sociology can be seen is in the rise and fall of dominating theories. Sociology formally begins in the United States in the 1890s with a long period of self-definition, emancipation from the other social sciences, and gradual establishment as a teaching subject in universities. The first dominant school of thought, the Chicago School, crystallized around World War I and continued until the early thirties. The second dominating school, the functionalists, succeeded the Chicago School in the forties and fifties after a period of interregnum. Functionalism declined in the late sixties, and no theory group succeeded in taking its place, though there were several claimants, and sociology was clearly undergoing massive internal change during the postfunctionalism years. Although not attempting to predict the future, I shall show why periods of interregnum follow the fall of powerful theory groups and how the current interregnum differs from the earlier one. I shall also suggest how the "ins versus outs" pattern might be broken, how the field might be integrated without a dominating group, and how the present uneasy interregnum might thereby be resolved.

METHOD

The first point of method has to do with the strands that intertwine to form the history of a science. I shall treat the flow of sociological history as having three determinants: ideas, theory groups, and control of the means of production. All three work together, in some wondrous way, to produce the stream of symbols we call the history of sociology.

The ideas themselves—whether theoretical, methodological, or substantive—have life histories of their own; to some extent they cause each other, and they are considerably more than shadows of underlying social processes. Their implications, exclusions, associations and emotional overtones have important symbolic force, and it is a mistake to dissolve the power of ideas into the politics of interest groups or the structure of social organization.

But ideas do not just float along like clouds. People have to think them, and it takes a subtle organization of people to develop ideas and increase their explanatory power. This point has been made persuasively by Nicholas Mullins in his *Theories and Theory Groups in Contemporary American Sociology* (1973), which has the striking merit of showing that ideas are cultivated and harvested by real groups of people. These people can be named, their scholarly interactions observed, and it can be shown that the growth and spread of ideas depends not just on their intrinsic merit but on the skill, strategy, and luck of group processes as well.

A major source of theory group strength, beyond the merit of ideas and the skill of group processes, is access to the means of intellectual production. In the economy generally the term "means of production" refers to productive property of any kind, but in the economy of a scholarly discipline the term refers only to the tools and productive property of that discipline. Among the more basic tools are professional jobs, access to journal publication, graduate students, access to university and commercial publishers, and money for research. In addition, in this day of government programs and learned society lobbying, basic tools include the control of the organizational and ceremonial structures of the major professional associations of the discipline.

To achieve domination, a theory must be reasonably strong in all three respects. It must have intellectual merit; it must be backed by a well-organized group; and the group must gain control of a large and balanced share of the means of intellectual production. An idea or theory that is unsuccessful is not necessarily less true or less meritorious than the successful ones. The key theorist may not have formed a group, or it may have been poorly organized and led, or it may have been unable to gain enough of the means of production to grow.[2] As we shall see, the interregnums are periods in which no theory group can put together this three-legged throne and sit on it.

A second point of method, which assumes several things, concerns the "ins versus outs" framework of analysis. It assumes that sociology has never had a theory so full of truth that almost everyone was convinced of it. Instead, the normal condition has been for there to be several opposing theories on all key questions. There has never been a full-scale paradigm in Thomas Kuhn's technical sense, though this term, or one like it, can be more loosely used in the social sciences (Kuhn, 1962). And perhaps in the nature of the case, unlike that of the natural sciences, there never will be that type of paradigm. In any event, the pattern of sociology has been one of rival theory groups competing over ideas, members, and the means of production.

This framework also assumes that the various groups of "outs" will initially pursue their criticisms of the "ins" as a series of separate and uncoordinated attacks on the weak spots of the dominating group. The outs will be intellectually divided from each other, and they will try to retain as much intellectual purity as possible. If, however, this unorganized set of little rebellions does not work, the various groups that constitute the outs may move toward coalitions, looking for similarities in their ideas, compatibilities in their methods, and ways of sharing or combining their meager means of production. It may be that much of the creativity in science is brought about by power considerations that dissolve old conceptual limits and force scholars to think the unthinkable.

Finally, this framework allows that the "dualization" of scientific power between dominating groups of ins and brooding sets of outs need not necessarily continue indefinitely. Sociology's interregnums, including the present one, are characterized by a wasteful jockeying for supremacy and a decline in the authority of the discipline. Perhaps the maturity of a discipline depends on its using its best insights simultaneously and finding unity in diversity, thereby breaking out of the "ins versus outs" pattern.

A third point of method has to do with the gains and risks that come from using a wide intellectual brush. To cover eighty years in one essay requires a great deal of selectivity and does not permit the detailed documentation that a smaller problem would allow. Major assertions will be documented, but at times I shall rely on common knowledge, historical summary, and my own interpretations. My quest will be for ideas rather than ideographic precision, and my assumption is that certain questions can never be raised, let alone answered, unless scholars sometimes use a wide brush. This means that in reviewing the relations among theory groups of the past I shall not use the same careful methods Mullins used in reviewing such groups in the present. His methods *could* be used, but this paper is a preliminary statement, and it is meant only to establish a framework for more detailed research.

In particular I shall not always be able to prove that a collection of scholars who followed the same intellectual orientation formed an interacting group in the strict sense of the word. At times the better term might be "grouping," which suggests some interaction but less than in a working group. Actually, Mullins has already done much of the work of this paper, for it is easy to refer to contemporary groupings such as symbolic interactionists, ethnomethodologists, and new causal theorists, since he showed the structures of these groups in some detail. In dealing with those of the more distant past, however, some descriptive precision will necessarily be sacrificed. If these losses are compensated by ideas that could not otherwise be constructed, the bargain will be favorable and the wide brush justified.

A final procedural matter concerns the weasel-word "positivist," which I shall often use. Ignoring the complex nineteenth-century history of this word, it is commonly and loosely used today for anyone who is on the highly quantified or mathematical side in sociology. I find this informal usage among the Weberians, Marxists, symbolic interactionists, and phenomenologists whom I know, as well as among others, and it is clearly a valid meaning of the term in the Wittgensteinian, language-game sense of meaning. For some purposes, however, this is sloppy usage of this term. More technically, positivism often means: (1) scientism, or the dictum that sociology must use natural science models outlawing empathy/gestalt/teleology/*verstehen*/typification/elective affinity/dialectics/functionalism, and so on, except as a prescientific heuristic device. In addition, subjective states—much as in Watsonian behaviorism—are inadmissible as data, except as they are externalized or objectified in questionnaire responses and the like. This is about the same as Parsons' definition of "positivism" in his *Structure of Social Action* (Parsons, 1937:61).

Or it can mean (2) seeing the world of symbols, in both culture and social structure, as "external and constraining" in a Durkheimian sense. This version of positivism opposes the "reality construction" argument of symbolic interactionism and phenomenology, holding that symbols are "out there" and not constantly constructed and reconstructed by interacting people (Ritzer, 1975a).

I shall make the assumption that the three definitions—highly quantified, scientistic, and social factist—tend to be found together; that is, the same people tend to have all three traits or methodological commitments, though they do not always go together, and there is some precision lost in using the term. I shall use it anyway, since it is in common use, with the understanding that more refined terms would be needed for more refined analysis. I shall not use the term to refer to the various less quantified and qualitative lines of empirical research: historical, case study, participant observation, functional analysis, comparative, phenomenological, and so on. Some of the people who pursue these lines of field work actually are positivists in either the scientistic or social fact senses of the word, though most are not, and I think my somewhat imprecise usage is adequate for the kind of sketch I have in mind.

THE EVOLUTIONARY PERIOD

The formal origin of American sociology can be dated to 1892, when Albion Small founded the first department of sociology at the new University of Chicago (Diner, 1975), although the field had been inching into existence for several decades, outside of universities and in other disciplines, and it is merely a convenience to use this late date. But if we think of Small as having founded the *role* of the sociologist, as opposed to the books and ideas of the field of sociology, we do have a precise date. Before the Chicago founding, there were almost no jobs in the United States for sociologists, and, in a way, there were no sociologists, except in an amateur or part-time manner. This is another way of saying a role comes into stable existence when someone will buy it, either on the market or in the state. Along with the sale—in this case to universities—there gradually came a whole culture of erudition, morality, tradition, ceremony, and legality, but if there had been no sale, the rich growth and development of sociology would not have come about.

Other universities were also adding sociology in the 1890s, but it was not until World War I that a dominating theoretical school was formed. For the twenty some years before then, organized sociology was busily attempting to give internal clarification to a role which had come unexpectedly, so to speak, with the Chicago founding. In other words, people were selling the role before they were quite sure what they were selling—before they had defined the field in a way that would liberate it from its origins in other bodies of thought and other social institutions.

Throughout the nineteenth century, especially after the Civil War, the idea was spreading that one could have systematic knowledge of, or perhaps a science of, society (Bernard and Bernard, 1943; Curti, 1964). The idea was often a political football, and there were differently flavored sociologies for Southern planters, Northern robber barrons, modernizing Protestant religions, trade unions, and social reformers. Though the idea of a science of society was everywhere, it was also nowhere, for it was confined to the borders of other roles and lacked its own niche in society (Becker and Barnes, 1961:vol. 3; Dorfman, 1934; Hofstadter, 1955). The Chicago founding, then, was the beginning of a role confluence in which a role that was poorly defined and part time within the confines of several other roles burst into its own structure (cf. Baker, Ferrell, and Quensel, 1975).[3]

However, the emancipation from these parental roles and the clarification of what was new and different in sociology—tasks which were necessary if sociology was to spread among universities—took a long time (Matthews, 1977: chap. 4). Since this role confluence is not well understood in the history of American sociology, I shall simply list what appear to be the major umbilical cords which the early sociologists had to cut.

Evolution

Darwin's theory of biological evolution was both a help and a hindrance to the founding of sociology. It helped by weakening traditional religion, which had its own, biblically based sociology, and which would have to be replaced by a secular substitute. But if biological evolution was itself to be the new sociology, there would be no need for a separate field of sociology. And, if changes in society and culture were interpreted strictly from a survival-of-the-fittest point of view, sociology would lose the crucial sponsorship of liberal religion, social reformers, and the liberal fringes of the other social sciences. Accordingly, one of the major tasks of early sociology, well met by Lester Ward in *Dynamic Sociology* (1883), was to temper the dog-eat-dog fatalism of social Darwinism by reinterpreting evolution to allow for reform, self-direction of society, and a cultural level of organization that transcended biology (Page, 1969; Hinkle and Hinkle, 1954; Goldman, 1956).

German Idealism

The evolutionism of Darwin and the British sociologist Herbert Spencer was only one of several intellectual streams leading to the confluence of sociology. In addition, many early sociologists took graduate work at German universities and learned a historicist version of social science which drew on elements of Hegelian and neo-Kantian idealism (Herbst, 1965). The German social sciences were at the opposite philosophical pole from the British, for, far from being materialistic or biological, they located the heart of the social in nonmaterial elements such as symbols, values, and meanings, and their quest was for the underlying patterns of meaning, stretched across large swatches of historical time (Reill, 1975; Aho, 1975).

These students returned to the United States just as American philosophy was shifting from various forms of idealism to the more materialistic philosophy of pragmatism. In his article on "The Philosophies of Royce, James and Dewey in Their American Setting," George Herbert Mead (1964b:371-91) interprets the philosophical shift, in which he was a central participant, as the gradual adoption of a culture fitting to a democratic capitalist society, free of feudal institutions and influences. Mead thought idealism was more suited to an aristocratic, monarchical society, and pragmatism more suitable for a democracy. In any case, the German-trained social scientists found themselves under pressure to Americanize their ideas, which meant shifting theories and methods to something closer to pragmatism, and they did so by joining the pragmatists in the loose school of thought called reform Darwinism (Goldman, 1956:chap. 5; Jones, 1972).[4]

Economics

German sociology was largely an expansion of economics to take account of economically important social forces which were not themselves economic. Max Weber's sociology comes from this process, and there is no clear line between his economics and his sociology. Similarly, in the United States early sociology grew within economics, although more for reasons of practical reform and less of theory than in Germany. The result was that in the United States,

sociologists had difficulty breaking out of economics departments and forming their own academic departments, for this breaking away required a defen-
sible intellectual justification (Baker, Ferrell, and Quensel, 1975). It had to be
shown that the subject matter of sociology was not just the "leftovers," as the
Harvard economist Thomas N. Carver had said (Small, 1910:8-10), but was a
legitimate field of investigation.

The early American sociologists pursued a number of conceptual lines to
make their theoretical escape from economics, using such noneconomic ideas
as "process," "forms," "groups," "society," and "culture." Although the
ideas of Simmel, and eventually Durkheim, were useful for uncoupling the
field from economics, sociologists were not completely successful in making
this escape, and to this day there are signs that economics would like to swallow
chunks of sociology (Olson, 1968).

Ethical Commitment

Early sociology was also initially close to a variety of committed social movements, religious bodies, and pressure groups that wanted to use sociological
knowledge to achieve specific political and ethical ends. These groups ranged
from the small Marxist parties to Social Gospel Protestantism, Progressive social reform associations, and conservative business organizations (Bernard
and Bernard, 1943; Matthews, 1977). But there were dangers in getting caught
in the cross fire. The early Chicago sociologists could almost literally feel the
heat, and as an English professor from that early Chicago period recalls:

The chief excitement of the summer of 1894 was the strike which, beginning with the
workers at Pullman, came to involve all the railroads having connections at Chicago.
Night after night we saw the western sky red with the light of burning cars. Grant Park
was white with the tents of soldiers sent by President Cleveland on the pretext that the
strikers were interfering with the mails, a charge hotly denied by Governor Altgeld.
(Lovett, 1948:68)

To achieve autonomy and self-direction the early sociologists had to devise a
formula of objective science and ethical-political neutrality which would release them from the moral authority of these sponsoring groups and movements. The trick was to find an identity which would allow intellectual independence without offending too many powerful groups too much. The practical result was more a matter of finding the safe political center—away from the
sharp ideological edges of the left and right—than one of avoiding political implications altogether, and the early sociologists eventually put together a field
which was mildly reformist, without being too close to either socialism or busi-
ness-dictated conservatism. This search for a safe centrism was the practical
meaning of ethical neutrality; yet despite the moral and political difficulties of
this cumbersome escape from commitment, it proved a workable way of a-

chieving enough moral autonomy to allow for professional, self-governing controls (Becker, 1971).

These four umbilical cords, as well as some others, were not easily cut. The result was that American sociology spent over two decades on a kind of shakedown cruise in which it gradually achieved enough autonomy to steer its own ship. World War I was important for the crystallization of sociology, for it gave focus to a number of social problems—particularly that of assimilating the numerous big-city immigrants—that sociologists would be asked to solve. The role of sociologists had finally become a workable, productive role, and the mutation occurred at the University of Chicago, the place where the role had first been created in the 1890s.

THE CHICAGO SCHOOL

The Chicago School's reign, broadly conceived, extended from World War I to the founding of the rival *American Sociological Review* in 1936, though its best years were the twenties. The intellectual or theoretical unity of this school has always been difficult for scholars to put their fingers on. The key members were Albion Small, born in 1854 and declining by the early twenties but still in power as editor of the *American Journal of Sociology* and lifetime department head; W. I. Thomas, who left in 1918, just as the school was being formed, but whose ideas and empirical style remained influential throughout the period; Robert Park, who was the intellectual center point and leading member of the school; Ernest W. Burgess, whose career began with a brilliant nineteenth-century style dissertation against social Darwinism and eventually stretched all the way to the high-speed computer; and Ellsworth Faris, who succeeded Small as department chairman in 1926 and served as a crucial link to Mead and the pragmatists in other departments (Carey, 1975; Matthews, 1977; Short, 1971; Dibble, 1975; Diner, 1975; Burgess and Bogue, 1963; Shils, 1970; Faris, 1967; Rucker, 1969; Cavan, 1972).

It is not difficult to see the group basis of the Chicago School: their Ph.D.'s out teaching and getting into reciprocity arrangements with their faculty back at Chicago, their annual get-togethers at the Society for Social Research convention held every summer after 1920, their arrangements to teach summer school on each other's campuses, and their breakfasts and caucuses at the annual meetings of the American Sociological Society. Nor is it difficult to see their enormous control over the key means of intellectual production. The major journal was theirs; they attracted excellent graduate students; their Ph.D.'s chaired departments and controlled jobs on numerous campuses; they controlled the ASS through permanently occupying the office of secretary-treasurer, usually being well represented among the other offices too; and in 1923 the Laura Spelman Rockefeller Fund began giving substantial sums for social research at Chicago.[5] But the intellectual unity of the school is more difficult to get at.

Perhaps the best way to put it is to say they were all symbolic interactionists in the generic, pre-Blumerian sense of the word, though this is not entirely fair to Herbert Blumer, who coined the term in 1937 (Blumer, 1937) and gave it much of its modern meaning. Nevertheless, they all saw symbols and personalities as emerging from interaction; they were all broadly oriented to language; they all worked in research media fitting these premises; and they all agreed that society was largely meaning and meaning systems were self-confirming truths (Faris, 1967; Carey, 1975; Rucker, 1969).

What seems to have occurred with this group, epistemologically, is that they created a merger of German historical idealism, which was moving toward materialism in the United States, and philosophical pragmatism, which, with William James, was moving away from materialism.[6] The numerous, German-trained social scientists in America during the late nineteenth century found that historicism—with its primary method of *verstehen*, primary explanation in values and meanings, and exclusively ideographic or individualizing conclusions—did not fit comfortably into native American social science. This poor fit was due partly to an extraneous factor; for these young scholars often returned from Germany with "soft" socialist ideals, more Bismarckian than Marxian, for which America's business elites were far from ready (Goldman, 1956:80). But it was also due to the pervasive evolutionary tone of native American social science, which had been selectively adapted from the writings of Spencer and the more complex Darwinian notions of early pragmatists (Hinkle and Hinkle, 1954). Small found it difficult to make the shift toward reform Darwinism and pragmatism, but Park had little problem moving from Windelband's historicism to an eclecticism which included pragmatism (Herbst, 1959; Dibble, 1975; Becker, 1971; Matthews, 1977; Coser, 1977).

In contrast to this hardening of historicism, pragmatism, which began with Charles Saunders Peirce in the late 1870s (Mills, 1964) as a slight variant of British empiricism, was becoming soft, Germanic, and culturally oriented in the hands of William James. The "will to believe" was introduced by James, and he worked with an idea much like the one W. I. and Dorothy Thomas were later to articulate in saying "if men define situations as real, they are real in their consequences" (Thomas and Thomas, 1928:572). James worked with both forms of pragmatism: the materialistic, hard version originally introduced by Peirce, and his own, religiously open softer form. Seemingly unaware that he was working with two pragmatisms, James could move, effortlessly, from hard empiricism to symbolic interactionism, taking his readers with him (Henle, 1951:125-27; Lovejoy, 1963:6-10). James Dewey and Mead took tough pragmatism halfway to idealism, meeting Park, Small and the other German historicists who were coming from the opposite direction.

This epistemological convergence was the American counterpart of the European convergence, Talcott Parsons later saw, between Durkheim, Weber, and others. Both convergences were attacks on classical economics and overly rational views of life; both were cases of idealists and materialists meeting each other halfway in dualism; and both centered on the importance of symbolic definitions of social reality. In his 1937 *Structure of Social Action*, Parsons made no reference to the American side of the turn-of-the-century symbolic convergence, for his studies were primarily in European social thought and he was not closely familiar with early American sociology (Parsons, 1975). But some University of Chicago sociologists were unhappy about his omission, and this lost opportunity appears to have weakened the possibility of an eventual collaboration or coalition between the Chicago School and functionalism (Faris, 1953; Wirth, 1969; Janowitz, 1967).

In any case, the Chicago School entered the twenties with an orientation toward sociology that was united in the loose but powerful form of a family resemblance. They did not share the same philosophy of science in all respects, but they all had enough traits in common to give them a sense of intellectual kinship and family solidarity. This loose unity not only characterized their philosophy of science and epistemology, but their methods and substantive theory as well.[7]

The thread running through their methods was the study of the single case, whether an individual or a group, with special attention to the symbolic culture and subjective definitions of the case. They were looking, not for laws but for patterns, ideal types and gestalts, and they used the insights of case analysis, not primarily for defining variables and pursuing later statistical analysis but for enlarging the case and searching for bigger patterns. This may have been one reason it seemed difficult to move their research beyond the city of Chicago, into the college towns where many of their Ph.D.'s had jobs.[8]

Small was always hospitable toward case analysis, for his Johns Hopkins training had been in that vein; his dissertation had been a case study of the American Continental Congress (Herbst, 1959:231), and his eventual theory of social process, modeled closely after Ratzenhofer's conflict theory, was well suited for case analysis (Aho, 1975). But it was Thomas who most clearly merged the case study with the study of subjective definitions. As Thomas tells the story (Thomas, 1973:250), he happened to find a long personal letter in the trash behind his apartment one day, and this chance occurrence led him to his studies of ethnic groups, particularly the Polish, by way of their letters back to the old country. Thomas seemed to enjoy putting on a hard-boiled, atheoretical front at times—as did Park—but the use of the emotionally condensed written document was such a good fit for the orientation of the Chicago School that if Thomas had not happened to find that letter, one gets the impression it would have eventually found him.

Park was also inclined toward the urban case, for his German training under Windelband had glorified the cultural case, and his journalistic instincts also inclined him toward particulars (Park, 1973; Matthews, 1977:chap. 4). Park and Thomas were much alike in many ways, and it is a sadness that Thomas had to leave, just when they got going, thereby depriving them of a decade of collegiality.[9] But the Chicago twenties proceeded as though Thomas were still there, and the study of the urban case, particularly the ethnic or offbeat neighborhood, was the backbone of the dozens of studies carried out during that decade. Burgess was the most marginal to the group in his methodology, for he did a lot of mapping of social problems on a map of Chicago. These maps of insanity, crime, delinquency, alcoholism, marriage breakup, and such, were on the same map, and fit into the same broad theory of urban process, that the case study people were working with, but nevertheless Burgess was the member least associated with the case study (Bogue, 1974).

In addition to epistemology and methods, the Chicago School also shared broad theoretical ideas, particularly as these are summed up in the notion of "process" (Kress, 1970:chap. 3). The term "process" should be distinguished from two opposed ideas. In contrast to the notion of structure and fixity, process indicates movement, change, and constant flow. In contrast to teleology and final causes, it suggests openness in direction and uncertainty in outcome.

The idea of process led the Chicago people to other ideas that were well suited to the study of their major concrete problem, the understanding and control of Chicago's ethnic groups. For the understanding of problems *within* these groups, they used concepts such as interests, wishes, attitudes, values, and definitions of the situation, all understood as open processes and not scores on a test (Fleming, 1967:324). For problems *among* these groups, they used the more macroscopic concepts of conflict, competition, accommodation, and assimilation. The problems within the groups were related to those among the groups, and this whole theoretical apparatus was imposed on the map of Chicago, which showed the spatial relations among ethnic groups and their processes (Park and Burgess, 1924; Matthews, 1977).

The first, dominating school of sociologists, then, had an incredibly deep and balanced structure of scientific resources. They had plenty of bright people in close collaboration; they had the most privileged access to the major means of intellectual production; and they shared an orientation in epistemology, methods, and theory that made them a vibrant intellectual community. What went wrong?

Nothing went wrong through most of the 1920s, but eventually time created a number of changes that brought increasing numbers and power to the various non-Chicago "outs," particularly the Giddings Columbia Ph.D.'s and those who preferred statistics to the case study (cf. House, 1936:chaps. 32 and 38). Although his formal ideas had limited influence, Franklin H. Giddings

has not been given his due in the history of American sociology. His psychological impact on students and his zeal for quantification had enormous consequences (Lipset, 1955:285-88). In the years just before World War I, the
"F.H.G. Club," a discussion group centered in the Columbia graduate department, included the following members, with year of Ph.D given after the name:
William Ogburn, 1912, Howard Odum, 1910, F. Stuart Chapin, 1911, James
Lichtenberger, 1909, John Gillin, 1906, Frank Hankins, 1908, A. A. Tenney,
1907, and Charles Ghelke, 1915, among others (Columbia University, 1931;
Odum, 1951:15). Maurice Parmalee had a 1909 Columbia degree, and he was
a leader of the anti-Chicago forces (House, 1936:n. 2), but Odum does not list
him as a member of this elite club of devoted Giddings students.

   The F.H.G. Club members were singularly successful in American sociology, with the first six of those listed previously becoming ASS presidents:
Lichtenberger, 1922, Gillin, 1926, Ogburn, 1929, Odum, 1930, Chapin, 1935,
and Hankins, 1938. In contrast to Small, Giddings did not hire his best students. The home department remained modest in quality, except for the charismatic Giddings, though other social science departments at Columbia provided a strong backup for sociology.[10] What the great Giddings students did,
however, was to build and strengthen their own Ph.D.-producing departments
at other universities: Lichtenberger at Pennsylvania, Chapin at Minnesota,
Odum at North Carolina, and Gillin at Wisconsin, to mention the major outposts. Ogburn, the most talented of the big six, was hired by Chicago in 1927,
and although everyone agreed that this was a coup, it was not entirely clear
which side had made the coup. The Giddings people, then, had a powerful, decentralized network, controlling most eastern campuses and making inroads
in the Midwest.

   Small, rather than sending out the best people as missionaries, hired them,
or hired them back. This list, with year of Chicago Ph.D., included: George
Vincent, 1896, W. I. Thomas, 1896, E. W. Burgess, 1913, and during Ellsworth
Faris' chairmanship, Louis Wirth, 1926, Herbert Blumer, 1928, and Everett
Hughes, 1928, among others. Of course Chicago also sent out numerous excel-
lent students, many of whom headed departments, *but not strong Ph.D.-pro-
ducing departments like Columbia's outposts*. The outlying departments in
the Midwest and the West may have been sending their best graduates back to
Chicago itself, rather than developing strong graduate programs of their own.
Beyond this many Chicago Ph.D.'s did not do much writing after the dissertation, possibly finding Park's naturalistic method difficult to reproduce outside
Chicago, in the college towns of the Midwest. This may also have been a result
of their dependency on Park. Nels Anderson is reported to have said, "Park
has two kinds of students. Some he drains so dry, they never can piss another
drop" (Matthews, 1977:109).

   The result of these contrasting placement patterns was that, while Chicago
had a strong center and a modest periphery, Columbia had a weak center and a

mighty periphery, with the key outpost departments establishing hinterlands of their own. This pattern led to several advantages for Columbia people in their long-term rivalry with Chicago. It gave them flexibility, for the various departmental styles, all relatively statistical, could go in different concrete directions. It gave them a "low profile," allowing Chapin to suggest in a 1934 article (Chapin, 1934), on the overproduction of Ph.D.'s, that both Chicago and Columbia lower their production of Ph.D.'s. Tit for tat, he was slyly saying: We'll reduce our center if you reduce yours. And above all, it gave them a Ph.D.-producing apparatus that gradually outpopulated, and outvoted, the Chicago machine.

Columbia's center-periphery style also led to a paradox concerning the prestige of the department. In 1925 a national poll of thirty-five prominent sociologists picked Columbia as second in excellence after Chicago from a list of fourteen departments (Hughes, 1925:29-30; Keniston, 1959:146). But by that time the department had so many enemies in other departments within Columbia that, after Giddings' retirement in 1928, President Nicholas Murray Butler held an evening meeting of several department chairmen and senior professors to decide whether to abolish the sociology department (MacIver, 1968:98-99). The historians wanted to kill it, but the "renowned John Dewey made an effective plea to the effect that the sociological approach was different from and as significant as the historic, economic or political approach. There was a majority in favor of retention. The department was saved" (MacIver, 1968:99). MacIver, with his classical, theoretical bent, was made chairman in 1929, thereby initiating a basic change in department tone. Theodore Abel, another theorist, was hired in 1929, and Robert Lynd came in as full professor in 1931 (Lipset, 1955). This combination had problems of its own, since MacIver the theorist and Lynd the empiricist clashed, but it meant that the Giddings statistical pattern was deflected (Abel, 1977). In the early forties, Columbia would experience still another basic change, as Merton and Lazarsfeld joined the department, combined their styles, and brought about the great Columbia fifties.

But to return to the "Columbia versus Chicago" theme, this "Columbia" was primarily that of Giddings and his powerful students in other departments throughout the country. The Columbia of the MacIver-Lynd period, beginning in 1929, also tended to be anti-Chicago, though for different reasons than those of the Giddings group. Park had written a ruinous review of MacIver's *Community* in the *American Journal of Sociology* (Park, 1918:542-44), and MacIver found it so harmful, both psychologically and professionally, that he devoted a poignant page to it in his autobiography, published fifty years after the incident (MacIver, 1968:87; Bierstedt, 1977). We can sum up the Giddings-MacIver difference by saying Giddings and his group were opposed to Chicago from the methodologically hard side, and *MacIver from a side even softer than that of Chicago and Park.*

In addition to the Giddings group outpopulating Chicago, the coming of the

Great Depression hurt the Chicago people, for it led to the cutting off of the extremely "fluid" Laura Spelman Rockefeller money, and, perhaps more seriously, it changed the great national concern from one of Americanizing the immigrants to one of dealing with mass unemployment (Matthews, 1977:110-13; Fosdick, 1952:207-8). The Chicago School's orientation was especially built for the study of ethnicity, or, we might say, status politics, and when the times moved from status to class politics, the theory was creaky and out of focus.

The study of class, with its key economic variables, was in some ways more suited to quantitative methods and less limited to the case study than ethnic research had been. William Ogburn, the 1927 addition to Chicago's department, was at the forefront of statistical work in sociology, but he had little respect for case studies, and his scientistic leanings seemed almost too radical a break with the earlier Chicago tradition. This discontinuity showed in the 1930 Ph.D. dissertation of his student, Samuel Stouffer, which argued the statistical study of attitudes to be superior to the case study. Stouffer's notion of attitude was much narrower than the one W. I. Thomas and the Chicago School had used (Fleming, 1967:324), but the result of Stouffer's influential thesis was that all case studies came to be viewed as, at best, a prescientific heuristic, rather than a source of valid knowledge in their own right, as they had previously been regarded at Chicago (Faris, 1967:114-15).

Ogburn's epistemological slant is nicely captured by the motto he chose, as chairman of the Committee on Symbolism, to be engraved on the bay of the new University of Chicago social science building in 1929. The phrase, from the English physicist Lord Kelvin, read: "When you cannot measure . . . , your knowledge is . . . meagre . . . and . . . unsatisfactory. . . ." In the original passage, Kelvin had restricted his remarks to the physical sciences, though Ogburn had evidently gotten the quote from someone else and did not realize it had been taken out of context (Karl, 1974:154-55; Kelvin, 1889:73-74).

Both Stouffer's dissertation and Ogburn's orientation suggested that perhaps the Chicago twenties of Park and Burgess had been "meagre and unsatisfactory," and the other Chicago people were never able to reconstruct their epistemology to make room for both the case study and statistics, or, put differently, for both Park and Ogburn. Here they were paying for their years of reliance on their family resemblance and their neglect of stating positively and profoundly their philosophy of science. When the family resemblance broke down with the addition of the powerful Ogburn, they were unable to figure out why or to create some new and larger structure of intellectual kinship.

By 1930, the Chicago School was losing its scholarly edge, and the outs were getting increasingly bold. At the December 1930 meetings in Cleveland, W. P. Meroney of Baylor gave a paper criticizing the dominance of the "Midwest," which seems to have been a code word for Chicago. Meroney showed, statistically, that the Midwest had been overrepresented on annual convention programs, committees, and in high office during the previous twenty-five-year existence of the society. He concluded that:

The extra margin in the activities of this Society on the part of the Middle West group is obvious from the standpoint of experience and of the recorded facts. Its greater unity and solidarity as a group in the Society are probably natural and normal in view of the location in the Middle West of the official organ of the Society, the *American Journal of Sociology*, and the like location there of the official headquarters of the Society. Had these been located elsewhere through the years, the story would probably have been different. (Meroney, 1930:66-67)

At these same meetings, the eastern sociologists came in with a strong sense of sectionalism. Just the previous May they had formed the Eastern Sociological Conference, which was to become the Eastern Sociological Society (*American Journal of Sociology*, News and Notes, 1930:124-25; Odum, 1951:365). During the 1930 meetings, an incident occurred that evidently made many easterners unhappy and confirmed their feeling that American sociology needed more journals, more regional societies, and a more open structure. When Robert MacIver—who had become something of a symbol for eastern sociology—had gotten about three-fourths through with his important paper entitled "Is Sociology a Natural Science?" (MacIver, 1931), the chairman of his session, without having given any warning (Abel, 1977), declared that MacIver had run out of time. When the audience shouted its disapproval, the chairman backed down and MacIver was allowed to finish, but the incident was much talked about, and it confirmed the easterners' feeling that the ASS needed a complete restructuring. [11] The incident also illustrates a point made earlier: that out-groups of different theoretical orientations will sometimes combine forces, primarily on the basis of sharing opposition to the ins.

The 1930 convention appears to have been crucial for the crystallization of the outs, for shortly afterward two letters of petition, signed by nine sociologists, were printed in the *American Journal of Sociology*. One asked for discussion of how the society could get editorial control of the official journal of the society, the *American Journal of Sociology*, which, of course, was owned and controlled by the University of Chicago Press. The second asked that the society's nominating committee announce its slate of candidates, not at the same business meeting during which the election was to take place, but one day earlier, so that members could have time to think about nominations from the floor (Parmalee et al., 1931:468-69; Martindale, 1976b:72-74). These letters, dated May 5, 1931, represented a public surfacing of discontent that had probably been growing for some time, though events at the 1930 meetings seem to have been the precipitating cause. The nine signatories and their ages were: the group's chairman, Maurice Parmalee, 49; A. A. Tenney, 55; Theodore Abel, 35; Frank Hankins, 54; Henry Fairchild, 51; Maurice Davie, 38; Thomas

N. Carver, 66; Pitirim Sorokin, 42; and C. G. Dittmer, 46. These nine were all considered easterners, for the first four had Columbia Ph.D.'s, with Tenney and Abel being on Columbia's staff at the time; Fairchild and Davie were both Yale Ph.D's; Carver the economist and Sorokin were both at Harvard; and Dittmer, who had done some work under Giddings, was at New York University.

At the December 1931 meetings, L. L. Bernard, who had a Chicago Ph.D. (1910), but was no longer in the Chicago camp, was elected president of the society. A resolution at the business meeting of that convention empowered Bernard to appoint a committee "to consider a plan for the control of the official journal and the other publications of the American Sociological Society" (*American Journal of Sociology*, News and Notes, 1932:784). This committee, which reported at the 1933 meetings, listed several options: adopting *Social Forces* or *Sociology and Social Research* as the official journal of the society, if possible; allowing members to choose either *Social Forces, Sociology and Social Research*, or the *American Journal of Sociology* with their membership; or starting a new journal (ASS Publications Committee Report, n.d.). Since the University of Chicago Press refused to give editorial control of the *American Journal of Sociology* to the ASS, the obvious fourth possibility of letting things continue as they were was not treated seriously in the report.

This committee report led to more committees, whose reports I have been unable to obtain because, if they exist at all, they are in the archives of the American Sociological Association. At this writing (November 1977) these archives are inaccessible in closed boxes, awaiting transfer to the Library of Congress (Hans Mauksch, 1977). There is another series of committee reports on the society's structure, electoral rules and so on, which ran parallel to the Publications Committee's reports, and which are also inaccessible to scholars at the present time. The final Publications Committee's report, however, which did get published (*American Sociological Review*, 1936:122-25), proposed the publication of a new, bimonthly journal to be called the *American Sociological Review* (conspicuously subtitled "The Official Journal of the American Sociological Society"). The report of this committee, chaired by Meroney, was passed by a vote of 78 to 42 at the business meeting of December 28, 1935 (*American Sociological Review*, 1936:122), though it is difficult to interpret this vote. For, as Robert E. L. Faris recalls the meeting (Faris, 1977), a number of Chicago people, including Robert Park, were supporting the new journal by now, and their vote was added to that of the anti-Chicago people. This final vote, therefore, was evidently anticlimactic, for the more contested issues had been fought out in the conventions of 1933 and 1934. Whatever committee reports and documents from those two conventions that may exist are in the papers of deceased sociologists and the ASA archives.

Although there are some gaps and fuzzy points in this story, commonly referred to as the "*ASR* coup," the outcome is clear. The Chicago School had fallen like a mighty oak: ideas, social organization, and now the means of production, all weakened, diminished, and divided. The Chicago group fought back as well as they could. Burgess, the new *AJS* editor, published a strong, proud editorial in the July 1936 (p. 102) issue, and the Chicago people constructed a standby organization, the Sociological Research Association (Faris, 1967:121-22), in case the insurgents deflected the society from its scholarly purposes. Chicago sociology continued strong, though less united than before. But the group that had risen in the teens and dominated during the twenties had now fallen, or been nudged, off the throne and other groups would get a shot at replacing them.

FUNCTIONALISM

The period from the decline of the Chicago School until the rise of functionalism extended from the mid-thirties to the late forties or early fifties, and during these years there was a confused situation: Chicago was down but by no means out; the positivists were increasing their control of the means of production but were unable to work out their larger ideas effectively; and the functionalists were only gradually constructing their intellectual web, increasing their numbers and finding footholds in departments, publishing outlets, and funding sources.

When the *ASR* was founded in December 1935, Parsons was thirty-three years old, did not have an American degree but a more modest German Ph.D., had a job under the unsympathetic chairmanship of Pitirim Sorokin, and though he was in his ninth year as instructor at Harvard, prospects for tenure were still in doubt (Parsons, 1970:827, 835). He clearly was not in a position to be exerting much power at that 1935 ASS convention, or at the more important ones going back to 1931. However, his department was strongly anti-Chicago, for both Sorokin and the Harvard economist Thomas N. Carver had been among the nine signatories of the 1931 Parmalee letters, and Parsons was to omit all reference to the early Chicago School in his 1937 *Structure of Social Action*. But Parsons was not noticeably involved with the Giddings positivists either. On the contrary, he organized this work so that it could be interpreted as antipositivist in two senses of the word: the utilitarianism of classical economics and the statistical operationalism of the Giddings students. The high intellectual message was framed in European categories and turn-of-the-century theoretical struggles, but there was a more down-to-earth message for the neighborhood American positivists.

The positivist leaders appear to have ignored the book—it was so long and clumsily written that its importance could easily be overlooked—but the book's influence steadily increased. In retrospect it looks as though key positivists such as Ogburn, Chapin, Lundberg, and Odum never fully realized the power of Parsons' critique of their philosophy of science, or how influential it was in checking their rise to theoretical domination.

Parsons was clearly cutting a third path, which was neither the Chicago School nor Columbia. Harvard was big and powerful enough to stand above the long-standing Chicago-Columbia rivalry of American sociology, and the functionalism that came from the pen of Parsons made both Chicago and the positivists look provincial.

Unlike the group beginnings of the Chicago School, functionalism was initially a one-man show, originating in classic style as a group of devoted graduate students sat at the feet, or rather the side, of a great teacher. Eventually, Robert Merton achieved something like equal partnership with Parsons as a leader of functional theory—or, in Merton's preferred term, "functional analysis"—but during the late thirties and forties, Parsons was the sole dominating figure.

Not that Parsons was in no way beholden to his predecessors or seniors. His key intellectual achievement was to show important parallels between the theories of Durkheim and Weber, two great thinkers whose French-German national rivalries prevented them from appreciating and using each other's work. Parsons was the first to be able to use the genius of both, and his ability to do so indicates the addition of no little genius of his own. Yet, in the last analysis, it was an achievement of intellectual brokerage, and if we want to look for a theory group behind Parsons, we would have to point to these very turn-of-the-century figures who were theoretically isolated from each other until Parsons fitted them together.12

Parsons was also beholden to a group of senior professors, all "outside members" of the sociology department, who went over Sorokin's head to get Parsons his assistant professorship in 1936. This led to a promise of tenure the next year (Parsons, 1970:832). The dependency was primarily one of academic politics, in the narrow sense, and not one of intellectual ties, though Parsons' key sponsor, the physiologist L. J. Henderson, did work closely with Parsons on the text of *The Structure of Social Action* (Parsons, 1970:832).

But these Parsonian ties were not those of a working theory group, as those of the early Chicago people had been. The closest thing Parsons had to a theory group, unlike the Chicago School, was his circle of early graduate students (Parsons, 1970:833). The mimeographed notes from his 1936-37 meetings report a series of evening discussions and beer-sipping sessions, in which Parsons presided as an intellectual giant, and a dozen or so bright young men engaged him in debating and clarifying his new theory (Parsons' Sociological Group: Reports of Meetings, 1936-37). The "scribes" for the nine meetings were listed as: Bierstedt, Davis, Devereux, McKain, Hartshorne, Merton, Hopkins, Smullyan, and Wilson, with the names DeNood and Knox appearing in the text. The theory itself was the central wedge for this group, and the sheer power of the ideas gradually strengthened and enlarged the group. The means of production were scarce during these late depression years, and this paucity of resources, combined with the interruption of World War II, may have prevented the functionalists from rising to power sooner.

It is not easy to capture Parsons' key premises or core insights. We could take him on his own terms and say he clarified the problem of order—how human beings, lacking instincts, nevertheless avoid the war of all against all—and that he achieved this clarification by showing how Durkheim, Weber, and others converged on a fundamentally moral interpretation of society. We could also follow some of Parsons' critics and say he found new justification for capitalism, befitting the historical shift from market to oligopoly—in his terms, from utilitarianism to voluntarism—coming just as the worldwide depression and the move toward war intensified the need to find something nice to say about this economic system (Gouldner, 1970).

Parsons may have been both these things, but we might get a clearer idea of what he said if we look at what he did not quite say. He was trying to figure out how these millions of self-interested, competitive human beings, picturing them as the economists and major social thinkers of the nineteenth century saw them, avoid destroying each other and manage to maintain cooperative human societies. They are not ants or wasps with built-in genetic mechanisms of cooperation. On the contrary, they are almost totally plastic and instinct free, except of course for the need to satisfy their fundamental drives and bodily needs. The economists had invoked the "invisible hand," or the market as their explanation for order, cooperation, and social harmony, but this was a tautological, nonempirical answer in the first place, and, given the twentieth-century rise of oligopoly and decline of the market, it made even less sense in the dark days of the 1930s.

Parsons found his solution by piecing together certain texts of Durkheim, who challenged the classical economists, and Weber, who faced the contemporary Marxists. Both argued for a moral matrix to economic life. Thus a war of all against all is avoided by a process of moral socialization, in which people's antisocial impulses are inhibited, allowing harmonious behavior in society; and captialism avoids internal conflict by being embedded in a normative context that prevents conflict and contradiction.

However, Parsons exaggerated the moral component in these two classical theorists, particularly Weber (Pope, 1973:407-8; Pope, Cohen, and Hazelrigg, 1975:422). He also underrated the importance they both placed on shared beliefs and cognitions for holding a society together (Warner, 1978). The classic solutions to the problem of social order are: (1) the utilitarian theory of social contract and exchange, (2) the Italian elitist and Marxist theory of coercion and cultural manipulation, and (3) the Freudian-Parsonian theory of moral internalization and normative restraint.

But there is a fourth solution, scattered in the writings of Simmel (Levine,

1971:xv-xx) and Mead as well as Durkheim and Weber, which emphasizes the ordering effects of cognitive consensus and shared meanings (O'Neill, 1972). This consensus includes not only the truths of physical science, but also those of everyday life, extending from the ordinary and routine to the life defining and ultimate. Garfinkel pointed out the importance and fragility of routine cognitive consensus by performing experiments that broke this consensus, thereby releasing intense disorder (Garfinkel, 1967). Weber, coming at it from the other end, showed the relativity of cognition in ultimate questions, pointing out that the overarching ideas were "switchmen," which directed human interests along one moral track rather than another (Weber, 1915:280). He traced the divergencies between Asian and European development to differences in deeply embedded beliefs, which had historically ordered the moral and social systems of these societies.

But the issue was the same, both at Garfinkel's micro- and Weber's macroextreme: Definitions of reality, both physical and social, and how we can act toward this reality, are constructed by interaction in society, and these constructions constitute an important part of the glue that holds a society together. This insight, which was always used but rarely articulated by the Chicago School, was restated, piercingly, by a modern member of their group. Erving Goffman shed new light on the cognitive interpretation of order by showing how psychologically painful and existentially threatening it can be to live with an emotionally disturbed person. "Insanity of place" is one continuous Garfinkel experiment, showing both the fragility of everyday meaning systems and the sadness of those who stray from them (Goffman, 1971).

All four solutions to the problem of social order appear to be partly right. People in societies coerce, exchange, morally oblige, and cognitively define, giving them a highly flexible, living instrument that can shift from one basis of unity to another as circumstances require. Of course, societies are sometimes on their last legs, and they fall apart, get conquered, or undergo revolution, but until that end point is reached, societies can tolerate intense levels of social and moral conflict and still muddle through. This muddling through is due, not only to the unifying effects of exchange and coercion, but also to those of the shared cognitive world of language and beliefs.

This cognitive sharing is at the core of Durkheim's collective conscience, which might better be translated as "consciousness" at this point. Durkheim's rituals created the master cognitive categories as well as the moral ones, and although the organic or modern society may experience a thinning out and an individualizing of the moral component of the collective conscience, there remains a shared cognitive consciousness which controls us all, and outside of which lies, not moral deviance, but insanity (Durkheim, 1915:23-33; Warner, 1978).[13]

Eventually Parsons' inability to recognize the importance of the nonscientific cognitive side of life, and how these cognitions tie a society together, became the great weak spot, making him vulnerable to the criticisms of all competing theory groups. Not only did he underrate the cognitive basis of order, he overrated the moral basis, and these two errors were of a piece and fed on each other. Accordingly, criticism could be aimed at either side of this "Parsonian dilemma." The left of center sociologists criticized Parsons for his unrealistic postulate of shared morality and values (Mills, 1959; Lockwood, 1956; Dahrendorf, 1958; Horowitz, 1962). The Chicago School, and eventually the phenomenologists, criticized him for being unappreciative of the softer modes of cognition and reality construction (Becker, 1963:130; Faris, 1953; Blumer, 1975; Berger and Luckmann, 1967:17; Cicourel, 1974a:21). In addition, the positivist leader George Lundberg pointed out that Parsons had never actually enlarged his theory of knowledge past positivism (Lundberg, 1956).

But this discussion of Parsons' key arguments and their weak spots is made from hindsight, and the critical attacks did not become serious until toward the end of functionalism's twenty years of supremacy. In the early period, when Parsons was constructing his ingenious action theory and extending it, in the *Social System*, it was by far the most impressive theory on the scene. With these ideas and this theoretical commitment, then, Parsons started a theory group that expanded its influence at Harvard, as he found allies among his colleagues in neighboring departments and increased his ties with graduate students.

A breakthrough came in 1941, when Robert Merton left Tulane for an appointment at Columbia (Lipset, 1955). Merton was in many ways a critic of Parsons, and I could have listed him among those who rejected value consensus, but he was also Parsons' student and he shared his broad functional method. Merton's appointment was followed, the next year, by Sorokin's resignation of the department chairmanship at Harvard (Sorokin, 1963:251) and by Parsons' succession to that powerful office in 1944 (Parsons, 1970:841). The functionalists now had strong positions in two departments, particularly after Kingsley Davis joined Merton at Columbia in 1948, giving them access to a large number of elite graduate students.

By the forties it was becoming clear that one of functionalism's weaknesses was its inability to produce clear hypotheses, find a workable method, and give direction to empirical research. Even though Parsons was the most driving and productive theorist American sociology had ever seen, as an empirical researcher (Rocher, 1975:17-18) he was all thumbs, and, in this respect, a poor role model for his students.

As his earlier action theory gradually became a theory of social structure, he borrowed from the anthropologists the idea that the functional needs of society cause specific social structures, such as the family or the state, to come into and remain in existence. This was just an extension of the earlier idea that economic action is controlled by a moral matrix, for now the morality itself is explained as a response to the needs of society (Parsons, 1951). Whatever the empirical adequacy of this theory, its natural method was to search intuitively for goodness of fit or elective affinity between structures and functions. Many of Parsons' early students (Mullins, 1973:51) were able to use this method for the analysis of specific institutions and structures, such as aspects of kinship, the family, science, the university, social stratification, and bureaucracy, but not everyone had the bent of mind this method required.

Merton at Columbia evidently sensed these methodological inadequacies, for he had been working with middle-range ideas, including that of "unanticipated consequences," for many years (Merton, 1936), and he was moving toward a major theoretical statement of his own. In 1949, Merton published *Social Theory and Social Structure*, which emphasized the more concrete or "middle-range" level of abstraction, stayed close to empirical data, remained theoretically open to non- or dysfunctional elements, and developed the versatile idea of latent functions. Merton's functionalism also seemed more open to the political left than Parsons'. This ideological flexibility probably gave Merton's writings an appeal that Parsons' work lacked, though when the antiwar, leftist 1960s came, even Merton's functionalism could not contain the highly critical sentiments of many younger sociologists.

As a guide to research Merton's method was quite successful, although it remained fundamentally intuitive. Despite his elegant codification of the method (Merton, 1957:chap. 1), it rested on a flash of insight or "black box" in which the analyst finds an isomorphism between a structure and a need or function, and this lack of logical clarification meant that it remained at the level of discovery or heuristic.

Throughout the interregnum of the late thirties and forties, the positivists had done well with the means of production, enjoying easy access to the new *American Sociological Review* (Kuklick, 1973), and finding research opportunities with the Roosevelt administration (House, 1936:393; Lyons, 1969: chaps. 3-4). They built on the increasing importance of statistics in graduate training, but could never produce the genius who could build a theory out of the numbers. In particular, George Lundberg's attempt to formalize positivist sociology under the theory of operationalism was unsuccessful (Kuklick, 1973; Blalock, 1968:6). During sociology's long, post-Chicago School interregnum, the positivists had a method but no theory, and the rising functionalists had a theory but no method. On principle each side was opposed to the other, but practical needs won out, and the forties gradually saw an alliance between functionalism and the positivists in which the latter were officially the junior partners, but would eventually become strong enough to take over the firm.

When Merton was hired at Columbia, Paul Lazarsfeld, the brilliant statistical positivist, was hired with him. As mentioned earlier, Columbia was sharply polarized between a theoretical wing, led by MacIver, and an empiricist wing, led by Robert Lynd. The simultaneous hiring of Merton and Lazarsfeld was meant both as a temporary compromise between the two groups and as a means of keeping the fight going indefinitely. But Merton and Lazarsfeld somehow reached across this academic no man's land and became personal friends. This human feeling for each other seems to have had a great deal to do with the eventual close collaboration between functionalism and positivism (Hunt, 1961). At Harvard, Parsons also needed a research specialist; so Samuel Stouffer, a student of Ogburn, was hired, and he functioned as a can-do researcher, much as Lazarsfeld did at Columbia. These empiricists—Stouffer and Lazarsfeld—translated the language of structure and function into that of cause and effect. Although the logical juncture between the two languages was never too clear, the partnership of positivism and functionalism worked remarkably well, particularly at Columbia, where Lazarsfeld's European erudition gave him theoretical as well as methodological skills.

This partnership contrasts with the earlier tension between positivism and the case study tradition at Chicago. For Ogburn and Stouffer, on that occasion, it had been the case study *versus* statistics, or, at best, *in the service* of statistics (Faris, 1967:115). Perhaps by this later period, after Lundberg's operationalism fiasco, the positivists knew they could not go it alone. Also, the notion of "function," for all its ambiguities, may have been a bit more disciplined than Chicago's "process," and easier to translate into variable language. Nevertheless, it is a good question why the Merton-Lazarsfeld combination clicked and Park-Ogburn did not. The personal situation was vastly different, of course, but there is still the unyielding theoretical question of why an intellectual challenge that was almost identical in the two cases led to growth in the one department and trouble in the other.

But the Merton codification of theory and research—referred to by one reviewer as the "codification of Parsons and Lazarsfeld" (Bierstedt, 1950: 141)—was not without problems. In the fifties a series of papers by logical positivists attempted to clarify the relation between functional analysis and that of cause and effect (Nagel, 1956; Hempel and Oppenheim, 1953; Hempel, 1959). The result was, in some ways, a strengthening of functionalism, for now it could be translated into another logical tradition. But there were costs, for little uniqueness was left to functionalism after Nagel and Hempel had finished with it. Its only remaining purpose was to suggest ideas for positivists to test, and perhaps the positivists could figure out a way of finding these ideas on their own.

Merton accepted this division of labor, as he had always regarded functional analysis as a method and not a theory, but Parsons regarded it as the real thing, and the critique of the logicians put Parsons' functionalism in a state of logical ambiguity. But for both theorists, the critique meant that from then on, the existence of functional relationships would have to be proved, not simply announced, and they were to be proved on positivism's terms. Correlations, time order, and the control of third factors would have to be brought into any functional analysis that claimed valid findings. This logical synthesis remained a little woolly, until Stinchcombe's striking clarification, though it came a bit late in the game to have much effect (Stinchcombe, 1968:80-100).

The more visible critique of functionalism, particularly the Parsonian version, came from a variety of conflict positions, becoming a rising chorus by the sixties and eventually doing enormous damage to functionalism's moral legitimacy. I am using the notion of conflict in a broad sense, and if we consider how the glue of moral consensus permeates every dimension, level, nook, and cranny of Parsons' theory, we can see that any number of conflict arguments can be used against it.

The strongest was the macro-argument that conflict is basic to the overall organization of society, as evidenced by the way large-scale change occurs, the way force and repression are routinely used, and the way classes and status groups oppose each other (Mills, 1959: Lockwood, 1956; Dahrendorf, 1958; Horowitz, 1962; Gouldner, 1970). As the sixties wore on and conflicts within American society rose to the surface, others picked up the argument and the times gave it enormous cogency. Another line of macro-argument came from the Weberians around Reinhard Bendix at Berkeley, some of whom were political conservatives, but who nevertheless interpreted Weber in a conflict manner (Bendix, 1962; Collins, 1968; Roth, 1968).

At the level of micro-interaction, functionalism was also drawing criticism that drew on process, change, and conflict. The symbolic interactionists, who flourished again under Blumer and Hughes in Chicago's late forties and fifties, in a kind of second summer, criticized Parsons for picturing ordinary interaction in a too rigid, role-determined, and precut fashion. The drama of life, they observed, is not read from a script but is extemporaneous. They pointed to negotiation and, more daringly, to a kind of cognitive reality construction, in which conflict and emergence were generous ingredients (Blumer, 1969; Becker, 1963; Scott and Lyon, 1968; Wrong, 1961). And the phenomenologists, particularly those around Garfinkel and Cicourel on the West Coast, were so struck by the inherent ambiguity and ineffability of ordinary experience, deeply examined, and by its openness to conflicting definitions, that they regarded functionalism as totally misguided (Garfinkel, 1964; Cicourel, 1974a:21). Even the exchange theorist at Harvard, George Homans, challenged the postulate of moral consensus by dissolving it in the ulterior motive of self-interest (Homans, 1967:51).

By the end of the sixties it was clear that, although no vote had been taken at the ASA business meeting, functionalism was no longer king. Something else was happening. What that something was did not become clear right away, for it took a while for the dust to settle. But when it did, it was apparent that despite all the sixties' hoopla, the conflict forces, whether together or one by one, were not to be the big winners. To almost everyone's surprise it was to be, of all people, old Joe, the friendly methodologist, always available to touch up your questionnaire and quite knowledgeable about these new-fangled computers. It was to be the junior partners, the descendants of Stouffer, Lazarsfeld, and other positivists, who seemed so firmly under control during functionalism's heyday (Mullins, 1973:chap. 9). Like the black power drama of the sixties in which Rochester becomes a serious character and kills Jack Benny, old Joe, the fumbling methodologist, who could expect to wait a good long time to make full professor, since he did not actually study anything, stood up to full height, laid his cards on the table and walked off with the game.

CONTEMPORARY INTERREGNUM

It seems almost necessary to put it facetiously, as I just did, to capture the drama of how unexpectedly the positivists moved ahead in the late sixties. The intense sociological discussion of that decade had been primarily over theory, ideology, values, and American politics, and the last thing anyone expected was a *methodological* resolution of the issue. Yet, in retrospect, it should be no surprise. A positivist breakaway was always possible in the shaky Parsons-Merton-Lazarsfeld coalition, and there were developments within the positivist group which gradually strengthened their position, particularly in relation to the means of production.

The importance of the computer as a means of production grew steadily throughout those years. High-speed computation allowed the statistical treatment of a whole new range of quantitative problems and encouraged the development and diffusion of new statistical procedures. This increased the importance of quantitative data analysis of all kinds and caused more emphasis to be placed on statistics and mathematics in the graduate curriculum.

Alongside the new computer technology there was a kind of mathematics lobby, from at least the mid-fifties, working to increase the role of quantification in all the social sciences. The Social Science Research Council (SRRC) was an organizer and a clearinghouse for this process. In 1974 Frederick Mosteller, a Harvard statistician, wrote of "The Role of the Social Science Research Council in the Advance of Mathematics in the Social Sciences," as follows:

The current level of mathematical training for social scientists in this country was not quickly achieved, nor did it grow by itself through natural evolution; instead it has come about through a long, fairly deliberate process that has depended upon the ideas and contributions of a great many people and organizations. (Mosteller, 1974:17)

Mosteller goes on to describe a series of SSRC-sponsored committees, conferences, subsidized textbooks, monographs, summer training sessions, and workshops, funded at various points by Carnegie, Ford, Russell Sage, and particularly the National Science Foundation.

Within sociology an important informal group, which came to be known as the Committee on Sociological Training, was formed in the mid-sixties

(Schuessler, 1966:82), leading, through a series of conferences and subcommittees, to the critical Carmel Conference on applied sociology, held in December 1972. Karl Schuessler's prologue to that conference is as follows:

The Carmel Conference was not without a history. In one view, it all started with an informal meeting of a dozen or so sociologists in Washington in the spring of 1965. The occasion for that meeting was the concern in some circles that sociologists were relatively unsophisticated in research design, as evinced by their proposals to federal funding agencies, and that possibly their graduate training was inadequate. Whatever the validity of that charge, it was decided by the group to initiate and to maintain a national dialogue among sociologists, insofar as practicable, on problems in graduate training and the quality of social research. (Schuessler, 1975:2)

This group was not primarily a math lobby but more an economic lobby, pursuing the laudable goal of expanding the monetary means of production for sociologists.[14] But since Uncle Sam favored descriptively precise, quantitative sociology, the indirect effect of their efforts was to quantify the graduate curriculum still more and to enhance the power of the positivist wing. The new courses were not simply added to the existing curriculum, as in a plus-sum game. For every add there was a drop in this zero-sum game, and almost no one was asking what the long-run effects would be for sociology or what intellectual capabilities were being sacrificed to make room for the federal money (Useem, 1976a, 1976b; Bernard, 1977:9).

In addition to the influence of these planning groups and the computer, the politicization of the sixties had consequences for the means of intellectual production. Federal social programs expanded, and along with them came new opportunities for social research on these programs. It was the poor and the dark ethnic groups—the constituency, in a way, of many of the conflict sociologists—whose protests brought these programs into existence. But these sociologists would not get the research opportunities. Instead, they would primarily go to survey researchers and other highly quantitative sociologists.

In a second way the positivists gained from the political sixties. Some moderate and conservative intellectuals blamed the rise in protest partly on sociological theories which criticized American society. Moynihan's *Maximum Feasible Misunderstanding* makes this point. With great force he blames the Merton-Cloward-Ohlin thesis of blocked opportunity, which was behind the poverty program's original emphasis on the participation of the poor, for contributing to rising expectations and social disorder (Moynihan, 1969:50-53). Moynihan's message to social science was that it should no longer apply theories and propose solutions to social problems, but devote itself solely to the quantitative evaluation of programs set up by the government. As he bluntly put it: *"The role of social science lies not in the formulation of social policy, but in the measurement of its results"* (Moynihan, 1969:193, italics in original).

The core scholarly group or network in this quantitative expansion was the "new causal theorists," as Nicholas Mullins (Mullins, 1973:chap. 9) calls them, whose intellectual leaders were Hubert M. Blalock, Jr., and Otis Dudley Duncan. Blau and Duncan's *American Occupational Structure* (1967), was a strong display of how regression analysis could put order into a mass of demographic data, placing the correlations in a "path," which had some resemblance to a sequential process. Part of the expansive style of the new causal people was to use equal-interval statistics on ordinal data, disregarding a logical norm that had been respected by the more cautious Lazarsfeld-style tabular analysts, whose methods the new groups tended to replace in the major journals. A second line of intellectual expansion was in the rethinking of the thorny problem of validity, which had always placed a cloud over much quantitative research, for it could not be proved that tests and scales actually measured the abstract variable or property they purported to measure. Blalock in particular was giving thought to validity (Blalock, 1968:7-13), but though he came at it in a more sophisticated manner than Lundberg had done in the thirties, the cloud was as big as ever, and his solution appeared to be a kind of neo-operationalism.[15]

In late 1972 when the Carmel Conference assembled, the increased influence of the federal government over the development of sociology was apparent. The conference was attended by about sixty prominent sociologists, all present or former National Institute of Mental Health (NIMH) training program directors, and the list was understandably characterized by a lack of theorists. The message of this conference, which is not easily captured from the editors' prologue and epilogue, seems to have been that the government would be phasing out the NIMH training grants—a mainstay of graduate support for many years—but that new money would be available for the execution of applied research. A corollary was that graduate departments might start thinking about revising their curriculums in an applied, quantitative direction.

It should be remembered that the term "applied research" had undergone an astonishing change in meaning from the mid-sixties, largely due to the redefinition that Moynihan and other government spokesmen had given it. In 1965 Gouldner had defined it as "above all concerned with the prediction and production of social and cultural change" (Gouldner and Miller, 1965:8). His enthusiastic, lordly conception of its role was probably about typical for those hopeful times. By the 1970s it referred solely to the measurement of ongoing social programs, leaving the predicting, producing, and changing to an earlier era (Janowitz, 1972; Street, 1976).

The tension and ambiguity of this conference is suggested by the post-conference analysis of Robert Hall, a National Science Foundation executive, and one of the two government representatives at the conference.

The reaction of the participants in the early stages of the conference to this ambiguous but threatening situation was a kind of elementary collective behavior.... Rumors were

flying as people tried to clarify what the conference was all about. . . . Lacking an au-
thoritative statement, participants began improvising plausible stories about the
"real" meaning of the conference and trying (sometimes in a rather hostile, aggressive
tone) to get the "real" purpose stated openly. Thus, there seemed to be established, early in the conference, a tone that inhibited detached, deliberate analysis of training issues, and encouraged hostile expression against the administration responsible for cutting training grants and against any sociologist so spineless or stupid (so the beliefs
seem to be) as to yield to governmental pressures. . . . One of the important values in
contemporary sociology is a rather *chaotic pluralism*. There seemed to be a powerful
fear that some *single style of sociology* was going to be imposed on sociologists; and
hence the conference became preeminently defensive—partly a *defense of chaos*, and
partly a defense of particular styles of sociology practiced by those present. It was difficult to tell which was feared more—the Washington threat or the well-meaning efforts
of sociologists who responded to the Washington threat in some unified way. (My italics, but ellipses in original; see Demerath, Larsen, and Schuessler, 1975:340-41.)

Whatever the meaning and impact of this strange conference, it clearly was
not meant to promote the "chaotic pluralism" that the NSF's representative
Robert Hall saw in sociology. Hall's statement does not indicate whether he
and the federal administration he represented were more opposed to chaos or
pluralism, or whether they could even tell the difference. In any case, the winners of this conference were clearly Pat Moynihan's narrowly blinkered engi-
neers.

While all this was going on and the positivists were increasing their control
over the means of production, the more pluralistic and qualitative field researchers and the theorists were in disarray, still divided by the conflict-func-
tionalism fight of the sixties, split into several uncommunicating groups, and
slipping in their share of the means of production.

A serious problem was what to make of the new West Coast phenomenologists, the enthnomethodologists around Harold Garfinkel, the cognitive sociologists around Aaron Cicourel, and the conversation analysts around Harvey
Sacks, before his death in 1975. The East Coast phenomenologists, following
Alfred Schutz and Peter Berger, had proved at least minimally compatible with
established sociology, but the West Coast groups did not find easy relationship
with any established macro-theories. Yet these social phenomenologists were
mining the cognitive insight in new ways, exploring the construction and operation of cognitive consensus in micro-situations, and their findings could be
renewing for theory. The West Coast groups did not even find easy communication with what appeared to be their first cousins, the symbolic interactionists, though Mead's discussion of the "inner conversation" and the "I" and
"me" were deeply phenomenological[16] (Denzin, 1970; Zimmerman and Wieder, 1970; Natanson, 1973:56-62) and Goffman's work displayed a brilliant
synthesis of symbolic interactionism and phenomenology. Finally, these phenomenologists felt quite distant from the Parsonian functionalists, even

though Garfinkel had been a devoted student of Parsons and had developed an important side of action theory that Parsons, in another lost opportunity, had allowed to lie fallow.

Another problem for the theorists was what to make of the theoretical Marxists. Were they intellectually incompetent and biased, or were they fellow theorists and scholars? Parsons regarded Marxist sociologists as not really seeking truth and not really sociologists, though the Sorokin Award had gone to two intellectual Marxists: Immanuel Wallerstein for his *Modern World System*, in 1975, and to Perry Anderson for his *Considerations on Western Marxism*, in 1977 (Parsons, 1973; *Daily Illini*, April 5, 1973). The theorists would clearly have to bracket their politics and interact as scholars if they were to combine their work into some meaningful whole.

By the mid-seventies, then, the theorists were still performing their function of intellectual overview, the direction of research and interpretation of data, but they were not doing it with one voice or even in the same language. Unlike the *lingua franca* of the Chicago School, which had united sociology in the twenties, or that of functionalism, which was spoken in the fifties and early sixties, the speech of the seventies showed the linguistic confusion of an interregnum. Coser faced up to this confusion in his 1975 ASA presidential address (see Coser, this volume) by inviting sociology to return to the center, avoiding the extremes of ethnomethodology and new causal theory. But neither of these two wings of sociology would go away, and the problem seemed more one of integrating all the vital lines in the field than in choosing among them.

CONCLUDING COMMENT

Perhaps these divided theorists and theory groups could find a common meeting ground by taking a profound and sustained look at the classic problem of order, and how they each contribute something toward its solution. Different groups give primacy to different insights. The *utilitarian* insight is developed by exchange theorists, behavioristic sociologists, and the new causal theorists, whose random sample had the same logical structure as that of the market.[17] The role of *coercion* in order is shown by Weberians, Marxists, and the more eclectic comparative-historical sociologists. The role of *morality and values* is shown by the Durkheimians, the Parsonians, and some interpreters of Mead. The *cognitive* basis of order is shown by the symbolic interactionists, the various schools of phenomenology, and the newer interpretations of Weber and Durkheim. The followers of Merton fit at several points, and the Merton of the self-fulfilling prophecy has strong phenomenological overtones. The details of this pattern are, of course, unclear and in process, but the broad picture, which envisages theories and theory groups attacking the same basic problem from different angles, constitutes a basis of unity that sociologists could build on.

The interregnum of the seventies, then, like that of the thirties and early forties, shows the signs of ? theoretical vacuum. When a powerful theory, such as that of the Chicago School or Parsonian functionalism, falls, there is a long period of theoretical confusion. Theorists are slow to find the best framework within which to restate their ideas and findings. Communication has to build up among neighboring theory groups first; translators who know more than one theoretical language must appear; and some larger model or language, in which all important insights find a place, must gradually be built (for an example of an impressive theoretical synthesis, cf. Collins' *Conflict Sociology*, 1975).

The positivists could not be expected to do this theoretical work, for their methodology, which is finely attuned to maximize descriptive accuracy and quantitative analysis, is the wrong tool for theoretical work. Theory construction, which was impressively codified in Arthur Stinchcombe's *Constructing Social Theories*, shows something of the formal methodology embedded in the work of the great theorists, but it does not lead to substantive theory itself. And the cumulation of survey findings and quantitative analysis can never be piled high enough to build a theory.

The interregnum of the seventies, to return to the problem of the three-legged throne, was a period of sharp status inconsistency among competing theory groups. The positivists had amassed an impressive share of the means of production, particularly federal money, and they were also well represented in the top journals, but they had not been able to squeeze a theory out of the numbers. The theorists, and the many lines of empirical research that are not highly quantified, had less impressive shares of the means of production, but they had the ideas, the intellectual high ground, and, as Coser's address suggests, still stood at the center of the sociological Establishment. It looked as though no group was in a position to construct the combination of ideas, social organization, and means of production that would give sociology another dominating theory group and end the interregnum.

In the meantime the field of sociology was having serious problems. Undergraduate enrollments were badly slipping; big money was getting harder to come by; and technical sociology was having trouble defining its relation to a self-governing, democratic citizenry (Wiley, 1977:422-24). If the theorists could broaden the basis of unity, empirical research could increase its significance and once again lead to profound explanation. But it looked unlikely that theory and research would come closer until the theorists began working toward a new synthesis. The possibilities for these lines of growth were there, but the sociologists were slow to do the necessary intellectual work.

No giant had emerged from the aftermath of functionalism, and it did not look as though one was soon to come. Perhaps this time sociologists would drop the old pattern of "ins and outs" and "rise and fall" to build a new sociology with what they had. This is the crisis of sociology that Gouldner knew would follow the fall of Parsonian functionalism, though Gouldner could not be correct in all details (Gouldner, 1970). Only the theorists could begin the resolution of this crisis, and to do so they would have to stop making "nothing but" explanations and learn to see their separate insights as part of a larger whole. Historical analysis suggests that this is a workable way for sociology to find its unity and strength after the postfunctionalism confusion. And theoretical analysis suggests that this can be done by returning to the problem of social order and by constructing a more comprehensive solution to the problem, which can give guidance, direction, and meaning to empirical research.

NOTES

1. This is a revised version of a paper originally given at the monthly colloquium of the Theory Group of the University of Illinois, an informal group of professors from the departments of sociology, educational policy studies, speech communication, business administration, and anthropology. For comments on earlier sections and drafts I am indebted to Paul J. Baker, Aaron Cicourel, Randall Collins, Lewis Coser, Richard Kraus, Don Martindale, Stephen McNamee, Robert Merton, Nicholas Mullins, James Short, R. Stephen Warner, David Westby, Thomas P. Wilson, and especially Norman Denzin, though the responsibility for this essay remains mine.

2. The formulation of this three-part division has been influenced by Edward Shils (1970) and Joseph Ben-David (1971), and their concept of the "institutionalization" of science.

3. The term "role confluence," and much of the interpretation that goes with it, was suggested to me by Paul J. Baker.

4. For a perceptive discussion of an American Kantian sociologist, whose voluminous writings were rendered obsolete and forgotten by the shift in American philosophy, see Jones, 1972.

5. This money was given, not just to sociology, but to a group of departments that formed the Local Community Research Committee. The amount was $25,000, contingent on matching funds, the first year. In the second and subsequent years, there was an additional $50,000 flat grant (Burgess and Bogue, 1964:6). The money evidently stopped in 1929 or 1930 (Fosdick, 1952:198-99).

6. The idea of historicism-pragmatism convergence was first presented by Herbst (1959, 1965) and later developed by Carey, to whom my discussion is particularly indebted (1975:163-67).

7. Small's closeness to pragmatism was selective and uneven. He was close to Dewey's ethics (Herbst, 1959:244), but he regarded Mead's social psychology, which he evidently accepted, as psychology and not sociology (Dibble, 1975:102, n. 6).

8. In a personal communication James Short disagrees with my interpretation of the Chicago case studies, arguing that these studies often did lead to subsequent statistical analysis, particularly in criminology. See Short, 1971.

9. Thomas was unceremoniously fired, following newspaper publicity, when he was arrested in 1918 for renting a hotel room with a woman who was not his wife, although the facts of the case are not at all clear. World War II was still going on, and Thomas' wife of the time was a pacifist. Janowitz (1966:xiv-xv) suggests the possibility that the

federal agents, who became involved in the case, were trying to embarass Mrs. Thomas by hurting her husband.

10. Giddings was at his charismatic best, according to Abel (1977), who attended Columbia in the mid-twenties, in giving formal lectures. The "course" was not only crammed with students, but the entire staff was expected to attend, along with the department secretary, who sat at Giddings' feet taking official notes. "F.H.G." himself would often come attired in formal academic dress, that is, cap and gown.

11. The incident of MacIver's speech at the 1930 meetings needs more looking into. Neither Faris (1977) nor Blumer (1977) could recall the incident, though they both had attended the 1930 convention, Faris as a graduate student and Blumer as the secretary of the society. Both being from Chicago, they allowed that it may well have happened, though they wondered whether the easterners had not blown it out of proportion.

It might be clarifying to have the name of the chairman of MacIver's session, that is, the person who did the timekeeping. I have been unable to get a copy of the program, which was not completely published, and Abel did not recall the name of the timekeeper. The importance of Abel's recollection is that he is the only living survivor of the nine men who signed the important 1931 Parmalee letters, as we shall see. Abel did not remember much about the circumstances under which they were signed, and he feels the founding of the ASR was overdetermined and inevitable in any case, though he did single out the MacIver incident as one thing that led to the signatures. A somewhat different interpretation of the founding of the ASR is given in Lengermann (1978), which came to my attention too late to be incorporated into the present article.

12. In March 1975, Parsons spoke at the University of California at San Diego (La Jolla) on his intellectual autobiography, including the circumstances that led to the writing of the *Structure of Social Action*. Afterward at dinner, someone asked him why, after hundreds of American students had been going to Germany for decades, he was the one to come home with a theoretical synthesis. Parsons replied that he was the first to go over "after the War," and I thought this was an illuminating comment. Both Weber and Durkheim had been dead for several years; their writings were "in," so to speak; and there was a bit of temporal distance on their contributions. Perhaps there was only that one brief moment, in the middle of Weimar Germany's twenties, when you could get a clear view of all of European social thought. Yet obviously Parsons deserves more credit than simply having been in the right place at the right time.

Since there are sections of this paper that might be interpreted as anti-Parsonian— though I am attempting to use the evenhandedness of an umpire, who calls them as he sees them—I would like to mention that I sent an earlier draft to Parsons, inviting his comment. He did not respond.

13. My discussion of the cognitive basis of order is indebted to Warner (1978) and to several personal conversations with him.

14. The original group that met in Washington, D.C., in 1965 included: Robert Bales, Edgar Borgatta, Ernest Campbell, James A. Davis, David Gold, Robert Hall, Albert Reiss, Peter Rossi, Karl Schuessler, James Short, and Nathaniel Siegel (Schuessler, 1966:82).

15. The critical assessment of neo-operationalism, which is just beginning in sociology, might well use Bierstedt's critique of Lundberg (Bierstedt, 1974:41-72) as a point of departure. Bierstedt summarized his criticism of operationalism by saying that it "erased the distinctions between nominal and real definitions on the one hand and be-

tween cardinal and ordinal measurement on the other, and that the erasures were in fact required by the theory" (Bierstedt, 1974:8).

16. When Mead shifts his analysis from interpersonal to intrapersonal or intrapsychic conversation, he stays with the vocabulary of role taking, the collapsed or incipient act, and so on, but the words do not mean the same thing, and he is making a gestalt shift from pragmatism to phenomenology, reminiscent of the one William James made in shifting his criteria of meaning from the consequences of a statement to the consequences of *belief* in a statement (Mead, 1974:173-78, 1964a:142-49; Henle, 1951:125-27).

17. The sample and the market are both characterized by (a) a multiplicity of units, (b) roughly homogeneous in size and power, (c) causally independent of each other in the property being observed, (d) which find order from randomness and chance. Just as price fixing and oligopoly lead to "market imperfections" in the economy, bureaucratization leads to "sample imperfections" in the society at large. To the extent that a society is characterized by atomized markets and samples, new causal theory is often a fitting and powerful tool, but for institutional analysis, the importance of which increases in a bureaucratizing world, other empirical styles are more fitting and powerful.

PART II

ONTOLOGY AND SOCIOLOGY

Each of the three essays that comprise this part focuses on the ontological dimension of scientific investigation, namely: *What* is to be studied? This, then, is the realm of theory. The issue under consideration is that of identifying the very substance to be studied and, in turn, the subject matter of the discipline.

Perhaps the most basic ontological issue facing sociology concerns one's unit of analysis, whether it is the individual, the group, or a combination of the two. It is this topic which is discussed in the Bealer essay. Coser, in turn, explores what he refers to as the "substance" of sociology, and its relationship to various methodological techniques and procedures. Finally, Blalock delineates those qualities or characteristics which "good" theory ought to possess. Questions of ontology again become paramount by virtue of the fact that what one chooses to study will directly affect the ease or difficulty experienced in achieving the qualities which Blalock puts forth.

The central premise of Bealer's essay "Ontology in American Sociology: Whence and Whither?" is that a clear delineation of the specific set of events, phenomena, or behavior under investigation is a crucial first step in any form of scientific inquiry. To quote Bealer, "What sociologists define as their pertinent reality unquestionably has important consequences for theorizing and researching. Employing the realist (group)-nominalist (individual) distinction, Bealer then sets about tracing the ontological posture of several leading sociologists from Comte to the present.

First to be discussed is the predominantly realist ontological position taken by classical European scholars such as Comte, Durkheim, Spencer, Marx, Weber, and Simmel. Gradually, the emphasis shifts to the writings of early American sociologists, particularly members of the Chicago School. In general, the works of Ward, Cooley, Small, Mead, and others are seen as signaling a shift to nominalism, or at the very least, a more dualistic or hybrid ontological stance which combines both the realist and nominalist perspectives. Bealer concludes the "whence" portion of his essay, on the ontological changes which have taken place throughout the history of the discipline, by attempting to interpret the complex role of functionalism in American sociology. After carefully analyzing the "functionalism" of Parsons, which he contrasts to the "structuralism" of Merton, Bealer concludes that the traditional nominalistic bent of American sociology, recently thought to have *reappeared*, has never really disappeared. Instead, not unlike its highly empirical orientation, American sociology has never strayed very far from its basically nominalistic ontological posture.

In the final section of his essay, "whither" the reality of sociology, Bealer conjectures as to the predominant future ontological orientation of the discipline. Here Bealer is of the opinion that unless more sociologists openly and earnestly address themselves to issues of an ontological nature, the science of sociology may well undergo radical changes. Furthermore, because of various methodological constraints (whether real or imagined), Bealer sees little likelihood of a major return to the realist perspective of our European founders. It is on this note that Bealer ends by ironically observing that "a realist orientation is the better ontological candidate for getting us (sociology) to a true scientific status (vis-à-vis prediction) than is a nominalist view."

Using Diana Crane's treatise on the diffusion of knowledge within scientific communities as a backdrop, Coser's essay "Two Methods in Search of a Substance" warns sociology of "the growth of both narrow, routine activities, and of sect-like, esoteric ruminations." Coser views each of these two broad maladies as portending a decline in the discipline.

As concerns the narrow and routine activities in which many present-day sociologists are engaged, Coser registers alarm over what appears to be a marked emphasis on the use of precise measurement and sophisticated statistical procedures at the expense of addressing substantive issues. Moreover, such powerful and elaborate statistical operations, while expedient and more easily published in the major journals, appear to be leading the discipline to focus upon certain issues at the expense of others. As an example, Coser cites the tendency of highly sophisticated statistical studies in social stratification to stress "distributive" rather than "relational" aspects of social class. In short, not only is the methodological tail wagging the theoretical dog, but it is leading the animal in a certain direction!

In the latter portion of his essay, Coser voices his dismay at the sect-like nature of ethnomethodology. Much like the abstract empirical approach discussed earlier, it too is said to lack any theoretical content or substantive relevance for sociology. Instead, Coser finds the issues addressed by many ethnomethodologists to be trivial, their vocabulary idiosyncratic and noncommunicative, and the focus of their inquiries to decry a concern for latent structures.

Blalock's essay "Dilemmas and Strategies of Theory Construction" begins with this assertion: "Problems of conceptualization, measurement, and generalizability constitute the most serious hurdles confronting contemporary sociology." Thus although issues of data analysis and funding remain legitimate areas of concern, Blalock nevertheless believes there to be a more pressing need to address the aforementioned topics if sociological theory is to grow and mature.

Prior to embarking on a discussion of the various "internal criteria" to be taken into consideration in assessing a theory's "adequacy," Blalock distinguishes among the four basic ways in which a theory's "utility" can be judged: importance, predictability, manipulation potential, and generalizability. Then, Blalock discusses, in some detail, the manner in which the internal criteria of precision, internal consistency, parsimony, generalizability, falsifiability, and complexity affect one another and, in turn, the adequacy of one's theory. Of import, concerning these criteria, is Blalock's observation as to the processual nature of theory construction. Thus Blalock states that "it is often a matter of judgment as to which ones (criteria) should receive the greater attention at a given stage of the development of scientific inquiry."

Blalock concludes his essay by outlining two basic strategies (i.e., situation vs. model manipulation) that may be used in knowledge systemization. Although each has its strengths and weaknesses, the potential pitfalls of each are explicated and their solutions discussed. Of importance is the fact that neither method is a panacea and that, in practice, the assumptions underlying each approach need to be made *explicit*. It is this latter request that stands as a basic goal of metasociology and of this volume.

Robert C. Bealer

ONTOLOGY IN AMERICAN SOCIOLOGY: WHENCE AND WHITHER?

"If men define situations as real they are real in their consequences" (Volkart, 1951:81). This hoary axion in the sociologist's bag—attributed to the pioneer W. I. Thomas—is an appropriate entry for my discussion of ontology. Although the dictum has been generated to apply to the behavior of others, that is, persons of interest to the sociologist, there is no reason to exclude the idea when the behavior of the sociologist *qua* sociologist is focal. Such a focus is precisely the thrust of this essay. In simplest terms—the level toward which I shall try always to push the analysis—the matter of ontology comes down to the basic notions, assumptions, presuppositions, metaphysical choices, ideas (call them what you will) as to the nature of existential phenomena that the sociologist should be or is studying. Put otherwise, what the devil does the sociologist mean to signal in the everyday world of perception when she or he makes an analysis and calls it "sociological"? If the sociologist is to have any reasonable hearing in the courts of intellectual endeavor and, more importantly, empirical science, the implied causal proposition given by Thomas about the effects of "reality" defining must apply to the sociologist as well as to our subjects. I believe it does. What sociologists define as their pertinent reality unquestionably has important consequences for theorizing and researching. We need something on which to gaze, to think about, to explore. Exactly what that something is represents a fundamental ontological question for sociology—and a continuing polemic (Ellis, 1977). It is my purpose to chart the course of ontology in sociology and, along the way, to comment on certain aspects of the issue.

The answer posed by history to the sociologist's ontological question is diverse by label and often dichotomous: nominalism-realism (Snizek, 1975;

Wolff, 1959; Warriner, 1956); individual-group (Allport, 1965); individual-ism-collectivism (O'Neill, 1973); existentialism-sociologism (Tiryakian, 1962); methodological individualism-metaphysical holism (Brodbeck, 1968); atomis-tic-holistic (Cohen, 1968); psychological reduction-social facts (Fallding, 1968); behavioral-ecological perspectives (Duncan and Schnore, 1959a); lev-els of analysis in social theory (Edel, 1959); micro-macroscopic sociology (Et-zioni, 1965; Merton, 1970). This list is not complete, nor is the point of discus-sion indexed by the terms singular. For example, it is the case that the dictum attributed to Thomas speaks most clearly to an aspect of ontology I shall *not* be addressing directly, that is, the perspective from which the definition of reality is taken. Do we (as sociologists) go to the person as actor and try to get his or her definition of perceived reality, or can we ignore this datum and go to the struc-ture of things as they "really are," whether recognized by actors or not (cf. Braybrooke, 1965; Katz, 1976:7-14)? The former alternative grants impor-tance to the subjective viewpoint that the latter denies.[1] The granting of im-portance to the individual's view of the world is at the heart of a humanist stance (Bruyn, 1966), a tradition that emphasizes the uniqueness of people and events, of the freedom for the individual to choose that which will be her or his destiny (Berger and Luckmann, 1967). Indeed, the viewpoint is logically anti-thetical to a science of human behavior and, historically, this aspect of ontolo-gy has sharply divided the field (cf. Parsons, 1949). A subject-object dimension for ontology is clearly important; however, I will not push out on this plane ex-cept tangentially.

The task I have set is to cast ontology's historical trace in sociology and to suggest some reasons why the choices made about one's ultimate subject mat-ter may have been as they were. To help complete my task, it is imperative to specify a reference point. Throughout the chapter I shall focus on the Ameri-can case. In part, this reflects my own failings as well as space limitations. But the focus is not impertinent. As Alvin Gouldner cogently observes: "To much of the world today, sociology is practically synonymous with American sociolo-gy. . . . Its techniques are everywhere emulated, and its theories shape the terms in which world discussion of sociology is cast and the issues around which intel-lectual debate centers" (Gouldner, 1970:22). In the nature of the case, then, the topic of ontology may prove to be slippery—water through the fingers—but it does have a course. Well, at least, it can be made so.[2] Let us start at the head-waters so to speak: What position did the founders of sociology take? What changes may have transpired over time?

WHENCE THE REALITY OF SOCIOLOGY?

Phase I: Our Early Forebears

If sociology was sired by August Comte, the background to the act was tur-moil. As noted by Raymond Aaron (1965:61): "Comte believed that modern society was in crisis; as a result one social order was disappearing and another social order was being born. . . . The function of sociology . . . [was] to understand the necessary, indispensable, and inevitable course of history in such a way as to promote the realization of the new order." At the same time, Comte personally was profoundly conservative. He was not happy with the apparent breakup of the established structure and its disengagement of the individual from traditional group controls. Thus he cast sociology as the guide to giving exit from chaos and entrance to a new stability. The "positive" society envisioned by Comte was, in Nisbet's (1966:58) words, "simply medievalism minus Christianity," with the sociologist as the new priest-king. The particulars of Comte's thought (Simpson, 1969) are not germane, but following Nisbet (1966:59) we can note that "Comte made everything human above the level of the purely physiological derive from society . . . at the base of Comte's sociology lies his total rejection of individualism as a perspective." The removal of the individual from sociological consideration as a meaningful, significant entity may have been a wish-fulfilling aspect to Comte's own personal desires, but this sense of reality was a legacy with a long shadow over subsequent French work.

In many ways, Durkheim and Comte were nearly identical twins in reference to ontology. Durkheim's intellectual interests had a strong continuity and singularity. Beginning with *The Division of Labor* (1893), he left no doubts as to where the sociologist should be oriented—society as a unique phenomenon, not understandable at the level of individual motivation or acts. Indeed, the realist theme so generally associated with Durkheim was there set: the social structure which exists prior to and external from the individual determines what the members of society do. Structure—recognizable as "collective conscience"—must be focal to sociology. In *The Rules of Sociological Method* (1895) Durkheim tried to outline exactly how such a problem interest was to be handled by an appropriate scientific methodology. Put otherwise, if society was a social fact and only social facts could be used to explain them, one had to know how to identify them, use them in explanation, and establish proofs. This broadly outlines Durkheim's treatment of materials in *The Rules*. With the metasociological exposition of sociological procedure behind him, Durkheim then went on to himself conduct empirical studies—the significance of varying group structure on the very being or not of members, *Suicide* (1897). And, in *The Elementary Forms of the Religious Life* (1912), Durkheim tried to establish the functions of religion for society. He argued these as the affirmation and continuous renewal of the priority and moral right of the group to member loyalty.

Clearly, the atmosphere of sociology in France was realist in bent and empiricist in preference. The situation concurrently in England was more muddled despite an opportunity for unity given by the dominance of a single person. A competitor to Comte was Herbert Spencer, a man whose presence was unusually long and overwhelming to English "sociological" thought. His writings helped immensely to popularize Darwinian notions in application to the social. Spencer not only talked programmatically about tying all human knowledge together—as did Comte—he spent a lifetime trying to do it.

Spencer formulated an encompassing theory of reality including the physical, the biological, and the social. The mainspring in all was the "law" of evolution. Society, as an organism, a thing in a sense of literalness that could set agreeably with the French positivists, was at the core of Spencerian thought one would reasonably call sociological. Spencer tried to explicate how societies evolved from small, simple, uncomplicated structures to large, complex, and differentiated forms. His global philosophical perspective and substantive analysis was compatible with a realist sociology. However, Spencer did not stop his speculations within this framework. As suggested by Werner Stark, Spencer:

... developed a second social theory, diametrically opposed to the first ... society [he wrote] is nothing in itself. It is not a scheme which exists before the individuals and into which they must fit themselves; it is not a kind of organism endowed with ontological reality; it is not a thing. It is merely the mutual relationships which obtain between the individuals ... who alone are real in the ontological sense of the word. (Stark, 1961:517-18)

Spencer the nominalist! What is the true Spencer?

The ambiguity to his ontology is patent even as it is certain that the utilitarian mode of thought expressed as nominalism was more consistent with the political philosophy of laissez-faire for which Spencer was a vociferous advocate. He was a staunch defender of the idea that human intervention in the evolving social structure would likely be mischievous rather than helpful. This political doctrine fitted the needs of England's expanding industrial order and its capitalist ruling class, but it did not sell well in American sociology, which from the outset had strong meliorative drives.

The third leg of the classical European influence in sociology is found in Germany, and the writings of Marx. Like both Comte and Durkheim, Marx was a thoroughgoing realist. As best seen in the *Communist Manifesto* (1848) and *Capital* (1867-79), he, too, wished to explore the changing social order extant in Western Europe resulting from the Industrial Revolution. In trying to account for the sweep of history as an expression of economic interests:

Marx was not concerned with the maximization of individual self-interest upon which utilitarian interest theories commonly rest. He was not concerned with the private drives and propensities of individuals but rather with the collective interests of particular categories of men playing their peculiar roles on the social scene. "Individuals are [he said in the preface to *Capital*] dealt with only insofar as they are the personifications of economic categories." (Jessor, 1975:121)

Unlike the French, Marx showed his German intellectual inheritance. Positivism had no appeal. Rather, a certain quality of the idealistic tradition associated with German thought of various orders came through strongly in Marx's writing. "Class interests" and related ideas were palpable reality to Marx just as surely as the actor's notions about his or her own situation were dismissed as opium dreams unless they coincided with the social order depicted by Marx. And although Marxist and French sociology differed widely on how to study the phenomenon of note, they were singular in knowing to what they were not to be oriented as reality: the individual.

The presence of Marx in Germany was intellectually enormous. Certainly, the specter of Marx was manifest to Max Weber. His sociological writings have a sensitivity to nuance and alterantives that is outstanding. Still, it is clear that Weber was not antithetical to a realistic perspective.

His most general problem simply was to understand the social order of his being. Like Durkheim, Weber was intensely interested in the role played by religion in societal operation. He insisted (*The Protestant Ethic and the Spirit of Capitalism*, 1904) that the ideology and practice of ascetic Protestant religious groups provided an important impetus to the success of capitalist economic organization in Western Europe, with the specific interplay between the two institutional orders being an expression of the larger global movement of all societies to rationalization.

The use of ideal types by Weber was not confined to the unique historical events of which the Protestant Ethic was an example. He also acted upon another strand of thoughtways common to German sociology—call it "formal" or "analytical." That is, Weber also developed general ideal types as in his now famous modes of social action and types of authority. This element of Weber's sociology, however, was less prominent than in certain other German writers and clearly had to have a subsidiary impact on the development of American sociology. As important as Weber has come to be for sociology, it must be remembered that wide awareness of the man by Americans came relatively recently; his works were not translated into English prior to 1930.

By contrast, Georg Simmel's thought was early available to Americans (e.g., Simmel, 1909, 1910), and, by intellectual generation, he preceded Weber. Simmel's name is traditionally linked to "formal" sociology. He took for his analyses the historical record and sweep of human history—as did all the classic workers in the field. The contents of history provided the particulars for expression of deeper, constant, and universal forms of interactional association, to which, Simmel argued, sociologists should pay attention. He believed that sociology could, by looking to the discovery of invariances in forms of association, find a unique place not contested by any other of the already established social science professions.

In such an endeavor, Simmel was unwilling to accept either extreme of the realist-nominalist polarity; he was quite willing and able personally to provide

analyses consistent with both views. He argued at once against the reductionism of the nominalist or the magic of emergence crucial to the realist. The
ontological principle espoused by this cagey German was cast in the commonsense terms of viewing an object.

> We obtain different pictures . . . when we see it at a distance of two, or of five, or of ten
> yards. At each distance, however, the picture is "correct" in its particular way . . . a view
> gained at any distance whatever has its own justification. It cannot be replaced or cor-
> rected by any other view emerging at another distance. In a similar way, when we look at
> human life from a certain distance, we see each individual in his precise differentiation
> from all others. But if we increase our distance, the single individual disappears, and
> there emerges, instead, the picture of a "society" with its own forms and colors. (Sim-
> mel, 1950:7-8)

The position taken by Simmel suited American tastes and values. In effect, it
was a position that said "put your money down and take your pick!" American
sociologists from the outset tended to go effectively with nominalism.

If we date the appearance in 1883 of Lester Ward's *Dynamic Sociology* as
the birth of the American breed line, one can see the beginnings of a disclina-
tion to a realist view. Like many of his peers in Europe, particularly Spencer,
Ward's interest focused on cosmic evolution within which social evolution took
a place of compatibility. Ward tried to explain social phenomena on a philosophical base of total reality. In so doing, however, he insisted on the unique
character of social evolution due to mankind's rational faculties. Humans, as
individuals trained through education in science and executing rational judgment, could change the course of evolutionary development. Ward's passionate embrace of the differential mind as locus of the social was reflected among
his American compatriots in various ways.

Franklin Giddings saw society as essentially a psychic phenomenon and followed Ward's lead in positing volition to be the key in the matter. Giddings'
famous concept of "consciousness of kind" was proposed as the major motivational principle underlying the shared thoughts and common ideas identifiable as a social mind, that is, society. In a similar way, one finds Albion Small
using "interest" as the pivot of his sociological thinking. Interests were seen as
the simplest motivational modes guiding human conduct. At any particular
time the individual's behavior was seen as the outcome of a persisting struggle
internally among numerous interests, whereas society was merely the net outcome of various individuals' acting out their own interest dominated drives. A
certain degree of conflict theorizing is embryonic in Small, though the more
enduring, pertinent quality was his enunciation of a key component to
American sociology's ontology: "Individual and society are not means to each
other, but phases of each other. A society is a combining of the activities of persons. A person is a center of conscious impulses which realize themselves fully
only in society" (Timasheff, 1957:65).

This dualistic conceptualization of ontological reality has been symptomatic of American orientations from the start and has persisted down to the present. The perspective received perhaps its most famous statement in the work of Charles Horton Cooley. In *Human Nature and the Social Order* (1902) he wrote: "Society and individuals do not denote separate phenomena, but are simply the collective and distributive aspects of the same thing." Despite the ostensible parity posed by this equation, Cooley went on to posit in the same book his memorable notion of the "looking-glass self." The nominalist tilt is clear in Cooley's formulation and is underscored by the methodological position usually associated with this important pioneer: sympathetic understanding. This is just another term for the *verstehen* (understanding) directive previously encountered in regard to Weber. The inherent logic of *verstehen* (Abel, 1948) forces one to stumble whenever movement beyond the person and his or her motivation is tried. To emphasize empathy is, perhaps, implicitly to be pushed toward nominalism. In any case, one finds that Cooley confined his own attempts at empirical observations to children's play groups and immortalized these in his writings on "the primary group"—collectivities to be sure, and, as such, a representative of "society," but those about which one can still detect easily and obviously a sense of individuality to each of the constituent members. Cooley, then, provided a sterling example for later generations of American sociologists on taking on ontological middle ground which attempted to synthesize the realist and nominalist perspectives.

But why such a choice? In answer one can point to the pioneers in the field and cite, as has been done briefly, some of their specific ideas. Those sociological ideas and stances form part of the most immediate milieu that latter workers must make peace with. The cultural mix once begun is part of the determinance for culture continued. Indeed, it must be accepted as a powerful factor lest we as sociologists belie by our own behavior what we otherwise argue is true: Culture *is* an important explanatory idea. With that said, one can yet ask a bit more fundamental question: What accounts for the tilt of American sociology *originally* away from a realist bent toward nominalism?

If one accepts the apparent consensual view that sociology arose originally in Europe in response to the upheavals of the time and place, then a reasonable extension would cite the same kinds of factors and be forced to note dissimilarities in qualities. America was a relative babe in arms to the lineal kin of nations from which its white settlers were drawn. The comparative freedom from history gave this country a particular capability to bypass sociological collectivism as a pertinent—and appealing—phenomenon. As noted by Martindale (1976a:122), "settlement . . . was dominated by North European middle-class urbanites. They had to contend neither with an established aristocracy and a traditional church hierarchy above them nor with proletarian masses and a peasantry below." The obvious emphasis on control of person inherent in a realist mode of thought lacked a ready referent in the American context. Originally, the Indians as "aliens" and nature as a harsh enemy were the main targets of attention; neither was translated into a point of internal societal contest, for their subjugation was nearly unanimously agreed upon. To own attempts at empirical observations to childrens' play groups and immornization was by groups trying to cast off oppression from external authority, be it civil or religious. Moreover, it is sometimes forgotten that American society predated by some years the profound turmoil engendered by the French Revolution, with its shock and significance to European sociology. The United States had changed its political order early in the name of self-determination. The ideals of rugged individualism and free choice were incorporated in the national psyche at its birth and were given a conspicuous bolster by the continued availability of the frontier (Turner, 1894). Whether myth or reality, the idea of the person having the right to make the choices that will be his or her destiny has been a strong flavor in the American experience from the outset (Rischin, 1965). It is perhaps not surprising that the realist orientation of the Continental classical sociologists was muted in crossing the sea.

Phase II: Dominance by Chicago

The willingness of Americans to look at micro-sociological details—to take society as a given, as unproblematic, to probe at the parts as over against the whole, to be happier moving away from rather than toward a realist orientation—was vividly apparent in the maturation of "Chicago sociology" beyond what I have just called the first phase of the discipline. As Albion Small was the catalyst for Chicago's infancy, Robert Park and Ernest Burgess were critical to adolescence and young adulthood.

The basic orientation of the Chicago school as the 1920s opened was laid down, more than in any document, in Park and Burgess' *Science of Society* [sic: *Sociology*, 1921] which drew heavily for its orientation on the neo-Kantianism of Simmel. It thrust the social process into central focus and urged a program of systematic, objective, empirical research. (Martindale, 1976a:136)

The vehicle of their program was the notion of human ecology. At the theoretical level they proposed to study the city with the key ecological idea, taken from biology, of natural patterns of spatial distribution. Distinct patterning to land use was believed to result from the Darwinian struggle among competing units for survival within an environment of limited resources and differential capability of competitors to adjust. Dominance focused through the economic order was the structural mode defining the outcome to the competition. The fabric of social structure as large scale, impersonal, exterior and constraining, coercive and Darwinian was realist in view and could trace a comfortable path of continuity with European roots. But ecology was only half the story.

The Chicago School divided social organization into two parts, the biotic and the cultural.

At the biotic level, in the social as in the natural environment, competition was the guiding process. On the cultural level, communication and consensus between members of society were the distinctive processes. The guiding laws at the cultural level were those of tradition and the moral order; at the biotic, those of survival. The cultural level, which Park called society, was in a sense a superstructure that depended on the biotic, or what Park called community. The two levels were connected so that what occurred at the lower level had consequences for the higher. (Reissman, 1964:102)

Ecological study, strictly speaking, was limited to the biotic. In this way Park hoped to avoid and circumvent the complexities of "society." The Parkian definition of "community" removed the individual as significant and made human motives superfluous, except for the implicit directives of economic man oriented to maximal efficiency in land use. Quite the opposite was true regarding "society." Here the essence of things was the individual as a moral creature engaged in commerce with his fellows through the medium of roles guided by normative consensus. The bifurcation yet bracketing of problems and orientations for the sociologist carried forward the previously seen tendency of American sociology to take both horns of the ontological dilemma. Simmel's advice on being all things at once, ontologically, was witnessed in Park's program for sociology. However, the fancy footwork that a Simmel could give to keep this egalitarian choice operative was not evinced. The bifurcation of tasks was not successfully bracketed.

Human ecology as the study strictly of spatial patterning at the symbiotic subsocial level was carried forward. Burgess enunciated his famous hypothesis of the city as an organization of five concentric circles. Though developed originally as a description for the city of Chicago, it was meant to apply to other American cities as well, being an intended generalized account of dominance. Yet, although human ecology represented one of the clearest expressions of a realistic orientation in American sociology and showed a certain continuity, it was generally regarded as suspect by sociologists. The sense of peripheral status was apparent among the human ecologists themselves and elicited a decided defensiveness in their now-and-again metasociological writing (cf. Duncan and Schnore, 1959a, 1959b; Hawley, 1950b). The more important point at this juncture, however, is to note that the realist thrust to Chicago sociology was largely blunted *from the outset.*

Park suggested that sociological research should begin with what he termed "community" for practical reasons—and a bold one in the light of most sociological thinking. "The community [said Park, 1952:182] is a visible object. One can point it out, define its territorial limits, and plot its constituent elements, its population, and its institutions on maps." In a word, the community, the subsocial, was a thing more readily identifiable and subject to ease of methodological manipulation than was the social, his "society." Precisely the opposite kind of argument is more typical in sociology, with a realist view emerging as less concrete. Whether Park's peers shared his sentiment is questionable, for the major vector of Chicago sociology was not to an enrichment of the realist ontology palpable in ecology per se. Although often moving in the name of "community," much of the Chicago sociological work was an elaboration of Park's "society" construct.

Taking a note from Simmel, the Chicago School tried to get at the forms of sociation comprising the dynamics of social organization: competition, conflict, cooperation, succession, assimilation, and so on. This urge was muted and strained by filtering through a methodological sensitivity for detailing content—the specifics of time and place. Whereas Simmel was able to flit amid historical and contemporary examples to derive at least some general ideas to stand the test of time, the typical Chicago sociologist felt obliged to document, describe, and heavily detail *the* city (Chicago) and its inhabitants in staunch empiricist terms. The drive toward scientific respectability beating in the breasts of sociologists should never be underestimated and least of all at this particular time of the field's development. Although the positivistic claims of the French pioneers were always appealing to Americans, it was during this stage that there was, in Leon Bramson's (1971:74) apt words, a concerned "search for a methodology which would guarantee the scientific status of the discipline." The natural-science-inspired sense of exploratory description exploded in prominence—and why not? Almost anything carefully laid out would appear to be more scientific than the speculative ruminations of the homegrown forefathers, even granting that the American pioneers from the first were more inclined to look first before they conjectured.

The methodological-ontological impetus to description was supplemented and strengthened by the fact that Chicago hatched a theoretical orientation mandating a less than global perspective. Symbolic interactionism was instigated, primarily out of the fertile thoughts of George Herbert Mead, and lurked constantly as a humanistically more appealing imagery for sociology than ecology ever did. The former allowed for the warmth of the human as a blood-and-guts person with feelings, goals, desires, emotions, all the kinds of things that ecology dismissed as unnecessary to its rationale. In this regard, *Mind, Self, and Society* (1934) contains the most distilled of Mead's notions and is the medium by which he is generally identified.

If one question could do justice to Mead's seminal ideas—as surely as it cannot—it would be this: What is the process, inside the mind and with subsequent linkages to external events, that generates the person as self? Mead could not be happy with the kind of view—a realist one—that sees the individual coerced always to compliant action by external, antecedent forces presented to the actor as an inflexible given. As Clint Jessor has noted on Mead's behalf:

Social organization may shape a situation or provide some preexisting definition of it by virtue of the shared symbols people coming to the situation already possess. But the situation is not always prestructured, so there is usually room for reinterpretation. At bottom, only individuals, separately or together, act. And unless we understand the interpretation process in terms of the acting unit, we will pursue a groundless sociology and miss the realities in which individuals create and manage new institutions. (Jessor, 1975:304)

"Society," for Mead, was basically people—each with his or her own sense of self—engaging in mutually aware interaction, that presupposed communication of shared meanings which sustained such a system. Society was most vitally a universe of symbols and symbolic action; it was the aggregate traced out of selves.

That symbolic interactionism arose when it did at Chicago had fateful significance for American sociology. As lamented by the famous ecologist Amos Hawley (1950b) and vouched for by many others (Parsons, 1949; Hinkle and Hinkle, 1954; Mills, 1959; Bramson, 1971; Leventman, 1971), "in the literature of the 20th Century . . . the main preoccupation [of sociology] has been with the individual organism as affected by the social situation" or, stated more cogently, how the self is imparted and altered via socialization. No small part of the characterization applicable to America's second phase of development was attributable to the acceptance of symbolic interactionism and its strong disinclination to a realist ontology.

I shall not try to detail further the particulars of American sociology's development from roughly World War I through World War II, the chronological span one might assign to identify the second phase of its evolvement. We can note in passing that the Chicago hegemony was diffused somewhat to other schools in the Midwest. And, toward the end of the period, a certain stirring of change became manifest. It was symbolized, most dramatically, with the establishment in 1936 of the *American Sociological Review* as the official professional voice of the field—a role unquestionably played by the *American Journal of Sociology* since its inception four decades earlier. The move was a deliberate attempt to molt the Chicago influence (Faris, 1970). Yet, like the nation's isolationism at large, sociology during the period tended to insular dominance (cf. Martindale, 1976:135-40). Sociology, like most institutional orders of society, leaned to lethargy in moving away from the course originally traced and deepened with time's passage.

In that light one must reemphasize the place of meliorative goals in motivating American sociology from the outset. A desire to know in order to do characterized many in the field and provided a base of support to obtain resources for empirical research. Before a person can change something, he must know the parameters of the situation and where circumstances will allow him to go. The liaison between reform-minded academic sociologists and government agency personnel quickened during this period and was galvanized, first, by the Great Depression of the 1930s and, second, by the mammoth impetus to empirical research afforded by the virtual engulfment of sociology by the federal government's demands for World War II contribution (Martindale, 1976a:132-35; Bowers, 1967:250-55). Whatever faults to the coupling, one thing is sure: the primary emphasis was on research orientation. What C. Wright Mills (1959) would thunder at as "abstracted empiricism" was solidified on the bedrock of rank-and-file approval (cf. Lazarsfeld et al., 1967).

Phase III: The Muddle of Functionalism

Following World War II, sociology exploded from a relative handful of practitioners to a legion spawned by the opportunities for employment. One could try to detail the various shadings of ontological positions given by sociologists, young and old alike, in marginally differentiating themselves from their kind in the academic game of status seeking. However, after Stark (1961:515), I find that, past nuance, there are only three ontological choices possible for the sociologist: (1) accept a realist view and reject nominalism; (2) reverse these preferences; (3) amalgamate and try to take both positions at once. The foregoing sketch has set down the historical current of American character that favors the third—as a program, even though the mode of actual work is more likely to be the second. Some comment about the most recent phase of American sociology is in order, since the period has particularly muddled ontology.

Martindale (1976a:140) notes that, toward the close of the second period, the "variations on elementarism [nominalism], was showing fracture lines. The first intimations of a native form of theoretical collectivism were manifest." Functionalism is the referent for the latter; Talcott Parsons is the acclaimed messiah (Gouldner, 1970). Parsons became the hub of sociological efforts at Harvard and was vital to that school's ascendance in the profession, reflecting the more general thrust of sociology outward from its heartland home to a new prominence on both coasts.

Parsons was instrumental in opening American sociology to the works of Max Weber. He translated Weber's *Ethnic* and made that material a critical part of the claimed convergence of theory among an elite cross section of European social thought—German, French (Durkheim), British (Marshall) and Italian (Pareto)—dissected in *The Structure of Social Action* (1937). Parsons tried to educe a scheme he called a "voluntaristic theory of action" from the two great Continental traditions: positivism and idealism. Parsons' classic book was relatively dormant in peer interest until its reissue by the Free Press in 1949. In short order there followed *The Social System* (1951) and *Toward a General Theory of Action* (1952); a prolific writer was put into orbit (cf. Loomis and Loomis, 1965:327-441). The substance of Parsons' work is not germane except in one sense. A major complaint against his "theory" from the outset has been a claimed failure to provide substance, to substitute misguidedly a conceptual framework and its manipulation toward logical closure as over against explanation, even description of concrete—time and place—events. Parsons' ontology needs a closer look.

His choice was the traditionally American one of trying to straddle ontology's horns. Not only was Parsons willing to find strong convergence within the polyglot of sociology, but the essence of his "general theory" was to insist on homology across the historically given levels of abstraction by which the social creature called "man" had been analyzed—as biological organism (Parsons, 1959), personality, group or society, and culture. Parsons granted a measure of worth to viewing human behavior at all levels as long as the ultimate goal of union became paramount. The medium for homology was the posited insistence that at all levels the structure in reference faced the same general types of functioning problems of adaptation, goal attainment, integration, and pattern maintenance-tension management. History was taken as showing the sociologist to be preeminent in studying the "social system," Parsons' term bracketing group and society.[3] It is revealing to note that although Parsons characteristically cojoined "social system" to "society," his only extended reference to empirical materials in his landmark treatment of sociology's purpose was to the two-person relationship of doctor and patient (Parsons, 1951). A simple, face-to-face brace of role players is no different from the congeries of two billion comprising Chinese society! The ontologically tinged sleight of hand equating such phenomena makes eminent sense if someone is pragmatically trying to sell his peers on their need to accept his point of view. With the legacy of nominalist inclination in American sociology, analyzing "society" as a particular, miniscule role-set is appealing, though some would insist that such a maneuver is an abomination and abortive. Indeed, Parsons' prime antagonism has come from so-called conflict theory, which basically charges that Parsons' work (and functionalism as a whole) stresses harmony, cooperation, continuity, and persistence in social matters to the neglect of disharmony, conflict, disjointure, and change because he persists in not vigorously taking a realist perspective in general and, more specifically, that of Marxian analysis (cf. Demerath and Peterson, 1967; Gouldner, 1970).

To sort out the claims of Parsons and his critics is futile, partly because so many of the discussions talk past each other, whether deliberately or otherwise. Moreover, the rubric of "functionalism" (and equal terms like "structural functional") has been appropriated to so many different modes of analyses that the terminology has tended to lose all meaning (Davis, 1959). Still sociologists continue the terminology, and in the present context it can help to distinguish an important difference. "Functionalism" as a label identifies those sociologists who are more willing than most to consider a realist claim as having merit, those who will claim to cast their vision of the social through the lens of society (Maines, 1977:235). As one might expect, however, and returning to Simmel's metaphor of sociology, there are views and there are views! Demerath has wisely observed:

There are certainly distinctions within structural-functionalism itself . . . [it] includes distinct subspecies with distinct consequences . . . a crucial difference between subspecies is whether the analyst is primarily interested in a particular "part" (a discrete institution) or in the configuration of the "whole" (the total society). (Demerath, 1967:502)

Clearly, the latter position is the heritage of classical sociology. Clearly, also, it is less represented in recent American sociology except, perhaps, as it seems to be the favored whipping boy of the many "talks about" functionalism.

To suggest that functionalism may not be as dominant as it is commonly thought to be (Gouldner, 1970; Coser, 1976) is not easy to establish or prove unequivocally, even given the amount of criticism that was leveled against it. Some comments, however, are possible, and so that some of the bombast can be avoided and misunderstanding allayed, I must reaffirm the distinction made by Demerath (1967:517) and note his further words that "the *structuralist* [whom he identifies as one subspecie exemplified par excellence by R. K. Merton's work] is more likely . . . to be conservative in his emphasis on the individual and his vulnerability to teleology." That is, the structuralist makes the actor's ends-in-view, motivations, and purposes central to analysis. By contrast, "the *functionalist* [Parsons as an exemplar, has a] lack of particularism, but is liberal in his stress on the collectivity and his aversion to teleology." My claim applies to the "functionalist" rather than the "structuralist."

The fit of Merton's "structuralist" brand of "functionalism" to the inherited ontological line of American sociology just sketched makes for a comfortable fit. His position on middle-range theorizing—as a conscious antidote to the "grand theory" (Mills, 1959:25-49) of a Parsons and a direct catalyst for empirical research—is revered except by certain iconoclasts (Willer, 1967:xiii-xx); his call corresponds to what is being already attempted. His emphasis in tracing an institutional structure—upward to its functions for societal operation, yes, but more often and influentially, downward to the individual's behavior as in "reference group theory" (Merton, 1957:225-386)—is witnessed in the interests of professional sociologists because he is a magnificent codifier (e.g., Merton, 1957:12-84) and reflective of rank-and-file proclivities. Thus if one looks at the cumulative indexes of the *American Journal of Sociology*, 1895-1965 and 1966-70, articles on "institutions" abound, and always have. By the same token, "personality" is well represented and overrides a heading like "society" by a factor of approximately 10 to 1. Again, in the first volume, an entry like "culture, norms and values" exceeds "culture, comparative study" by literally 100 to 1. If functionalism is the dominant contended, it seems strange to find it so little in evidence in the journal writings of practitioners outside one's coterie. Put bluntly, where does one find even an attempt made to use Parsonian "theory" directly in research? The pattern variables (Parsons, 1951:58-67), probably the most likely of his ideas to be converted easily to a direct research use, have evinced only a scattered handful of tries at operationalization (e.g., Williams, 1961:91-92; Nall, 1962; Dean, 1967), and all have used a role level of analysis in application to persons rather than characterizing society per se. In a word, Parsons's functionalist theory does not seem to have had the criticalness often claimed.

One further comment can allow me to both provide further evidence about the foregoing matter and add a needed frame to the movie of ontology in American sociology. Coser (1976:147) claims that although a Parsonian-type functionalism dominated the scene from "the early 1940s until roughly the middle of the 1960s," this has been replaced by a resurgence of micro-sociological theories, especially "a psychological exchange perspective" (p. 154). The latter part of the claim can stand as reasonably accurate, but the former part is another matter. If Parsonian "theory" was as entrenched as Coser implies, it would be difficult to appreciate the means for an abrupt reversion back to a clearly nominalist ontology. However, if "functionalism" was more talk than action (research) and a veneer imperfectly placed over the antique wormholes of an empiricist, nominalist preference, the "change" is understandable: There was, in fact, no radical shift at all in American sociology's basic course.

All the furor surrounding "functionalism" tends to obscure the truly identifying character of American sociology—its empirical bent, its "hard science" view, its commitment to research, its striving for quantification and methodological sophistication, the continuing ascendance of positivism begun with Comte. Put in the terms of C. Wright Mills' searing analysis of two decades ago (1959), neither the "sociological imagination" he preferred nor the "grand theory" he despised has marched forward in any way to begin to challenge the supremacy of "abstracted empiricism," which he also loathed (cf. McKinney, 1957; Lazarsfeld et al., 1967; Willer and Willer, 1973). Love it or hate it, American sociology is Comtean in one sense and, however unfortunate it may be, no more characterized by sound scientific theory now than at its outset.

Recently, I had the opportunity to evaluate carefully the state of theory since 1965 in regard to the subfield of rural sociology, as revealed by the contents of the journal by the same name (Bealer, 1975). One would be hard-pressed to find any branch of sociology more resolutely given over to empirical research than is rural sociology. Although by some criteria advancement was evident and is probably indicative for other fields as well, a sad conclusion had to be made:

I doubt that one can find many corroborated empirical generalizations floating about in the pages of the journal; even less likely to be found are the lawlike relationships that a Merton would reserve for the honorific label of theory. We may, if we wish, be upset by the lack. However, I would urge perspective:

> Despite the many volumes dealing with the history of sociological theory and despite the plethora of empirical investigations, sociologists (including the writer) may discuss the logical criteria of sociological laws without citing a single instance which fully satisfies these criteria. (Merton, 1957:96)

First uttered nearly 30 years ago and unchanged through the various editions of his work, Merton's observation seems yet valid. The failing of *Rural Sociology* to pass muster for adequacy of theory on the generalization sense of meaning for the term is not unique. It is just that the field seems far more willing to chance the pain of self-appraisal (Bealer, 1969) and thus be aware of its own limits. (Bealer, 1975:472)

If we can find few, if any, sound empirical generalizations anywhere in sociology, it is not untoward to fail at identifying established scientific laws; the precondition for the latter is the former. "Laws" are explanations of empirical phenomena witnessed as "generalizations."

I stated at the outset of this section that American sociologists would like to think of the third period (the present) as a state of theoretical maturation. It is certain to me that a lot of talk about theory has transpired, much of it centering on "functionalism." Equally, in the past decade, much has been written counseling the need to join research and theory construction via mathematical models (e.g., Coleman, 1964; Bielby and Hauser, 1977). Yet the reality persisting is that we still have no viable, scientifically sound theory, and this may not be unrelated to ontology.

WHITHER THE REALITY OF SOCIOLOGY?

The sketch just drawn of ontology's history in American sociology has tried to show that despite a strong realist orientation to the European forebears of the field and a certain realist cast to some of the early American sociologists, this perspective never had strong support in the United States. Having asked about the past, it seems appropriate now to ask about the future. The cogency of the inquiry has been heightened by some recent events outside the realm of sociology, specifically, the appearance of sociobiology (Wilson, 1975). Based on this, Lee Ellis (1977) has contended that doom will result for the field of sociology if it continues what he considers to be a misguided allegiance to a nonreductionist position on ontology. Ellis' plea, like that of Homans (1961, 1964) earlier, is to go beyond the actor even as person to the other side of possibility. That is, he urges us to get beneath the person to the biological level. The pith of sociology becomes genetics or, possibly, molecular chemistry. Ellis argues that unless such a radical reductionist move occurs, a step taken beyond the present ontology, sociobiology will preempt the discipline.

It is not my purpose to argue at length with Ellis. But certain remarks are in order. Possibly sociology will succumb in the near future to sociobiology. If this occurs, however, I suspect it will not be for the reasons Ellis cites. I would submit that most persons calling themselves sociologists are today: (1) not realist in orientation and, certainly, (2) not openly interested in ontology. Both of these facts need brief examination, for whatever the pitfalls of predicting the future, one thing is certain: Tomorrow's events must take off from today's history. Moreover, I take it as a reasonable *hypothesis*, in the "functionalist" tradition, that the best prediction to be made about the state of any social order is continuity (Bealer et al., 1965). Systems tend to maintain the status quo. A Parsonite is unabashed by such an assumption; an antagonist is likely to scream loudly at the asininity of the choice and yet, when such a person comes to write political or popular (lay-oriented) sociological treatises, he constantly bemoans the unchanging character to society, the futility of assailing the "Establishment," the perpetuation of power groups, and the continuing failure of America's real structure to realize the ideal (cf. much of the writing in *Society* nee *Trans-Action*). One could suggest that the critics of "functionalism" mute the vitality of their own criticism most tellingly by their otherwise given complaints about lack of change.

My prognosis assumes that *both* "nominalists"[4] and realists in sociology presently tend overtly to trivialize and degrade concern over ontological levels of analysis. They do so by insisting that there is no real issue. Who wants to be caught dead—let alone alive—peering after the vacuous? Sociology has long suffered the pangs of inferiority feelings within the scientific community (Sjoberg, 1959; Ehrlich, 1962); why give your enemies more ammunition? Letting ontology rest seems to strike a common thread of agreement.

Some years ago O. D. Duncan and Leo Schnore, two leading figures in the human ecology realm, set about the task of explicating the assumptions of this almost ideal-typical manifestation of a realist view that also incorporates a strong empirical research component. One hears from them (Duncan and Schnore, 1959a:144): "Our intention . . . is not to engage in bootless argument regarding the ultimate reality of either the individual or the aggregate . . . both are abstractions and thus unreal in equal degree. As Cooley noted . . . the individual and the group are but aspects of the same reality." Having said this, however, the human ecologist has been prone to follow Amos Hawley's classical strategy—enunciated as follows:

The individual in [human ecology] . . . has no place . . . he enters as a theoretical postulate and as a unit of enumeration, but not as a [meaningful] . . . variable. . . . I think it entirely possible to state a sociological problem in such a way that motives, attitudes, and other social-psychological variables cannot [and should not] enter as data. (Hawley, 1950b)

That is precisely what has occurred in the research of the human ecologist (Willits et al., 1974:335). The outcome is to deny effectively the allegation of unitedness. The individual and society may be different sides of a single coin but only one side ever appears as worth one's attention. Or, put otherwise, the distinction between individual and aggregate may be a bootless argument, but the difference does seem to be quite consequential in terms of what gets done, is thought about, or is written.

No better public demonstration of this is known to me than that displayed in the exchange between Duncan and Schnore (1959a, 1959b) and Peter Rossi (1959). Both parties wound up talking past each other because of a fundamental disagreement on ontology. The most intriguing and instructive aspect to the exchange is that the antagonists seemed to be aware of the point at issue but awareness *could not* provide grounds for reconciliation—awareness is important (Bealer, 1963) but no panacea. Thus Duncan and Schnore aver:

In all likelihood he [Rossi] does not mean what we mean in declaring that the job of sociology is to explain social organization. Perhaps Rossi really means by "social organization" a fabric of mutual understanding and consensual meanings shared by a set of persons. If this is the case, it is difficult indeed to reach any fundamental agreement, since the conception of social organization set forth in our paper does not involve such subjective [individual-level] elements. (Duncan and Schnore, 1959b:151)

Difficult, indeed. Duncan and Schnore (1959b:150) snarl at Rossi: "[His] pronouncement that 'behavior . . . is motivated, and men seek goals through social organization—goals which cannot be irrelevant to social organization [is sententious].' Whatever the basis for this statement, it does not have to be accepted as an axiom." Clearly, Duncan and Schnore are not willing to give their assent. Without it, the combatants are likely to remain just that—locking horns and shouting.

On the other side of the ontological issue, the nominalist plurality in sociology is likely to nod in agreement with Peter Berger and Thomas Luckmann's (1967:61) words that: "Society is a human product. Society is an objective reality. Man is a social product . . . an analysis of the social world that leaves out any one of these three moments will be distortive." True, perhaps. Yet the linkage between society as an objective reality and the human as a social product is the connection of overwhelming significance—as noted previously. Dual reality may be acknowledged formally by the contemporary nominalist but the singularity of the person bending to social reality ("society") is the hallmark of modern sociology. Who, then, in the proper name of the field, is going to waste much time or effort in following out the Berger and Luckmann link that individuals make (create, control) the society?

There are some, of course. Berger and Luckmann (1967) are two such people. Indeed, it is precisely because "contemporary American sociology tends toward leaving out the first moment [i.e., society is a human product]" (Berger and Luckmann, 1967:197-98) that those authors felt the need to write their rally call for a humanistic perspective. In general, the phenomenological-existential-ethnomethodological writers are joinable in terms of their common plea that modern social science pay attention to the undeniable fact that human beings make and continue to remake the social order in which they live. The plea has vitality only because the opposite fact is often and easily bantered about. Modernization, urbanization, secularization, bureaucratization, and all kinds of other "izations" can be blithefully cited as uncontrolled and uncontrollable forces projected as "out there" and forming the inextricable milieu to which the person adjusts—with some degree of alienation (Olson, 1963). Social determinism, though unrecognized, is an uncomfortably close realization in much of the ideology of modern sociology (Bealer, 1970). Culture, subculture, counterculture, social class, reference group, as examples, are taken as explanatory ideas par excellence. Crime, delinquency, poverty, adolescent behavior, professional behavior, neurosis, birth rates, ambition, mobility, and practically anything else we choose to name is due to a received (or anticipated and oriented to) tradition, set of norms, shared values, and so on, in whose face the individual is plastic and putty. The human being is no more or less than what culture and society make them.

Yet, paradoxically, the realist perspective witnessed by this thrust is largely neutralized by two related strategies characteristically invoked as maxims: (1) "Society does nothing to people; people do things to one another in terms of some society [as a set of norms]" (Levy, 1966:4); and (2) given people oriented one to another, we accept with a vengeance that "if men define situations as real, they are real in their consequences" (Volkart, 1951:81). With these assumptions, one logically emphasizes attitudes, beliefs, cognitive structures, values, preferences, orientations, perceptions or whatever kind of related term you might wish to use to denote the overriding urge to get inside the skin and skull of others to know what they think and value and seek. Getting the individual's view on existential reality is the modus operandi for the overwhelming bulk of sociological research (Willer, 1967; Stokes and Miller, 1975; Webb et al., 1966). But this kind of strategy fails to reach the heart of a critical matter. As Duncan and Schnore (1959b:153) noted years ago: "Granted that a substantial portion of the variation in individual behavior is demonstrably conditioned by variation in social structure [i.e., "society" and its norms] we ought then to be curious about the determinants of social structure itself." That presently is largely lacking; it is needed to have a truly realist perspective.

Are we likely to get there in the future? One has to be pessimistic for a very simple reason: methodology. Above all, sociology today is procedures and techniques oriented—we are empiricists. There is a tremendous stone cast in the road for acceptance of a realist orientation by the widely embraced canons of an empiricist methodology—call it, "finger the group" failure.

As John McKinney (1957:190) has noted: "Empiricism . . . indicates an attitude complex characterized by the utmost faith in the senses, firm belief in the power of observation, willingness to be ruled by observable evidence and belief that scientific conclusions should never get beyond the realm of extrapolation." In such a context, how can you touch, see, hear, smell, taste a group or society, as you can, in an intuitively obvious way, a person? Is this perhaps the fundamental reason why sociology tends so often to be essentially nominalist? We *can* know without question whether we have touched, seen, heard, smelled, or, yes, tasted a person. But where exactly is the group, such that the same kinds of direct sense impressions of it are possible? Is it any wonder that people seem so real, whereas groups are a fiction? In contrast to the immediately obvious impression of a person as real, a sociologistic (or realist) view is inevitably revealed as abstract, inferred, theoretical. The person seems less so—and never mind the nicety that the person is inferred from the regularity of behavior in the biological organism just as society is an inference of the same sort from the actions of persons only one order of abstraction more removed from the perceptual. The choice of ontology is not simply a rational matter. There are degrees of "sin." For the empiricist-oriented sociologist, it follows that the further removed from the senses, the greater the potential for sin. "Salvation" is obvious! Perhaps not.

The case of human ecology is interesting in this context. The firm view of this school against a nominalist stance has already been shown; yet the field is staunchly empiricist (cf. Schnore, 1965; Hawley, 1950a, 1971). The apparent effervescence of society as a construct seems to be dispelled by such persons via the ever-present reliance on census materials as data sources. The obvious "thingness" to all those thick, abundant, and constantly produced volumes may be this faction's route to stilling the nagging doubts about concreteness so often plaguing a realist persuasion. Moreover, past a bit of humor here, there is coming from this perspective a methodological antidote to the "finger failure." It is that old saw—"finger me the victim"!

We know factually that—as an example—suicide rates tend to be stable except as they are made to vary by known factors (Labovitz, 1968). The relative stability in rates or incidence of behaviors within a defined population despite the inevitable turnover of specific persons is a cornerstone of realist thinking (Warriner, 1956). It is persuasive by contrast with the equally well-known fact that predicting exactly which person(s) within a population will commit the act (suicide) making up the rate is exceedingly difficult and prone to error. From delinquency and crime through mental health to social mobility and other measures of "success," the record of sociology's ability to explain statistically, let alone empirically sort out, exactly which persons will do what is dismal (Lazarsfeld et al., 1967; Schuessler, 1971). One might even suggest that the failure will continue unabated because the existential nature of the case decrees it (Bartholomew, 1975).

If emergence exists in the human case because "society" is only individuals meeting one another and interacting with but partly shared perceptual frames —as the socialization literature substantiates (Goslin, 1969)—and if there is that important residue of freedom to the human psyche and opportunity for individuality the phenomenologists and like-minded analysts constantly press upon our consciousness, can there ever be anything but high-order indeterminancy for individual acts (Bartholomew, 1975)? Why then bark up the tree of the realist? That it is easier presently to measure aspects of the person, to identify him or her as an empirical object and meet, thereby, the trappings of an empiricist philosophy may just be siren enticements to long-term fertility. Put another way, in atomic physics (de Broglie, 1953), and many other areas of science, events in the aggregate show high stability even though at the more specific level of this or that act there is high instability. The phenomenon is not a source of despair or anguish but of comfort. Perhaps one could argue that if we want to use prediction as the *sine qua non* for sociology's performance, a realist orientation is the better ontological candidate for getting us to a true scientific status than is a nominalist view.

NOTES

1. Within the camp of those who would grant import to getting subjective dispositions, a major point of difference lies in how one handles the data collected. Freudian analysts, as an example, are vividly interested in virtually every aspect of the subjective —dreams, thoughts, feelings, speech patterns of the patient—*but* the analyst (as "scientist") has to reinterpret their "true" meanings (Hall and Lindzey, 1957:29-75). By contrast, most of survey research in sociology takes the subjective—as "attitudes," "opinions," "orientations," "values," or related terms—as basically a true datum, not requiring reinterpretation. Thus the long history of an attitude-behavior disjunction (Schuman and Johnson, 1976) has been written largely as a methodological matter. If the predictive ability of attitudes for other behavior forms is not generally very good—as has been the record to date—the fault is seen as a failure in methods of measurement, not as an issue, perhaps, of ontological supposition.

2. I must confess to a basically "structuralist" view of science (Katz, 1976:10). We impose regularity—more or less—on the existential world of raw data and experience. Such construction, as noted by and elaborated in McKinney (1966:5), "is a means of reducing diversities and complexities of phenomena to a generally coherent level. Consequently it does not [literally] describe or represent any course of action . . . in uniqueness, but does represent an . . . empirically relevent course of action." There is no escape in science from the typification process just summarized. And there is no danger, as long as we do not reify our conjectures, or, put otherwise, we must recognize that an ideal-typical construct is being presented. In stroking the lines of major differences among the designated philosophical sets, a certain degree of looking past details must occur. The dimension space of ontology is not singular, nor is there uniformity among those who would dissect it. Among the better attempts by one who wants to stay close to nuance and details is that by W. L. Wallace (1969: 1-59).

3. Just what relationship sociology bears to other disciplines and orders of study has been subject to vacillation and dispute. Broadly, two alternatives have emerged: (a) sociology is the capstone social science integrating the knowledge of more specialized fields, especially through the construct of society; (b) sociology covers those aspects of

human social situations not laid claim to by other fields, such as economics or political science (cf. Timasheff, 1957:4-9). Sociology clearly began with the first alternative, but would appear to have gravitated toward the second. In this regard, it should be noted that Parsons' claim to a general theory framework, enunciated by a sociologist to sociologists, implies something of a return for the field to its original position. In this, perhaps, we have a late-blooming, unwilling answer to the contemptuous question with which Parsons (1949:3) opened *The Structure of Social Action*: "Who reads [and believes] Spencer?" Despite his disclaimers, the answer may be Talcott Parsons—it just took a long time for it to become manifest!

4. I use the quotes to alert the reader to a special meaning of the term. The grayness of history, as contrasted with the black-and-white tones that characterize the kind of ideal-typical picture used in the exposition, prompts the alert. As will be seen, a more literal approximation to the mean on ontology among present-day sociologists is to accept a basic realist premise and then turn one's back immediately upon it.

I need also to note the work of Snizek (1975). He classified 81 percent of the 1,434 studies he examined as "realist" or "quasi-realist" in perspective. The figure is high in the context of various characterizations of American sociology as nominalist. The difference may be due to the way Snizek classified his materials. I would argue: (a) that it is often difficult to discover a researcher's ontological view from the name given to the variables used; and (b) that it is not so much the kinds of variables one invokes as it is what one does with them that reveals the sociologist's true ontological position.

Lewis A. Coser

TWO METHODS IN
SEARCH OF A
SUBSTANCE

This essay is an exercise in the uses of controversy. It deals with two major methodological orientations in contemporary sociology and examines them critically. The reader should bear in mind, however, that methodological approaches in other areas, such as the sociology of science or the study of complex organizations, might lend themselves equally well to similar critical reflections. My major attempt in this paper has not been to start a quarrel with particular orientations, but rather to raise questions that seem relevant to the general sociological enterprise at this juncture. I am perturbed about present developments in American sociology which seem to foster the growth of both narrow, routine activities, and of sectlike, esoteric ruminations. Although on the surface these two trends are dissimilar, together they are an expression of crisis and fatigue within the discipline and its theoretical underpinnings. I shall eschew statesmanlike weighing of the pros and cons of the issues to be considered and shall attempt instead to express bluntly certain of my misgivings and alarms about these recent trends in our common enterprise; let the chips fall where they may.

Building on other students of science, Diana Crane (1972) has argued that scientific disciplines typically go through various states of growth accompanied by a series of changes in the characteristics of scientific knowledge and of the scientific community involved in the study of the area. In stage one, important discoveries provide models for future work and attract new enthusiastic scientists. In the next stage, a few highly productive scientists recruit and train students, set priorities for research and maintain informal contacts with one another. All this leads to rapid growth in both membership and publications. But in later stages the seminal ideas become exhausted and the original theories no longer seem sufficient. At this point, a gradual decline in both membership and publication sets in, and those who remain develop increasingly narrow, specialized, though often methodologically highly refined, interests. Unless fresh theoretical leads are produced at this point to inspire new growth, the field gradually declines.

The findings of Crane and others in the sociology of science typically refer not to a whole branch of knowledge but only to subfields within such branches. It would therefore be wrong to apply these findings to sociology as a whole, composed as it is of a wide variety of subareas each with its own pattern and rhythm of growth. Nevertheless, permit me roughly, and perhaps rashly, to sketch what I consider to be the present condition of sociology as a whole.

By and large, we are still in the second stage of growth, the stage of lively development, of creative ability, and innovative effervescence. Yet there now appear a number of danger signs suggesting that the fat years of the past may be followed by lean years, by years of normal science with a vengeance, in which not only the mediocre minds but even the minds of the best are hitched to quotidian endeavors and routine activities. This seems portended by the recent insistence among many sociologists on the primacy of precise measurement over substantive issues.

The germ of the idea for this address came to me earlier this year when a friend of mine, the editor of a major sociological journal, explained with some pride that, no matter what the substantive merits of the paper might be, he would refuse to accept contributions using old-fashioned tabular methods rather than modern techniques of regression and path analysis. I gather, for I have respect for his opinion, that he meant that he would not accept articles requiring modern methods of data analysis that do not make use of such techniques. Yet, though his intentions are undoubtedly excellent, I submit that such an orientation is likely to have a dynamic of its own and that, inadvertently perhaps, it will lead to a situation in which the methodological tail wags the substantive dog, in which as Robert Bierstedt (1974:316) once put it, methods would be considered the independent and substantive issues the dependent variable.

My friend's voice is, of course, not a lonely one. In fact, he expressed what is tacitly assumed or openly asserted by a growing number of our colleagues. Fascinated by new tools of research, such as computers, that have come to be available in the last decades, and spellbound by the apparently irresistible appeal of techniques that allow measures of a precision hitherto unattainable, many of our colleagues are in danger of forgetting that measurements are, after all, but a means toward better analysis and explanation. If concepts and theoretical notions are weak, no measurement, however precise, will advance an explanatory science.

The fallacy of misplaced precision consists in believing that one can compensate for theoretical weakness by methodological strength. Concern with precision in measurement before theoretical clarification of what is worth measuring and what is not, and before one clearly knows what one is measuring, is a roadblock to progress in sociological analysis. Too many enthusiastic researchers seem to be in the same situation as Saint Augustine when he wrote, on the concept of time, "For so it is Oh Lord, My God, I measure it but what it is I measure I do not know" (Saint Augustine, 1953:35).[2]

No doubt, modern methods of research have immeasurably advanced sociological inquiry. Only sociological Luddites would argue that computers be smashed and path diagrams outlawed. What I am concerned with is not the uses, but rather the abuses of these instruments of research. They serve us well in certain areas of inquiry, but they can become Frankenstein monsters when they are applied indiscriminately and, above all, when their availability dictates the problem choices of the investigator so that trivial problems are treated with the utmost refinement.

The sheer availability of new methods encourages their use and seems to release the user from the obligation to decide whether his problem or findings are worthy of attention. By way of illustrating this, let me quote from the summary of a recent paper by Oksanan and Spencer (1975) in one of the official journals of our association, the *American Sociologist*: "A rather large degree of explanatory power has been achieved by our regression model, in terms of overall goodness of fit and in terms of significant variables. It is of considerable interest to learn that high school performance is an invariably significant indicator of 'success' in the [college] courses examined." Abraham Kaplan's (1964: 28) delightful formulation of the Law of the Instrument comes to mind here: "Give a small boy a hammer, and he will find that everything he encounters needs pounding."

The fact is that though in principle these new methods and technologies could help us achieve greater theoretical sophistication, they are used as "magic helpers," as a shortcut to, or even replacement for, theoretical analysis rather than as a means for furthering it. An insistence on the use of these refined methods, no matter what, makes it fall prey to Kaplan's law.

It would be easy, and perhaps entertaining, to go on quoting similar instances, but each of us can easily supply other examples. Let me instead return to the serious problems now faced by our discipline, many of which have been created, or at least accentuated, by the revolution in methodology and research technology.

Our new methodological tools may well be adaptable to deal with a great variety of topics and problems, and I hope they are. However, the data needed for path or regression analyses are much harder to come by in some areas than in others, and in many of them it would take a great deal of sophistication to discover and handle usable indicators. Consequently, under the pressure to publish to avoid perishing, or to gain promotion, or simply to obtain the narcissistic gratification that comes from seeing one's name in print, it is more attractive to do what is quick and easy. This is so in every scholarly field and even in the healing arts. In psychiatry, for example, it leads to prescribing drugs instead of psychotherapy, often not as result of deliberate choice between alternative diagnoses and prognoses, but simply because drug therapy is easy to administer and promises quick results, superficial though they may be. In the world of scholarships, moreover, not only the choice of technique but even the choice of the problem tends to be determined by what is quick and easy rather than by theoretical considerations or an evaluation of the importance of the questions that are raised. Moreover, the uses of a sophisticated technological and methodological apparatus give assurance, but often deceptive assurance, to the researcher.

Sociology is not advanced enough solely to rely on precisely measured variables. Qualitative observations on a small universe can provide theoretical leads that may at a later stage become amenable to more refined statistical treatment. To refrain from using descriptive data because they may lend themselves only to tabular presentation will not only diminish our theoretical powers but will retard the refinement of statistical analysis as well.

Training the new generation of sociologists not to bother with problems about which data are hard to come by, and to concentrate on areas in which data can be easily gathered, will result, in the worst of cases, in the piling up of useless information and, in the best cases, in a kind of tunnel vision in which some problems are explored exhaustively whereas others are not even perceived.

There is at least some evidence that we tend to produce young sociologists with superior research skills but with a trained incapacity to think in theoretically innovative ways. Much of our present way of training as well as our system of rewards for scientific contributions encourages our students to eschew the risks of theoretical work and to search instead for the security that comes with proceeding along a well-traveled course, chartered though it may be by ever more refined instruments of navigation. J. E. McGrath and I. Altman (1966) have shown this in instructive detail for small-group research, but it applies in other areas as well.

Careers, especially those of people with modest ambitions, can be more easily advanced through quantity rather than quality of publication. This leads to an emphasis on methodological rigor, not on theoretical substance. One way to publish rapidly is to apply "the [same] procedure, task, or piece of equipment over and over, introducing new variables or slight modification of old variables, and thereby generate a host of studies rather quickly" (McGrath and Altman, 1966:87). The formulation of theories, moreover, is time consuming, and may not lend itself easily to publication in journals increasingly geared to publishing empirical research, and to reject "soft" theoretical papers. There exist, then, a number of factors in our present systems of training and of rewards that exercise pressures on incoming generations of sociologists to refine their methods at the expense of developing innovative lines.

This is not inherent in methods per se, but it is, let me emphasize again at the risk of repetition, a temptation for lesser minds. And here as elsewhere inflation has set in. However, it is important to note that even the better minds, those who have been able to use the new methods innovatively, are *nolens volens* geared to deal with problems, important as they may be, for which these methods promise quick results. Even in the serious work that is being done with the help of the new statistical techniques there lurks the danger of one-sided emphasis.

Stratification studies of recent years will illustrate this point. This field has benefited a great deal from modern path analytical methods whose power is perhaps shown at its best in Blau and Duncan's *The American Occupational Structure* (1967). Path analysis allows these authors systematically to trace the impact of factors such as father's occupation, father's educational attainments, and son's education and first job on the son's placement in the occupational hierarchy. It allows for the first time the assessment in precise detail of the ways in which occupational status in a modern industrial society is based on a combination of achieved and ascribed characteristics. It permits, in fact, the assessment of the contributions of social inheritance and individual effort in the attainment of socioeconomic status.

Yet, to use an important distinction made by John Goldthorpe (1972), this research contributes to the understanding of the *distributive*, not to the *relational*, aspects of social class. The focus is predominantly on the impact on individual careers of differences in parental resources, access to educational institutions and the like, or they center attention upon individual characteristics of people variously placed in the class structure. There is no concern here with the ways in which differential class power and social advantage operate in predictable and routine ways, through specifiable social interactions between classes or interest groups, to give shape to determinate social structures and to create differential life chances. The first and only entry under path analysis in the 1966-70 Index to the *American Sociological Review* (vols. 31-35) refers to a paper by Hodge and Treiman (1968) tracing the effects of the social participation of parents on that of their offspring. There were only two papers analyzing problems in social stratification with the aid of path analytical methods in the 1973 (vol. 38) volume of the *American Sociological Review*, and both (Kelley, 1973, and Jackman and Jackman, 1973) deal with the *distributional* aspects of social stratification or with the characteristics of individuals in the class hierarchy.

Yet a class system is not only a distributive system, in which individuals are assigned to their respective niches in terms of background and training, nor is its analytical significance exhausted by individual characteristics of people who make their way within it; it is also a system that is shaped by the interaction between various classes and interest groups differentially located within the social structure. It is a system, moreover, in which command and coercion play major parts. Classes and other socioeconomic groups use their resources so as effectively to maintain or advance their positions and to maximize the distribution of material and social benefits to their advantage. Exclusive concern with the distributive aspects of stratification directs attention away from the sociopolitical mechanisms through which members of different strata monopolize chances by reducing the chances of others. Max Weber, building on Karl Marx, saw this with exemplary clarity when he stated that:

It is the most elemental economic fact that the way in which disposition over material property is distributed among a plurality of people . . . in itself creates specific life chances. According to the law of marginal utility this mode of distribution excludes the non-owners from competing for highly valued goods. . . . It increases . . . the power [of the propertied] in price wars with those who, being propertyless, have nothing to offer but their labor. . . . (Gerth and Mills, 1947:181)

One need not accept Marx's dichotomous scheme of class analysis in order to agree that classes are linked in asymmetrical relationships. The notion of a class of owners of the means of production is dialectically bound to the notion of a class of non-owners. Just as in the classical Indian caste system, as Louis Dumont (1970) has shown, the purity of the Brahmans is inseparable from the impurity of the untouchables, so the central characteristics of the class systems is not that there are propertied and the propertyless but that they are mutually interdependent. Randall Collins, arguing against a narrowly defined sociology of poverty, puts the matter well when he writes, "Why some people are poor is only one aspect of the same question as to why some people are rich: a generalized explanation of the distribution of wealth is called for if one is to have a testable explanation of either particular" (Collins, 1975:17).

A system of stratification consists in relationships between groups or categories of men and women which sustain, or alter, their respective access to life chances. It is one thing to investigate the ways in which, for example, people manage to attain the status position of medical practitioners in American society, and quite another to analyze the institutions that help the American Medical Association to monopolize the market for health care by restricting access. What needs analysis is not merely the ladder to medical success but those institutional factors that contribute to the maintenance of a system of medical service that effectively minimizes the life chances of the poor (Kelman, 1974).

Analysis of the distributional aspects of stratification systems can dispense with considerations of social and political power; concern with the relational aspects, however, directs attention to the power contentions that make for the relationships which establish differential class privileges, and create patterned conflicts between unequally benefited contenders. When no question is asked about who benefits from existing social and political arrangements, stratification research, no matter how sophisticated its methodological tools, presents a "bowdlerized" version of social reality. When the causes and consequences of differential location in the class structure remain unanalyzed, the whole area of research so brilliantly opened up by Robert K. Merton's (1968: chaps. 6 and 7) seminal anomie paradigm remains unexplored.

I am not arguing, let this be clearly understood, that concern with the structures of power and exploitation is necessarily better than preoccupation with the pathways to individual mobility. There is surely a need for both types of studies. I believe, however, that the methodological tools that are available help focus on the latter. It must be added—lest I be accused of technological determinism—that such restrictions are also rooted in the prevailing American ideology of individual achievement. But taken together, the ideology, combined with the use of statistical methods in limited areas, prevents the growth of our discipline and curtails our ability to strive for a full accounting and explanation of the major societal forces that shape our common destiny and determine our life chances. If the computer and the new methodological tools we possess now are not yet adequate for handling some of the issues I have raised, then let us at least press forward with theoretical explorations even if they must later be refined or modified by more precise empirical research. Let us not continue on a path about which one may say with the poet Roy Campbell (1955:198): "They use the snaffle and the curb all right. But where is the bloody horse."

Another symptom of the decline of a discipline, as Diana Crane (1972) indicates, is exclusive insistence on one particular dimension of reality and one particular mode of analysis by cliques or sects who fail to communicate with the larger body, or with one another. Under such conditions, a community of scholars will gradually dissolve through splitting up into a variety of camps of ever more restricted esoteric and specialized sects, jealously fighting each other and proclaiming that they alone possess the keys to the kingdom, whereas others are not just in error, but in sin. Under such conditions the only dialogue between antagonistic camps is a dialogue of the deaf. Such tendencies have also become apparent in the past few years of the history of our discipline. This brings me to my second topic of examination, the assessment of ethnomethodology.

If I understand correctly, ethnomethodology aims at a descriptive reconstruction of the cognitive map in people's minds which enables them to make sense of their everyday activities and encounters. It is a method that endeavors to penetrate to the deeper layers of the categorical and perceptual apparatus that is used in the construction of diverse realities. The method also aims at a rigorous description of ordinary linguistic usage and speech acts. As such it seems aggressively and programmatically devoid of theoretical content of sociological relevance. Limiting itself by a self-denying ordinance to the concrete observation of communicative codes, subjective categorizations, and conversational gestures, it underplays the behavioral aspects of goal-directed social interaction. It focuses instead on descriptions of definitions of the situation, meaning structures, conversational exchanges, and the mutual modification of images of self in such interchanges. Ignoring institutional factors in general, and the centrality of power in social interaction in particular, it is restricted to the descriptive tracing of the ways in which both individual actors and students of their activities account for their actions.

Ethnomethodologists put particular stress on the contextuality of accounts and meanings, their embedment in the interactive context, their "situated" nature. Given the constitutive situatedness of any act, it is asserted that no objective generalizing approach is possible in the social sciences, which by their very nature can only provide ideographic description. In some versions of ethnomethodology, intersubjectivity is consciously neglected so that one ends up with a view of individual actors as monads without windows enclosed in their private and unsharable universes of meanings.

As distinct from path analysis and similar methods, ethnomethodology has not found ready acceptance within our discipline; in fact, it has never sought such acceptance. It has consciously limited its appeal to devoted followers united in the knowledge that they possess a special kind of insight denied to outsiders.

Ethnomethodology claims access to types of knowledge not accessible to the sociological *vulgus*. Write Zimmerman and Pollner (1970), for example, on the ethnomethodological reduction, one of the mainstays of the method: "The reduction does not generate research that may be regarded as an extension, refinement, or correction of extant sociological inquiry. . . . The reduction constitutes as its phenomenon an order of affairs that has no identifiable counterpart in contemporary social science." More typically still than the oft-repeated insistence that ethnomethodology has a unique subject matter is the esoteric and particularistic nature of the pronouncements of its practitioners. Consider, for example, a paper by David Sudnow, entitled "Temporal Parameters of Interpersonal Observation," which turns out to deal with the glances people exchange with one another or direct at the passing scene. It is concerned, as the author elegantly puts it, with "the issue of glance timing importance" (1972: 273).

Let us consider the situation of "walking across the street," where an orientation to be clearly so seen is held by virtue of the noted presence of a rapidly approaching vehicle. Here a familiar traffic situation may be regularly imagined where a mere and single glance is expected, where the sufficiency of the mere and single glance is criterial [*sic*] for bringing off safe passage . . . and where, as a consequence, the concern for a correspondence between the "details" of what we are doing and what we are seen at a single glance to be doing, may be of paramount concern. (Sudnow, 1972:269)

When I try to explain to my four-year-old grandson that he should always be careful when crossing a street, I say to him, "Always watch for passing cars." I do not think that Sudnow's jargon conveys anything more. Each field, to be sure, must construct its own defined terms, but what is developed here is a restricted code of communications rather than open scientific vocabulary (Bernstein, 1971).

It is much too facile simply to poke fun at a group of people who profess central concern with the linguistic aspects of interactive processes and yet seem unable to handle the vernacular. But the fact is that such language diseases have sociological significance in the development of particularistic communities of True Believers. To begin with, esoteric language erects barriers against outsiders and confirms to the insiders that they have indeed a hold on some special truth. But there is more; such jargon, as the philosopher Susanne Langer puts it, "is language which is more technical than the ideas it serves to express" (1967:36), so that it can successfully camouflage relatively trivial ideas. Moreover, esoteric jargon may serve to bind the neophyte to his newfound anchorage. People tend to value highly those activities in which they have invested a great deal. Having invested considerable time and energy in mastering an esoteric vocabulary, people are loath, even when some disillusionment has already set in, to admit to themselves that what has cost them so much might, after all, be devoid of genuine value. Hence the particularistic vocabulary is not due to happenstance; it serves significant functions in marking boundaries and holding members.

Yet another characteristic with obvious functional value that ethnomethodologists share with similar close groupings in other scholarly areas is the characteristic habit of limiting their footnote references almost exclusively to members of the ingroup or to nonsociologists, while quoting other sociologists mainly in order to show the errors of their way. There is, in addition, a peculiar propensity to refer to as yet unpublished manuscripts, to lecture notes and research notebooks.

It will be recognized that the characteristics I have outlined are those of a sect rather than of a field of specialization. I here define a sect as a group that has separated in protest from a larger body and emphasizes an esoteric and "pure" doctrine that is said to have been abandoned or ignored by the wider body. Sects are typically closed systems, usually led by charismatic leaders and their immediate followers. They attempt to reduce communication with the outside world to a minimum while engaging in highly intense interactions among the True Believers (Coser, 1974). Sects develop a special particularistic language, distinctive norms of relevance, and specialized behavior patterns that effectively set off the believers from the unconverted, serve as a badge of special status, and highlight their members' differentiation from the larger body of which they once formed a part.[3]

Yet what is functional for the sect is, by the same token, dysfunctional for those who are not among the elect. Blockage of the flow of communication is among the most serious impediments of scientific developments. A science is utterly dependent on the free exchange of information among its practitioners. Preciseness and economy in information flow make for growth, and blockages lead to decline (cf. Crane, 1972). But the language of ethnomethodology, as James Coleman (1968:130) once put it, makes for "an extraordinarily high ratio of reading time to information transfer." More generally, an esoteric language can only serve to dissociate a body of people who were once united in common pursuits. As in the story of Babel in Genesis, "And the Lord said, 'Behold they are one people, and they have one language; and this is only the beginning of what they will do. . . . Come, let us go down, and there confuse their language, that they may not understand one another's speech.'"

Even though the sect is still quite young, the splits and fissures that typically beset sectarian developments have already set in. I do not profess to be knowledgeable about the detailed grounds of these developments (see Attewell, 1974, for an excellent mapping and critique), but shall only sketch some of them very roughly. At present, the ethnomethodology of Garfinkel differs significantly from that of Sacks, which, in turn, is far removed from the concerns of Blum or the researches of Cicourel. Some versions are, in fact, solipsistic; others attend to intersubjective meanings; some admit the existence of invariant rules and procedures that transcend situations; others deny the possibility of any analysis that is not situation specific. Some find philosophical anchorage in the German idealistic tradition and its Husserlian offshoots; others make use of British linguistic philosophy and seem to have replaced the guidance of Alfred Schuetz with that of Ludwig Wittgenstein. Some concentrate on the analysis of unique events; others attend to invariant properties of situated actions. The only things all of them still seem to hold in common is the rejection of the possibility of an objective study and explanation of society and history, and a celebration of that long-dead war-horse of German idealistic philosophy, the transcendental ego.

Concern with the hypertrophy of wordage among ethnomethodologists and their other sectarian characteristics should, however, not preempt all of our attention. It is axiomatic among sociologists of knowledge that the origin of ideas does not prejudice their validity. It is possible that important and fruitful ideas may indeed develop in sectarian milieus. This has, in fact, often been the case, from the inception of puritanism to the emergence of psychoanalysis in the Viennese sect of Freud's immediate disciples.

Yet, when one turns to the problems that ethnomethodology tries to illuminate, one is struck, for the most part, by their embarrassing triviality. We have already encountered Sudnow's "glancing research." Schegloff (1968) has spent productive years studying the ways in which people manage to begin and end their telephone conversations. I am not denying that "Studies of the Routine Grounds of Everyday Activities" (Garfinkel, 1967) may uncover significant and valuable matters, but in my considered judgment what has so far been dug up is mostly dross or interminable methodological disquisitions and polemics. Bittner's (1967) fine studies of the police or Cicourel's (1968) analysis of juvenile justice and a very few other good studies are not enough to justify the enormous ballyhoo surrounding ethnomethodology.

In general, it would seem to me that we deal here with a massive cop out, a determined refusal to undertake research that would indicate the extent to which our lives are affected by the socioeconomic context in which they are embedded. It amounts to an orgy of subjectivism, a self-indulgent enterprise in which perpetual methodological analysis and self-analysis lead to infinite regress, where the discovery of the ineffable qualities of the mind of analyst and analysand and their private construction of reality serves to obscure the tangible qualities of the world "out there." By limiting itself to trying to discover what is in the actors' minds, it blocks the way to an investigation of those central aspects of their lives about which they know very little. By attempting to describe the manifest content of people's experiences, ethnomethodologists neglect that central area of sociological analysis which deals with latent structures. The analysis of ever more refined minutiae of reality construction, and the assertion that one cannot possibly understand larger social structures before all these minutiae have been exhaustively mapped, irresistibly brings to mind Dr. Johnson's pregnant observation that "You don't have to eat the whole ox to know that the meat is tough."

Path analysis, as has been shown, is a method that found quick acceptance among wide circles in the sociological discipline because it provided technical means for more precise measurements hitherto unavailable; ethnomethodology, in contrast, found acceptance only among a small number of practitioners huddled around a charismatic leader and his apostles. The first was widely communicated through the various informational networks, both personal and impersonal, available to sociologists; the second developed particularistic codes of communication that effectively restricted access to all but the insiders. Yet what both have in common is a hypertrophy of method at the expense of substantive theory. The first has been used as an encouragement to neglect important areas of inquiry even while it has brought about greater precision of measurement in other areas, some important, some trivial. The second lends itself at best to atheoretical mappings of cognitive categories, and deliberately eschews concern with most of the matters that sociology has been centrally concerned with ever since Auguste Comte. In both cases, I submit, preoccupation with method largely has led to a neglect of significance and substance. And yet our discipline will be judged in the last analysis on the basis of the substantive enlightenment which it is able to supply about the social structures in which we are enmeshed and which largely condition the course of our lives. If we neglect that major task, if we refuse the challenge to answer these questions, we shall forfeit our birthright and degenerate into congeries of rival sects and specialized researchers who will learn more and more about less and less.

NOTES

1. Portions of this essay first appeared in the *American Sociological Review*, December 1975, and are reprinted with permission of the author and the American Sociological Association.

2. In fairness to Saint Augustine, modern physics tends to agree with his position. "Time is a primitive element in the logical structure of physics," state W. H. Cannon and O. G. Jensen (1975), and "consequently physics does not explicitly define time but rather specifies operational procedures for its measurement in units of seconds."

3. For an earlier analysis of sectlike characteristics in sociology compare Coser (1955).

Hubert M. Blalock

DILEMMAS AND STRATEGIES OF THEORY CONSTRUCTION

Before we begin talking about strategies of theory construction, it is well to ask the prior question: What are the desirable characteristics that a "good" theory ought to have, from both the standpoint of its practical utility and also that of its internal structure and relationship to data analysis? Whenever one enumerates a number of distinct criteria, we may anticipate that there will be a number of incompatibilities among them or, at least, a set of conflicting demands that are difficult to satisfy simultaneously. We shall therefore want to examine such incompatibilities and their implications for one's strategy of theory construction.

The major thrust of our argument will be that problems of conceptualization, measurement, and generalizability constitute the most serious hurdles confronting contemporary sociology. Many problems of data *analysis*, as well as the formal rules for making theoretical and causal inferences on the basis of one's data, are now reasonably well understood, though there remains the pedagogic problem of communicating this technical literature to the practicing sociologist.[1] Furthermore, computer technology and available "packaged" programs make it possible for the data analyst to conduct highly sophisticated types of analyses at a relatively low cost.

To be sure, improvements in these areas of knowledge can and should be made, but it appears unlikely that sociologists will be in a position to take effective advantage of them unless and until our data-collection procedures, measurement-error theories, and conceptualization efforts are drastically improved. In short, there is a definite lag in, or underdevelopment of, certain areas of our methodological and theoretical knowledge that poses very serious problems for the advancement of the sociological enterprise. These need to be faced head on, with the recognition that there will be many a priori assumptions and methodological complexities that need to be brought out into the open.

Though we shall not really focus on the question of a theory's utility, it is important at the outset to distinguish among four meanings that may be attached to this notion. First, one may be referring to the social *importance* of the set of "dependent" variables that the theory sets out to explain. Basically, one may ask: If the theory under consideration were to provide a perfect explanation of the phenomena in question, and if on the basis of this theory a policy maker was able to make basic changes in these phenomena, would this really matter to a significant number of actors? Does the theory deal with an important topic or a trivial one? Answers to these questions obviously lie beyond the scope of the scientific method, though this of course does not imply that they cannot be addressed by some other means.

A second notion of utility basically compares the degree of knowledge provided by the theory in question with that of its competitors, including common sense or folk wisdom. Here the question being asked is: Does this theory provide any important insights or *predictions* beyond those that could be obtained more simply by extrapolating past trends into the future or by commonsense reasoning? For example, one may "predict" behavior at some future time merely by looking at past behaviors. Such predictions are likely to be faulty to the degree that the situation or context is altered. But even so, the best available theory may provide no better a predictive mechanism, although its explanatory power (in a causal sense) may be far superior. If so, the theory would be judged to have little practical utility, at least for limited and short-term projections into the future.

A third meaning of utility may be expressed in terms of the degree to which the major explanatory variables in the theory can actually be *manipulated* in the policy-making arena. Thus a theory about planetary motions would have no "utility" in this sense, even though it enabled one to predict these motions with an extremely high degree of accuracy. A theory that explained deviant behavior in terms of the individual's family background and early socialization would have little utility to a policy maker who was prevented from manipulating these variables. By contrast, a theory that explained deviance in terms of school variables or police behaviors might have a greater chance of leading to policy alterations that could actually affect the levels of the dependent variables.

There is also a fourth meaning of the term "utility" that is perhaps most closely linked to the first and that will have a more direct bearing on our own discussion. This is the notion that a theory is useful to the degree that it can be *generalized* to cover a diversity of phenomena that otherwise appear totally to be unrelated to each other. Presumably, also, such phenomena would have to be judged individually important in the first sense we have described. This criterion of generalizability is obviously crucial whenever the phenomena being studied are undergoing rapid change, so that what is defined as an important social problem one day may become less "relevant" at another time, only to reappear as an important phenomenon in slightly different guise at a still later time. In other words, if society's problems are undergoing rapid changes, it becomes all the more important that theories developed to explain one of these phenomena also be applicable to others. If this cannot be accomplished, the social scientist may never be able to catch up with these changes. Once a theory becomes adequate in terms of its explanatory power, there may no longer be any interest in it unless it can be extended to cover other phenomena under new conditions.

SOME "INTERNAL" CRITERIA FOR ASSESSING A THEORY'S ADEQUACY

The remaining criteria we shall identify are familiar ones in discussions of scientific methodology, namely, parsimony, internal or logical consistency, precision, completeness, and rejectability. In brief, a "good" theory should be parsimonious or relatively simple, logically consistent, capable of making precise predictions, as complete or self-contained as possible in the sense of including virtually all of the important explanatory variables, and capable of being falsified.

Such an ideal theory is obviously extremely difficult to construct, to say nothing of being adequately tested. Nevertheless, it remains a kind of prototype model to be approximated as closely as possible. Since the criteria are multiple, any given theory may satisfy one criterion much better than another, and therefore it becomes partly a matter of taste as to which criteria are given the most weight. Since theory construction is really a *process* that lacks a clear-cut beginning and ending, and since one may always hope that certain unmet criteria will eventually be satisfied, it is often a matter of judgment as to which ones should receive the greater attention at a given stage of the development of scientific inquiry. We may anticipate that there will be no general consensus on this matter and that various strategy combinations need to be attempted.

Parsimony, Internal Consistency, and Generalizability

We see no basic incompatibility between the objectives of constructing theories that are both parsimonious and logically or mathematically consistent. In fact, the typical strategy for constructing mathematical models of empirical processes is to begin with as small a number of assumptions or axioms as possible, to use as few primitive concepts as necessary, and then to define other concepts in terms of these and to derive internally consistent theorems from the axioms and definitions. One then compares the predictions from the theorems (and sometimes even the axioms themselves) with actual empirical results, using some sort of goodness-of-fit criterion to decide upon the adequacy of the model. If the model does not fit or correspond to the data, the theory is modified, sometimes by changing one of the axioms but often by admitting greater complexity into the theory. One then extracts the implications of this revised theory by a deductive process, once more comparing the implications with the data, and proceeding to make the theory increasingly "realistic" in terms of its ability to predict to increasingly complex phenomena in the real world. (See Leik, this volume.)

Such deductive systems may be constructed at varying levels of specificity, with different implications for the precision of their predictions. Thus if we merely say that Y is a function of X, this says practically nothing about what we may expect, except that if X varies, Y will also vary in *some* systematic fashion. If we add to this statement the restriction that Y is a positive monotonic function of X, then we know that if X increases, Y cannot decrease. If we say that Y is a "strictly" monotonic function of X, then Y must always increase (and cannot remain constant) if X increases. If we say that Y is a linear function of X with the equation $Y = a + bX$, then we place a further restriction on the relationship between X and Y. Finally, if we specify the numerical values of the parameters in the equation, say, by setting $Y = 5 + 6X$, then we make a prediction about Y that is totally unambiguous, provided that we know the value of X. Such a "theory" is, of course, also much more easily rejected than any of the previous less specific versions.

Considerations of parsimony also enter in when we say that we hope to find a general theory that accounts for a number of diverse phenomena, each of which may be explained by a more limited theory that turns out to be a special case of the more general theory. Thus Newton's laws of motion account for a diversity of phenomena, including the planetary orbits as well as the distance a falling body travels in a given amount of time in the presence of the earth's gravitational field. Without this more general law one could, for instance, obtain separate laws appropriate for falling bodies that are near the earth's surface, on the moon, and so forth. Each of these "laws" would be found to have the same equational form, namely $S = 1/2\, gt^2$, where g takes on a different value for each planet or other heavenly body. Furthermore, the laws of motion also account for other apparently different phenomena, such as the periodicity of a pendulum of a given length. A very small number of equations and empirical constants can thus be used to account for a diversity of phenomena and with a high degree of precision.

Precision and Falsifiability

Although it may be to the advantage of an individual theorist to present a theory that is totally untestable and therefore incapable of being rejected, this is obviously not to the advantage of the discipline, nor to the unfortunate persons who must read and digest a large number of such theories. Obviously, the more precise the predictions made by a theory, the easier it will be to prove them wrong. Therefore, a theory that makes a large number of precise predictions that have been put to the test and have not been falsified is a theory in which one can have considerably more faith than one that makes an equal number of very imprecise predictions.

This relationship between precision and falsifiability depends, however, on two additional conditions. First, the theory must specify the *conditions* under which the predictions are expected to hold, and of course these conditions must at least be approximated either in a laboratory setting or in some relatively simple natural one. For example, although a "perfect vacuum" remains an idealization, it can, nevertheless, be approximated to a high degree in a laboratory setting. Certain very specific kinds of predictions, however, may require extremely unusual kinds of events, so that crucial tests of the theory may have to await the passage of time before such events can be actualized.

Second, a precise prediction cannot be verified unless measurement accuracy is at least of the same order of magnitude as are the differences in predictions made by the theory and its principal rivals. Thus certain kinds of crucial tests of a theory may have to await refinements in measurement. This rather obvious point has very important implications for the testing and construction of sociological theories. Imagine, for example, a theory precise enough to predict that, in a given setting, the proportion of "alienated" blacks will be greater than the comparable proportion of "alienated" whites by exactly .23067. Without a theoretical definition of "alienation" capable of being linked unambiguously with a precise operational definition, such a theory—although precise—would be unrejectable. True, if one were to obtain a higher proportion of alienated whites than blacks, one could say that the prediction had been falsified, but only if the measured values of alienation were assumed to "represent" adequately the underlying concept. Clearly, when we consider precision, we must face up to the problem of "slippage" between the theoretical constructs and their indicators.

In the presence of inadequate measurements, the falsifiability of a theory would seem to depend primarily on its ability to make a large *number* of relatively imprecise predictions, each of which would not be expected on the basis of some relatively simple rival theory or common sense. If the theory only makes one or two very imprecise predictions that can actually be tested, then there will remain a very large number of rival alternatives that may also make such predictions.

In order for a theory to make relatively precise predictions, it must also be logically tight or basically mathematical in nature. That is, the conclusions (predictions) must be *deduced* from a set of assumptions. We rule out of consideration, in this connection, simple predictions that take the form: Predict X at time t from X at time $t - 1$, though as we noted in our introductory remarks such a prediction based on past values may actually be much more accurate than one based on a theoretical model. The kinds of theories and predictions we ordinarily find in sociology, however, are usually very "loose" ones from the standpoint of logical or mathematical rigor. Most commonly, one sees a verbal discussion followed by a series of hypotheses that *seem* to stem from this discussion and that merely predict the *direction* of a relationship between two variables, with conditions unspecified. This usually means that certain of the predictions may be verified and others falsified without the theory, as a totality, having to be rejected in favor of a particular alternative. During early stages of theory development, this sort of partial verification is to be expected. The trick is to make the process a cumulative one, rather than one that is merely highly elusive and vague.

Generalizability, Complexity, and Precision

Let us look once again at the situation in physics, the science which serves as a prototype of a discipline with a well-developed, semideductive, set of theories capable of making very precise predictions under well-defined conditions. The measurement of many variables in physics is *considerably* facilitated through the existence of relatively simple and highly general laws that interrelate the variables. It has been pointed out that there are only six "fundamental," operationally distinct, measures that underlie the derived measurement of fully 100 other basic concepts (Krantz et al., 1971:455). Thus if mass, distance, time intervals, temperature, charge, and angle have been measured, virtually all other ratio-scale variables may then be "measured" in terms of them. Velocity is defined as distance/time, acceleration as a change in velocity per unit of time, force as mass times acceleration, density as mass/volume (or mass/distance cubed), and so forth.

This use of derived concepts is not just based on arbitrary decisions, however. If one were to define "density" as mass squared/volume, or as mass/surface area, this would indeed create a new concept. But the utility of the notion of density depends upon a *homogeneity* property of pure substances. Namely, if one takes the mass of a given quantity of this substance (say, water or iron) and divides it by the volume, the result is a *constant* that is universally applicable for that substance. Likewise, pure copper or silver has a specific conductivity coefficient or a rate of expansion that remains virtually constant under a broad range of circumstances. In fact, we use this constancy of rates of expansion to devise instruments that give indirect measures of temperature, which are theoretically defined in terms of heat energy but generally measured in terms of things such as the height of a column of mercury. It turns out that virtually all of the important derived concepts in physics can be defined in terms of *multiplicative* functions of the fundamentally measured concepts, each with an integer exponent of relatively small size (e.g., distance -3 or time^2). This is a truly remarkable fact or property of "Nature" that we can hardly expect to hold in the case of sociology, or indeed hardly any of the less exact sciences.

There is, however, a property roughly analogous to the homogeneity assumption so necessary in the field of physics. Consider the simple regression equation $Y = a + \beta X + \varepsilon$, where we conventionally assume that the disturbance term ε has a specified probability distribution. The coefficients a and β are *constants* that we assume hold for *some* population to which we wish to generalize. If we give these coefficients causal interpretations, referring to them as "structural parameters," then we assume that all members of this population are characterized by these same parameters. That is, they act in a homogeneous fashion with respect to changes in X. A unit change in X can be expected to produce a change of β units in Y.

Now suppose we wish to increase the scope of the generalization, in the sense that we wish to apply it to some broader population. To do so, if we wish to retain the same law, we must also assume that members of this broader population will respond in the same fashion as those in the original population. That is, the coefficient β applies to the entire expanded population. If we do not wish to make this assumption, and instead wish to allow for the possibility that the larger population is *heterogeneous* with respect to the appropriate structural parameters, then we must use a different coefficient to represent each subpopulation that has a distinctive response. This is directly analogous to using a different density coefficient for each homogeneous substance. The parameter in the original equation becomes a *variable*, the value of which needs to be explained. This of course complicates the original equation.[2]

Thus unless "Nature" has been extremely kind to us, we must expect that our laws will become increasingly complex whenever we wish to extend the scope of our generalizations. We have illustrated this point in connection with populations of differing types, but the same principle holds for increasing the scope of our generalizations in terms of the types of *behaviors* being considered. A law that is useful in explaining a single type of aggression or deviant behavior will ordinarily be much simpler than one that can be used to explain a diversity of forms of aggression or types of deviance. *If we choose to keep the law simple while at the same time expanding the scope of the generalization, then we must pay the price of decreased precision*! This poses a fundamental dilemma for the social scientist, and we may anticipate the attempts to resolve it will take different forms.

It is important to emphasize that *some* homogeneity assumptions will always have to be made in any given theoretical model or actual piece of research. That is, certain constants in equations must be estimated empirically from some set of data, whether this be on supposedly homogeneous subjects (e.g., white males between the ages forty and forty-five) or based on repeated measurements on the same subject (whose properties are assumed to remain constant). The point we wish to emphasize is that the *realism* of these homogeneity assumptions is a function of the scope of generalization. The broader this scope, the less realistic they are likely to be, and therefore the greater the imprecision inherent in the theory.

Looking at the matter another way, since all scientific measurements are indirect to varying degrees, we require an "auxiliary" measurement theory to pin down the linkage between, on the one hand, our theoretical variables, true scores, latent variables, or whatever other term is used to describe the constructs that appear in our theories, and, on the other hand, our measured scores, research operations, indicators, or other terms that refer to the actual measurement process. (See Blalock, 1968.) These auxiliary theories vary with respect to their complexity, generality, and adequacy. Whenever they are highly complex, appropriate to only a narrow range of phenomena, or of questionable validity, verification of the theory will be made especially difficult. In effect, the adequacy of the measurement assumptions will be confounded with the adequacy of the substantive theory, so that it becomes exceedingly difficult to establish which is faulty.

In physics the measurement theories are simpler and more readily justified on independent grounds than in sociology and the other social sciences. Thus we have noted that the measurement of temperature is facilitated considerably by well-established laws specifying the linkage between the expansion rates of certain pure substances (e.g., mercury or copper) and the application of heat energy. In contrast, many basic concepts in sociology are defined in such a way that much more complex causal laws are needed to justify the linkage between "true" and measured variables. The literature on multiple indicators and the causal approach to measurement error is developing at a rapid rate and is far too complex to be summarized here.[3] The implications of this literature are becoming increasingly clear, however. Not only are the links between concepts and their measurements much more indirect and subject to greater dispute than we had previously imagined, but even strictly random measurement errors create serious problems for theory verification and parameter estimation.

We may illustrate in terms of two forms of behavior, namely, "aggression" and "discrimination." As long as one confines one's attention to extremely simple situations, these concepts may be given definitions that permit relatively straightforward research operations enabling one to count instances of their occurrence. Thus an observer may be instructed to count the number of times that young children hit, bite, kick, spit upon, or verbally abuse other children, as instances of "aggression." But with more subtle adult behaviors and situations involving prolonged contact with many instances of delayed reactions, it becomes much more difficult to specify what one means by aggression.

Often, a theoretical definition of a behavior is given which depends upon some assessment of motivation, or intent to produce certain consequences, such as injury of another party. In the case of "discrimination," definitions commonly refer to differential behavior "based on" racial, ethnic, sexual, or other characteristics; or behaviors "resulting in" inequalities of various kinds. But in these more complex situations, in which there may be several motives underlying each form of behavior, and in which consequences are delayed or are functions of *several* jointly operative factors, one's measurement theory becomes correspondingly complex. In such situations, there is increased opportunity for "slippage" between construct and measure.

The fact that our auxiliary measurement theories vary from one situation to the next has basic implications for considerations of strategy. If one measures distance, time, mass, and temperature, in basically the same ways in simple laboratory settings as in more complex naturally occurring ones, it becomes possible to arrive at laws appropriate to this greater complexity by a process of adding complexities, a few at a time, until the more complex processes are better understood. Thus one may first establish empirical laws in situations approximating those specified by the ideal (e.g., the perfect vacuum, the frictionless pulley). Then one introduces complications to allow for motion through substances that resist this motion, coefficients of friction in pulleys, slight changes in temperature or imperfections in insulating bodies, and so forth. *The essential point in all these instances is that the measurement theory remains fixed as one passes from the more simple to the more complex situations*. This permits one to modify the laws by adding further terms to equations, as for example, by allowing for the viscosity of the medium through which the body is moving. This constancy of the measurement theory, in turn, permits one to establish empirical laws of varying degrees of complexity that are not confounded with changes in the measurement theory.

By contrast, if we must change our operational definition of "aggression" as we move from the laboratory to a natural setting, or from a simple play situation to a much more complex situation involving relationships between dominant and subordinate groups, then we have two things changing at once—the substantive situation *and* the measurement operations. *If* we had well-established laws that could be used to relate the several different measurement operations, there would be no special problem. But in the absence of such laws, the problem of generalizing our findings from one situation to the next becomes confused by this confounding of measurements with substantive differences. It makes the strategy of moving systematically from simple to more complex situations a much more tricky affair.

The problem is not completely hopeless, but the solution—if there is one—must depend upon our ability to make our measurement assumptions as explicit as possible. As we shall see in the next section, it will *never* be possible to justify all such measurement assumptions on strictly empirical grounds; hence certain a priori assumptions must always be made. The best we can hope for is that social scientists will learn to bring these assumptions out into the open, where the implications of differing sets of assumptions can be systematically studied.

IMPLICATIONS FOR THEORY CONSTRUCTION

Before addressing the more specific question of what implications the foregoing considerations have for the construction of sociological theories with desirable characteristics, let us return briefly to the matter of a theory's practical utility. If we asked the layman just what it is about physics or chemistry that appears to justify their support, I suspect the answer would be in terms of tangible products or "gadgets" that have been developed as a result of the application of principles of physics—things like telephones, refrigerators, electric lights, TV, airplanes, and hydrogen bombs. By contrast, the answer to a similar question about the utility of botany and zoology would most likely be in terms of the understanding they provide for applications in medicine, the control of pests, or the improvement of livestock quality or crop yields. Such answers of course grossly oversimplify a very complex set of possible elaborations, exceptions, and misgivings about the advantages and disadvantages of each of these applications. But they will serve to illustrate several basic points that seem to have implications for our own field, in particular, and the social sciences, more generally.

Many if not most of the "gadgets" that are produced as a result of applications of knowledge about basic physical or chemical properties are useful precisely because they have been constructed to be relatively *simple* and *insulated* systems that behave in predictable ways because of the fact that they are not tampered with unless and until some breakdown occurs. Similarly, knowledge of the chemical properties of alloys, plastics, and other "nonnatural" products enables the manufacturer to produce goods with highly predictable properties based on studies of nearly identical (homogeneous) replicas. In short, the success of these ventures depends very heavily on our ability to *create* relatively simple but nevertheless highly useful entities or systems that then *supplement* those found naturally in the "real world."

To be sure, knowledge of physical and chemical processes is also used to predict and perhaps control natural events such as floods, earthquakes, forest fires, or tornadoes. These highly complex natural events seem most difficult to explain, however, precisely because they are so complex and involve so many unknown parameters. The human body is also highly complex and shares with naturally occurring events the common property that scientists are as yet unable to construct simpler counterparts. Instead, they attempt to *find* these counterparts in nature and study their component parts and behaviors in order to reach conclusions that are intended to apply to the more complex organisms that are the real subjects of interest. The success of this strategy depends, then, on generalizing from the simple to the complex, rather than in building a set of simpler devices that, themselves, have direct utility.

I am prepared to bet that the utility of the social sciences will be much more similar to that of the biological sciences than the physical sciences in these regards. That is, it does not appear likely that we will be given the opportunity to create our own simplified mini-systems that themselves have direct utility. Exceptions may occur, however. As, for example, the possibility of constructing semi-isolated correctional institutions, small experimental colleges, or specialized hospitals. But, for the most part, the systems that we "create" are much more likely to be tampered with, to grow or develop more or less naturally, and to be subjected to interactions with other relatively complex systems that cannot be treated in isolation. Those we are able to construct and isolate will be primarily useful for the insights they provide for the study of more complex systems, just as studies of earthworms and fruit flies are primarily useful because biologists are able to generalize findings to more important populations (as defined of course by human beings).

Two Basic Strategies for the Systematization of Knowledge

Two rather general strategies of attack on "important" social questions seem possible. Most individual social scientists will only be able to concentrate on the one or the other, but somehow ways must be found to work back and forth between them in such a fashion that the literatures developed do not become mutually incomprehensible or irrelevant. As we shall see, problems of conceptualization and measurement lie at the core of this problem of integration, which is made especially difficult as a result of the indirectness of measurement and our inability to rely on relatively simple auxiliary measurement theories.

The first basic strategy is exemplified by small-group laboratory research in which the investigator creates a highly simplified social system that is intended to represent certain selected aspects of a more complex reality. Empirical data are collected *on this system*, or its components, and hypotheses tested and resulting relationships described. One then attempts to extrapolate the findings to more important or more general systems by basically appealing to the reader's sense of analogy, and by making certain simplifying assumptions about the other variables that may be operating in this more complex reality. The process cumulates through a series of replications involving slight variations, some of which are either intended or noticed ex post facto, whereas others must be treated as though they were random variations. Gradually, then, complexities are introduced in the *empirical* setting until there is a reasonable approximation to the more complex situation of interest.

The second strategy involves studying the more complex situation directly but doing so through a process of developing theoretical *models* of this reality.

The predictions of these models can then be tested by means of sets of data that pertain directly to this same situation. One begins with relatively simple models that give very inadequate predictions, gradually increasing the complexity and realism of the models until a reasonably good fit can be obtained. Thus the simplications produced by the scientists are not in the situations themselves, but in the representations or models of these situations. Unfortunately, there will always be a number of equally plausible models that fit the data almost equally well, making it necessary to choose among them on a priori grounds, or on the basis of assumptions justified in terms of *other* pieces of empirical information.

In the ideal, both strategies will in principle "work," but this is of little interest unless the ideal can be approximated. Likewise, it is merely a pious pronouncement to assert that one should work back and forth from the one strategy to the other, or to "triangulate" among their findings. Nor can one say that one strategy is superior to the other under most circumstances. One may expect that, since the data-collection strategies differ considerably between the two approaches, one will encounter very different sorts of practical problems that will vary in their seriousness according to the circumstances. We shall therefore not attempt to specify strengths and deficiencies, as these are the subject matter of standard treatments of research methods. Rather, we shall focus on the problem of the nature of the hurdles that tend to prevent us from routinely passing back and forth between these approaches.

The "burden of proof" faced by those who attempt the first strategy consists of demonstrating generalizability. The advantage of this strategy consists of the ability of the investigator to concentrate on a relatively small number of variables and to simplify the measurement of these variables via a measurement theory that is realistic for the setting under investigation, but often not so for more complex situations. Measurement problems are solved at the expense of generalizability. As long as the level of abstraction remains low, it may even appear that measurement problems are entirely routine and reduced to recordings of very simple acts, such as button pushing or responses to paper-and-pencil tests.

A key question that investigators studying these simple situations need to ask is: Does the measurement strategy being employed depend in some essential way on the simplicity of the setting? A yes answer to this question implies the need for very careful attention to the problem of finding alternative ways of conceptualizing the variables so that a clear distinction is made between those variables that can be measured reasonably directly in many different contexts, and those that may have to be treated as unmeasured in some contexts and measured in others. For example, we have noted that many kinds of behaviors are defined in such a way that intent or motivation is built into the definition. Thus aggression may be defined as behavior the intent of which is to injure another party. Alternative definitions may stress the effects or consequences of the behaviors. For example, one may define aggression as behaviors that generally result in injury. Still another kind of definition may require replications under highly standardized conditions. Regardless of the way the concept is defined, it becomes essential to ask what kinds of measurement complications will result when one shifts the focus of attention from very simple situations to more complex ones.

Considerations of parsimony may conflict, here, with those of generalizability. Where measurement complications appear insurmountable in complex situations it may be tempting to develop a different set of concepts in order to distinguish them from those that are more appropriate to simpler settings. This will either complicate the resulting theory or make it extremely difficult to translate from one set of concepts to another. Where feasible, it seems wise to make a clear-cut distinction between measured and unmeasured variables in any given study, and then to attempt to specify one's assumptions about possible biases, and other implications, of omitting the latter from one's empirical investigations.

In examining behaviors it may sometimes be possible to make a clear-cut distinction between a motivational state or attitude (that may be unmeasured) and the behavior it is thought to produce. For instance, one *could* define "avoidance" as behavior motivated to reduce contact with another individual. But it might be wiser to distinguish between two variables, one of which is the intent (to reduce contact); and the other is the behavior itself (conceptualized in terms of physical movements away from another person or perhaps the erection of barriers to contact). This kind of distinction complicates one's causal model but may permit one to make a relatively more clear-cut distinction between measured and unmeasured variables. In very simple situations, as, for example, those in which avoidance may take only one or two forms and the motivation is "obvious," this kind of theoretical conceptualization problem may never arise. But if the goal is to generalize to situations of greater complexity, sooner or later the difficulty of reconceptualizing basic variables will arise.

The second strategy of developing *models* of the more complex situations also has its pitfalls, two of which deserve special emphasis. The first is the danger of remaining entirely on the descriptive level and of becoming overly concerned with details and "capturing" the full complexity of the situation. This temptation is especially real in those fields, such as history, cultural anthropology, and psychiatry, in which scholarly norms stress the need to report endless details and in which the investigator may expect severe criticism for getting a few facts wrong or for omitting certain standard subjects. There is here a conflict between the admittedly desirable goal of providing accurate facts for the benefit of those who may later incorporate them into a theoretical body of knowledge and the objective of furthering the development of this theory itself. Ideally, a division of labor is possible, but unfortunately it often happens that the detailed descriptions are noncomparable and therefore almost impossible to "add up." The theory never gets developed or remains in an extremely elementary state.

The obvious strategy in this instance is that of very explicitly making comparisons among two or more situations that are sufficiently different to bring out variations as well as similarities. Perhaps the classic works of Max Weber are our best models of such a strategy. But this approach, too, has its drawbacks unless there is a reasonable degree of consensus on basic concepts and their measurement. The temptation is to make the "comparisons" primarily implicit, by merely juxtaposing several descriptive accounts in sequence and then writing a single summary statement that rather loosely calls attention to similarities and differences, rather than attempting to construct an explicit theory suggested by these comparisons. A series of such summary chapters by authors who all use different terminologies may not advance us very far unless other investigators use these statements as *starting points* for their own comparative analysis. Furthermore, unless detailed attention is given to questions of conceptualization and measurement, the theories are likely to remain so entirely flexible as to defy their rejection. If there is one major shortcoming of the body of literature that is generally included in most courses on "sociological theory," it is this inattention to the obvious problems of measurement that these theories would require if anyone seriously were to put them to the test.

The second danger or temptation we encounter in studies of complex situations is that of permitting one's data limitations to determine one's theory. That is, whenever one discovers that certain variables cannot be measured in the study at hand, it is tempting to believe that these are not important variables, or that they may rather simply be absorbed into the error terms in one's equations. One sees in the journal literature many path diagrams involving six or eight variables, whereas even a minimally realistic theory would undoubtedly require twenty or thirty. There are now available, as research models, several excellent empirical studies that do not involve these defects, and the recent literature on measurement errors has sensitized our profession to the problem.[4] Nevertheless, the tendency to omit variables from one's theory on the grounds of empirical expediency remains a serious problem for the discipline. It is presumably one of the reasons for the extremely oversimplified condemnation of the entire approach in Lewis Coser's (1975) presidential address to the American Sociological Association. (See Coser, this volume.)

This problem might not be too serious if investigators each omitted a different set of variables, with the omissions of one complementing those of another. But where a single data-collection strategy predominates, it becomes likely that certain kinds of variables are *systematically* overlooked—not because they are really believed to be theoretically unimportant but merely because no one is in a good position to tap them empirically. Thus if surveys tend to favor the study of attitudes or opinions over actual behavior, or if they must rely on getting at only those past behaviors that are easily recalled, then many kinds of behaviors and past events will be systematically neglected.

Similarly, most surveys tend to neglect contextual variables, in effect treating each respondent as if he or she were operating in isolation. (See Blau, this volume.) Where measured, contextual variables are likely to be represented very imperfectly in terms of subgroup means or the respondents' *perceptions* of behaviors and attitudes of their relatives or friends. An adolescent may be asked about the deviant behaviors of his or her best friends, these being correlated with own characteristics. Perceptions and actual behaviors thus become confounded. To be sure, this may be a necessary consequence of practical research constraints, but this does not mean that one's *theory* also has to neglect the distinctions.

The implication is that a clear-cut distinction needs to be made in the theory construction process between one's theoretical model, which contains *both* measured and unmeasured variables, and one's actual data analysis that necessarily must be confined to the measured variables. Once more, the growing body of literature on the causal approach to measurement errors enables one to extract the implications of unmeasured variables contained in such models, and even to estimate certain coefficients interrelating these unmeasured variables provided that there are not too many unknowns introduced into the equations.

This need to include both measured and unmeasured variables in one's models of complex processes introduces additional complexities into the theories, thereby conflicting with the objective of achieving parsimony. Obviously, the number of "real life" situations that sociologists can attempt to describe is almost endless. Here it is essential to focus on the objective of "data reduction," or the process of identifying a reasonably smaller number of *dimensions* common to as many comparable situations as possible. A self-conscious effort to ask about variations in *degree*, as well as kind, will aid in this process.

Basically, when comparing a number of different complex situations—say, five or six forms of social conflict—one must explicitly ask: Are there a relatively small number of distinct *ways* in which these situations or behaviors either differ or are similar, and how could I begin to measure the dimensions involved? Here a knowledge of recent developments in the scaling literature is important, not only in terms of immediate applications but also because of the indirect benefits gained by wrestling with strategies of data reduction that require *theoretical models* of the processes involved.[5]

CONCLUDING REMARKS

Regardless of whether one follows the strategy of tackling relatively simple situations, adding gradually to their complexity, or that of developing relatively simple models of complex processes and working to increase the complexity of these models, it seems essential to move back and forth between the simple and more complex versions of either strategy. If one attempts to begin very simply, without an overview picture of the complexities that will later be encountered, it becomes almost impossible to decide *which* simplifications to introduce. In other words, one needs to have the complex theory in order to decide what to eliminate or to provide a theoretical justification for introducing the simplifications. Otherwise, the simplifications may be prematurely introduced or based on research expediencies rather than theoretical considerations. But how do we get to this more complex theory if we cannot begin simply and build up? This is of course our dilemma in a nutshell!

Our most general advice basically boils down to two fundamental points. First, our theories and assumptions need to be made *explicit*, as painful as this process may be. Second, we must wrestle with problems of conceptualization and measurement applied to sufficiently diverse phenomena that our theoretical propositions and tests of these theories are both reasonably precise and generalizable, insofar as these desired characteristics are not incompatible owing to the nature of the real world phenomena we are studying.

Stated so generally, this advice undoubtedly sounds platitudinous. But I believe that we are not in the process of acting on it, as a scholarly discipline, even though some of our individual members may be doing so. What seems required is a *self-conscious and coordinated effort* to focus on the basic concepts in the field, their clarity, overlap, inclusiveness, and implications for measurement strategies. The technical tools for theory building and data analysis are reasonably available, but many kinds of slippery and elusive conceptual problems remain at least as formidable as they were several decades ago. Here is where progress must be made if we are to achieve a true integration of theory and research.

NOTES

1. For discussions of theory construction that stress causal analyses see Blalock (1969), Duncan (1975), Goldberger and Duncan (1973), Heise (1975), Namboodiri, Carter, and Blalock (1975), and Stinchcombe (1968).

2. Leik, in his essay in this volume, stresses the desirability of examining equations that are more complex in form than the simple linear equation, a point with which I heartily agree. It needs to be pointed out, however, that even in the case of more complex nonlinear equations *some* constants must be introduced and hence some homogeneity properties assumed. It is misleading to claim that path-analytic approaches, or the more general structural-equation approaches of econometricians, are not adaptable to the use of such nonlinear equations, although it is true that most *sociological* applications have introduced this particular kind of simplifying assumption. It would be my own strong suspicion, however, that the kinds of errors produced by the linearity restriction are far less serious, in most instances, than those that are forced on the inves-

tigator who chooses to reduce the number of *variables* to only three or four and who also fails to allow for measurement errors in some explicit fashion.

3. See especially Costner (1969), Hauser and Goldberger (1971), Jöreskog (1970), Long (1976), and Namboodiri, Carter, and Blalock (1975).

4. See especially the recent stratification literature stimulated by Blau and Duncan (1967) and Duncan, Featherman, and Duncan (1972).

5. See especially Coombs (1964), Krantz et al. (1971), and Shepard et al. (1972).

PART III

EPISTEMOLOGY AND SOCIOLOGY

The essays in this part, by Blau, Cicourel, and Leik, are concerned with the epistemological choices made by practicing sociologists. The material included here is part and parcel of a theory of knowledge for sociology. In particular, this set of essays addresses the following two questions: What are the limitations, sources, and validity of sociological knowledge? What are the criteria by which such issues can be evaluated? Certainly, the three papers in this section do not exhaust the germane issues. However, they are not intended to represent a full elaboration of all phases of sociological inquiry. But they do present a cross section of the epistemological concerns confronting the contemporary sociologist.

In his article "Levels and Types of Structural Effects," Peter Blau addresses himself to core questions of sociology: How does the encompassing social structure affect its component parts? Is the nature of the effect the same at all levels of social structure? How does one go about separating out the influence of structure at various levels? Blau's initial contribution to the analysis of the impact of group structure on individual behavior is well known. To understand this impact is to realize that group structure exerts an influence on the conduct of individuals in the group, independent of that exerted by an individual's own attributes. The independent structural effects are of two primary types (or a combination of the two), each representing a different mediating mechanism between the attributes of the social environment and those of the individual. If the group structure parallels or reinforces the effects of the individual's own attributes, the structural effect is direct. In short, the direct structural effects are mediated by classic exchange processes in social interaction which then generate group pressures. Conversely, if the prevailing attributes in the social environment are having opposite effects from the individual's own attributes, an inverse structural effect is present. In this situation, the social environment is being mediated by the social significance of relative standing and the comparison process it engenders (e.g., relative deprivation).

Since social structures constitute nesting series with successive levels of structure, Blau goes on to argue that the same logic applies at all levels of social structure. There exist not only structural effects on individuals but also higher-order structural effects with respect to social groups and organizations. Further, these higher-order structural effects can be explained in the same theoretical terms as the lower-order effects on individuals. To demonstrate the validity of his theoretical argument, Blau analyzes the impact of university structure on the actions of professional schools within the larger university context.

In his article "Field Research: The Need for Stronger Theory and More Control over the Data Base," Aaron Cicourel is concerned with a very different issue in the conduct of inquiry: How does one improve field research? An important step would be the strengthening of theoretical concepts with the simultaneous acquisition of needed control over the methods of data collection and minimization of reactive error. The key to such improvement, for Cicourel, is the development and employment of an interactive model. The form of such a model would allow a linkage among sundry levels of data and analysis, and the forms of reasoning employed in field research. Such a model would force the researcher to be explicit about both the sources and structure of information that constitute the data base.

There is always more than just the context of observation that influences what we see and how we interpret it. Indeed, there is always pre- and post-processing of external information as well as the actual information processing that goes on during participant observation. All of the aforementioned information sources are necessary parts of field research. This information is acquired from various sources and hence represents differing types of knowledge. Linguistic knowledge is a key to understanding the immediate setting, whereas lexical knowledge enables the researcher to go beyond simple categorization of phenomena to explanation or interpretation. Practical knowledge, on the other hand, allows for understanding information, both verbal and visual, not covered by lexical knowledge. As Cicourel points out, this coexistence of information in an interactional setting disallows the possibility of the researcher directly addressing all aspects of the information at the same time or in the same way. Hence if we are to create valid field notes and analyze them effectively, we need to address explicitly the interaction of these theoretical levels. Cicourel recommends making use of all relevant relationships between cultural experiences and reasoning, and their representation in memory and observable symbolic form, as a way of addressing the problem. In other words, it is necessary to address the organization of memory and the forms of reasoning as part of field research. By making use of the structure of language and how that structure varies according to cultural groups in social contexts, the researcher not only benefits from the richness of language but also the ethnographic settings. Only by explicitly handling this interaction via abductive reasoning will the field researcher maximize validity in the creation of field notes and subsequent professional papers.

In "Let's Work Inductively, Too," Robert Leik addresses yet another problem faced by the sociological practitioner: How, during the development and maturation of a theory, can the sociologists go about making certain that the end product will maximally satisfy the various criteria for a "good theory"?

Building on Blalock's essay in Part II, Leik acknowledges that in order to be efficacious at organizing accumulated knowledge and guiding further inquiry, theories need to satisfy various criteria. In addition, since most of these criteria are subject to logical or empirical examination, it is quite possible to establish guidelines for determining when theoretical efforts are wanting. If the theory is assessed as being in some way deficient, then presumably corrective action should be taken. It is at this corrective-action state that Leik sees major deficiencies in contemporary methodology. The problem is one of "deductive tunnel vision." The deductive side of retroduction has become so prominent in contemporary attempts at theory development that repair of theory through inductive procedures seldom, if ever, comes to mind. Leik explicates the issue and a possible solution in terms of two general problems: theoretical form and conceptual generality.

One of the ever-present problems of sociologists is the tendency to think primarily in terms of monotonic linear forms. From a strictly theoretical position this is probably a deficiency. Many, if not most, sociologically relevant relationships are probably better represented by some other theoretical form, for example, exponential or power curves. This becomes particularly true with time series data. Hence, until we move beyond the very limited linear form, it is likely that our empirical research will continue to misrepresent most social relationships. Furthermore, the opportunity for generalization, by subsuming specific relationships under more general forms, cannot be realized until the linear mind-set changes. Yet the linear model will not be shed easily, since it is both easily used and a powerful tool for *deducing* and *testing* consequences of theoretical formulations. But what if the data do not fit the model? This currently poses a serious problem, since this predilection for deductive power and easy estimation using canned computer routines precludes the serious theoretical reexamination which nonlinear forms would require. Instead, one simply redraws the path diagram or adds more variables to the extant model. Such patch-work can never be successful. The solution proposed by Leik is an emphasis on *basic equations*.

In contrast to incorporating a large number of variables in a multiple regression equation, a theory of equations would specify a basic relationship and then focus on the variety of ways in which other variables influence the basic equations. This inductive approach, argues Leik, results in parameters that are substantively more interpretable, allows opportunity for conceptual generalizations, and is particularly suited to the analysis of time series data and policy research.

The voluminous literature in contemporary methodology suggests that sociologists are interested in epistemological questions facing the discipline. It also is clear that Blau, Cicourel, and Leik do not agree on the relative importance of the issues. In the past, this has been due to the metasociological choice made by these sociologists. Whereas Blau and Leik take the summarization of data for granted, Cicourel makes this his focus of interest. Yet Cicourel is not concerned with documenting emergence; but he does share a similar interest with Leik in suggesting a strategy for theory construction.

Peter M. Blau

LEVELS AND TYPES OF STRUCTURAL EFFECTS: THE IMPACT OF UNIVERSITY STRUCTURE ON PROFESSIONAL SCHOOLS [1]

Social structures constitute nesting series with successive levels of structure. The micro-structures of interpersonal relations in families, neighborhoods, and work groups are parts of the structures of interrelated groups in communities and organizations. The interrelated communities and organizations in turn compose the macro-structure of society. An important sociological question is how the encompassing social structure affects its component parts—how individuals are influenced by the characteristics of their groups, organizations, communities, and societies, or how subunits of organizations are influenced by the characteristics of their roof organizations. Answering this question raises problems in empirical research because the operational indicators of social structure are often aggregate attributes of individuals, for example, average income or the proportion of old people in a community. To say that the class structure or the age structure influences conduct implies something more than the fact that differences in class position or in age among persons affect their conduct. It implies that in addition to these differences there are also differences in conduct among communities attributable to differences in the class distribution or the age distribution. For example, middle-class persons behave differently depending on whether they live in predominantly middle-class or working-class communities. The problem is to separate the influences of the aggregate community attributes from those of the corresponding attributes of individuals.

Durkheim (1938) emphasizes that social facts exert external constraints on individuals. His empirical indicators of social facts are usually rates of individual attributes or behavior, for instance, divorce rates. A major thesis of Durkheim's (1951:259-76) is that the weakness of the marital bond in a society, as indicated by its high divorce rate, engenders anomie. The anomie, in turn, is manifest in a high suicide rate. Testing this proposition empirically requires that the hypothesized external constraints of the strength of the marital institution in society be analytically distinguished from the influences the personalities or experiences of divorced individuals have on their likelihood of committing suicide. Only the latter influences are revealed by the finding that divorced persons have a higher suicide rate than married ones. Further, that societies with high divorce rates also have high suicide rates may simply reflect the higher suicide rate of divorced as opposed to married individuals. Empirical corroboration of the proposition that society's strong marital institution is a protection against anomie and suicide requires evidence that even married persons have higher suicide rates in societies where divorce is frequent than in those where it is rare. Durkheim shows this to be the case for men, though not for women.

THE NOTION OF STRUCTURAL EFFECTS

The concept of structural effects was originally introduced (Blau, 1957, 1960) to refer to the influences on conduct exerted by the distribution of attributes in a group, independent of the influences exerted by an individual's own attributes. Making explicit the procedure implicit in Durkheim's analysis of divorce and suicide rates, a structural effect is ascertained by demonstrating that the prevalence of a social attribute in a group influences group members whether or not they themselves have this attribute.[2] Structural effects can, of course, only be observed by comparing numerous collectivities to show that the proportion of members with a given attribute is related to a dependent variable when the same attribute is held constant for individuals. For instance, social workers in a public welfare agency who had positive attitudes toward clients were more likely than others to provide casework services to clients. But, regardless of their own attitudes, those in work groups most of whose members had positive attitudes were also more likely to provide these services than those in other groups. In short, a caseworker's treatment of clients was influenced by co-workers' attitudes toward clients as well as by his own attitudes. Similarly, a study of the Great Books program (Davis, 1961:105-8) reports that members of discussion groups were less likely to drop out if they participated actively in the discussions. But whatever their own participation level, they tended not to drop out if most other members of their group participated actively. Not only a person's own active participation but also that of other members in her group makes the discussions more interesting and furnishes incentives for remaining in the program.

Such findings imply structural effects on conduct, that is, influences on conduct resulting from the external constraints exerted by the attributes and behavior of others in one's social environment. The inference is that the orientation of fellow workers to clients, for instance, creates group pressures that influence the individual's treatment of clients, independent of her own orientation. To be sure, this inference might be wrong because the empirical relationship on which it rests may be spurious. Thus if the orientation of supervisors toward welfare greatly influences both the attitudes to and the treatment of clients in work groups, it would produce a correlation between the attitudes of fellow workers and treatment of clients although the former does not actually influence the latter; that is, it would produce a spurious correlation. Other factors that are correlated with the dependent variable should, therefore, be controlled to detect spurious relationships and increase the probable validity of the inference that the persisting relationship between the prevalence of an attribute in groups and the dependent variable reveals a structural effect.[3]

The concept of social structure refers to the interrelations among elements in a larger whole, to the relations among individuals in a group, or to the relations among groups, and among their members, in a larger collectivity or the entire society. This raises the question of why the influence of the prevalence of an attribute in people's social environment on their conduct is termed a structural effect. Why not simply call it a compositional effect, as Davis (1961:9-12) does, inasmuch as they are effects of the group composition? The reason is that the influences of the composition of people's social environment on their conduct are interpreted by making the assumption that these influences are mediated by the relations among people. Although there is no direct evidence on the mediating influence of social relations, this assumption is highly plausible, indeed, virtually inescapable. If the characteristics of others in one's social environment influence one's conduct, it clearly implies that something about one's relations to others transmits this influence. It does not mean, however, that the influences of the social environment are necessarily transmitted in direct social interaction. They may be so transmitted, resulting from social pressures and sanctions communicated in direct contacts, but they may also result from the fact that the attributes of others in people's environment, jointly with their own attributes, govern their positions in relation to others and their relative standing among them. Two types of structural effect—direct and inverse ones—reveal these two different mediating mechanisms.

HIGHER-ORDER STRUCTURAL EFFECTS

The structural effect of the prevailing attributes in the social environment may parallel and reinforce the effect of people's own attributes on their conduct. Such direct structural effects have already been illustrated. Another example is provided by Berelson and colleagues (1954:98-101): The proportion of friends who are Republicans increases the likelihood of voting Republican, for Democrats as well as Republicans, reinforcing the influence of own party identification on the likelihood of voting for a Republican candidate. However, the attributes of others in a collectivity and people's own attributes sometimes influence them in opposite ways. A well-known case of such inverse structural effects is reported by Stouffer and colleagues (1949:250-54): Noncommissioned officers were more satisfied than privates with the army's promotion system, but a large proportion of noncommissioned officers in an outfit reduced satisfaction with promotions. Similarly, Davis (1966) finds that the abilities of college students are directly related to their expectations of going to graduate school, but the average students' abilities in a college are inversely related to these expectations.[4]

As a matter of fact, the same attribute may have some direct and some inverse structural effects, as observed in a study of universities and colleges (Blau, 1973:109-28). Faculty members with superior qualifications were more likely than others to be involved in research. Moreover, independent of own qualifications and various conditions related to research involvement, the larger the proportion of colleagues at their institution who had superior qualifications, the more likely were faculty members to be involved in research. Thus the influence of colleagues' qualifications reinforces that of one's own on research involvement. Academics with superior qualifications are more interested in research, but whether this interest is stimulated or stifled depends on the colleague climate. At academic institutions where most of the faculty is oriented toward research, the discussions among colleagues about research—about the problems encountered and the discoveries made—furnish social support and approval for engaging in it. In colleague groups with little interest in research, scholarly endeavors are often discouraged and ridiculed with phrases such as "publish or perish." These processes of social exchange engender social pressures either to become involved in research or not to do so, depending on the prevalence of scholarly qualifications and interests in the colleague group. Direct structural effects generally can be explained in terms of such exchange processes in direct social interaction that create group pressures.

The influence of the qualifications of faculty members on their commitment to their own institution reveals a different pattern, however, and must be explained in different terms. Faculty members with superior qualifications expressed less allegiance than others to their college or university. But a large proportion of colleagues at their institution who had superior qualifications strengthened the allegiance of other faculty to that institution. This strengthening occurred independent of various other conditions that affected allegiance. Why do colleagues' and own attributes have opposite effects on individuals in this instance? Superior qualifications and the research accomplishments that tend to accompany them command prestige in academia. This makes faculty members attractive both to other institutions and to colleagues at their own institution. Many such faculty members enhance an academic institution's reputation and the allegiance of others to it. However, the wider prestige of these faculty members encourages a cosmopolitan orientation which limits their local allegiance, and it also places them in demand at other institutions. In cyclical fashion, this external demand further weakens their commitment to their own institution. In other words, what governs the local allegiance of faculty members is their relative standing among the faculty group. The low qualifications and scholarly accomplishments of faculty members themselves and the high ones of their colleagues have the same implication of reducing their relative standing among colleagues. Lower relative standing tends to strengthen local allegiance because many colleagues whose academic standing is superior to one's own make an institution an attractive place.

The principle that can explain inverse structural effects generally is that people's own status attributes and the corresponding ones of others in their social environment have opposite consequences for their relative standing and for the attitudes and conduct affected by relative standing. Although a person's status is typically measured in absolute terms—qualifications, rank, income, prestige score—its influence is relative to the status of others, this being inherent in the meaning of social status. The high absolute status of egos and the low one of alters have parallel, not opposite, significance for egos and for alters, because both raise egos' relative standing and lower alters'. Relative standing governs reference-group comparisons (Merton, 1968:279-334), which is why high relative standing makes soldiers more satisfied with promotions and college students more confident in having sufficient abilities for graduate school. Whereas direct structural effects are mediated by exchange processes in social interaction generating group pressures, inverse structural effects are mediated by the social significance of relative standing and the comparison processes it engenders.

Groups and organizations as well as individuals are affected by the social context in which they exist. So far, only structural effects on individuals have been considered. But there are also higher-order structural effects of the wider social contexts on the groups and organizations within it. For instance, a study of employment security agencies observes (Blau and Schoenherr, 1971:222-23) that the span of control of supervisors in local offices became wider with the increasing size of the local office. Additionally, independent of office size and other conditions, the span of control widened with the increasing size of the state agency to which the office belongs. Large agencies tend to have large local offices, and the span of control in large offices tends to be wide because the larger number of employees performing similar tasks there makes it possible to assign more of them to a single supervisor. Hence, a wide supervisory span of control is the prevailing practice in large agencies, whereas a narrow one is more common in small ones. These standard practices create normative pressures that influence span of control independent of office size. The direct structural effect is mediated by social pressures, which in formal organizations tend to be administrative pressures.

We turn now to an analysis of higher-order structural effects. Specifically, we shall examine the influences exerted by characteristics of universities, controlling corresponding characteristics of their professional schools, on other characteristics of these schools. The unit of analysis is the professional school. Data are available for a large number of schools in 18 different professions located in 309 different universities. The issue posed is whether higher-order structural effects can be explained in the same theoretical terms as lower-order ones on individuals. That is, can direct structural effects of universities on their schools be attributed to reinforcing social pressures and inverse ones to relative standing?

DATA AND PROCEDURES

Data were collected through questionnaires mailed to the deans of all 1,250 American accredited, university-affiliated professional schools in 18 fields. The 18 types of professional schools are: architecture, business, dentistry, education, engineering, forestry, journalism, law, library science, medicine, music, nursing, optometry, pharmacy, public health, social work, theology, and veterinary medicine. The mailing was based on lists provided by the accrediting associations of the various professions in 1972. Those that were not university affiliated and those that were departments rather than schools were eliminated. To check on response bias by comparing initial respondents (53 percent) with nonrespondents, a random sample of nonrespondents was selected for intensive follow-ups. Using a shortened questionnaire and telephone interviews, 93 percent (106 of 114) of the nonrespondent sample completed returns. Comparisons of these answers with those of the original respondents revealed significant differences on only a few items, none of which is used in this paper. Shorter questionnaires were also sent to other nonrespondents. The final response rate is 76 percent (948 of 1,250 deans), but data on considerably fewer cases are available on numerous variables, owing partly to the shortened follow-up schedule. Most of the information requested from the deans is factual, such as numbers of undergraduates, graduate students, and faculty, though some depends on their judgment, for example, how much influence the central administration has over various specified decisions. Data on the university to which the school belongs were obtained from published sources (notably Furniss, 1973).

Many variables are straightforward and need no explication, but some should be briefly described. The measure of the power of the central administration is the unweighted sum of the dean's rating on a seven-point score of the central administration's influence in four areas: new tenure appointments, degree requirements, what hours classes meet, and which courses are taught. The operational criterion of the school's autonomy is an eight-point (0-7) score, one point each given for the dean's answer that the school (1) is financially independent of the university; (2) has discretion over spending its budget; (3) has its own board; (4) has discretion over admissions; (5) does not need university approval for granting tenure; (6) has discretion over professional degree requirements; (7) has discretion over Ph.D. requirements. The index of faculty qualifications is the proportion of faculty members who have doctorates or other advanced professional degrees. Inside student recruitment is operationally defined as the proportion of the school's graduate students who have undergraduate degrees from the same university. Faculty size is measured by summing the number of full-time and one-half the number of half-time faculty members (used in logarithmic transformation). The dichotomy roughly indicating a university's reputation is whether at least one department received a rating as one of the best in the study by Roose and Anderson (1970; coded from Petrowski et al., 1973).

One variable of special importance is how advanced the training is that the professional school provides. This variable is indicated by the proportion of its students who are graduate students. A body of specialized abstract knowledge and the advanced training needed to acquire it are widely considered to be character-defining traits of professions that distinguish them from other occupations (see, e.g., Goode, 1969). Unless the performance of occupational tasks requires training beyond high school, it is unlikely that the members of an occupation are socially acknowledged to be professionals. But how advanced the training is varies among professions, among their practitioners, and among their schools. The old, established professions, like law, medicine, and the ministry, require advanced degrees of their practitioners, and virtually all their schools enroll only graduate students. Schools of dentistry and of library science also have hardly any undergraduates. In other fields, however, both undergraduate and graduate education is provided, and there are considerable variations among the schools within most professions in the extent to which they concentrate on undergraduate or on graduate training. The average proportion of graduate students for all schools is 44 percent.

Advanced training of graduate students differs from undergraduate education in a variety of ways. There is more emphasis on research and scholarship, less on teaching. Advanced training is more specialized, requiring greater resources, superior faculty qualifications, less coordination with other departments and schools, and more autonomy in instruction than does undergraduate education. It focuses on a body of abstract knowledge and the universalistic standards governing it. These universalistic standards demand that personal considerations are set aside in applying the knowledge. Finally, graduate instruction tends to command more prestige than undergraduate teaching. This is true for the faculty members engaged in it, the schools providing it, and the entire university (the correlation between a university's reputation and the proportion of graduate students in it is .36).

Thus the amount of graduate training in a professional school has some implications for its relative standing as well as other implications for practices that have no bearing on relative standing. The theoretical expectation is that the amount of graduate training in the university has inverse structural effects on conditions in its professional schools that depend on their relative standing. At the same time, the amount of graduate training is expected to have direct structural effects on conditions that do not depend on relative standing and that are subject to external pressures and influences. To discover such a structural effect on a given condition in professional schools, however, other characteristics of universities and of schools that influence this condition must be controlled. As indicated previously, the control is necessary lest a spurious relationship between graduate work in the university and this condition in its schools be erroneously interpreted as a structural effect. Regression analysis is used for this purpose, which permits examining simultaneously the relationships of a considerable number of independent variables to a dependent variable. In every regression analysis of a dependent variable characterizing schools, the independent variables introduced are all the attributes of universities and of schools themselves that have appreciable relationships with it under controls. These net relationships indicate direct effects on the dependent variable. (All regression coefficients—beta weights—reported are more than twice their standard error, since those that do not meet this criterion have been eliminated in preliminary analyses.) Attention centers on these beta weights, which reveal the relations existing under controls. The other influences on the characteristics of professional schools are of substantive interest, and controlling them increases confidence that the structural effects observed are not spurious.[5]

Professional schools of eighteen different types are combined in the analysis, since concern is with influences of universities on professional schools generally, not with the distinctive circumstances of teachers colleges and schools of engineering or any other particular type. But combining different types raises another problem of spuriousness: An influence attributed to variations among all schools in the proportion of graduate students (or another independent variable) may actually be produced by differences among types, inasmuch as some types have many and others few graduate students. To illustrate, it is as though one were to conclude from the empirical correlation between a person's height and ability to bear children that being tall influences this ability, not knowing that it is determined by sex. Actually, of course, sex is correlated with height, thus producing a spurious correlation between height and child bearing. The danger of making such false inferences exists whenever, and only when, some types are appreciably correlated with the dependent variable as well as one of the independent variables under consideration. Controlling the relevant types averts this danger. To accomplish the necessary control the eighteen types of professional schools are represented by dummy variables. Type of school is controlled in all cases in which a dummy variable and the dependent variable have a correlation of (plus or minus) .10 or more and a significant relationship persists when other factors are controlled.

REINFORCING SOCIAL PRESSURES

Table 1 indicates conditions in universities and professional schools that influence the proportion of students in a school who are members of minority groups, as reported by the dean. Universities with high standards of recruitment for students and faculty tend to have few minority students in their professional schools. Both SAT scores (sum of verbal and mathematical tests) and the formal qualifications of the faculty in the university are inversely related to the percent of minority students in its schools (rows 1 and 2 in the table). One reason undoubtedly is that the disadvantaged circumstances and inferior educational preparations of most minority members make it difficult for them to meet high admission standards. But this does not account for the influence of faculty as well as student standards. Another reason may well be that universities with high standards, fearful of compromising them, base admission in academically doubtful cases on background factors. By so doing they introduce a bias, perhaps inadvertently, against minority students. Besides, high academic standards conflict with the different standards required for commitment to affirmative action to recruit minority students to the school.

Table 1.
REGRESSION ANALYSIS OF PERCENT MINORITY STUDENTS

Independent Variable	Beta Weight	Zero-Order Correlation
UNIVERSITY		
1. Freshmen SAT	−.32	−.19
2. Faculty qualifications	−.12	−.12
3. Graduate students (%)	.21	.08
SCHOOL		
4. Graduate students (%)	.09	.17
5. Departments (#)	.18	.14
6. Female students (%)	.09	.10
7. Administration—faculty ratio	.12	.12
8. Social work[a]	.18	.22
9. Theology[a]	.10	.12

$R^2 = .21$ $N = 580$
[a] Dummy Variable

The inference that commitment to affirmative action not to discriminate plays a role here is lent some support by another finding. Affirmative action is designed to protect women as well as minorities against discrimination. The proportion of female students in a school is positively, though weakly, related to the proportion of minority students (row 6), which suggests that commitment to affirmative action tends to reduce discrimination against both women and minorities. To be sure, some professions, like nursing, comprise mostly women, whereas others, like engineering, comprise mostly men. This is reflected in the sex composition of different types of schools. But the differences among types of professional schools in sex composition cannot account for the observed relationship between the proportion of female and the proportion of minority students, because the type of school, if significantly related to the proportion of minority students, is controlled in the regression analysis.

Two types of professional schools indeed have disproportionate numbers of minority students: schools of social work and theological seminaries (rows 8 and 9). On the average, 19 percent of the students in these two kinds of schools are minority members. The average for all schools is less than one-half of that. Blacks and other minorities may be more attracted to the ministry and to social work than to other professions. But being attracted to a profession does not assure acceptance in its schools. The stress on social ethics and responsibility for the underprivileged in theology and social work probably makes most members of these professions extremely conscious of programs that fight injustice and seek to make up for discrimination. This orientation is reflected in the acceptance of disproportionate numbers of minority students in the schools in these two fields.

The more advanced and specialized the training a professional school offers, the larger is the proportion of its minority students (rows 4 and 5). The percent of graduate students is the measure of advanced training, and the number of departments (or subunits with another name) is considered to be indicative of specialization (many departments usually imply that one can major in narrower specialties). Advanced specialized pursuits organize knowledge in terms of universalistic principles, and this universalistic orientation to life may well make it less likely that particularistic preferences introduce a more or less subtle bias against minorities into admission decisions. There is less concern with the student's total personality in graduate work than in undergraduate education, which may also reduce the likelihood that the different cultural background of minorities adversely affects the chances of their acceptance. It seems to be easier for minority members to get into graduate school once they have completed college than to be accepted as undergraduates in professional schools. Minority members who have overcome their initial handicaps and graduated from college have thereby improved their opportunities of advancing further.

A large proportion of graduate students in the university increases the chances of minority members of being accepted in the university's professional schools, quite independent of the proportion of graduate students in these schools and other conditions (row 3). This finding, given the controls, implies that undergraduates as well as graduate students are more likely to be accepted in professional schools if their universities have relatively large proportions of graduate students. Indeed, the university's graduate students exert considerably more influence than the school's own on the proportion of minority students in the school (compare the beta weights in rows 3 and 4). This finding conforms to theoretical expectations.

For various reasons suggested, and possibly others, accepting minority students is more prevalent in graduate schools than on the undergraduate level. In universities with mostly undergraduates, therefore, the school that admits substantial numbers of minority students is a deviant case. In universities with many graduate students, however, most departments and schools tend to admit a considerable proportion of minority students. This tendency makes the admission of minorities the prevailing norm and failure to admit virtually any minority students a deviant practice. The prevailing standard to accept minority students creates social pressures to accept them. This pressure increases their chances of admission on the undergraduate as well as the graduate level. In formal organizations like universities, conformity with prevailing norms results not merely from informal pressures but also from the actions of administrators interested in standardizing procedures. The significance of administrative action for enforcing compliance with affirmative action and admitting minority students is indicated by the finding that a large complement of administrators increases the proportion of minority students in a school (row 7).

The acceptance of relatively large proportions of minority students depends on normative standards, which makes it subject to external pressures. These external pressures are reflected in a direct structural effect on admission policy. Power, on the other hand, is a status attribute, and the significance of status depends on relative standing. One would therefore expect to discover an inverse structural effect when analyzing the influences exercised by the university's administration over various matters in a professional school. Actually, however, advanced training has a direct structural effect on the influence of the central administration over school affairs (Table 2). The proportion of graduate students in a school somewhat reduces the power of the central administration in its affairs (row 4). The proportion of graduate students in the rest of the university has some additional effect reducing the power of the central administration (row 3). Before interpreting this unexpected finding, other conditions affecting the university's control over professional schools are briefly examined.

Professional schools with predominantly male faculties are more independent of the university administration than others (row 5). A possible reason is

Table 2.

REGRESSION ANALYSIS OF POWER OF CENTRAL
ADMINISTRATION

Independent Variable	Beta Weight	Zero-Order Correlation
UNIVERSITY		
1. Affluence (revenue per student)	−.12	−.16
2. Faculty size (log)	−.13	−.24
3. Graduate students (%)	−.11	−.23
SCHOOL		
4. Graduate students (%)	−.10	−.24
5. Male faculty (%)	−.17	−.22
6. Administrative ranks (#)	−.15	−.26

$R^2 = .18$ $N = 647$

that the types of professional schools with many women on their faculties, such as nursing, library science, and social work, are less well established. Because of their relatively recent appearance they command less prestige than older professional schools with predominantly male faculties (e.g., theological seminaries and law schools). It is also possible that the finding reflects a sexist bias of university administrators, most of whom are men. A hierarchically organized administrative staff of a school strengthens its own and weakens the central administration's power to decide its affairs. This is indicated by the negative beta weight of the number of administrative ranks within the school (row 6). The size of a school, although strongly correlated with the number of administrative ranks ($r = .44$), exerts no direct impact on the influence of the central administration. The large size of the university, however, reduces the influence of the central administration over schools (row 2), and so does the university's affluence (row 1). The large size of an organization, which implies that large numbers of decisions must be made, creates pressures on top administrators to decentralize decision making, as has been found in research on various kinds of organizations (Blau and Schoenherr, 1971:129-31; Mansfield, 1973).

Let us turn now to the unexpected finding that advanced training has a direct structural effect on the influence of the university administration over the affairs of professional schools (rows 3 and 4). To explain it one must first distinguish between the distribution of power and the degree of centralization in an organization. The distribution of power is what depends on relative standing. Higher ranks in an organization exercise more authority than lower ones. Further, the relative standing of subunits is expected to affect the influence of their administrators in the university. But the degree to which power is *generally* decentralized in an organization depends, naturally, on conditions other than a subunit's relative standing. One of these, as we just saw, is the large size of an organization. Another is the nature of the responsibilities, how much coordination they require on the one hand, and how much autonomy for subunits and individuals on the other. These requirements may vary among subunits. It was previously suggested that specialized advanced training requires less coordination among departments and schools than undergraduate education and more autonomy in planning the educational programs, which are so divergent in different fields. This is reflected in the finding that schools that offer more advanced training are less subject to the authority of the central administration than other schools (row 4). In universities with few graduate students, centralized control is the administrative standard. In universities with relatively large numbers of graduate students more decentralization prevails. These prevailing standards affect the power the university exercises over a school independent of the extent of graduate training in the school (indicated by the beta weight of the percent of graduate students in the university—row 3).

The interpretation of these findings in terms of the need for autonomy is supported by parallel results of advanced training in the regression analysis of another variable, the one designated as autonomy. A school's autonomy, as operationally defined, is not simply the opposite of the influence of the central administration in its affairs. Different items are used to measure the two (although two of the seven items are similar; see above). The two are not strongly correlated (−.19). With the exception of advanced training, the conditions that affect the power of the central administration over a school do not affect its autonomy, as measured, and other conditions influence the latter but not the former. Law schools have the most autonomy,[6] and schools of education have the least (Table 3, rows 4 and 5). Universities with superior reputations give less autonomy to their schools than other universities (row 1). The only other factors discovered to affect a school's autonomy are the two pertaining to advanced training. Schools with much graduate training have more autonomy than others (row 3), in accordance with the interpretation suggested. Granting a school substantial autonomy is, consequently, exceptional in universities having mostly undergraduates but standard administrative practice in those having many graduate students. This administrative standard of the university exerts considerable influence on the autonomy of its schools regardless of the amount of their graduate work (row 2).

RELATIVE SOCIAL STANDING

The academic qualifications of a school's faculty are measured by the proportion who have doctorates or advanced professional degrees. In some fields,

Table 3.

REGRESSION ANALYSIS OF SCHOOL AUTONOMY

Independent Variable	Beta Weight	Zero-Order Correlation
UNIVERSITY		
1. Reputation[a]	−.21	−.10
2. Graduate students (%)	.22	.23
SCHOOL		
3. Graduate students (%)	.13	.27
4. Law[a]	.13	.23
5. Education[a]	−.09	−.14

$R^2 = .15$ $N = 561$
[a]Dummy Variable

however, advanced professional degrees are rarely if ever given—architecture and nursing are examples—though a few faculty members may have Ph.D.'s in related disciplines. Besides, academic degrees have little significance in some professional schools compared with other qualifications; an obvious illustration is a school of music concentrating on performance. Six types of professional schools generally have fewer faculty members with advanced degrees than other types: those in architecture (14 percent on the average), journalism (32), library science (41), music (22), nursing (12), and social work (32). In all other types of professional schools the average proportion of the faculty with advanced degrees is more than three-fifths, and differences among them are essentially accounted for by other factors.

In the regression analysis of the formal qualifications of a school's faculty in Table 4, the six types with disproportionately few faculty members who have advanced degrees are controlled (rows 5-10). Another variable that is controlled is the proportion of the entire university's faculty who have advanced degrees. This variable is related to the proportion having advanced degrees in schools (row 1), in part because the proportions in professional schools contribute to the total proportion in the university. Besides, the relationship is probably partly due to the demand for high academic qualifications in the university, which affects faculty recruitment in its schools.

The age of a professional school increases the proportion of its faculty with advanced degrees (row 4), and so does the extent of graduate training in it (row 3).[7] Although the beta weight and partial correlation of age are small (.09 and .14, respectively), the zero-order correlation is substantial (.35), which indicates that the conditions controlled reduce the influence of school's age on its faculty's academic qualifications. A major reason why older professional schools tend to have more faculty members with advanced degrees than newer

Table 4.

REGRESSION ANALYSIS OF SCHOOL'S FACULTY QUALIFICATIONS

Independent Variable	Beta Weight	Zero-Order Correlation
UNIVERSITY		
1. Faculty Qualifications	.23	.22
2. Graduate students (%)	−.09	.10
SCHOOL		
3. Graduate students (%)	.23	.35
4. Age (years)	.09	.35
5. Architecture[a]	−.36	−.32
6. Journalism[a]	−.20	−.14
7. Library science[a]	−.22	−.10
8. Music[a]	−.30	−.24
9. Nursing[a]	−.48	−.45
10. Social work[a]	−.32	−.19

$R^2 = .68$ $N = 703$
[a] Dummy Variable

ones is that advanced degrees are generally infrequent in newer professions and their more recently established schools, notably nursing and social work. But some direct effect of a school's age on its faculty's degrees persists when the type of school and other conditions are controlled. This suggests that a professional school's tradition of long standing facilitates the recruitment of faculty with superior academic qualifications. The amount of graduate work in a school, too, may help in recruiting faculty with advanced degrees. Faculty members with lengthy academic training often prefer working with some graduate students to teaching exclusively undergraduates. Another factor contributing to the relationship between graduate education and faculty degrees in a school is that instructors of graduate students are in many places required to have advanced degrees.

A large proportion of graduate students in the university, in contrast to a large proportion in the school itself, is negatively related to the formal qualifications of the school's faculty (compare rows 2 and 3). This inverse higher-order structural effect can be explained in terms of the theoretical principles derived from the analysis of inverse structural effects on individual conduct. Greater resources tend to be needed to employ faculty members with advanced degrees than those without, not only because they typically get higher salaries but also because more of them are engaged in research which requires costly facilities. Graduate training commands more prestige than undergraduate teaching, owing to the characteristics of the professions (like medicine and law), of the schools, and of the faculty members associated with graduate training. Extensive graduate training in a school gives it a legitimate claim on sufficient university resources to recruit faculty members with advanced degrees, inasmuch as persons training graduate students are expected to have completed graduate training themselves, and the prestige and influence such a school commands helps it to implement that claim. Many graduate students in a university imply that many of its schools provide extensive graduate training. Holding constant a school's own proportion of graduate students, numerous other schools in its university with large proportions of graduate students (represented by the beta weight in row 2) lower its relative standing. This probably reduces its chances in the competition among schools for university resources to recruit faculty, which is reflected in an adverse effect on the academic qualifications of its faculty.

Finally, Table 5 presents the results of the regression analysis of inside student recruitment, indicated by the proportion of a professional school's graduate students who have undergraduate degrees from the same university (28 percent on the average). Schools of social work are least likely to recruit their students from their own universities (row 7). Three variables pertaining to economic conditions affect insider recruitment. A professional school's affiliation with a public university (row 1), its affiliation with a poor university (row 2), and its low faculty salaries (row 6) increase the likelihood that its students have undergraduate degrees from its own university. An underlying factor in all three relationships may well be the economic circumstances of students (on

Table 5.

REGRESSION ANALYSIS OF INSIDE STUDENT RECRUITMENT

Independent Variable	Beta Weight	Zero-Order Correlation
UNIVERSITY		
1. Public[a]	.20	.30
2. Affluence (revenue per student)	−.16	−.19
3. Graduate students (%)	−.13	−.26
SCHOOL		
4. Graduate students (%)	.13	−.14
5. Total enrollment (log)	.23	.29
6. Faculty salary	−.13	−.13
7. Social work[a]	−.09	−.13

$R^2 = .20$ $N = 513$
[a] Dummy Variable

which no data are here available). Public universities, with their lower tuition, unquestionably have more students who are poor than most private ones. Universities with low revenues per student undoubtedly also have more poor students than affluent universities, since higher tuition rates tend to raise revenues per student. That poorly paid faculties and poor students in a school are associated is less certain, though it is not entirely implausible. In any case, poor students are less likely than affluent ones to go to graduate school, and, if they do, they probably are more likely to go to one in their own university, because their meager resources restrict their alternative opportunities, and perhaps because their chances to obtain scholarships at their own university are better. Another reason for the observed relationships is that public universities usually give student applicants from their own state preferential treatment, making it more difficult to switch to another university. A further possibility is that poorer academic institutions have fewer resources for outside recruitment.

A large student enrollment in a professional school increases the proportion of its graduate students who have degrees from its own university (row 5), and so does a large proportion of graduate students in it (row 4). The two findings together imply that a large number of graduate students in a school make it most likely that these students have undergraduate degrees from the same university, and possibly from the same school. The number of places in the graduate program of a professional school apparently governs the rate of admission of graduates from its own university.

The proportion of graduate students in a university, on the other hand, reduces the proportion of its graduates in its professional schools (row 3). This inverse structural effect of graduate students on inside recruitment can be explained in the same theoretical terms as that on faculty academic qualifications. Many graduate students of a school raise, whereas many graduate students of other schools in the university lower, its relative standing and its visibility in the university community as a conspicuous place to go for graduate work. The attraction a school's graduate program has for the students in a university depends on its relative standing and visibility in the university. This interpretation of the findings from the perspective of student attraction can be complemented by an interpretation from the perspective of school admissions needs. The large graduate program of a professional school increases its demand for student applicants to fill all the places, making it more likely for students from the university to be admitted. But the large graduate programs of other schools in the university increase their demands for students and reduce any given school's competitive advantage in inside recruitment. The supply of candidates for graduate schools as well as the demand for them affects admissions. The negative influence of the percent of graduate students in the university on insider recruitment (row 3) is equivalent to a positive influence of the percent of undergraduates in the university on it. This implies that a large supply of potential candidates for graduate schools by a university's undergraduate programs increases the likelihood of inside recruitment by professional schools.

CONCLUSIONS

The problem posed in this paper is whether higher-order structural effects of universities on their professional schools can be explained in terms of the same theoretical principles earlier advanced to explain structural effects on the conduct and attitudes of individuals. The concept of structural effects refers to the influences on people exerted by the attributes of others in their environment, independent of their own attributes. These influences are assumed to be transmitted by the structure of social relations among people. The attributes of their associates and people's own attributes sometimes influence them in parallel ways (direct structural effects), but the two sometimes influence them in opposite ways (inverse structural effects). Direct structural effects have been explained on the basis of reinforcing social pressures resulting from prevailing practices. Thus the prevailing orientation to clients among fellow workers in a welfare agency exerts social pressures that reinforce the effect of a caseworker's own corresponding orientation (or counteract that of her own opposite orientation) on her treatment of clients. Inverse structural effects have been explained on the basis of the significance of relative standing. For instance, superior abilities of fellow students decrease, whereas a college student's own superior abilities increase, his expectation of going to graduate school. This results from the fact that the former lower and the latter raise his relative standing, which affects his self-image and expectations.

Professional schools that concentrate on training graduate students admit more minority students, are more independent of the central administration, and have more autonomy than those that have mostly undergraduate students. In addition, the extent of undergraduate training in a university exerts independent parallel effects on these conditions in its schools. In universities with few graduate students, the prevailing practices are not to admit many minority students and not to give much independence and autonomy to schools. In universities with many graduate students the opposite practices prevail. These standard practices in a university exert influences in their own right on the admission of minority students and the independence and autonomy granted schools, reinforcing the influences of a school's extent of graduate training. In short, the social pressures of prevailing standards can account for the direct structural effects observed, except that in formal organizations the pressures are largely administrative rather than primarily informal ones.

The more a professional school concentrates on graduate training, the higher are the academic qualifications of its faculty, and the larger is the proportion of its graduate students who have undergraduate degrees from its own university. However, the more the other schools in the university concentrate on graduate training, the lower are the academic qualifications of a given school's faculty, and the smaller is the proportion of its graduate students who have graduated from this university. Much graduate training in a school raises, whereas much graduate training in the other schools of its university lowers, its relative standing as a graduate school in the university. A school's relative standing governs its chances for success in the competition for university funds to recruit faculty with high academic qualifications and in the competition for recruiting graduate students among the university's undergraduates. Thus relative standing can account for the inverse structural effects observed.

Higher-order structural effects on organizational components appear to be explainable by the same principles as structural effects on individual conduct. Showing that an interpretative scheme is applicable to new findings, though it increases confidence in it, does not prove it, of course. Moreover, a caveat should be mentioned in conclusion. Direct structural effects have been attributed to social pressures, but the term is slightly misleading, inasmuch as it suggests the pressures of negative social sanctions. Social rewards also may produce pressures that engender direct structural effects. An example is the findings by Davis (1961) cited earlier that both a person's own active participation in a discussion group and that of other members reduces that person's chances of leaving the group. Others' as well as own participation make the discussions more rewarding, engendering pressures to remain in the group, though no negative sanctions penalizing deviants are involved.

NOTES

1. I gratefully acknowledge grant SOC71-03671 from the National Science Foundation, which supported this research.

2. Structural effects are a special case of the "contextual propositions" discussed by Lazarsfeld (1959:69-73).

3. The validity of the inference that a structural effect has been observed also rests on the correctness of the assumptions about causal sequence made, that is, the assumption that the structural property is the antecedent and the dependent variable the consequence.

4. A third type of structural effect is a contingency effect, when the influence of a person's own attribute depends on the prevalence of this attribute in the collectivity, but this type is not discussed in the present paper.

5. To be sure, controlling other conditions only increases the probability that an imputed structural effect is not spurious—it does not assure that it is not. The possibility always remains that it is the spurious result of still other factors on which no information is available and which therefore could not be controlled. Besides, correlated errors of the structural and the corresponding individual variable may artificially raise their coefficients.

6. Medical schools have second-most autonomy, but no more than the large proportion of their graduate students would predict, whereas law schools have even more than accounted for by their entirely graduate student body.

7. Both of these findings replicate results obtained in another study of academic institutions (Blau, 1973:82-84).

Aaron V. Cicourel

FIELD RESEARCH: THE NEED FOR STRONGER THEORY AND MORE CONTROL OVER THE DATA BASE

Field research seeks to portray some domain or activity of social life in a way that minimizes the researcher's influence on the data collected. In field research, the investigator often focuses on an inductive explanation of the local conditions observed. This stress on inductive procedures is often a result of weak theory that contains highly plausible but rather abstract concepts about the nature of social interaction and social institutions.

The researcher's presence in a social setting as a participant and observer inevitably produces a reaction on the part of those being studied. The reaction occurs despite the gradual feeling of the investigator, after continuous field work, that his or her presence is being taken for granted. Field researchers often seek to satisfy problems of validity by gradually "slipping into" or "drifting" into a taken-for-granted status in the group or setting being studied. As a rather large literature now exists on these topics, I shall avoid covering these familiar issues here.

I want to devote most of this essay to a brief description of the ways in which we might improve field research by strengthening our theoretical concepts, and by seeking more control over the methods with which we obtain and analyze data. Field work is a necessary aspect of social research, but considerable theoretical sophistication is needed if we are to make our recording, elicitation, and analysis of data more precise and valid across groups and cultures.

The theoretical concepts I shall recommend are primarily concerned with language and cognition. A better understanding of linguistic and cognitive structures will enable us to improve our analysis of the verbal (and eventually nonverbal) data that are basic aspects of all field research. The key theoretical notion to be described is that of an interactive model that seeks to link different levels of data and analysis to the forms of reasoning employed in field research. The model forces the researcher to be more explicit about the sources and structure of information that make up a data base, while also indicating the logic of analysis that is being imposed on the empirical materials used.

The methods recommended for the analysis of the linguistic materials that are gathered in field work are a variation of correlational techniques that are applied to discourse or conversations. The general idea is to establish rules of covariation between, say, social class and the sound patterns of a language, or ethnic or cultural identity and the use of a particular language code. The establishment of covariation rules is usually part of a limited field study, but the method can be extended easily to include a survey research format and aggregated tables. In the final section I indicate how we might go beyond these methods by seeking an analysis of the same data base using a strategy that, at first glance, seems to be weaker than the correlational method. The recommended strategy, however, is congruent with the cognitive and sociocultural processes necessary for comprehending and producing the social interaction of interest in field research. The strategy can also be linked to more algorithmic analysis of the textual materials or summarizations sometimes used in organizational studies.

AN INTERACTIVE MODEL

Doing field research always means being exposed to several sources of information that cannot all be attended and comprehended simultaneously. The field researcher must integrate the different sources of information during and after participation and observation in some group. Perception, language use, and periodic physical movement in a social context always presuppose acts of consciousness and the activation of stored information about specific and general types of knowledge. A person's prior experiences and thoughts about specific types of knowledge, as well as general knowledge stored in memory, are integral aspects of interpreting participant observer activities and the creation of field notes. Field notes are summarizations of interpretations at the time of experience and the interaction of this comprehension with later thinking about the activities. The further classification of field notes becomes the findings discussed in reports and professional papers.

Studies based on field research seldom refer to the preprocessing of information that goes on during participant observation, and the way such thoughts can be altered or sustained by the language used in field notes. Field work, therefore, requires a continuous process of negotiation in which the intentions, content, and significance of what is observed of others, and experienced and reflected on by oneself as researcher, comprise sources of information that become selectively incorporated into field notes. We also create additional inferences based on field notes and experiences that are stored in memory but not always recorded in summarized form as data.

The field researcher must rely on several types of information such as: special sound patterns, syntactic structures, semantic knowledge, and the pragmatics of the social setting. He or she must also make use of inductive inferences and information, deductive inferences, and what Peirce (1931-35) called abductive reasoning, that is, where the observation of facts in testing hypotheses is part of the particular (emergent) circumstances that exist at the time of observation. Participant observation depends on abductive reasoning and a use of tacit knowledge that is not always made explicit in writing down field notes or their elaboration at a later time.

The basic idea of an interactive model is that several levels of information are examined by several types of logical reasoning. The model seeks to formalize the way deductive hypotheses are affected by inductive reasoning. To this model we add the notion of abductive reasoning and the influence of tacit knowledge in order to deal adequately with the complex problems posed by field research. The particular circumstances that exist at the time of observation are integral elements of all field research inferences and the subsequent field notes that are created. Peirce's notion of abduction is useful here because it refers to the inferential step of first stating and then reflecting on a hypothesis that would choose among several possible explanations of some set of facts. In the case of field research this inferential step may require formulating a hypothesis from among several, possibly ambiguous, observations whose factual status remains, and was, unclear at the time they were experienced. Clarifying observations may require additional information from informants and later observations.

Rumelhart (forthcoming) has proposed a model of story grammar to explain how we recall brief stories and summarize them. The way persons are said to comprehend stories is described as identical to the way they select and verify conceptual schemata or knowledge of concepts when these persons seek to account for or explain a situation or text. Stated in other words, the way a subject understands a situation or the passage of a text or story can be equated to the selection and verification of the abstract representations or schemata that can be identified as characterizing the key elements of the situation, story, or text. As in Peirce's notion of creating facts and making guesses under conditions of hypothesis testing, the idea of summarization becomes a central aspect of comprehension. Field studies summarize different sources of information available to participants during interaction based on informants' talking about past events to the field researcher.

A central aspect of Rumelhart's analysis of brief stories is to view stories as problem-solving episodes in which something happens to the protagonist of the story that creates a goal for him or her to achieve. We can ask, how do field researchers use their knowledge of concepts to link an initiating event with a goal while also identifying appropriate methods for achieving the goal? Do field notes identify the knowledge and procedures used by subjects studied to select subgoals and methods for their attainment? In other words, do field notes display a structure that is similar to the way subjects remember a story or the way textual reports are written? If we can show a relationship between field notes and models of story or text grammars, then we have a more powerful tool available for understanding how a researcher is able to comprehend and report on his or her experiences. The models can also tell us something about the limits of this type of observation and inference. The study of story grammars reveals formal algorithmic structures that can be compared to the way field notes summarize a range of experiences and the researcher's thinking about these activities. The reliability and validity of remarks by informants also can be studied by reference to a story grammar model.

A related but different model addresses reading as an activity that reflects on the interaction of information from sensory, syntactic, semantic, and pragmatic sources. Rumelhart (n.d.) stresses the significance of metapredicate or higher-level predicates in the processing of data-driven or inductive information. We proceed from features to letters to spelling patterns and visual word displays, word meanings, and sentence meanings. Similarly, a higher-order predicate like the title of a chapter or the title of a section provides a context for remembering or understanding particular sentences or words.

The interaction of lower and higher levels of predication or information forces us to recognize how knowledge that is external to what is experienced in participant observation and conversational exchanges is a necessary part of all field research. The choice of particular words and the clarity and organization of speech influence the knowledge we utilize in our understanding of subsequent visual and speech perception.

In the Rumelhart model of reading, a "message center" is postulated that is monitored to see whether hypotheses emerge that contribute to particular areas of knowledge based on information from a set of parallel interacting processes. The message center receives sources of information that can be viewed as a parallel processing system that gives attention to different forms of stored knowledge in order to provide for the interpretation of different aspects of incoming information. A "pattern synthesizer" receives sensory and nonsensory knowledge about the current contextual situation. Different levels of analysis provide both information and constraints on the building of an interpretation of the different sources of knowledge that reach the message center. Rumelhart's model of reading is designed to deal primarily with linguistic sources of knowledge while postulating pragmatic aspects of the setting and the role of higher-order or metapredicates.

The field researcher faces several levels of information from the setting that can only be attended differentially or periodically (Cicourel, 1977b). Linguistic sources may be central for an understanding of the immediate setting, but lexical knowledge that enables the researcher to claim that something is a member or instance of some category is not sufficient to explain the interpretations that are made. A person's practical knowledge (Miller, 1976) is needed to clarify utterances and visual information not available from lexical knowledge. The rule-governed aspects of sound patterns, syntax, and lexical knowledge are embedded in an interactional setting that includes practical knowledge from the situation and from memory, and belief systems used as meta- or higher-level predicates. Not all aspects of the different sources of information can be addressed directly by a participant observer (much less any native participant of social interaction). Aspects of syntax, lexical knowledge, and conversational turn-taking devices may assume an "automatic" status; they can play a minor role in the comprehension of a setting, and in the subsequent field notes and memory of the participant observer. A tape recording of some period of interaction, however, may reveal patterns of syntactic, semantic, and turn-taking structures that can suggest significant information for a more general level of understanding using higher-order or metapredicates. We need to know more about the interaction of these theoretical levels if we are to create and analyze field notes effectively.

The use of field research procedures poses a complex problem for the sociologist. On the one hand we can be confident of observing and reflecting on very rich sources of information, but, on the other hand, we lack clear conceptual and methodological procedures for extracting the maximum knowledge from the valuable and sensitizing field settings on which we rely for data. Research projects that are dependent on survey procedures do not avoid similar difficulties. These later procedures generate considerable information from a method that virtually eliminates the rich sources of knowledge available from participant observation, while simultaneously ignoring the difficult issues posed by the interactive model recommended here. Yet both methods involve some form of field research. We cannot pursue the matter further except to note that these two types of field research require similar theoretical clarification.

RECENT METHODS USED IN FIELD RESEARCH

During the past fifteen years considerable field research in sociology has come to include the use of audio and video recorders. Some researchers have included audio and video or film recordings to expand the kinds of data available in participant observation and interviewing. Others have used these materials to focus on the discovery of rules governing conversational or nonverbal exchanges while deliberately ignoring the participant observer and interviewing conditions of field work which include the role of the organizational context and its structure. The ethnographic or organizational setting is a central aspect of all field research, especially as a rich source of current and historical institutional knowledge about higher-order or metapredicates that influence the structure of social interaction and the talk that occurs therein.

Current work on language use in interaction derives from several papers and books on ordinary language philosophy, componential analysis and ethnographic semantics, the ethnography of speaking, child language acquisition, ethnomethodology, and the analysis of turn-taking in conversations. Recent research on developmental psycholinguistics and sociolinguistics has given the study of language use in natural settings a stronger methodological focus because this work makes use of measurement techniques that are fairly explicit, yet retain a clear relationship to the early work in philosophy, anthropology, linguistics, psychology, and sociology.

The recent research I have addressed here deals with the classification of utterances and language use between persons of different cognitive, linguistic, social status, and sociocultural capacities. Other studies exist that also include additional variables, but for present purposes the studies of parent-child and child-child interaction are adequate for recommending linguistic methods to the field researcher in sociology.

When the field researcher records field notes, they invariably will contain statements that describe settings, persons, social relationships, theoretical inferences, methodological problems, and allude to factual circumstances observed during the course of the research. The many statements that make up field notes provide a coherent account of diverse activities that are amenable to a kind of story grammar analysis. We need to identify the independent sources of information that come to be described in summary form in the field notes. We can use some of the measures to be described shortly to provide an independent assessment of what is observed during participant observation. The story grammar (concerned with the constituent structures of a text) and the classification of language used in natural social interaction settings do not provide us with more subtle measures that are congruent with the intent of field researchers interested in daily social life in different organizational and institutional settings. But current measures are unavoidable in our search for theory and methods that more adequately address the structure and emergent aspects of social life.

Two broad aspects of the study of language use in natural settings can be identified: first, the kinds of abilities or capacities that can be attributed to the speakers and listeners when we contrast their remarks and reactions to each other; second, the functional classification of meaning in context which the researcher produces in an effort to obtain consistent measures of the interaction. The functional classification enables the researcher to make inferences about the speaker's or listener's capabilities as a member of some community or group. This classification is similar to the use of questionnaires with or without fixed-choice responses. The meaning of utterances or responses to questions is coded by reference to lexical knowledge or the conventional meanings that are expressed by dictionaries and what seems appropriate in some context of interaction. The questionnaire items, however, refer to hypothetical possibilities that insist the respondent subscribe to questions or summaries that may not coincide with the subject's memory of his or her experiences. The psycholinguistic and sociolinguistic research requires the coding of actual displays of daily life.

There is a similarity between the measures used by Bales (1950) in coding small-group interaction and the functional assignment of meaning in context to utterances produced by parents and children to each other. But again there is a difference. Bales' categories include several elements that are assumed to reveal negative affect, like showing antagonism, tension, and disagreeing; and positive affect, like showing agreement, friendliness, simple attention, and the release of tension. Other remarks are coded as neutral questions and statements such as seeking instructions, opinions, or information, and giving information or opinions. The syntactic and semantic bases of the Bales classification procedure have not been clarified or addressed explicitly. The philosopher of language, the linguistic anthropologist, the psycholinguist, and the sociolinguist—all seek to justify their classification of utterances by reference to explicit concepts about language structure and use. This latter group often alludes to, although it doesn't always use, nonverbal aspects of communication which also can be used to classify utterances.

Recent research in psycholinguistics and sociolinguistics (Shipley et al., 1969; Snow, 1972; Blount, 1972; Phillips, 1973; Shatz and Gelman, 1973; Cicourel, 1973, forthcoming [a], forthcoming [b]; Newport, forthcoming; Newport et al., forthcoming; Gelman and Shatz, n.d.; Corsaro, n.d.) has noted that speakers and listeners adjust their speech to, and understanding of, the other person in terms of the competence each attributes to the other. Speech may be preorganized for the listener under the assumption that the latter is only capable of certain narrow conceptions of the world and restrictive processing capacities. Specifically, this can mean the use of structural simplicity (i.e., simple, declarative utterances), standardized vocabularies that avoid difficult terms, and more repetitious variations in speech that lead to certain lexical and syntactic selections and speech styles. The social and conversational status of speakers and listeners can produce differences in the frequency of sentence types used in speech exchanges. Particular speech acts are identified and certain cooperative principles seem to be followed in seeking to influence others and in conveying specific intentions (Searle, 1969; Grice, 1975; Lakoff, 1973). Attempts have been made to identify the way topics are introduced and changed, the way requests are made and denied, and the general way participants of casual conversation gain the right to speak, take turns at speaking, tell jokes, and begin to close and finally terminate speech exchanges (Sacks et al., 1974; Goffman, 1975).

An important assumption in the use of audio-taped dialogues in natural set-

tings is that the participants will reveal, through their talk, systems of reference, one or more domains or bodies of knowledge, and particular vocabularies and styles of speech. When field researchers use informants for in-depth
interviews, they must often begin the exchange by introducing categories that
may not be congruent with those of the informant. But after having introduced
a few categories that are designed to explore and then pinpoint aspects of some
domain of knowledge, the researcher should then use the native's categories to
pursue the relevant particulars that make up a relevant domain (Black and
Metzger, 1965). The use of dialogues in natural settings assumes that these exchanges are sufficiently self-contained and internally consistent so as to reveal
aspects of various domains of knowledge (including elements of their boundaries, the abilities of speakers and listeners to introduce and sustain topics, the
capacity to employ different communicational structures), while also observing social and cultural rules and beliefs about the community and the world at
large. The tapes can provide the basis for pursuing the elicitation strategies of
ethnographic semantics and seeking organizational records and information
that are referenced in the recorded talk.

The field researcher seeks stable utterances that may or may not occur in
pairs like questions and responses. He or she looks for speech acts that ask for
clarification, that correct the expressive form of an utterance, that ask for
additional information, that illustrate the speaker's knowledge of normative
rules used in social interaction, and the way a speech exchange reveals knowledge of social positions and of objects and events of the community and larger
society.

A careful examination of the transcripts of natural settings will show the use
of imperatives or direct commands or warnings, often accompanied by nonverbal information such as particular facial expressions, added stress to the
voice, and a loud emphatic tone as the utterance ends. This type of utterance
can be used to describe and clarify the authority and power relationships
among the participants of the interaction.

Informative statements that clarify or add knowledge to some topic or activity, or statements that express general or personal observations about aspects of
the setting, can be used to construct a general picture of which participants are
most informed and active in keeping things oriented toward specific issues or
values. Individual utterances and sequences of conversation can provide the
documentation for general impressions that have been inferred from participant observation.

The researcher's general knowledge about the group or community being
studied becomes background information necessary for understanding discourse in which local requests or permission to do something occur, and occa-
sions where the listener is asked to join the speaker in joint action. This also
can be true for answers or accounts in conversation that presume a prior question or an attempt on the part of a speaker to explain a previous action or the

failure to do something. Similarly, the use of tag questions, or declaratives that have been made interrogatives by adding a tag marker at the end ("We're still sharing the expenses, right?"), appear to be a way of seeking an understanding with a listener by giving the listener a chance to respond. This type of utterance presupposes prior interaction.

The reader will notice that the coding of a dialogue or conversation according to its functional meaning in context is not unlike all coding procedures used in social research. The coding strategies I have outlined assume that the researcher is able to use his abilities as a native speaker, or knowledge of a native speaker's capabilities and practices, to recognize different utterances as requests for information instead of commands ("Are you planning to finish the reports today?"), or as requests for clarification instead of attempts to irritate someone or remind persons of moral or other commitments. The coding is highly dependent on the ethnographic information or higher-level predicates used by the researcher. This information can be obtained through participant observation and a knowledge of social institutions. Classifying utterances also depends on judgments or evaluations that are dependent on the context of extended social interaction.

Traditional coding procedures in demographic and survey research are a function of judgments or evaluations that are independent of the possibly changing social context of the original interviews. Coders seldom have access to information about the circumstances or experiences of the respondents that contributed to the responses given to the interviewer or reported in a self-administered questionnaire.

The coding activities that are necessary aspects of measurement in small-group research are seldom sensitive to the local conditions of interaction. These activities do not always describe and use information about the ethnographic setting created by researchers and understood by experimental subjects, nor do they make explicit a reliance on the lexical stability of linguistic expressions as a source of information for the measures used.

The methods recommended in this essay depend on the stability and structure of linguistic utterances and particular types of expressions that are cultivated by all groups and communities. A clear advantage of these methods consists of making use of the necessary relationship between cultural experiences and reasoning, and their representation in memory and observable symbolic form. By examining and using the structure of language and its variations by cultural groups in social contexts, the field researcher benefits from the richness of the language used in social interaction, while acknowledging the fact that we do not always mean what we say or say what we mean.

If we are to build on existing strategies of research in sociology, we must recognize that all of the coding practices described or alluded to in the foregoing material can be clarified by exploring the connection between what we say or ask respondents to report or scale, and the role of memory, forms of reasoning, and the levels of meaning that are presupposed. But, in field research, we are preoccupied with legitimate problems of gaining access to a group or community, faithfully recording field notes that reveal substantive, theoretical, and methodological issues, and coding our tape-recorded dialogues according to their functional meaning in context. Similarly field research, like all other forms of research, must be concerned with the assembly of cross-tabulated, aggregated, categorized utterances.

The notion of an interactive model becomes necessary for adequate field research. Several levels of analysis are presupposed in the analysis of speech acts, elicitation frames and responses from ethnographic semantics, field notes, general interviewing, the coding of fixed-choice responses, and information from vital statistics and census data. Every time we code something, we presume a knowledge of higher-level or metapredicates about the persons, group, or community we study. We can engage in elementary classification using low-level empirical materials, but moving up an inductive chain forces us to create or invoke new or prior knowledge. Our memory and forms of reasoning are indispensable for organizing our experiences and observations, creating question-answer response sets, and coding utterances in terms of local and external contextual knowledge. Arguing for the necessity of addressing the organization of memory and forms of reasoning as part of our field research is easier to say than to demonstrate. In the next two sections, I shall illustrate the problem by reference to some examples from recent research.

EXTENDED DISCOURSE AND INFORMATION PROCESSING

Measurement, in field research and all studies that require coding operations, like those found in the use of census materials, sample surveys, and small-group research, depends on presuppositions which are normal aspects of organizing and analyzing sources of information that comprise a data base. These presuppositions include a number of unexamined concepts and variables; the structure and use of language; several cognitive processes including selective perception, memory limitations involving what is stored, the format of storage, and the conditions that allow for retrieval of information; and the forms of reasoning employed that influence the interpretation of cultural beliefs and social rules which prevail in organizational settings.

If we are committed to survey research, a study of educational achievement by social class and ethnicity will seldom include participant observation in classrooms, peer groups, and the home experiences of a cohort of students. The organizational and cultural context of classroom, peer group, and family life can be inferred from several sources of information, but a survey will focus on questionnaire items to operationalize presumed sources of influence on educational achievement.

If we are partial to participant observation, a study of the activities of an esoteric group in a common setting will lead to intensive field research. Case studies are devoted primarily to intensive participant observation within the group and in-depth interviews with key informants. They seldom include a careful study of the comparative-historical literature and documents on similar groups. In field research it is not always common practice to examine higher-level or metapredicates derived from a more complex organizational context or from the comparative-historical literature.

The moral of the previous passages is that it is often very difficult to design our research so that we can use diverse measures and also be attentive to the presuppositions that can undermine the significance of the inferences we make from a data base. We seek research that generates measures which satisfy a subset of sociologists who find them acceptable vis-à-vis the standards of peer review and journal publication. In the pursuit of one or more of the accepted methodological strategies, sociology is a necessary aspect of sociological careers; nevertheless, it also contributes to a gradual growth in knowledge. But it is not the case that the majority of the papers and proposals that meet the standards of peer review for grants and journals are incorporated and accepted as part of the theoretical knowledge of the discipline.

Questionnaire items, field notes, and units of speech are central to social research despite the fact that they often are coded without explicit reference to theory. Each type of measure, when aggregated, provides us with explanations of key issues in sociology. We seldom feel that sociologists need to examine presuppositions about language structure and use, the perception, storage, and retrieval of information, and the way forms of reasoning influence cultural belief systems and the structure of activities in organizational or ethnographic settings.

But participants of interaction cannot invoke, at random, various forms of speech acts and vocabularies when faced with specific ethnographic or organizational settings. External knowledge and constraints always influence social interaction. We recognize that the participant's knowledge and memory of concepts and prior activities will influence a social exchange (i.e., an interview or the filling out of a questionnaire) just as these conditions affect the field researcher's notes. We can also acknowledge the role of different forms of reasoning which can be used under different organizational conditions or when certain beliefs are being discussed or challenged. But it is difficult to see how all of these notions can or should be made part of traditional social research strategies that focus on correlational or covariation measures whose identifiable payoff is assured.

The socialization of children has been studied by interviewing mothers with detailed questionnaires. Others have engaged in extensive ethnographic research at the village or household level. We can also examine parent-child interaction to study the child's ability to express common cultural knowledge about his or her daily life experiences, including activities that form part of the tape-recorded exchange. The child reveals knowledge about cars, elevators, brushing one's teeth, and the inappropriateness of aspects of a story (Cicourel, 1977b, forthcoming [a]). Tape recordings of parent-child interaction can help us understand some of the complex issues in the socialization of children, including parental, relatives', and friends' conceptions of how they would like to see the child grow up. The microcosm of daily interaction invariably includes rather commonplace as well as more dramatic sources of information, and further provides us with materials about a family's attempts to socialize children that may or may not be consistent with information from interviews and implicit ideas about conceptions of the larger society the child must gradually enter.

The reader should note that all of my tapes and observations reveal the requests for clarification or information, predicate complements, interrogatives, and similar illocutionary expressions that are identified in the literature cited earlier. We can specify the assignment of functional meaning in context and covariation in language use whereby an utterance can be seen as performing a function in a particular setting, according to the assumption that a certain rule must be known by the participants of the interaction. Context here is usually defined in local terms as what preceded and followed a particular utterance.

In prior work on parent-child interaction I was also concerned with attempts by subjects to create remarks or summary statements for my benefit. The quality of the data base cannot be taken for granted despite the ability of coders to produce reliably similar outcomes. The obtrusiveness of the tape recorder or video camera and/or the researcher is not a serious obstacle, but these conditions cannot be assumed to be irrelevant. But it may be necessary for the researcher to examine extensive discourse between parent and child to make decisions about the significance of coding procedures which give relative autonomy or independence to particular utterances and turns. The contrastive analysis of speech that is based on the logic of covariation is not always relevant for understanding the gist of extended discourse. The assignment of functional meaning in context can obscure the reasoning that must be used by the researcher in deciding that certain passages are idle chatter, or presuppose prior dialogue or knowledge. But aggregate measures of, say, mean length of utterance, or requests for information, provide important general findings about the structure of a family, a group, or an organization. The study of these collectivities can be pursued differently by examining extended discourse.

The careful examination of extended discourse, as a set of information-processing strategies and schemata or knowledge of concepts, can help us understand those presuppositions about cognition, language, and social structure which we must explore conceptually and empirically if we are to understand our use of field research techniques to collect and analyze data. Mother-child discourse reveals higher-level predicates that mark the way different schemata or knowledge of concepts are used by the mother and child in the same dialogue.

The mother is often engaged in specific tasks like washing clothes, dusting, ironing, and mending clothes, and if more than one child is present, the children can engage in conversations that include or exclude the mother. The mother may address only one child without naming her or him, or both children, yet use schemata that may not be comprehensible to both of them.

In another paper (Cicourel, 1977b), I described a young mother and university student talking to her three-and-one-half-year-old daughter while the mother was preparing the child's lunch. Topics seemed to emerge from what the mother was doing at the time of interaction and from what seemed to be ad hoc remarks by the child about objects and events that spontaneously appeared without prior context. I inferred a whining, singsong intonation to the child's voice that did not sound like an inquisitive child pestering her mother with relentless questions about a myriad of perceived and imagined conditions or objects. My further assumption, that the child's voice sounded belabored and somewhat mechanical or indifferent, is based on initial information inductively derived that was coded as higher-level predicates I later called "belabored" and "indifferent."

The dialogue deals with contents of the refrigerator, a shopping trip, a discussion about the child's saying she wanted to play with an apple, and other utterances that can be easily coded but not always interpreted with confidence. The coding operation involves an interpretation that can be faithful to certain presuppositions but this does not mean that each coded utterance makes sense within the context of extended discourse and other possible presuppositions. But the mother's talk, in the initial portion of discourse just described, seems to fit one important observation made by Newport, Newport et al., Gelman and Shatz, Blount, and many others, that speakers seem to adjust their speech according to the capabilities and social status of the listener.

We can also interpret the dialogue just alluded to as a special kind of monologue. The conditions I have in mind are common in parent-child interaction. The mother's remarks satisfy our expectations of polite discourse and "motherese," but her explanations do not seem to be oriented to the child's inability to understand what might be expected from her when she enters nursery school. The specific issue of sharing "things with people" when playing with other children seems to be produced for the mother's benefit. The child's ability to produce responses that can be coded easily does not help us understand how a level of communicative competence can be displayed that simulates, but is not equivalent to, the knowledge we associate with the adult level of comprehension we can attribute to the mother's speech (Cicourel, 1977b). The child possesses the ability to produce sophisticated utterances when seen from the perspective of an adult. But we are uncertain about what we can presume the child understands of the mother's utterances, and we are also unclear as to what the mother assumes the child can comprehend. Subsuming information-al particulars under normative categories does not mean that the child (or all adults) can explain the representation used despite the ability to use standard-ized native expressions. In our analysis of natural settings, the convenience of using or creating particular units of speech makes it difficult for us to take se-riously the more complex cognitive-cultural processes that orient the inter-pretation of lower-order levels of predication. These complex processes in-clude the ability, during extended discourse, to create narrative summaries that reveal hierarchical structural elements. These hierarchical elements can be formally represented in algorithmic models and are of interest because they occur in the same settings in which abductive interpretations, based on local-ly perceived conditions, are made spontaneously.

THE USE OF HIGHER-LEVEL PREDICATES IN MEDICAL INTERVIEWING

The medical interview provides us with a convenient setting within which we can trace the way higher-level or metapredicates influence face-to-face social interaction. The writing of a medical history enables us to observe the way higher-level predicates transform linguistic and nonverbal sources of informa-tion into orderly accounts that reveal social relationships among doctor, pa-tient, and others, while, at the same time, producing declarative statements about a patient's problems and diagnosis. Prior work (Cicourel, 1974b, 1975, 1977a, 1977b) describes the physician's summarization of a medical interview based on conditions of (1) recalling the exchange, with or without notes, at a later time, and (2) compiling the summary over the course of the interview.

When the transcript of an interview is contrasted with the written medical history, we can observe discrepancies in the way information is created under one set of conditions, and then transformed (under subsequent conditions) into standardized statements that give the interview a coherence that is not jus-tified by the circumstances of the actual dialogue. But this coherence satisfies organizational requirements whose analysis by other researchers ignores the original interview data base. A general pattern of interviewing is often followed vis-à-vis specific topics such as the prenatal period of a pregnancy, the delivery, and postpartum activities. The physician can use a general strategy to elimin-ate or explore specific problems, but many important inferences are not re-vealed until the written summary is completed. The doctor, for example, may ignore the patient's reasoning and attempts to present his or her factual know-ledge, beliefs, and values, but instead focus on a strategy of interrogation and conversation that produces a standardized medical history other physicians can "understand."

The parallels with field research are fairly obvious. Indirect "interviewing," based on participation in a group, can lead to summary field notes. The organization of notes is influenced by prior experiences in the group or community studied, and by the ideas or tentative hypotheses we have formulated from other studies. When we do in-depth interviews with key informants, and write up our notes when there is more time and fewer interferences, we are engaged in producing a data base that is similar to that of the physician. The doctor continually makes inferences about a patient's condition despite the fact that the patient's responses are ignored, or the fact that the patient's remarks are not understood. Yet the ways in which we make such evaluations depend on the interaction of several levels of comprehension and the production of speech and nonverbal behavior which are not an explicit part of our conceptual thinking and measurement strategies.

The doctor's interview strategy includes the use of higher-level or metapredicates based on prior training, a knowledge of considerable literature, and clinical experience of cases that are assumed to be part of general patterns that might enable the physician to subsume the present case and emergent conditions of the interview itself. A deductive strategy must interact with inductive experiences produced by the interview. Field researchers assume that the focus of the work should be on the conditions of interaction encountered in the natural setting. In many studies the researcher has little choice but to begin this way; however the interactive model calls our attention to the fact that "bottom up" or inductive procedures cannot be sustained. Inductive or data-driven strategies can lead to excessive data combinations that can be included in many higher-level concepts. It is also difficult to identify the discovery procedures that are used. The subtle ways in which we invoke higher-level or metapredicates, either tacitly during participant observation, or perhaps explicitly when writing field notes or classifying them, should not become a virtue of field work. We can strengthen our research by making the theoretical ideas we tacitly use during participant observation, and while taking notes, an explicit part of an interactional model. Such a model recognizes the problem-solving aspects of field research. The model recognizes the ways in which representational systems operate as part of our memory, and the ways in which we communicate using oral, nonverbal, and written exchanges.

The field researcher utilizes participant observation, field notes, in-depth or casual interviews with informants, and the elaboration of these sources of information, to create a data base. Such procedures can either reveal or mask the kinds of interpretations placed on a person's experiences, notes, and the questions or probes employed. The explicit study of interpretational and summarization procedures, as they occur during interaction, interviews, and taking notes or elaborating upon them, is a necessary step for improving the conceptual basis of our studies and for producing a more precise data base.

CONCLUDING NOTE

This essay has called the reader's attention to linguistic, cognitive, and sociocultural elements that can improve the conceptual and measurement conditions of field research and our understanding of the ways in which we perceive and process information in all sociological research. Specific recommendations were made about the importance and use of methods for the analysis of discourse or conversation in natural settings. Some cautions were registered concerning the limits of using only correlational or covariation models for the measurement of sociolinguistic data.

An interactive model that draws from work on story grammars and reading was suggested to enhance the conceptual basis of field research. This model calls attention to the necessary interaction between lower levels of analysis, or micro-data based on the local context of interaction, and the identification of measurement units and higher-level or metapredicates that are always part of the processing of information. The interactive model directs our attention to the way each person or field researcher uses different factual knowledge and cultural values and beliefs in actual social settings when reflecting on and/or summarizing past experiences. A central point of the paper, therefore, is that useful correlational methods or the analysis of covariation can obscure more basic processes involved in the comprehension and production of social interaction. An understanding of these basic cognitive, cultural, and linguistic processes is necessary if we are to improve the study of natural settings. This strategy will allow us to avoid using research and measurement procedures whose convenience and obvious utility can mask or obscure the phenomena we claim is of interest.

Robert K. Leik

LET'S WORK
INDUCTIVELY, TOO

Most sociologists will agree that theories contain concepts and the relationships which link those concepts. Some might add that boundary conditions need also be specified. There is by no means unanimity as to where those components come from. In fact, most efforts at developing theories reflect quite different origins for the separate parts. Concepts typically come from a combination of experience and intuition of the theorist, filtered through both current and traditional concepts of the discipline. When relationships are made explicit, they most often follow expedient conventions for the sake of simplifying deductions. Boundaries, if they are addressed at all, are likely to be qualifications about the types of cases to which the theory applies or the external conditions which must hold for the theory to obtain. Occasionally, boundaries are established on the basis of observed success or failure of the theory in explaining data.

At their best, theories provide for organizing accumulated knowledge and guiding further inquiry into more productive paths. It is generally agreed that to be most effective at these tasks, theories need to satisfy various criteria. Blalock's essay in this volume reviews such criteria; they will not be restated here. What needs to be addressed is how we go about satisfying those criteria more completely as theories develop and mature. That is, how do we successively approximate good theory?

Usefulness, suggests Blalock, implies importance, comparative effectiveness with respect to competing theories, potential for policy guidance by using manipulable explanatory variables, and/or generalizability. Clearly, *"importance* of the set of 'dependent' variables that the theory sets out to explain"

(Blalock, 1977:2) is at least partially dependent upon the concept of the theory. Someone trying to explain family violence, for example, may be thought of as doing more important work than someone trying to explain popularity of the latest pop vocalist. The question concerns societal priorities, and is not itself subject to rules of theory construction and evaluation.

Potential for guiding policy also concerns what concepts the theory contains. As with importance, it cannot be evaluated by logical or scientific criteria. On the other hand, effectiveness concerns explanatory power and generalizability concerns boundary conditions. Both can be assessed by objective empirical analysis.

Regarding Blalock's internal criteria, all are subject to logical or empirical examination. Consequently, except for importance and policy utility, it is possible to establish clear rules for determining how good a theory is. Those rules are, for the most part, well laid out in the literature on theory construction (e.g., Blalock, 1969; Burr, 1973; Reynolds, 1971) and data analysis. We have gotten quite good at telling when our theoretical efforts are wanting. What then?

Presumably discovering that our theory is in some way inadequate implies "back to the drawing board." Some steps must be taken to correct deficiencies unless we are willing either to toss out the whole effort or to live with the inadequacy. One of the major deficiencies of current methodological literature is a lack of guidance on how to attack the deficiencies.

The foregoing comments amount to saying that the deductive aspects of theory development have flourished, particularly since Zetterberg's (1958 and subsequent editions) lucid arguments for axiomatic theory. Subsequently, the causal modeling literature (Blalock, 1971; Heise, 1975), especially path analysis, has been much in vogue. On the other hand, our inductive prowess has languished. The deductive approach to theory construction has come to dominate our notions of theory so that both new theoretical efforts and attempts at repair of existing theories evidence creative blinders.

Consider the issue of generalizability raised in Blalock's paper. Parsimonious theories are simple ones, usually involving few variables. They may be elegant but are usually not general enough. The most common solution? Add more variables or more causal paths. In the current mode of structural modeling, that solution quickly creates a cobweb on the path diagram. Often, however, such remodeling of the path diagram will accomplish nothing, since it is the form of the theory itself which is restricting generalization.

Alternatively, it may be that the concepts are too narrowly defined. In order to generalize, some theories need to broaden their conceptual base. But as Blalock points out, just using broader concepts will likely reduce predictive or descriptive accuracy unless further theoretical work accompanies the generalization. The tendency to treat operationalizations of subconcepts as simply alternative indicators of a more general concept tends to preclude such additional theoretical work.

This chapter will focus on possible approaches to the two problems just raised: theoretical form and conceptual generality. The emphasis of the ensuing discussion should be seen as an argument for a more versatile, mathematical approach to theory; an approach that is organized so that concepts and theoretical forms more readily admit the inductive side of what Hanson (1958, 1960) has called retroduction.

Retroduction incorporates both induction and deduction. Deduction involves logical determination of the consequences of theoretical statements, and hence enables explicit testing of the theory. Induction involves subsuming observed patterns or restricted propositions or concepts under more general propositions or concepts. Presumably, we work both ways, alternatively deducing consequences and testing them, then inducing broader, more general forms. This dual process, retroduction, should provide an iterative approach to increasingly accurate and general theory. Clearly, retroduction cannot proceed on deductive power alone.

THINKING ABOUT RATES OF CHANGE

In order to discuss general forms of theoretical propositions, it will be helpful to consider an idea normally introduced only in calculus courses: the rate of change of one variable dependent upon change in another variable. The discussion will not require knowledge of calculus, however. Assume two variables, X and Y, such that a change in X is expected to produce a change in Y. For example, if X represents self-esteem and Y represents social participation, then we would be assuming that changes in self-esteem would result in changed levels of participation.

There are numerous ways to specify the relationship between X and Y. Most generally, they can be said to covary. Such a statement allows little explicit prediction, and can be rejected by evidence only if a change in X produces no response in Y. Therefore, a simple covariation hypothesis is both imprecise and difficult to test in a way that leads to improved formulation.

As a next form, let us suggest that Y is a (strong) monotonic increasing function of X. That statement means that if X increases, Y will always increase, and vice versa if X decreases. Monotonicity is more specific than simple covariation and admits more precise testing. Still, further specification is needed if we want to know more precisely how X influences Y. The most commonly specified monotonic form is linearity, at once a very precise and simple type of relation. Although it will be repetitious for many readers, let us examine linear relations in rate-of-change terms.

Equation 1 is a linear equation without error terms. As taught in standard courses on statistical method, a is called an "intercept," b a "slope"

$$Y_i = a + bX_i \qquad [1]$$

and i indicates that the equation applies to a population of cases, $i = 1, N$. Often the concepts of slope and intercept are poorly perceived from a theory construction point of view. Consider applying equation 1 to two different cases, case 1 and case 2, then subtracting the resulting equations.

$$Y_2 = a + bX_2$$
$$Y_1 = a + bX_1$$
$$\overline{Y_2 - Y_1 = b\ (X_2 - X_1\ )} \qquad [2]$$

Equation 2 states that the difference between the cases on variable Y is proportional to their differences on variable X. If 1 and 2 represent the same case measured at two different times, then the equation pertains to related changes in X and Y. That is, the change in Y is proportional to the change in X.

Since $X_2 - X_1$ could represent any time interval, let equation 2 be standardized by dividing by $X_2 - X_1$. Thus

$$\frac{Y_2 - Y_1}{X_2 - X_1} = b\ \frac{X_2 - X_1}{X_2 - X_1} = b \qquad [3]$$

If $Y_2 - Y_1$ is denoted ΔY, and $X_2 - X_1$ as ΔX, equation 3 becomes equation 4.

$$\frac{\Delta Y}{\Delta X} = b \qquad [4]$$

We now have a statement that the ratio of change in Y to change in X is constant (b). It does not matter what the values of X and Y might be prior to a change in X occurring; Y will always change in constant proportion to the change in X. The graph of such a relation, as the reader undoubtedly knows, is a straight line, as shown in Figure 1.

Can all relations reasonably be thought of as linear? Of course not. Psychophysics has demonstrated, for example, that the relation between physical stimulus and psychological perceived stimulus is not a linear, but a power relation (Stevens, 1957). Hamblin and his associates have explored the applicability of such a formulation to a wide variety of social relationships (Hamblin et al., 1973). What does a power curve look like? Equation 5 is a general example.

$$Y = bX^c \qquad [5]$$

Unfortunately, it is not as simple to develop an expression for $\Delta Y / \Delta X$ for a power curve as it is for a linear relation. Without delving into the requisite calculus, consider the power curve shown in Figure 2. If $\Delta Y / \Delta X$ is calculated for

Figure 1. Constant Rate of Change in Linear Relationships

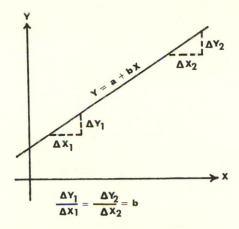

$$\frac{\Delta Y_1}{\Delta X_1} = \frac{\Delta Y_2}{\Delta X_2} = b$$

low values of X, it is obviously different from $\Delta Y / \Delta X$ calculated for high values of X. That is, the rate of change of Y with respect to a standardized change in X is not constant across the range of X values. The ratio $\Delta Y / \Delta X$ depends on X.

Suppose an infinitesimal slice of the curve in Figure 2 was examined in a powerful microscope. Theoretically, if the section were small enough, the curve segment would come out a straight line. Within that infinitesimal section, $\Delta Y / \Delta X$ would be constant. Differential calculus uses that notion to develop an infinitesimal analog to $\Delta Y / \Delta X$. That "differential" is written dY / dX and is read simply "dee Y dee X." It represents the rate of change of Y with respect to a standardized change of X anywhere on the curve. For the power curve of equation 5,

Figure 2. Variable Rate of Change in Curvilinear Relationships

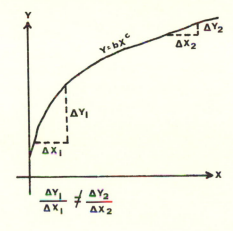

$$\frac{\Delta Y_1}{\Delta X_1} \neq \frac{\Delta Y_2}{\Delta X_2}$$

$$\frac{dY}{dX} = cbX^{b-1} \tag{6}$$

It is less important, for present purposes, to know how equation 6 was derived than it is to recognize that the rate of change of Y with respect to X depends upon X itself, a precise statement of our earlier informal conclusions.

Power curves represent only one of many possible nonlinear forms. Again without detailed pursuit, it is worth noting one other basic form. A family of curves of considerable utility is exponential equations. An example appears in equation 7, in which e is a mathematical constant, the base of natural logarithms.

$$Y = be^{cX} \tag{7}$$

The differential form of equation 7, representing the rate of change of Y with respect to X, depends on the value of Y, as shown in equation 8.

$$\frac{dY}{dX} = cY \tag{8}$$

The constant b in equation 7 turns out to be the value of Y before X began to change. A common use of such exponential forms (there are many variations) is to let the independent variable be time, usually replacing X with t. Then the rate of change of Y over time is a function of Y itself. Most growth processes, such as population growth, are of this form.

There are many nonlinear relationship forms other than power and exponential curves. The intention of this discussion is to be suggestive rather than exhaustive. In particular, it is likely that we shall misrepresent most social relationships unless we ask what factors influence the rate of change of a dependent variable with respect to one or more independent variables. Furthermore, we shall lose a major opportunity for generalization via subsuming specific relations under more general forms.

SOME COMMENTS ON LINEARITY

Before pursuing that statement further, it will help to ask why linearity is so often assumed and what consequences that assumption has. First, if there is not too pronounced nonlinearity in a graph of a relationship, a linear form is a reasonable first approximation. Especially when there is little basis for choosing specific theoretical nonlinear forms, linearity appears a reasonable assumption. Too often, though, there is no effort to check, either theoretically or empirically, on the appropriateness of the assumption.

A second basis for selecting linearity is that many structural relations are approximately linear in the major portion of the range of variables involved. That is, comparing across cases from a single time slice (cross-sectional data) often shows weak if any evidence for nonlinearity. There are notable exceptions, such as the relationship of income to many other variables. For many purposes, though, linearity represents a reasonable assumption for structural models.

There is a third, unfortunately more influential reason that linearity is so often assumed. When three or more variables are involved in a single system of relationships, if all relationships are assumed to be linear and additive, then a relatively simple set of equations can be written which contains all important deductions from the original assumptions. Further, if assumptions about prediction error and causal ordering are added to those of linearity and additivity, it is possible to relate all theoretical equations to correlations or covariances of measured variables. At that point, the linear regression coefficients (slopes) of the theory can all be estimated from actual data. Consequently, linear causal models are very powerful for *deducing* and *testing* consequences of theoretical formulations (see Blalock, 1971; Heise, 1975; Goldberger and Duncan, 1973). One need not even write out the equations, since others have done the work and provided computer packages such as SPSS to carry out analyses.

What has just been said is that too often linear models are used because of their deductive powers. Does that fact pose serious problems? Yes, especially in the limitations it creates for patching up a less-than-successful theory. If data do not fit the theoretical predictions very well, the fault could be—

1. that linearity does not obtain;
2. that error assumptions are incorrect;
3. that one or more crucial connections between variables were omitted;
4. that one or more variables not included in the theory are operating, confusing results;
5. that causal priorities among variables are not correctly specified.

When the only approach that the theorist feels comfortable with is linear structural modeling, then 1 in the preceding list will be rejected because it requires changing theoretical form. A predilection for the deductive power and simplicity of linear models forces assuming that fault lies elsewhere. Since faulty error assumptions are comparable to leaving out crucial variables, the common response to poor fit between theory and data is either to redraw the path diagram (new or redirected arrows) or to add variables.

The foregoing leaves one other route to theoretical revamping: that of concluding that measurement was inadequate. Note that if one assumes simply that measures are unreliable, there are no implications at the theoretical level.

On the other hand, if it is assumed that measurements were poor indicators of the underlying theoretical concepts, then one might return to the conceptual drawing board.

There is a current trend toward assuming that various measurement procedures simply provide alternative indicators of the same concept, leading to more complicated structural models but not necessarily to conceptual revamping. Again, the predilection for deductive power and manageable estimation and testing procedures tends to preclude serious theoretical reexamination.

BASIC EQUATIONS AND THEORIES OF RELATIONSHIPS

In contrast to an approach which attempts to incorporate a number of variables into a multiple regression formulation, as in path analysis, Hamblin has proposed emphasis on basic equations, involving only two or three variables usually. Let us examine, then augment, that approach. It will be convenient to quote or paraphrase portions of an earlier paper by Leik and Meeker (1974).

The type of theory to be developed always involves a basic relationship. There are five steps involved, the latter ones implying very extensive work. First, we choose a fairly simple question, such as how education influences income. For the time being, other variables can be ignored.

With the variables carefully selected, the second step is to determine as precisely as possible the curve which best relates them. There are two considerations here. The first is whether one curve provides better empirical fit than another; the second is whether the curve form has any theoretical significance or precedence. Diffusion processes, for example, can be expected to approximate logistic curves (Coleman, 1964; Dodd, 1955; Hamblin, 1973) while consequences of cumulative experience more probably provide logarithmic relationships and stimulus response processes follow power curves (Hamblin, 1971, 1973). (Leik and Meeker, 1974)

This second step will not produce a very general result, since the curve form will be established on limited data. Emphasis is on expressing the rate of change of one effect with respect to one cause, finding a general equation involving the variables of primary theoretical interest and having some plausible theoretical interpretation.

Once a basic equation has been found, there remain three steps in theory construction: providing theoretical interpretation of parameters of the equation, exploring generality of the equation, and developing a theory about the equation. Because interpretation of parameters is tied to the substantive sphere of the theory, a general discussion is at best somewhat vague. The primary concern is with translating the mathematical importance of the parameter (what it does in the equation) into a parallel substantive importance. One parameter in a learning curve, for example, might well be translated as learning ability; a parameter in a diffusion curve may be translated as the rate of "mixing" or "interacting" of the population. The best way to gain some feeling for translation of parameters is to study various discussions of existing mathematical models, for example, Bartholomew (1967), Berger, et al. (1974), Coleman (1964), Kemeney and Snell (1962), Hamblin (1973), Leik and Meeker (1974). Assuming that an equation and its interpretation has been worked out and found to fit a set of data (r^2 close to unity for predicting mean Y across the range of X), the next step is to explore that relationship under varying conditions of exogenous variables and for different populations. The question here is not so much whether the equation holds or does not hold as it is in what manner the parameters of the equation vary from one condition or population to another. If the equation is really a basic equation, in Hamblin's sense of an incipient law, then it will hold over a wide class of conditions and populations. If such generality of form is not found in subsequent work, it is likely either that the original formulation is faulty or that it represents a special case of some more complex form. In either event, lack of generality of form requires reexamination or reconceptualization of the basic process represented by the equation to determine a more widely applicable alternative.

Should the equation pass the crucial test of generality, it will be tempting to sit back and extoll the newly established "law." In our view, however, the real theory building task has only now been established. The next step is to *explore systematically the behavior of the parameters* of the equation under differing conditions and *to search for new equations which relate the parameters to the conditioning variables*. Thus it is not sufficient to assert simply that a parameter changes under variations in some exogenous variable, Z. The crucial task is to state precisely how Z influences the parameter. In this way, the basic or law-like relationship, which is the focus of research, is gradually built into a *theory of a relationship*. Both the process of theory development and the theorist's orientation to how variables explain things are different in this conception of theory building compared to the current causal model approach. (Leik and Meeker, 1974)

Note that, as Blalock pointed out, it is assumed that parameters will turn out not to be constant over all cases. Indeed, to overlook or minimize the importance of parameter variation under changes in exogenous conditions would be to miss a major opportunity for theoretical gain. To the extent that path-model-oriented theorists explore the same model for different populations or conditions, they have taken a first step in the indicated direction. The culmination of the process, though, should be establishing equations linking parameters to those external conditions.

It is obvious from the preceding that eventually a theory of a relationship contains as many variables as a path model can. Deductions and tests will be more difficult in many cases, and it may become necessary to work through data sequentially rather than seeking a single solution simultaneously for all parameters. Neither fact should be too discouraging because there are some unique benefits in the area of inductive development of theory.

The clearest characteristic of theories of relationships is that the basic equation form differs for theoretical reasons from one problem to the next. Consequently, when two areas of exploration produce comparable basic equations, there is a good possibility that they represent special cases of a more general form. That is, the *equation form becomes a clue to generalization*, to the necessary inductive side of retroduction.

A parallel consequence is that those variables which serve similarly in a basic equation or have a comparable effect on parameters of a basic equation are good candidates for conceptual generalization. *Variables that do the same type of job in the same type of process are possibly subforms of a single concept.*

Note that linear models provide no opportunity for either of the foregoing generalizations. All equations are linear—hence there are no subsets of similar form which provide leads to induction. Similarly, all variables act in the same way in linear models, except for their status as endogenous or exogenous. Further exploration of the uses of variables in equations should help clarify this point.

AFFECTING VARIABLES OR RELATIONSHIPS

One of the major differences between the theory-of-equations approach and path analysis concerns the use of conditioning or qualifying variables. All equations in multiple regression form specify variables affecting other variables. If interaction is present or theoretically expected, it is possible to include product terms as predictors of a dependent variable, but those terms are analytically treated as separate variables.

Assume that we began with a single linear equation showing Y dependent on X_1, then decided another variable, X_2, needed to be included in the theory. If all relations are linear, we have three options. First, X_2 can be added to X_1 to predict Y, making an ordinary multiple regression equation. Second, X_2 can be treated as multiplicative in its effects, resulting in the addition of an X_1X_2 product term. Third, if both approaches are assumed, then X_2 and X_1X_2 will both appear. Equations 9 through 11 illustrate these options.

$$Y = a + b_1X_1 + b_2X_2 \tag{9}$$

or

$$Y = a + b_1X_1 + b_2X_1X_2 \tag{10}$$

The combined form is

$$Y = a + b_1X_1 + b_2X_2 + b_3X_1X_2 \tag{11}$$

It is difficult to find a theoretically meaningful interpretation of the interaction terms in equations 10 and 11. In terms of rate of change, Y will change proportionate to changes in X_1 and X_2 and the product of their changes. Let us consider an alternative way of arriving at an interaction term.

Beginning with the basic X_1, Y equation, let us express the *slope* of Y on X_1 as a function of the new variable, X_2.

$$Y = a_1 + b_1 X_1 \qquad\qquad [12]$$

$$b_1 = a_2 + b_2 X_2 \qquad\qquad [13]$$

so that

$$Y = a_1 + b_1' X_1 + b_2' X_1 X_2 \qquad\qquad [14]$$

where $b_1' = a_2 b_1$ and $b_2' = b_1 b_2$. Obviously equation 14 is the same as equation 10, except for the way it can be interpreted. The equivalence of the two equations is due to both equation 12 and equation 13 being linear. It is also possible that a_1 could be expressed as a function of X_2. If both a_1 and b_1 are linear functions of X_2, then the result will be equivalent to equation 11.

If nonlinearity is admitted, much wider range of equations can result. For example, if the basic equation is exponential and the exponent coefficient of the equation—c, as shown in equation 7—is a linear function of another variable, X_2, then we could write

$$Y = b_1 e^{cX_1} \qquad\qquad [15]$$

$$c = a + b_2 X_2 \qquad\qquad [16]$$

These equations say that Y changes proportionate to its current value, as shown previously ($dY / dX_1 = cY$). They also say that the proportion, c, changes proportionate to any changes in X_2.

The result of substituting equation 16 into equation 15 produces a cumbersome exponent, but taking logarithms of both sides of that equation provides equation 17.

$$\ln Y = \ln b_1 + a X_1 + b_2 X_1 X_2 \qquad\qquad [17]$$

which looks just like equation 10 or 14 except that the dependent variable is logarithmic. It would indeed be difficult to find equation 17 by usual methods, or to interpret it if it were stumbled upon by chance, unlikely as that event would be. Interpretation is simple given the derivation of such a form from equations 15 and 16, and estimation of the parameters is quite easy.

The principal difference between approaches which should be recognized is the sensitivity, when working on a theory of a relationship, to diversity of forms which a basic equation can take, to different theoretical implications of those diverse forms, and to the variety of ways in which other variables can influence that basic equation. Clearly, the options for improving theoretical form and for discovering comparability which might suggest inductive generalization are far greater given the approach just discussed. Equally clearly, deductions from such a theory require more sophisticated mathematics, and procedures for estimating parameters and testing theoretical form are more difficult. It is hardly desirable to lose deductive power, but surely it would be desirable to gain inductive ability.

CHANGES OVER TIME—AN ILLUSTRATION

One of Blalock's criteria of usefulness, as noted at the outset, is that the theory contain manipulable explanatory variables, so that policy might be guided by the theory. An important consideration for that goal is that the theory be able to handle change over time produced by manipulation of such variables. Change over time returns us again to rate of change conceptualization, and to nonlinearity.

It can be argued that no process can remain linear over extended periods of time. Eventually linear functions will force dependent variables to exceed all reasonable boundaries. For short time periods linearity might be a reasonable first approximation, but the general consequence of change in any system is to set off events or processes which either augment or inhibit further change. These effects feed back on the rate of change of the dependent variable, systematically altering that rate over time or over the range of one or more of the system variables.

Given an orientation to change over time, an emphasis on policy applicability should create a renewed interest in sociology in time series data. We have had decades of urging to do longitudinal research, and there are now some longitudinal studies. Most such studies, however, provide only two to four time points. That is hardly enough to establish curve forms over time.

If analyses of time series are contemplated, it should be apparent that a theory-of-relationship approach is well suited. First find an appropriate basic equation form. The divorce curve over duration of marriage shown in Figure 3 provides a good example. A detailed analysis of that type of curve can be found in Leik (1977). The data are from California as reported by Schoen (1975).

To avoid lengthy discussion and complex equations, let us note informally the following characteristics of Figure 3.

1. The curve starts low, accelerates quickly, then reaches a peak at about year four. If we stopped at that point, the curve looks like an exponential growth process.
2. Beyond year four, the curve declines steadily at a decreasing rate. That segment looks like a declining exponential curve.

Figure 4 shows the appropriate types of curve for a and b separately, with their differential (i.e., rate of change) equations. It turns out that a single curve consisting of the product of those two curves fits Figure 3 very well ($r^2 = .987$).

**Figure 3. Probability of Divorce for All Males,
by Duration of Marriage**

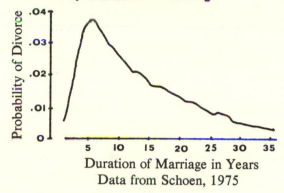

Duration of Marriage in Years
Data from Schoen, 1975

So far we have taken steps 1 (choose the variables) and 2 (find an appropriate curve). As to interpretation, it is plausible (though not necessarily compelling at this stage of knowledge) to argue that the probability of divorce declines proportionately with each further year invested in the marriage (part b) and the parameters of that part of the curve pertain to how high a probability existed at the outset and how rapidly the probability declined each year. That is, one parameter is risk at marriage and one is the effect of continuing success and investment.

Figure 4. Divorce Probability as a Product of Two Processes

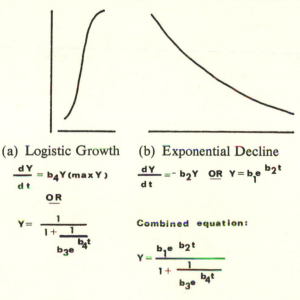

(a) Logistic Growth

$$\frac{dY}{dt} = b_4 Y (\max Y)$$

OR

$$Y = \frac{1}{1 + \frac{1}{b_3 e^{b_4 t}}}$$

(b) Exponential Decline

$$\frac{dY}{dt} = -b_2 Y \quad \underline{OR} \quad Y = b_1 e^{b_2 t}$$

Combined equation:

$$Y = \frac{b_1 e^{b_2 t}}{1 + \frac{1}{b_3 e^{b_4 t}}}$$

The growth curve portion (part a) seems to represent growth over the first few years of the full problem potential of the marriage. The parameters here represent the extent of evident problems at marriage and the rate at which those problems grow to maximum. In short, all parameters appear sensible.

What about generality of the curve? The Schoen data shown in Figure 3 represent average probabilities. Fortunately, Schoen's report also contains separate curves for twelve different ages at first marriage and for both males and females. One general equation, as just described, was separately fitted to these distributions with r^2 values from .735 to .953. At least for these data, the curve seems general.

The last step was limited by having only sex and age at marriage available as variables affecting parameters. Since divorce really involves both sexes, and their curves are nearly identical, only age at marriage was explored. Interestingly enough, three of the four parameters of the general curve, estimated for each of the twelve age-at-marriage curves, show apparent systematic change over age at marriage.

The maximum probability of divorce at outset is a clear power curve. As age at marriage increases (beginning at sixteen for females, eighteen for males), maximum probability of divorce drops rapidly but at a decreasing rate. Youngest marriages have the highest maximum; oldest the lowest.

The rate at which the divorce probability drops over duration of marriage appears constant for all ages at marriage. It is the only parameter not affected by age at marriage. The amount of potential problems which are evident at marriage appears exponentially dependent upon age at marriage, so that young marriages are cognizant of only a small portion of their potential difficulties. Finally, the rate at which problems grow during the first years of marriage is a somewhat more complicated exponential form.

When age at marriage is used to predict the parameters of the general equation, so that one general fit is attempted simultaneously for all twenty-four sex-by-age-at-marriage curves, r^2 values are still impressive: .624 to .942, averaging .840. Obviously, not all the data are well predicted, but 864 different probabilities are rather well re-created by one basic equation whose parameters are influenced by just one additional variable. If other data, such as race, religion, or status, were available, it would be reasonable to expect considerable improvement.

SUMMARY

There are many ways to analyze time series data, from the atheoretical approach of the Box-Jenkins (1976) models to highly complex theoretical formulations. If we are to pursue how trends over time are going to be affected by social or policy change, we need to begin use of such procedures. It seems to me that starting with a basic equation, then exploring and theorizing about its parameters, offers our best approach.

Whether dynamic or structural, policy relevant or not, our work cannot continue to ignore the inductive side of the retroductive process. By all means, let us keep all the deductive and testing power we can. Let us not blind ourselves by thinking that those are the only important aspects of theory building.

PART IV

TOWARD A
REFLEXIVE SOCIOLOGY

Perceptive attempts to gain insight into the activities of sociologists and of the discipline are both a boon and a burden. Indeed, as some sociologists have suggested, the dicipline's willingness to cast a cold eye on its own doings has not surpassed the willingness of any other group or individual. But although it may be difficult, even painful, sociologists must look at themselves sociologically. Methodological dualism must be set aside and sociologists must become both willing and able to assess what they do and why they do it. Employing the assumption of the necessity of a reflexive sociology, the articles in this section turn inward and begin the move toward self-awareness.

In his article "Toward a Clarification of the Interrelationship Between Theory and Research: Its Forms and Implications," William Snizek looks at the extent and nature of the relationships that empirically exist between any given theoretical orientation in sociology and coterminous methodological techniques. Employing a four-category typology based primarily on levels of analysis, individuals' theoretical orientations were classified as realist, quasi-realist, quasi-nominalist, or nominalist. The relevant question: Is there any systematic covariation between the aforementioned theoretical perspectives and (1) the type of data collection device employed and (2) the analysis technique employed?

Snizek's research, based upon 1,434 articles appearing in nine major sociological journals, concludes that a realist orientation is most often found to be used in conjunction with comparative-historical methods and less powerful analysis techniques. Conversely, the nominalist perspective is shown to have an affinity for the use of questionnaires, census data, and more statistically powerful analysis modes. Further, the nature of the aforementioned relationships tends to be asymmetrical depending upon the point at which one enters the research circle. Specifically, using asymmetric measures of association, Snizek finds some evidence to suggest that the theoretical orientation determines the data-collection mode, but that the analysis technique determines the theoretical orientation.

What are the implications and the problems for this theory-method fit? To the extent that the asymmetric nature of the analysis-theory link is valid, sociology as a discipline, Snizek feels, is moving toward the study of psychological subject matter. Further, to the extent that the theory-method covariation deviates from "optimum best fit," Snizek argues that various types of systematic fallacies or errors become increasingly likely. In particular, a less than optimal fit between a nominalist theoretical orientation and the use of group data can easily result in problems of the ecological fallacy variety. Conversely, when a staunch realist tries to make inferences to the group on the basis of individual data, the so-called Nosnibor fallacy becomes a problem. As viewed by Snizek, one potential solution to these kinds of problems is to "optimize" the theory-method fit. To accomplish this optimization requires an explicit recognition on the part of the research of the meta-sociological choices being made.

Edward Tiryakian addresses himself to a different aspect of sociological self-awareness: How can sociologists better understand the development of their own discipline? In the pages of "The Significance of Schools in the Development of Sociology," Tiryakian presents a Kuhnian-like schema which suggests that the development of socioloy has been neither smooth nor cumulative. Rather, the progressive development has been very irregular and discrete. Using the term "school" in a more stringent sense than Kuhn's notion of a scientific community, Tiryakian views the evolution of the discipline as simply the impact of periodic inspirations (usually methodological) from a very limited number of influential "schools." Hence if the objective is to understand more fully the development of sociology, the chronological-order approach (i.e., the great-man or the intellectual-history approach and the sociohistorical approach) needs to be supplemented by an analysis of the impact of various schools in sociology.

As conceptualized by Tiryakian, a school is a real entity. It is composed of a group of intellectuals whose inception and development period share a high degree of temporal and spatial overlap. The primary integating component of the school is a charismatic leader. It is from this founder-leader that a basic conception of reality, and an idea of how to approach such a reality, receives its genesis. Subsequently, the founder builds an entourage and jointly they formulate a larger, more highly structured paradigm. At still a later stage, the immediate entourage, as well as lay converts from the profession, undertake actual application of the paradigm to the understanding of sundry social phenomena. If the activities of a particular charismatic leader, his immediate followers, and peripheral patrons and auxiliaries are successful in terms of intergenerational socialization into the paradigm, the stage has been set for development (or at least change) in the discipline.

According to Tiryakian, the necessary components to produce successful schools in sociology have occurred only three times in "modern" times. These schools correspond roughly to three major sociological generations: pre-World War I, the interwar period, and the period from the late 1940s to the late 1960s. The schools are identified as the Durkheimian School, the Chicago School (largely under the leadership of Park), and the Parsonian School. After identifying the schools, Tiryakian goes on to compare and contrast them in terms of the aforementioned schema and to suggest deeper metascientific dimensions of schools that should be addressed.

In "Human Rights, Reflectivity, and the Sociology of Knowledge," Gideon Sjoberg and Ted Vaughan examine issues that they perceive as being pivotal to theory building and research, but also to humankind at large. Specifically, Sjoberg and Vaughan are concerned with the lack of attention given to the fundamental issues of ethics and human rights by contemporary American sociologists. The explanation for this inattention is found in a misplaced commitment to the "natural science model" and to a particular type of "positivism." A commitment to such a logico-deductive model forces attention on certain limited kinds of problems, specifically, those problems that lend themselves well to certain basic assumptions about the nature of reality. For example, belief that the social world is preexistent to, and independent of, the researcher's own construction of it will cause inordinate attention to be given to issues of quantifiability and value neutrality. In short, if attention is focused on the aforementioned kinds of problems, the result will be a forcing of fictitious order on social life. As a result of the forced ordering, reflectivity becomes impossible. Herein lies the real problem.

If the predominant research paradigm obviates the ability of sociologists to reflect backward and subsequently to make judgments as to how things should be, then alternative modes of action or alternative futures become impossible. Further, the identifiable alternatives to the natural science model (e.g., the Frankfurt School of critical theorists, the historicists, and the ethnomethodologists) are all inadequate when it comes to coping with issues of ethics and human rights. Sjoberg and Vaughan attempt to outline a remedy by sketching an alternative to the natural science model. The alternative model explicitly includes a realization of the social nature of the human mind and the necessity and ability, within structurally determined limits, of sociologists to be reflexive. Given this newfound reflexive capability, it then becomes the moral obligation of sociologists to examine puissant organizational structures that serve to inhibit human rights through their ability to curtail reflective thought. The methodological tool that will allow such an examination is "counterstream analysis" (e.g., the creation of alternative futures).

The essays included in this section give a vivid picture of what can happen if sociologists turn their perspective inward and analyze their own profession. Heretofore unexplicated assumptions and practices are addressed and their shortcomings discussed. Only through such reflexive efforts, though painful in many instances, can true or complete communication among scholars become a reality. And only through such communication can the discipline expect to progress.

William E. Snizek

TOWARD A CLARIFICATION OF THE INTERRELA- TIONSHIP BETWEEN THEORY AND RESEARCH: ITS FORM AND IMPLICATIONS

Contemporary efforts in sociology to delineate the nature of the interrelationship between theory and research owe a large debt to two essays written by Robert Merton (1957:85-117). Merton saw theory as having a guiding and codifying effect on research; research, in turn, was seen as reformulating, redefining, refocusing, and otherwise updating existing theory. More recent attempts (e.g., Snizek, 1975; Ritzer, 1975a, 1975b; and Martindale's essay in this volume) have tried to elaborate on Merton's problems: That is, specifically how do theory and research affect one another? How, for example, might the utilization of a particular theoretical orientation or perspective affect one's choice or use of various methodological techniques and procedures, and vice versa? That is the issue to be addressed in this essay. Let me begin the discussion by briefly summarizing some of my own findings regarding the matter (Snizek, 1975, 1976).

CLASSIFICATION OF THEORETICAL AND METHODOLOGICAL ORIENTATIONS

In an attempt to specify the nature of the interrelationship between theory and research, I spent three years initially categorizing, rechecking, and independently validating[1] the theoretical and methodological procedures employed by numerous sociologists in the journal articles which they authored. In all, 1,434 articles, appearing in nine major sociological journals and covering the period 1950-70, were classified.[2]

Using a typology first suggested by Warriner (1956), and later elaborated by Willits (1965), authors' theoretical orientations were differentiated into four general categories: realist, quasi realist, quasi nominalist, and nominalist. The realist theoretical orientation was viewed as one which primarily focused on the study of group properties and the discovery of structural laws. Each of the two "quasi" orientations was used to categorize those authors whose theoretical perspectives were essentially social psychological in nature. Authors using group properties in order to explain individual phenomena were classified as quasi realists; those using individual-level variables to explain group-level properties were categorized as quasi nominalists. Nominalists were considered as having an essentially psychological theoretical orientation. To quote Fallding (1968:47-48), "By 'nominalism' I mean the view that only psychological processes have a reality . . . interaction has no properties of its own apart from the properties of the individuals who mutually influence one another."

By way of summary and parallelism, the realist theoretical category just outlined is directly synonomous with Ritzer's (1975a, 1975b) "social factist" designation. Similarly, the two "quasi" positions, when combined without regard to the causal priority of the variables involved, are identical to Ritzer's "social definitionist" category. And, finally, the nominalist classification is Ritzer's "social behaviorist" designation. These similarities, in the taxonomic schemas of Ritzer and myself, may help to clarify the exact nature of the categories used in the study currently under discussion.

Regarding research methodology, two measures were used to index the relative degrees of empiricism of the authors whose works were surveyed. First, using categories suggested by both Thomlinson (1965:40-60) and Weinstein and Weinstein (1974:85-109), authors' principal techniques of data collection were classified according to the following categories: (1) historical method, using primarily library materials synthesized by the researcher; (2) informants; (3) observational techniques; (4) interviews; (5) questionnaires; (6) census materials, official output records, and police statistics; and (7) experimental techniques of either a laboratory or field variety. Secondly, distinctions were made based on the authors' use (or not) of various statistical tests of significance and/or measures of association. As in the case of the categories used to classify authors' data collection methods, a continuum was constructed, ranging from the least to the most empirical modes of data analysis. The categories comprising such a continuum were as follows: (1) no use of tests of significance and/or association; (2) use of qualitative statistics on either nominally or ordinally measured variables (e.g., chi square, gamma, Yule's Q); (3) the combined use of qualitative and quantitative variables (e.g., analysis of variance, omega); (4) use of quantitative variables with assumed interval measurement (e.g., correlation-regression analysis, path analysis, beta coefficients).

It should be noted that, in a strict or traditional sense (Kant, 1964), the term "empiricism" has been used to denote a reliance on experience and observation (Munch, 1957). The general nonempirical-empirical continua employed in this study, however, are based upon a broader meaning of the term. As used here, "empiricism" includes each research technique or procedure's amenability to, or use of, precise measurement or quantification, the ease or difficulty encountered in reproducing or replicating results, and the overall degree of intuitive interpretation required of the researcher in the utilization of data collected or analyzed through the use of such techniques or procedures. Each of the two continua described previously was shown, upon their use, to have both high face and predictive validity.[3]

OBSERVED COALESCENCE IN AUTHORS' THEORETICAL AND METHODOLOGICAL ORIENTATIONS

My analysis showed that authors who used a realist theoretical orientation in their writings were significantly more likely to employ relatively nonempirical research methods. By contrast, authors classified as nominalists in their theoretical perspective were found to utilize various of the more empirical research methods. Thus 54.7 percent of the realists, in contrast to only 9.2 percent of the nominalists, utilized historical procedures as their principal method of data collection. On the other hand, questionnaires, census, and experimental data collection methods were used by 63.8 percent of the nominalists, as opposed to only 19.7 percent of the realists (Snizek, 1975:Table 1). This same affinity was further evident when the types of statistical procedures utilized are related to authors' theoretical orientations. For example, 71.3 percent of the realists, as compared with only 25.5 percent of the nominalists, used no measure of statistical significance and/or association in their research. By contrast, 45.4 percent of the nominalists, as compared with only 3.2 percent of the realists, were shown to use correlational or path analysis in the analysis of their data (Snizek, 1975:Table 2).

Apart from the foregoing pattern, a greater tendency was shown for authors' theoretical orientations to determine ($\lambda_a = .290$), rather than be determined by ($\lambda_\beta = .061$), their method of data collection. By contrast, the methods of analysis employed by the authors of the articles surveyed were found more often to determine ($\lambda_\beta = .143$) the choice of a theoretical orientation than to be the result of a prior theoretical orientation ($\lambda_a = .049$). In brief, the interplay between theory and research, quite apart from its form, would appear to depend greatly upon the particular stage of the given research. When addressing the *data collection* stage of the research process, one's theoretical orientation appears to determine the method used. When the *data analysis* stage of the research process is considered, one's theoretical orientation was shown to be determined by, rather than to be the determinant of, the technique of data analysis selected.

POSSIBLE EXPLANATIONS FOR THE OBSERVED RELATIONSHIP BETWEEN THEORY AND RESEARCH

In order to place the observed relationship between theory and research in perspective, several characteristics of the realist, as well as the nominalist position, need to be stressed. First, it must be remembered that a realist orientation focuses on group properties, or structural phenomena if you will, rather than on individual attributes, as done by nominalists. Paul Lazarsfeld (1959:69) terms the former "contextual properties" of groups, the latter "primary properties" of individuals. By way of example, being a teacher in a conservative college or a worker in a large plant are contextual properties; being young or an extrovert are considered primary properties. Second, it should be kept in mind that the realist position is highly "inferential" in nature. Structure is indexed, not directly manifest. Thus Durkheim (1965), in his study of suicide, viewed individuals' marital statuses, religious affiliations, and the like, as being indicative of their varying degrees of integration within a group. Durkheim's conclusions regarding group solidarity or the integration of individuals into the group were arrived at in an inferential manner.

Given these characteristics, it is understandable that those persons who have chosen to operate on what is generally looked upon to be a more concrete,[4] less inferential level of analysis (i.e., the nominalist, as opposed to the realist) will also opt to employ the most precise (statistically powerful and sophisticated) research instruments possible (i.e., those of an empirical variety). Stated in terms of a cognitive consistency framework, to the extent that an individual researcher feels uneasy in studying emergent group properties (a realist mode of inquiry), so too is that individual likely to experience an uneasiness in using what are generally looked upon as less precise or less powerful research techniques (i.e., those representing a low degree of empiricism). Conversely, researchers who chose to study group properties and engage in a highly inferential mode of inquiry would appear least likely to feel compelled to use research methods and techniques of a highly empirical nature. In short, whereas the quantitatively oriented empiricist is often hesitant to engage in an interpretation of his data and instead would prefer to let the figures "speak" for themselves, the nonempirically oriented researcher must proceed in a largely logico-deductive manner and continually draw inferences from the available data. Thus the inferential nature of the realist perspective seriously diminishes the likelihood of its use by researchers bent on employing a highly empirical mode of inquiry.

On yet another level, the realist-nonempirical and nominalist-empirical linkages noted may, in part, be viewed as a function of both the *scope* and *defi-*

nition of the problems studied. Regarding scope, researchers of a realist theoretical orientation have tended to be *macro* in their focus, whereas nominalists have generally been *micro* in range. Take, for example, the often evoked societal emphases of individuals such as Sorokin, Parsons, Merton, Levy, and Williams, in contrast to the micro-perspective of Lewin, Cartwright, Heider, Hare, and others. Owing in large measure to a scarcity of quantitative data on macro-scale issues, the well-documented affinity of macro-analysis for a largely nonempirical approach[5] (and, conversely, of micro-investigation for highly empirical techniques) results in a residue of nonempirical realism (and empirical nominalism).

The way in which one defines the problem, and hence the variables under investigation, also bears upon the observed relationships between theoretical and methodological perspectives. That is to say, sociologists interested in engaging in a realist form of inquiry must manipulate their data, albeit often gathered from individuals, as an index of social structure. "Age, for example, may be treated as a personal trait by the nominalist, or as an aspect of social structure, such as potential for interaction, role demands, or experience, etc., by a realist" (Snizek, 1975:426). The choice as to how a variable will be used or interpreted resides with the researcher. Often, however, data on individuals are not analyzed in a realist manner. To quote Rossi (1959:149):

Our best-developed and most frequently employed techniques are based ultimately on data gathered from individuals. . . . The simplest, and, for that reason, the most attractive way of analyzing these data is in terms of individual differences. . . .

This last is perhaps the most serious problem facing the sociologist who wishes to study social organization. . . .

By way of summary, several possible explanations have been advanced for the relationships shown to exist between a realist theoretical orientation and the use of relatively nonempirical methodological procedures, as well as between nominalism and the use of highly empirical research techniques. Interestingly enough, further evidence and documentation regarding the existence of such linkages can be seen in the history of sociological thought. Martindale (1960), for example, in summarizing *The Nature and Types of Sociological Theory*, uses this idea to account for the eventual demise of the early positivistic organicist school. Basically, its downfall is attributed to an inconsistency between the organicist's theoretical and methodological orientations. That is to say, its organismic view of society, which represented a realist mode of orientation, was incompatible with a positivistic methodological approach. Similarly, the attempts of various proponents of pluralistic behaviorism, such as Chapin, Giddings, and Tarde, have met with, at best, limited success in attempting to use highly empirical or inductive techniques in studying collective behavior.

IMPLICATIONS

If the affinity between theory and research proposed in the foregoing is correct, and if the explanations offered to account for the relationship have some validity, a number of implications can be drawn.

The Discipline at Large

Given the well-documented (Brown and Gilmartin, 1969; Patel, 1972) trend in sociology toward the utilization of increasingly more empirical research procedures, the findings of this study imply the prime focus of sociology to be moving away from the study of group properties and structural laws, and instead toward the investigation of individual-level phenomena and properties. As long as American sociology continues to equate "scientific" sophistication with the blind employment of increasingly more empirical research methods and techniques, the sociological perspective is likely to move closer to that of psychology. As Blau (1969:52-53) has observed:

When the empirical measures used in sociological analysis refer, as they usually do, to individual conduct, such as committing suicide or getting divorced, special procedures must be devised to ascertain the associations between social facts . . . and not inadvertently to substitute for them associations between attributes of individuals.

The basic theoretical thrust of sociology toward a more psychological posture is further accentuated by the previously reported finding that authors' modes of statistical analysis were more likely to affect, than to be affected by, the theoretical perspective chosen. In short, the methodological tail, defined in terms of data analysis, appears, in many instances, to be wagging the theoretical dog. Or, as Coser and Bierstedt independently have observed, "the methodological tail wags the substantive dog" (Coser, 1975:692), and "methods would be considered the independent and substantive issues the dependent variable" (Bierstedt, 1974:316). When the methodological tail wagging the discipline is one of extreme empiricism and unbridled quantification, the documented linkages of nominalism-empiricism and realist-nonempiricism become even more telling.

Obviously, the employment, by various sociologists, of a more psychological theoretical orientation will delight some and appall others. That kind of evaluation is not at issue in this essay, for it concerns the rendering of a metasociological value judgment, the nature of which each of us as sociologists must, in time, make. What is pertinent is the fact that a basic shift in the theoretical focus of the discipline is occurring; as sociologists, we need to be made aware of this and its causes. Hopefully, the discussion thus far has served to do that. It now remains for each of us to consider the following questions: Is "scientific" sophistication necessarily equatable with the use of increasingly empirical research techniques, or can alternative, less empirical research procedures be used with comparable utility in furthering the "science" of sociology? Can appropriate care be taken, and procedures developed, so that data collected from individuals can be used to make inferences about groups concerning social facts? And, finally, can the assumptions underlying various sophisticated statistical procedures be made so evident as to avoid the inadvertent compromising of one's theoretical orientation? The answers each of us gives to these and other such questions will, in part, affect our metasociological judgments as concerns the choice of both a theoretical and a methodological perspective.

Understanding Sociology's Intellectual History

What we might call the principle of an *optimum best fit* between theoretical and methodological approaches can be used to comprehend better the particular career patterns of individual sociologists and, in turn, affords a means of understanding and interpreting the overall history of the discipline. Assuming that a majority of writers eventually arrive at an intellectual rapprochement or consistency in their theoretical-methodological approach, the documented affinity of the realist-nonempirical and nominalist-empirical orientations offers a means by which an author's works can be placed in proper perspective. Supplemented by a knowledge of factors such as time and type of prior academic training, outside funding dictates, and the identity of collaborators, one has a basis for understanding the theoretical-methodological approach already taken, or likely to be taken, by an author.

Note the career of George Homans as an example. According to Whitaker (1965:137), in works such as *English Villagers of the Thirteenth Century* (1941) and *The Human Group* (1950), Homans attempted to be both an empiricist and a functionalist. Given the realist bent of functionalism, such a pairing of theoretical and methodological approaches represents an inconsistency or poor fit. Thus one would expect a change in future works of either his theoretical or methodological stance (i.e., an attempt to bring theory in line with method, or vice versa). In Homans' case, he chose to alter his theoretical stance from realist to nominalist while keeping a rigid empiricist posture. Witness his avowed nominalist perspective as seen in works such as *Social Behavior: Its Elementary Forms* (1961), *Sentiments and Activities* (1962), "Bringing Men Back In" (1964), and "The Relevance of Psychology to the Explanation of Social Phenomena" (1970), plus his continued emphasis on the use of empirical methods such as operant conditioning and the experimental laboratory design.

Although Homans changed his theoretical orientation from realist to nominalist to get a better fit, Parsons would appear to have done just the opposite. In his earlier works, such as *The Structure of Social Action* (1937), Parsons advocated an antipositivist methodology coupled with a voluntaristic theory of action. As in the case of Homans, Parsons chose to change his theoretical stance in order to fit his method better. Thus in his later works, *Economy and Society* (1956), *Societies: Evolutionary and Comparative Perspectives* (1966), and *The System of Modern Societies* (1971), Parsons, although still nonempirical in his method, changed to the highly realistic theoretical perspective of macro-functionalism.

Similar metasociological analyses have been done on the careers of other leading sociologists. Of particular note is Braungart's (1976) essay on Weber, "A Metatheoretical Note on Max Weber's Political Sociology," and that of Stark (1961) on Spencer regarding his "Three Sociologies." Recent writings by Ritzer (1975a, 1975b) also represent signal attempts at delineating various intraparadigmatic theory-method linkages illustrated by the works of various exemplars. And although I disagree (Snizek, 1976) with Ritzer's theorizing about those linkages and his rather one-dimensional (i.e., unchanging) portrayal of various exemplars, I nevertheless applaud his investigating the interrelationship between theory and methods. Only if such research continues can we gain insight into the past, present, and future direction of sociology.

Toward this end, we probably need to increase our perspective to include various other orientations and procedures of a similar, though by no means identical, nature. Careful examination of the ontological (what to study) and epistemological (how to study) distinctions projected in Table 1 may reveal a tendency for linkages or coalescences to occur *within*, rather than *between*, columns. If realists are more likely to use relatively nonempirical research techniques, as discussed earlier, may they not also be prone toward deductive reasoning, use conceptual rather than operational definitions, and stress the importance of validity over reliability? Notice, it is *not* being suggested that realists fail to use operational definitions, nor that they have *no* interest in issues of reliability. Rather, it is being proposed that realists or holists will have a *greater tendency* to employ the aforementioned research methods and techniques, in contrast to their polar opposites.

In making such a proposal I am not arguing in favor of some form of syllogism or determinism. Unquestionably, attempts have been made throughout the course of sociology to combine or wed various of the polar opposites shown in Table 1. Take, for example, the positivistic organicist school of thought in early sociology (Martindale, 1960), Weber's attempts at combining prediction and explanation to yield understanding, and of linking objective possibility and causal relevance (meaning) in the construction of ideal types (Weber, 1949), or Znaniecki's attempts at establishing the technique of analytic induction (Robinson, 1951). For reasons too detailed to discuss in this essay, various of these attempts at synthesis have failed or have met with, at best, limited acceptance and success. In part, the explanation may once again come back to the notion of *optimum best fit*.

The Fallacies of Inquiry

If various theoretical orientations have an affinity or coalescence to certain research techniques or procedures—as I have presented evidence, in the form

Table 1.

VARIATIONS ON, AND CONCEPTS RELATED TO, THE DISTINCTIONS OF REALIST-NOMINALIST, AND NONEMPIRICAL-EMPIRICAL

Ontological Distinctions	
Nominalist	Realist
Mechanistic	Organismic
Elementarist	Holist
Individual	Group
Personality system	Social system

Epistemological Distinctions

General Methods or Approach	
Empiricist	Nonempiricist or rationalist
Positivist	Antipositivist
Inductive	Deductive
Quantitative	Qualitative
Outside observer	Subjective investigator

Specific Techniques or Practices	
Nominal definitions	Real definitions
Empirical closure	Logical closure
Part-type concepts	Analytic elements
Operational definitions	Conceptual definitions
Stress reliability	Stress validity

of both logical arguments and data—one might expect also to find patterning regarding errors in analysis. Put otherwise, to the extent that one's theoretical-methodological posture deviates from "best fits" or consistent positions, the likelihood of committing various fallacies or errors, whether logical or statistical, may increase dramatically. This is illustrated by Table 2.

The three major cells of the table (extending diagonally from upper left to lower right) were shown, by far, to be the most frequently employed combinations of theory and methods (Snizek, 1975). Furthermore, these pairings of theoretical and methodological orientations represent logically consistent linkages between theory and research. The remaining six cells (not boxed in) of the table indicate inconsistent pairings of theory and research. It is my suggestion that, by this fact, they afford the greatest probability of yielding questionable results or, at least, the committing of various kinds of errors in analysis.

Table 2.

POTENTIAL FALLACIES AND PITFALLS STEMMING FROM THE
ERRANT FIT BETWEEN THEORY AND METHODS

Theoretical Orientation	Methodological Approach		
	Low Empirical	Moderately Empirical	Highly Empirical
Realist	Consistent	Nosnibor fallacy	Nosnibor fallacy
Quasi realist Quasi nominalist	Errors of dummy-variable analysis	Consistent	Errors of collapsing data
Nominalist	Ecological fallacy	Ecological fallacy	Consistent

The lower left-hand corner of Table 2 indicates a type situation in which a psychological-theoretical orientation is being used in conjunction with a relatively low level of empiricism. Using grouped, semigrouped, and individual or ungrouped data, as a continuum of increasing empiricism, grouped data are here being employed in combination with a nominalist theoretical approach. In short, grouped data are being employed in hopes of explaining phenomena at the individual level. Without extremely careful interpretation (cf. Cartwright, 1969), such a condition can easily lead to what W. S. Robinson (1950), Selvin (1960), and others refer to as an Ecological fallacy. Such an error is simply drawing inferences about an individual's behavior on the bases of coincidence of two grouped properties. For example, even though countries with high proportions of Protestants may have high rates of suicide compared with nations with mainly Catholic populations, these data do not necessarily support the conclusion that religious affiliation is the cause of suicide, since there are no data presented on the religious affiliations of *each individual suicide* victim.

The temptation to commit an Ecological fallacy also seems likely in that circumstance depicted in the cell to the immediate right of that just discussed. Albeit a slightly better fit between theory and method than the cell to its left, the investigator whose research falls within this category is attempting, once again, to make nominalist-level inferences based upon data other than those of an individual or ungrouped nature.

The inverse of the situations just described can be found in the upper right and center cells of Table 2. Here the so-called Nosnibor fallacy (in honor of W. S. Robinson, spelled backward) is likely to occur. In this case the investigator attempts to draw group-level inferences based upon inappropriate individual-level data. Selvin (1960) points to the presence of this type error in Lazarsfeld and Thielens' (1958) study of *The Academic Mind*. At issue is their attempt to demonstrate a direct relationship between levels of productivity and apprehension among college *faculties* (a group-level variable). What they do, however, is compare the varying degree of apprehension of *professors* (individual-level data), who differ as to their rates of productivity. Since the productivity and the apprehension of a faculty is an aggregate or group concept (i.e., the proportion of a college's faculty that is productive or apprehensive), attempts to compare such variables based upon the average of individual professors, without regard to the faculty to which they belong, cannot legitimately be done given the research problem as posited. Once again, a poor fit between theory and method may lead to spurious or misleading findings (cf. Blalock, 1969:34).

Finally, there exist those situations in which an investigator wishes to pursue an essentially social-psychological-theoretical approach (of either a quasi-realist or quasi-nominalist variety), and is operating with data measured in either too elaborate or too general a fashion. In the former instance the investigator must aggregate or collapse certain data, thereby arriving at truly social indicators, in order to meet the theoretical demands stemming from the realist portion of the social-psychological approach employed. In the latter case, the investigator must attempt to dummy or raise artificially the level of precision of certain data in order to meet the theoretical assumptions underlying the nominalist portion of the social-psychological approach desired. Both procedures, collapsing data and dummy variable analysis, although not fallacies in the manner of those discussed previously, nonetheless present the researcher with numerous potential pitfalls. When collapsing data, for example, both the precision of measurement and later the power efficiency of those statistics which may be appropriately employed are each compromised. As concerns the use of dummy variables, Suits (1967) discusses various difficulties of their interpretation and the special steps which must be taken in securing a determinate solution when using such variables in regression equations.

In conclusion, although we are free as sociologists to choose whatever theoretical and methodological approaches we wish to employ in the conduct of our research, we should be conscious also of certain pitfalls which may accrue from the wedding of those approaches. Particularly in the case of the six inconsistent pairings of theory and method discussed in this section, the likelihood of committing a fallacy or measurement error may be heightened.

SUMMARY AND CONCLUSIONS

This essay has reviewed evidence indicating the existence of linkages between individuals' theoretical orientations and their methodological perspectives. Those persons using a realist theoretical approach are shown generally to employ a nonempirical methodology, whereas nominalists are found to utilize more empirical research techniques and procedures. Given certain parameters, which include a presumed desire on the part of individuals for some measure of cognitive consistency, the scope and definition of the problems studied, and the nature of the data most readily available for analysis, such linkages become somewhat more understandable. Finally, attention was focused on the implications which such theory-method interrelationships have for the discipline at large, an understanding of the history of sociology and the careers of its exemplars, and the potential fallacies which may attend various research efforts. It is this last point on which I would like to make some concluding remarks.

It is my contention that the linkages shown to exist in this essay, between theory and methods, represent a hypothesis about the likelihood or probability of falling prey to various fallacies or research errors in the conduct of inquiry. Obviously, not all researchers at all times operate from a so-called consistent (or optimum fit) theoretical-methodological posture. My own data certainly attest to that fact (Snizek, 1975). Precisely because of this, I would argue that, to the extent one deviates from an optimum or consistent fit between theoretical perspective and methodological approach, the likelihood of committing various fallacies or other errors increases.

To be sure, a consistent theoretical-methodological posture cannot *ensure* that one's investigation will be accurate or error free. Nor does the employment of an inconsistent theory-method posture irrevocably or necessarily doom one's investigation.[6] Rather, it merely serves to increase the likelihood that the researcher, owing to a less than optimum fit between theory and method, will be confronted with a disproportionate number of theoretical, measurement, statistical, grammatical,[7] and related problems requiring solution. Should the researcher be unaware of such problems, or knowing of their existences, be unable to arrive at their proper solution, spurious or otherwise misleading results are likely to occur. Hopefully, this essay has sensitized the reader to the importance of the interrelationship between theory and methods and the potential pitfalls which may result from an awareness or insensitivity in that regard.

Equally important, I have suggested a specific proposition of an empirical nature that those interested in the sociology of sociology could do well to investigate in the manner of research reported and reviewed at the outset of this essay. The consequences of assuming given metatheoretical choices need not remain—indeed, should not remain—merely a conjectural matter.

NOTES

1. Using a predesigned checklist of items, some thirty-two weeks were spent by the author and twenty-six graduate students in initially collecting the data for this study. Following collection of the data, considerable time and care were taken to check and recheck each student's categorization of the theoretical and methodological orientations used by the authors of the articles surveyed. Inter-interviewer reliability, in this connection, was shown to be .91 or higher, thus demonstrating considerable agreement as to the classification of authors' theoretical and methodological stances.

2. The nine journals surveyed were: *American Journal of Sociology, American Sociological Review, American Sociologist, Rural Sociology, Social Forces, Social Problems, Social Research, Sociological Inquiry,* and *Sociology*. Since a survey of all articles published in these journals during the period 1950-70 was not feasible, selection was restricted to five substantive areas, based on student interest: (a) stratification and mobility; (b) deviant behavior; (c) industrial sociology; (d) religion; and (e) the family. Ritzer's (1977a) remarks to the contrary, it is inconceivable that the nature of either the specific journals or the substantive areas surveyed could have biased the present study's findings. Rather, to have surveyed other journals or areas would appear to have given a markedly less representative picture of the discipline of sociology. Equally implausible is Ritzer's assertion that both the form and content of the *relationship* shown to exist between theory and research, as presented in this essay, is somehow an artifact of the journals surveyed. What journals better represent the discipline than those surveyed?

3. To assess predictive validity, pair-wise lambdas were computed between all possible combinations of categories used to represent each of the two continua of empiricism employed in the study. In each instance, ordinality was shown to be present in the categories as constructed (e.g., the use of no statistical tests of significance and/or association was shown to be less empirical than the use of contingency tables; the use of contingency tables less empirical than employment of an analysis of variance framework; etc.).

4. It is not being argued that the individual level of analysis *is* "more concrete or less abstract" than the group level of analysis, but rather that many researchers *perceive* such to be the case. For an excellent elaboration of this point see Warriner's (1956) comments on the tendency to treat a "conceptual entity as a perceptual entity."

5. Obviously, there are exceptions to these general linkages. See, for example, the work of Laumann (1973), which represents an attempt to investigate macro-structures empirically.

6. Once again I wish to underscore the fact that not all quantitatively oriented sociologists fall prey to the various errors and fallacies described previously, nor do they *necessarily* employ a nominalist theoretical orientation. A notable example in this regard are the writings of Peter Blau (1977, and his essay in this volume), who, like Durkheim, has continually managed to analyze quantitatively group or structural effects in a most perceptive and accurate fashion.

7. An example of the grammatical distinction referred to here is illustrated by the difference between the singular and plural possessive of the word "individual." The phrase "individual's attitudes" implies a nominalist theoretical approach, whereas "individuals' attitudes" represents the use of a realist- or group-level of analysis. Yet we often see such phrases used interchangeably, without regard to the varying meanings and implications each conveys.

Edward A. Tiryakian

THE SIGNIFICANCE OF SCHOOLS IN THE DEVELOPMENT OF SOCIOLOGY

The major intention of this essay is to challenge the customary way of interpreting and presenting the history of sociology, or rather its development. I shall do this by arguing that unlike the pre-Kuhnian image of the natural sciences, sociology's development is not adequately typified by a cumulative, progressive growth of empirical discoveries or facts generated and encompassed within an ever more refined or elegant body of theory. Rather, I would suggest, the growth of sociology is much more uneven and discontinuous, and to a large measure represents, or is a function of, periodic infusions brought about by a small number of major "schools." The major scientific contribution of each school, I would further propose, is a generalizable approach or method of investigating and representing social reality; that is, what fuels the development of the discipline is, more than anything else, general methodological innovations rather than either new theoretical models or new empirical observations. The articulation and the demonstration of the efficacy of a new methodology are much more a communal affair than that of the single individual. In later sections I shall expand on this thesis and indicate at some length an ideal-type approach to the concept of school. I shall then go on to illustrate this with what I consider to be the three major successive schools at the core of the development of sociology, as an academic discipline, in Western society. By making the school the unit of analysis in accounting for the development of sociology (as illustrative of the social sciences), I hope this essay will be seen as rendering a contribution to the sociology of sociology.

In a sense, this essay begins where Thomas Kuhn (1970a) ends in the second edition of his provocative analytical essay on the history of science. In his

"Postscript," Kuhn amplifies his conception of "paradigm" by bringing attention to the notion of "scientific community" as playing a noteworthy role in
the historical development of science. To quote Kuhn: "Having opened this
postscript by emphasizing the need to study the community structure of science, I shall close by underscoring the need for similar and, above all, for comparative study of the corresponding communities in other fields" (1970a:209).

It is gratifying for a sociologist to see a distinguished historian of science becoming aware of science as a social system, and one therefore which is
grounded in a broader sociohistorical matrix rather than being a sphere of
human thought and activity apart from the mundane social world.[1] Nevertheless, Kuhn's remarks are more suggestive than programmatic and are in need
of greater precision and elaboration. There seems to be as much ambiguity
surrounding the notion of "scientific community" as he admits there was in
the initial articulation of "paradigm."[2] What I should like to do at this juncture is to indicate various levels of generality involved in the concept of "scientific community" and within these locate that of "school."

Kuhn uses "scientific community" in a broad sense as "the practitioners of
a scientific specialty," but obviously this does not make precise the membership class intended. Thus "physicists" may be thought of as a generic scientific
community, "low-temperature physicists" as a more meaningful species within the larger aggregate in terms of members' professional identity and daily activities. In turn, "physicists" may be thought of as part of the community of
"scientists," for example, in the academic setting in distinguishing them from
"humanists." Kuhn does not specify what sort of community he has in mind as
figuring in the development of paradigms, but presumably it is one of a relatively small number within a discipline (such as low-temperature physicists,
econometricians, ethnomethodologists). He does refer to the communication
networks involving "communities of perhaps one hundred members, occasionally significantly fewer" (Kuhn, 1970a:178).

Without further specification, it would appear as if the notion of "community" entertained by Kuhn is that of a group of scientists having as a common
denominator a professional specialization in the division of labor of their discipline, who share a common intellectual or cognitive orientation to the subject
matter of their field (including a common language or jargon), and who may or
may not be aware of the presence and activities of members of that community
via various communication networks (specialized journals or newsletters, telephone and computer conversations, etc.).[3] This is essentially an assemblage of
widely scattered individuals who come together only occasionally, such as at
national or international meetings, externally funded conferences, and the
like.

I would suggest that this kind of scientific community, at least as an ideal
type, is a predominantly impersonal one, having as the basis of its existence little face-to-face interaction among its members (with little or no affective bonds

uniting them). It represents or corresponds to a certain image of science as comprised of distinct individuals each pursuing the same goals in their own laboratory cell. A more "humanized" view of scientific community might be that of the brotherhood of secret benefactors of mankind depicted by Bacon in *New Atlantis*, or, in yet another imagery, the scientific community is like the denomination, whose membership is voluntary and whose size, quality, and intensity of social bonds are intermediate between "church" and "sect." In dealing with the historical development of the natural sciences, it may be appropriate to refer to this sort of grouping as a "scientific community." However, in examining the development of the social sciences, or at least sociology, I wish to reserve the term "community," as approximating the sense of *communitas* for a more stringent use, namely that of "school."

Before explicating what I take as components of the concept of "school" in relation to the development of the social sciences, let me briefly note two much more common paths that have been used toward this purpose, at least in sociology. The first consists of various attempts to outline the history of sociology by discussing, in more or less chronological order, the thoughts of various historical figures who have exerted an intellectual influence at various times in the growth of sociology (with major figures receiving more attention than minor figures). A variant of this is an attempt to trace the history of certain key sociological concepts, for example, "action," "alienation," "status," and so on.

Both of these paths (and a combination thereof) have highly commendable followers and moreover appeal to the usual, customary way we approach history; it is history in terms of a "great man" approach or in terms of intellectual history (the diffusion of key notions or concepts over time, including their reappearance in settings other than their original point). Seeing sociology, then, as a succession of major figures, or even as a succession of major concepts which accumulate in a contemporary storage vault of intellectual treasures and legacies, is to approach the history of sociology in a nominalist vein.

A third path, which has become increasingly utilized in the present decade, is one which reflects the growth of the sociology of sociology; this alternative has as a general characteristic the examination of the historical development of sociology in terms of its relationships to its national setting. Following this path, we can organize and codify the development of sociology by grounding it in its sociohistorical setting, rather than treating it abstractly. Questions such as the following then become germane: Are there any traits or central tendencies which characterize the sociology of a given country and distinguish it from those of sociology in other countries, and, if so, how are these traits reflections of major situational exigencies faced by sociology in that setting? Do institutional variations from country to country in the teaching, training, and recruitment of sociologists lead to recognizable differences in the development and primary concerns of the respective sociologies? How do significant collective sociohistorical experiences of a country leave an imprint on the concerns and approaches of sociology? This approach will tend to identify national traits that give specificity to sociology on a country-by-country basis; different phases of development of sociology will perforce reflect major phases of national development, and the unit of historical analysis is thus a "national sociology," whether this be American, French, or Russian sociology (e.g., Tiryakian, 1971; Gurvitch and Moore, 1945).

This approach could become a genuine sociological perspective on the development of sociology, but there is need for methodological reflection and rigor which is usually not the case among its users. In many instances, this approach is a more or less chronological description of "who was who" in the history of the discipline in the country; the sociohistorical context for the most part remains so far in the background that "national" aspects of the development of sociology in the given country elude the reader. Yet, it is often the sociohistorical context which marks sociology at key historical points, or which marks sociologists as historical actors. Here I do not mean that a sociology-of-sociology or a sociology-of-knowledge approach will *reduce* the development of sociology to its national context; at the same time, the preoccupations of a sociology will certainly reflect the existential situation of sociologists qua actors in a given sociohistorical setting. And perhaps it may even be possible to treat sociological thought as an indicator of collective sentiments and aspirations at the national level—or at least as an indicator of collective representations of one social stratum, typically, that of liberal intellectuals.

A further major problem of treating the development of sociology in terms of its national setting is whether or not we can justify the assumption that a cohort analysis is applicable. That is to say, are we really dealing with the same sort of persons over time who are practicing sociologists in a given country? If not, then to bring out "national traits" or a "national character" of sociology may neglect the fact that the population of sociologists changes and becomes heterogeneous over time. For example, if one were to study the development of sociology in Canada, one would have to pay attention to its "Americanization" in the 1950s and 1960s and the changes this introduced in the profession and the curriculum. Or in another vein, whereas American sociology in its first generation (before 1914) and for a good deal of its second generation (up to World War II) consisted of a fairly culturally homogeneous group of American descendants of old British stock (and therefore oriented to the American historical experience), latter-day American sociology (post-World War II) is much more pluralistic in terms of ethnicity and value orientations. Therefore, the sociohistorical context will have differential impact and significance as the population changes composition (from homogeneity to heterogeneity). These are some of the factors I have in mind in cautioning that to examine the development of sociology in terms of its national context entails some formidable problems.

Perhaps one more problem must be realized before we can think of doing either a sociology of sociology or a sociological study of the development of sociology. And that is the following: We must come to think of sociology not as a system of ideas (sociological methods, sociological theories, sociological concepts), nor as a group of individuals who for the most part earn their living by doing sociology. Rather, we must see sociology as an institution (even as the level of institutionalization changes over time) and as a profession, consisting of differentiated structures, of established avenues of training, of vehicles of integration (journals, meetings, etc.) and of various major elements (theories, methods of analysis, and the like).

A good approximation of what I have in mind is a superb essay by Edward Shils (1970), "Tradition, Ecology, and Institution in the History of Sociology." The main focus of the analysis is neither sociological thought nor sociological "giants," but rather the institutional structures within which thought and individuals have interacted, both in Europe and in the United States. In the process of unfolding a synoptic treatment of the history of Western sociology, Shils makes clear that differential access to institutional support leads to differentials in the recognition and influence of individual sociologists. For example, though by far the greater mind, Mannheim's influence on sociology was much less than that of his contemporary and colleague Max Horkheimer, essentially because the latter was successful in obtaining a series of important institutional patronage, first in Germany and later in New York (Shils, 1970: 733-77). To complement Shils' sociological approach to the history of sociology, it would be well to have (easier said than done!) a similar synoptic treatment of the development of sociology in the Third World and other areas falling outside Europe and the United States (Latin America, Japan, Africa, etc.). It would be interesting to see the effects of colonial, neo-colonial, and post-colonial society on the institutional structures of sociologists; the factor of the "colonial situation," so well discussed by Balandier (1970) is as salient for societies outside the West as the factor of industrialization has been for the latter. If Western sociology, in its development, is to a crucial extent a continuing reflection on the ramifications of industrial society (from its inner core to its external limits or boundaries), so also might we take as the Ariadne thread for the development of non-Western sociology the ramifications of a colonial setting, even if this preoccupation engenders concern at different levels.[4] Naturally, not all features of the development of sociology outside the West can be subsumed under the problems of colonial society, anymore than the problems of industrial society can suffice for an accounting of sociology in Western society; nonetheless, each is a crucial entry point into sociology as a "total social phenomenon," to use the expression of Marcel Mauss.

ON THE CONCEPT OF SCHOOL

In between approaching the development of sociology at the global level or in polar fashion, accounting for it in terms of individual figures and key ideas, there stands what might be called, to borrow from Merton, an "approach of the middle range." This account of the development of sociology would see the main thrust of the development stemming from a small number of influential "schools"; as I shall make clear, I use the concept of "school" in the sense which I believe Kuhn intends for "scientific community," but I believe that "school" is a more general heuristic concept for purposes of historical analysis of a given discipline.

To be sure, to frame the development of sociology in terms of "schools" is not, as such, original with this writer. Thus a very important pioneering effort in delineating clusters in sociological thought is that done fifty years ago by Pitirim A. Sorokin in his *Contemporary Sociological Theories*. The organizing principle is a critical evaluation of a small number of "schools" (e.g., the anthropo-racial school, the sociologistic one, the psychological one, etc.), each forming a sort of classificatory genus with its major species. Sorokin's work performed a notable service in weaving various threads of scattered sociological thought into a coherent tapestry. It is essentially a typological approach to the historical development of sociology which has had later followers (Martindale, 1960).

It should be noted that Sorokin tacitly takes "school" in the sense of a "school of thought," that is, an intellectual grouping of individuals who may be separated in space and/or time but who share a certain recognizable approach, model, assumptive frame, and/or method. Persons comprising a "school" in this sense may or may not have been in contact with one another or known each other personally. So, for example, we can talk of a "sociobiology school" which would include Herbert Spencer, Alfred Espinas, and Pierre van den Berghe, or a "mathematical school" which would include Quetelet, Giddings, and Blalock, or an "exchange school" which would cluster Bentham, Adam Smith, Mauss, and Homans.

However, by "school" I understand a real group of intellectuals, a small community of persons whose origin and formative period can be localized in time and place. Let me advance this concept as an ideal typical one, which can be readily distinguished from that of the "school of thought" usage. The sense of school used in this essay is akin, though not identical, to that of school used in art history to designate a group of contemporaries sharing a certain style, technique, or set of symbolic expressions, and having at some point or other in time and space a high degree of interaction (e.g., the Florentine School, the Bauhaus School, the Fauves, the Impressionists, etc.). It is also fairly typical that the innovation in style, technique, and conceptualization which gives the school its primary identity is organized around a "master" and his pupils working together in an *atelier*, or workshop, or, in the case of literary schools, the workshop is one or more group journals or reviews. Examples here would be the school of Giotto or of Rubens, or even in the modern period the literary schools of Dadaism integrated around Tzara, and Surrealism around Breton.

Rather than use the term "master," which has an anachronistic ring to our democratic ears, let me suggest that a school has a primary role differentiation in terms of a *founder-leader* and his followers. In size, a school varies. Although there can be no absolute limits, I would suggest that by and large the membership of a school ranges from about one to three dozen members. To be sure, the size of a given school varies during the effective life of the particular community, and the life span of any given school is itself variable. Initially, fewer than a dozen might constitute the early core around the founder-leader; somewhat later, as the school becomes more visible in the larger scientific or intellectual community of which it is part, it will gradually increase its membership (with admittance to the group on an informal, ad hoc basis, pretty much regulated by the founder-leader deciding whether or not the prospective member should be taken on as another student).

The school is comparable in its formative stage, at least, to a religious community, a sect, or a brotherhood. It usually provides an intellectual sense of mission to its members. They are drawn together by a set of ideas, techniques, and normative dispositions expressed by the founder-leader which at the time of the school's beginning are at odds with prevailing views in the wider profession. The school may have a tacit sense of bringing salvation to the profession, that is, rescuing it from a state of stagnation and/or degradation; the school seeks to "put new clothes" on the profession, to modernize it, to renovate it, to give it a new beginning. The school may be looked down upon by the larger scientific community, ignored or repudiated for being nonscientific (which may mean no more than not doing what the majority of the members of the profession believe constitutes the activities of scientists in that profession). The school, in its debut, is denied entrance into the temple; its expressions and products are kept apart from the official organs of the profession, thereby leading the school to seek its own organs of public diffusion.[5]

Weber's notion of "charisma" is useful in further relating school as an ideal type to the religious community. Weber used charisma as an interpersonal attribute of leadership based upon extraordinary qualities welding leader to followers in affective communal bonds. The school does tend to have unity through the intellectual charisma of its founder, albeit a school of intellectuals may be prone to a greater degree of ambivalence in the relationships (e.g., the case of the original Freudian School) than a religious community, where abnegation, obedience, and devotion to the founder-leader are dispositions generated by a common orientation to the sacred. The founder-leader imparts a basic conception of reality or one of how to approach reality which wins the commitment of his followers and which they apply to their own investigations; in turn, their investigations tend to provide empirical validation to the basic conceptualization or "message." The latter becomes the core of the revolutionary paradigm which has a greater vitality than contrasting alternative conceptions and approaches current in the field or discipline. The successes (and productivity) of the new school begin to receive greater attention, from informal means (word-of-mouth propagation, for example) to more formal ones (publications in respected journals, invitations to address professional meetings at plenary sessions). As the school becomes more institutionally visible (analogous to the evolution of the religious community from sect to denomination), its membership size keeps increasing. Its core ideas (theories, methods, techniques) become popularized and no longer depend upon the founder directly teaching new recruits in face-to-face interaction. The charisma of the school becomes "routinized"; its ideas become part of the standard conceptions of the discipline. The more the school and its achievements become integrated into the discipline, the more depersonalized becomes its paradigm. New generations of the scientific community, as a whole, come to utilize freely ideas and techniques without awareness that these originated in a specific sociointellectual community. As the community becomes the orthodox party (and of course, this does not always happen, for many a sect remains that), the school faces the same paradoxes of institutionalization noted by O'Dea (1963) in the development of religious movements: from the dilemma of "single-mindedness versus mixed motivation" to that of "conversion versus coercion."

With depersonalization and increased usage of the paradigm beyond the original community, an element of the paradigm may get lost, namely, that which is a covert dimension, its *presuppositions*. By presuppositions I mean those often implicit ontological groundings of a general theory; presuppositions are not intellectual constructs like hypotheses, empirical propositions, and articulated theories. They are the existential as well as metaphysical foundations, the basic definitions of the situation, the basic approaches to reality which are not falsifiable by any rational or empirical means. For example, a cardinal presupposition of one sociological paradigm may be that religion is an effective force in the viability of any human society, the presupposition of another may be that what is institutionalized, particularly government, is necessarily corrupt and corrosive, and so forth. Each paradigm has a set of presuppositions which in part relate the school at its debut to its institutional and sociohistorical context, though the same objective context can give rise to quite different presuppositions and "definitions of the situation."[6] Over time, and with an increased and perforce more heterogeneous membership, the presuppositions of the school become blunted, diluted, trivialized, or compromised.[7] But since presuppositions are never fully articulated, it is always possible that the school may revitalize itself by a return to pristine presuppositions when investigations following a more articulate or explicit track of the paradigm seem fruitless, redundant, or, simply, from a scientific point of view, "uninteresting."

A school, then, consists of a scientific community integrated around a central figure, an intellectual charismatic leader, and a paradigm of empirical reality which is subject to investigation. The paradigm's core formulations are those of the founder-leader, but the full-blown paradigm is typically a collective enterprise, fashioned by the founder-leader and his immediate entourage. The applications of the paradigm to actual investigations are carried out by members of the entourage, but also may be undertaken at a subsequent stage by lay members of the profession (that is, by those having no contacts with the leader and actual members of the school but who can make use of a "manual" of instructions).

A school, however, has characteristics which can be further delineated. Very often, the founder-leader is one who, because he has such an intense, innovative way of conceptualizing the reality of the world, has trouble expressing himself in ordinary language. His immediate group of followers or associates may know perfectly well what he means because of intimate contacts with him; between them there is a spoken and unspoken universe of discourse understood by all. But for the scientific community at large and the wider public, the leader's message is esoteric and the paradigm itself may be unclear as to its broad outlines and significance. Thus there is often need for a role of "interpreter" (or popularizer): the person who knows the paradigm as an insider but who can translate it to outsiders so that they can see the relevance of the message. The interpreter role may also encompass the role of pragmatic organizer (i.e., the person who can organize the group or represent it effectively within the institutional context of the larger community). The founder-leader, or intellectual charismatic leader, is not necessarily a visionary without ability to organize the group in its everyday dealings, but he is expected to be more a "man of ideas," of "big ideas," and cannot maximize this activity while taking care of problems of organization. It is essential to find the right interpreter/popularizer if the school is to survive and have a major influence on the profession.

In addition to this differentiation, we can also suggest that social science schools have the following types of roles. Around the leader, the immediate entourage may have a small number of important "converts" who may be of the same generation as the leader, and therefore share his same historical situation (including what he finds disturbing about the present state of the discipline). They have received their early training elsewhere but upon coming into contact with him decide that his way of constructing or conceptualizing reality is a marked advance over the status quo. They and their contacts in other professional structures may give the school an immediate visibility and advantage over other fledgling groups lacking such "converts." As important, though, is that the entourage consists of students, younger than the leader, who become his trusted lieutenants as they imprint his paradigm early in their career. Later on, when the leader-founder is gone, they will have the task of training a new generation, and, in part, their authority will stem from having been associates of the charismatic founder. It is the lieutenants who are the effective agents of institutionalization. They are the ones who spread the doctrine by taking appointments at other institutions, who send new recruits to the master, who take offices in the professional associations, who get research grants, and so forth.

We may also discern another role, more on the periphery than at the center of the school, and that is of the "auxiliary"; like a chess pawn, he is a loyal foot soldier who assists the school in getting visibility and support, but who himself makes little if any intellectual contributions. The auxiliary may become a journal editor, a civil servant bureaucrat, a foundation executive, a textbook writer; sympathetic to the school's paradigm and having a modicum of personal contacts with the founder and/or members of the inner core, the auxiliary will help in the institutional and material support of the school. The auxiliary is a part of the community, but a background part. We might also invoke another ancillary role which is that of the *patron*, that is, a person who is not a member of the intellectual community but who provides important material assistance to the leader and the school; this may stem from personal ties with the leader, from commitment to the presuppositions of the school, from the seeking of prestige that comes from association with "scientists" even if one does not have the credentials, etc.

For the most part this defines the social structure of the school as a scientific community.[8] To study a school's role in the development of sociology, one must also take into account the *dynamics* of the school, that is, the problem of generations. A school that has an impact on the profession—and it is the successful schools which I claim are the major units in the development of sociology—is one which can socialize more than one generation. It is hard to pinpoint what constitutes one generation in the scientific community—perhaps five years, but usually no more than ten. A truly successful school, by these rough standards, is one which continues to recruit new members to its original founder and/or his lieutenants, and which continues to produce works of scientific eminence, for more than two or three generations.

What needs to be worked out are some of the qualitative changes that take place in a school as the generations succeed themselves, as the revolutionary paradigm becomes incorporated into the "normal science of the discipline." This includes questions of succession of leadership, role relationships among members of the school after departure of the leader, and the problem of whether commitment to the presuppositions can be maintained by new recruits of a later generation, particularly as the training itself becomes institutionalized and formalized. The dynamics of a school entail attention to the crises it may face from one generation to another, whether, for example, the crisis is in the nature of a schism between followers, the unexpected death of a key lieutenant or other core member, the defection of a key figure over basic presuppositions (as the case of Gaston Richard with the Durkheimians, of Jung with the Freudians), or any other external event which may objectively disrupt the ongoingness of the school (again, the case of World War I vis-à-vis the Durkheimians).

A successful school is one which becomes recognized by the wider scientific community as being "where the action is." Its figures are in demand in the profession; they secure key positions in the academic profession, and become appointed and elected to key offices of professional associations. They write the works which receive immediate attention. In effect, there is a quasi meritocracy operative in the discipline, with the members of the school setting the tone and major directions of research and publication. At any one time, the number of schools dominant in the profession, or in the main domain area of the discipline, is bound to be small. I am suggesting that advancement of the discipline, or rather its development (which may or may not be an advancement), typically occurs when one school emerges which sets the tone for the entire discipline. It is its figures and writings which receive the attention of the discipline, not only because their writings and research are "exciting" but also because the school has marshaled very important institutional resources (major sources of training and research grants, prestigious publications and equally prestigious appointments, etc.).

Of course, one discipline is not exhausted by a dominant school at a given time. There are "great men" who are cited and remembered, but whether their contributions continue to be important and influential is much more a function of whether their ideas, theories, and so on, are picked up and integrated within a school than whether their ideas stack up intellectually to the test of time.

Let me briefly summarize what I regard as propitious factors for the emergence of a school, that is, the prerequisites or necessary conditions for a school to achieve prominence in the development of sociology (and other social sciences).

At the rational, intellectual level, the conditions which Kuhn notes as prerequisites for a new paradigm to be accepted can be transposed to the social sciences with minor adjustments. Prior to a school's emergence, the accepted dominant model, theory, or method of approaching social reality has been on the scene for quite a while and is commonly accepted as the obvious way to approach sociology (practically as a "given" within the corpus of the discipline). There may be academic and research centers where alternative perspectives are prevalent, but these centers are not generating a great deal of attention and interest; such centers have a regional base or a restricted clientele. Insofar as they are integrated around a central figure and therefore do constitute a socio-intellectual community, they should be regarded as "schools" in our sense of the term, but insofar as they do not play a major role in the development of sociology at the national or intersocietal level, I shall refer to them as "minor schools." As instances of this phenomenon, I have in mind the schools of LePlay, Odum, and Lundberg.

For the "big picture," the state of the discipline as a whole on the eve of an intellectual takeover by a new school may be characterized by a sort of "anomie." There is either an intellectual void due to a plurality of orientations which are incapable of integrating, in a coherent fashion, the major dimensions and domain areas of the discipline, or else there may be a dominant prevailing orientation, but one in which there is little affective commitment to its premises (i.e., an orientation that has de facto legitimation as scientific orthodoxy but in which the applications follow the letter, and the spirit is missing among its practitioners).

Some phenomena are not considered as significant or important in terms of the dominant schema. Yet these are treated as important either by practitioners outside the discipline or by a practitioner within who has little recognition at home but who has extensive contacts outside the discipline with other points of view where the phenomena are treated as real, important, and vital. The intellectual innovator is able to take the new ideas, points of view, orientations, or whatnot from outside his discipline, synthesize, and integrate them within his discipline's major problem areas. The intellectual innovator is able to formulate a new conception of social reality, a "big picture," either at the ontological or epistemological level (or both) which makes room for the phenomena in question within a new model or paradigm. This orientation becomes the intellectual core of the social group which gathers around the innovator, and as it gathers momentum, the group may then become one of the schools whose inputs affect the course of the discipline.

Before seeking to apply this conceptualization to the actual development of sociology, let me conclude this section with a few remarks as to what is needed for a school to be successful, that is, to have a sustained impact which can be obvious to anyone doing or reading the history of the discipline.

First, and foremost, a school needs a founder-leader, an intellectual charismatic figure who has unshakable faith in the model, theory, and conceptualization of social reality which he seeks to establish; like a true prophet, he must be willing to be a *vox clamantis in deserto* against the voice of professional orthodoxy and respectability. Beyond this there is another quality he must possess. He must be willing to have students work closely under him; he must encourage their collaboration in developing together the paradigm whose outline and essential features he is responsible for. If the intellectual or social distance between innovator and those who come into contact with him is too great, or if the innovator does not impart cues that he is willing to have junior collaborators, associates, and lieutenants, then no school will be formed around him, irrespective of how brilliant his ideas may be. I should add that an intellectual giant or innovator may have a supporting figure close to him, a confidant, but that is not the same role as a lieutenant or junior collaborator; the confidant provides emotional support, friendship, and the like, but not critical intellectual feedback. A school, as I have conceptualized it, may have its Boswell (like Jones for the Freudian School), but if the innovator only has a Boswell, he has no school (and may want no school). In any case, the personality of the leader, along with his intellectual superiority and imagination, constitutes an irreducible component of any successful school.

Second, a school needs an institutional affiliation, typically an academic site of general excellence and preferably in a metropolitan area.[9] This makes it easier for the leader to have access to communication channels which inform him of the advanced state of the art in other disciplines, to communicate with colleagues in other disciplines, and to attract highly gifted students who have to pay some attention to later employment opportunities. It is possible that idealistic or ideological commitment to the normative dimension of the school's presuppositions may attract recruits to a leader irrespective of where he is, but as a school matures and grows, it needs certain institutional support and facilities for its members and their research.

Third, a school in the social sciences needs a journal, review, or other means of regularly publishing its research and theoretical developments beyond its inner core. Furthermore, as the group grows and scatters beyond its initial locale, a journal is one means of reaffirming its identity through continuing collaborative work.

Fourth, a school's identity is also provided by means of a document in the nature of a professional proclamation of its basic mode of perceiving and relating to the world. This is the functional equivalent of Luther's theses, of the Declaration of Independence, and the original Constitution, of the Principles of 1789, and of the Manifesto of 1848.

Undoubtedly, other factors may be adduced, but at least those already mentioned will prove to be useful in the sociological interpretation of schools as units of historical development. Let us now proceed to illustrate this conceptualization of schools with some concrete examples.

THREE SCHOOLS IN THE DEVELOPMENT OF MODERN SOCIOLOGY

It is not within the scope of this essay to attempt a rigorous interpretation of the development of sociology in terms of the school as the unit of analysis, or as the effective agent of social change of the discipline. Certainly, such a comprehensive history would have to begin at the very beginning of sociology, with the fascinating figure of Saint-Simon, who gathered around him the first sociological school, half sect and half scientific community (see Jones and Anservitz, 1975). For most of the nineteenth century, albeit Comte had given precision to the idea of "sociology," the latter was not really a discipline. There was no career training in sociology, no consensus as to what characterized sociology as an orientation to society. One could be a sociologist in the morning, a philosopher in the afternoon, and a literary critic in the evening, so to speak. There were groupings of persons around a leader, which in retrospect appear as protosociological schools, but their paramount concern was explicitly practical, either to improve the world through reform (such as the LePlay School) or to provide it an example of reconstruction by withdrawing from it (as some of the socialist schools) or to overthrow it (as the Marxist School). These schools do give some historical context to the development of sociology and therefore cannot be neglected in a comprehensive history of the discipline. But I would like to propose that modern sociology begins with a new phase of modern society, one that begins in the 1890s. It is here that sociology enters the academic arena on both sides of the Atlantic, and, with academic institutionalization, the paramount concern of professional sociologists becomes more to understand the social world than to change it.

Roughly speaking, the *modern* period of sociology is from a historical perspective marked by America's involvement in two imperalist wars: the Spanish-American War and the nondeclared war in Vietnam. The same year as the Spanish-American War, France is rocked by the Dreyfus affair, whose outcome does have important consequences for giving sociology strong institutional support in Paris. The crisis of Vietnam in the United States provides a climate of dissent which has important repercussions on American sociology, changing the tone of the profession very dramatically at the annual meetings in San Francisco in 1969. On the other side of the Atlantic, the May 1968 "events" in France and radical student activism in Germany and other countries also have repercussions, for it appears that much of the agitation is spawned in sociology departments. The present decade is the *contemporary* period, and like the stock market, the world order, and most of the other disciplines I know of, represents a very ambiguous and amorphous time in sociology's development.[10]

While we await for Godot, then, let me suggest that for the modern period, spanning roughly the biblical three score and ten years, or three major sociohistorical generations (that before World War I, the interwar one, and the generation from the late 1940s to the late 1960s), sociology's development has been profoundly marked by three schools.

The first is the *Durkheimian School*, drawn around the charismatic leadership of Emile Durkheim (1858-1917). I have discussed at length his ideas and his intellectual and social milieu elsewhere (Tiryakian, 1962, 1978) and will not repeat the individual aspects of this towering figure of modern sociology. Let me indicate, though, that one can hardly dissociate Durkheim in the development of sociology from the group of associates and students which formed an intellectual community par excellence. Durkheim was the charismatic intellectual leader whose vision of society as a reality *sui generis*, one having a moral infrastructure capable of scientific investigation, attracted the talents and energy of a group of gifted intellectuals (scientifically minded, academically oriented for the most part) who were seeking an alternative between moral anarchy, on the one hand, and traditional religious authority and society on the other. Durkheim's first recruit was his own nephew Marcel Mauss, and during Durkheim's first half of his university career, spent "in the province" at Bordeaux, the formative period of the school began.

Durkheim made the most of the university setting at Bordeaux, which allowed a great deal of interaction among faculties. Some of his colleagues and students came from the Faculty of Letters, others from the Faculty of Law. The early core group had received their training elsewhere or in disciplines other than sociology, but they found in Durkheim a man who could "put it together" and provide them with conceptual common denominators that helped to order and organize phenomena of their own research interests. Among the early joiners were Gaston Richard, François Simiand, Paul Lapie, Célestin Bouglé, Paul Fauconnet, and Edmond Doutté; then somewhat later came Antoine Meillet, Maurice Halbwachs, and Henri Hubert. Since Durkheim began his teaching at Bordeaux in 1887, had his doctorate awarded in 1893 (with the successful defense of his major thesis, *The Division of Labor*), and received his appointment to the Sorbonne in 1902, one can say that the formative period of the school was that of the first generation. Two very important publications belong to this period. The first is Durkheim's *Rules of (the) Sociological Method*, which he published in 1895. This is an important document because it is the methodological manifesto of the school's paradigm. Even if his followers did not always carry out their investigations to the letter of the treatise, it was an articulation of the general scientific endeavor of sociology, a general guide to the underlying frame of reference of *The Division of Labor* and *Suicide*. In brief, Durkheim's *Rules* provided a vital role in formulating a general methodology. The second publication was the launching of the famous *L'Année Sociologique*, whose book review section derived its logic of organization from the *Rules* and was intended as an integral aspect of making sociology a cumulative and comparative science of society.[11] Later on, the *Année* as a key medium of publication was differentiated into the *Année* and the *Travaux de l'Année*, the former devoted exclusively to reviews, the latter being a series of original monographs by members of the school.

Durkheim's followers were very involved in political affairs, being, in the main, committed republicans and/or democratic socialists. The Dreyfus affair was a national crisis which gave further solidarity to the group, rallying as a bloc behind the defense of Dreyfus (and behind him, to the defense of liberal republicanism). With the triumph of the cause over the traditionalist factions (essentially, the various groups of the right), the Durkheimian School received a wide array of institutional support from academic and governmental institutions, including those who before "the Affair" had been skeptical about sociological tenets. Many of the school's members became civil servants in the upper levels of the French educational system, with one, Paul Lapie, ultimately heading the University of Paris. Célestin Bouglé also had an important administrative position at the end of his career, as head of the Ecole Normale Supérieure de Paris, the training ground for the elite teaching corps of lycées. Bouglé is an important figure in the school because although not trained by Durkheim, he was the effective "popularizer" of the school, the one who could communicate and interpret the master's sociological teachings to a wider audience. Bouglé wrote several works dealing with equality and inequality that make use in their approach of the basic Durkheimian paradigm. As a popularizer, his manuals (such as *What Is Sociology?*) had an important function in giving continuity to the recruitment of students into a Durkheimian frame of reference. Bouglé, who was popular with all and whose political views, unlike some of the more progressive Durkheimians (Hertz, Simiand, Halbwachs, and Mauss), were liberal republican but not socialist, ultimately was appointed to Durkheim's chair at the Sorbonne.

The school was badly crippled by World War I; its leader and many of the more promising newer recruits died in the period 1914-18. The school did survive after the war and had an effective monopoly on French sociology. Its major publishing organ was revived for two issues, but Mauss lacked the organizational genius and discipline of Durkheim, and the *Année* could not continue as such. There was, in the 1930s, an attempt at differentiating it into various autonomous sections called collectively the *Annales Sociologiques*, and for a brief period the remaining members of the school (spanning several generations) met periodically and published as a forum for their discussions the *Bulletin de l'Institut Français de Sociologie*. The fall of Paris in 1940 brought to an end the Third Republic and for all practical purpose the Durkheimian School was at an end (though its last remaining survivor, Georges Davy, passed away only in 1976).

This, then, is a skeletal outline of the Durkheimian School. During the period 1894-1914, when sociology outside of France was struggling to differentiate itself from other disciplines or modes of thought (ranging from religion and moral philosophy to political economy), the Durkheimian School established sociology as a comparative, scientific discipline, autonomous from both humanistic and natural science disciplines. Its members adopted as sociologists an orientation of objectivity and rigor which was imparted to them by their charismatic leader. A division of labor around a central figure, a shared methodological orientation, and a high level of excellence and original research are some of the essential characteristics of the school. The same essential characteristics typify the other two schools which contributed enormously to the development of sociology. Due to space limitations, I shall make some brief comments about them.

For the interwar period, the development of sociology owes very much to the formation of the *Chicago School* (see Faris, 1968; Carey, 1975; and Matthews, 1976), which provided a new sense of integration to the discipline. Prior to World War I, the department of sociology had gathered several eminent figures, still recognized today in terms of their contributions to the corpus of the discipline (Veblen and Thomas, in particular). Later, the department jelled into a community marked by organic solidarity under the leadership of Robert Park (1864-1944). Park brought to American sociology important inputs from the wider world of ideas and the wider social world. Though not a great lecturer, he had the gift of drawing out of prospective students existential aspects of themselves which later became transformed into major research problems. Park's great innovation was a methodological one, namely, to view the city as a natural laboratory for sociological investigation and to frame this research in terms of an ecological model derived from botany. What served as a "manifesto" for the school, equivalent to Durkheim's *Rules*, was the famous textbook published jointly by Robert Park and Ernest Burgess, *Introduction to the Science of Sociology*; as Morris Janowitz (1970:xiii) has noted in his introduction to the recent student edition of this landmark volume, "it was a volume which conformed to the older format of a textbook and a treatise at the same time." It was, in effect, a general methodological treatise, providing students with the basic vocabulary and grammar of the discipline which codified structural and dynamic aspects of society. As students and associates of the school brought their pioneering field investigations to fruition, they found and utilized publication resources having the prestige of the University of Chicago, namely, the University Press, which published the various dissertations of Anderson, Mowrer, Wirth, Zorbaugh, Thrasher, Cressey, and others. They also had access to the oldest sociological journal, *The American Journal of Sociology*, which became much more a scholarly, professional scientific journal after World War I. Being located in Chicago also enabled members of the school, either at the doctoral or at the postdoctoral stage, to find employment in various civic and municipal agencies in need of those capable of assisting in the development of a complex and heterogeneous metropolis. Furthermore, the department became the main recruiting ground of sociologists for new departments of sociology stretching from the Rockies to the Appalachians.

In addition to the ecological model, which gave great methodological organization to dozens of specific field investigations, the Chicago School was also able to incorporate into its frame of reference a subjective or intersubjective dimension. W. I. Thomas and Robert Park, under the influence of Simmel and German idealism in the social sciences, made room for the subjective element in social life. This was greatly reinforced by inputs from George Herbert Mead, a colleague in the department of philosophy. Thus the school's paradigm made room for or incorporated both an external, objective approach, one that analyzed subjects in their everyday life situation, and another complementary approach, which looked at the inner, subjective elements of this *Lebenswelt*. This development was encouraged by Park and is reflected in distinguished students and lieutenants such as Wirth, Blumer, and Hughes, each of whom in turn trained a later generation of students.

All in all, the Chicago School made the strongest imprint in the period between the two wars. Its influence has continued to this day in the continuing use of field research, participant-observation, urban sociology, and the attention given to social psychological or intersubjective features of social organization and social processes. The school, however, after the passing of Park and the dispersion of its members, lost its inner cohesion. The core paradigm had lost its vitality by the onset of World War II. But for nearly twenty years, about the same time period as the Durkheimian School's great period of flourish, it had the greatest impact on the development of sociology.

I come now to the end of the trilogy with the *Parsonian School*, which is so much a part of the post-World War II scene that its major proponents and opponents are for the most part alive and kicking, making it difficult to garner objective detachment. 12 I shall select only a few features which make it comparable to the two schools previously discussed.

First of all, the school owes its existence to a charismatic intellectual leader, Talcott Parsons. Parsons received his initial training and his initial appointment in economics, and has had an amazing ability to enter into intellectual interchanges with leading figures in a great many other disciplines. These inputs from fields outside of sociology have enabled him to develop a much more global view about the relation of sociology to other sciences (social and natural) than almost any other modern sociologist. While formulating his basic paradigm in the 1930s, he was a "voice in the wilderness" at a time when American sociology was predominantly empirical, atheoretical, and positivistic; Parsons' central notion of "action," synthesizing elements from theories of four major European figures, was, in a sense, not that much of a radical departure from the native American tradition of pragmatism and voluntarism found in Mead, Park, Thomas, and Cooley. However, whereas these men had had illuminating insights, Parsons was to insist on the formulation of a *general theory* of action. Parsons tacitly drew on one of the basic aspirations of the sociological imagination, going back to Comte and Saint-Simon, namely, to provide a frame of reference for the unification of the (social) sciences. The manifesto or methodological treatise which stamped the Parsonian School was the work jointly edited with Edward Shils, *Toward a General Theory of Action* (1951). It is important to note that this is a collaborative venture with the treatise beginning by a "General Statement" cosigned by Parsons, Shils, Gordon Allport, Clyde Kluckhohn, Henry Murray, Robert Sears, Richard Sheldon, Samuel Stouffer, and Edward Tolman—eminent figures in sociology, social psychology, clinical psychology, and anthropology. Parsons in 1946 was the key figure in the establishment of a new interdisciplinary department at Harvard, the department of social relations. The school that gathered around him was highly interdisciplinary, and found an institutional structure in the department which allowed a great deal of interaction with specialists in other sciences.

Although Parsons had begun to draw some students around him in the mid- and late 1930s, it was with the end of the war and the beginning of a new department that the school became highly visible. America had come out of the war ready to reconstruct a shattered and exhausted world, and, appropriately, the Parsonian School felt that it had a mission to revive and reconstruct the behavioral sciences. For a period of about fifteen to twenty years, the Parsonian

School was the dominant center of conceptualization and theoretical analysis, and not only within sociology; it also profoundly marked theoretical formulations and modes of orientation to social phenomena in other disciplines (notably political science and social anthropology).

The school was very fortunate in finding, quite early, a major interpreter who took the rather recondite ideas and conceptualizations of Parsons and formulated them into a major statement. I mean, of course, Robert Merton who, like the early Durkheimians, had already completed his formal training (under Sorokin) before coming into contact with Parsons. The publication of his *Social Theory and Social Structure* (1949) provided the school with a wide public, who could now have a lucid explication of the method of analysis at the heart of Parsons' structural-functional approach. The collaboration of Parsons the theorist with Sam Stouffer the empirical researcher, and the similar pairing of Merton with Lazarsfeld, seemed ample proof that the new paradigm could integrate sociological analysis and research. Merton has also, by virtue of his erudition in the area of the natural sciences, added legitimation and respectability to sociology and to structural-functional analysis, for being accepted by natural scientists is an accolade sociologists long for!

Unlike the Durkheimians and the Chicagoans, the Parsonians did not establish their own scientific journal. However, they did have important formal channels of communication.[13] The *American Sociological Review* was a major vehicle of dissemination among prestigious journals (though it was never a captive organ). Equally important, the school found a figure who played a role similar to that of Felix Alcan in giving the Durkheimians a press which readily published their writings in book form and monographs. This was Jeremiah Kaplan, who launched his Free Press of Glencoe with the reissue of Parsons' *The Structure of Social Action* (McGraw-Hill, publisher of the 1937 edition, still had unsold copies by the end of the war) and with Merton's *Social Theory and Social Structure*, both in 1949. Kaplan's Free Press thereafter published almost all the works of Parsons and readily took those of other members of the school.

The Parsonian School, or the structural-functional school, provided a major integrating function for sociology as a discipline. At one level, it provided a general language for sociological analysis (a general medium of communication much like a computer language): the logic of structural-functional analysis, the core elements of social action differentiated into the pattern variables and the subsequent analysis of social systems into four major functional sectors, and so on. At another level, Parsons, along with core associates and lieutenants, integrated into the emergent paradigm various figures in the sociological tradition, notably Durkheim, Weber, and to a lesser extent Pareto, and made their writings take on a new vitality for contemporary sociology. Lastly, the Parsonian School helped to integrate sociology with other disciplines and also with broader global trends. Many of the Parsonians, or structural functionalists, such as David Schneider, Clifford Gertz, Wilbert Moore, Robert Bellah, Renee Fox, Marion Levy, Francis Sutton, found that the general frame of reference had relevance beyond the setting of American society; the cosmopolitan ethos of Harvard University (and other places on the Eastern seaboard which came to be populated with products of the Harvard school), coupled with an encouragement from the Department of Social Relations for students to do research on a comparative basis, resulted in a certain internationalization of American sociology.[14]

CONCLUDING REMARKS

In this essay I have sought to provide an outline for rethinking the history of sociology. It should be seen as an initial sketch, not as a finished canvas. To do a comparative analysis of schools as units of sociological development entails painstaking research, and is likely to require team research. We need, for example, to know a great deal about the biographical features of the members of a school: where they came from before joining the school, the nature of their association with the school, their subsequent career. We need to know what evolution took place in the school and its paradigm over time, as a function of generational changes. We also need to know the relationships of the school to its institutional and societal context. Lastly, we must ask which factors make for the ascendance and fall of a school from a central position in the discipline. Implicitly, the approach developed in this essay would suggest that during "normal" periods of sociology there is a core paradigm which has a hegemony over the main intellectual orientation of the discipline. This hegemony is established and maintained by an ongoing scientific community, the dominant school, which can be shown to have developed in actual interaction with one another at a given place at a given time. But the school does not exhaust the profession. If the school is dominant, it is a reflection that in science, like other areas of human endeavor, nothing succeeds like success, and success stems from demonstrated results and productivity, which are viewed as furthering the advancement of the discipline. The three schools we have emphasized are each characterized both by extremely capable intellectual charismatic leaders, who knew tacitly how to organize colleagues and students into an effective research team, and by extremely productive associates and students. The school, in its formative period, lives in the state of intellectual effervescence which is not so dissimilar in generating enthusiasm as that described by Durkheim in *The Elementary Forms*. There is imparted a certain hyperactivism to its members which is translated in an average rate of productivity much higher than that of other groups; it is not sheer quantity of output, however, but also a high level of first-rate contributions to the discipline.

To be sure, even while the school is flourishing in its greatest period of creativity and productivity, other individuals and other groups are active; they

cannot be ignored in the total picture of the history and development of sociology. But they lack the sustained impact, the concentrated set of intellectual
and professional activities of the dominant school. Some may be "dormant,"
like a colony of spores, which under altered environmental conditions surfaces
as a major grouping. To examine the relation of dominant schools to competing ones, or to individuals standing apart from schools but who are nevertheless seen as significant figures in the profession, would constitute another
dimension of a sociological account of the development of the discipline. There
is a vast array of related themes and topics involved in approaching the history
of sociology this way, particularly those which take us into deeper metascientific dimensions of major schools, such as the question of ideological elements in a school's presuppositions. In brief, there is a vast sociological undertaking involved in rethinking sociology sociologically. Hopefully, this essay will
have suggested some of the layers of the undertaking.

NOTES

1. Needless to say, the formulations of the sociology of science rest on the shoulders
of the giant of the field, Robert K. Merton.
2. See Kuhn (1970a:174), and also the excellent review essay of Dudley Shapere
(1971) entitled "The Paradigm Concept." But to point out an ambiguity in one element
of Kuhn's interpretation of scientific development is not intended as a negation of his
approach. Rather, it should be clear to the reader that the perspective which frames this
essay's approach to the development of sociology is entirely congruent with the general
thesis of Kuhn. That scientific progress is discontinuous, qualitative, and grounded in
sociopsychological factors making for the acceptance and rejection of paradigmatic
presuppositions is a perspective which has pronounced affinity with the structure of
Rostow's thesis for economic development, *The Stages of Economic Growth*, and with
various papers in the volume edited by Georges Balandier and Yvonne Roux entitled
Sociologie des Mutations, particularly those grouped in the first section pertaining to
theoretical aspects of the sociology of mutations.
3. Nicholas Mullins, in his *Theories and Theory Groups in Contemporary American Sociology*, elaborates as the second of a four-stage model of the development of scientific groups that of a "network stage." This stage, for Mullins, represents a certain
group formation, since scientific communications are "thickened" between those who
are attuned to a major problem, research idea, or other common stimulus. One can say
that A is a member of scientific community Y if most of his scientific communications
are first communicated to Y and most of his information about what is going on comes
from other members of Y; stated in different terms, A is a member of scientific community Y to the extent that members of Y constitute his "significant others" in terms of his
scientific communications.
4. For example, if one simply looks at typical anthropological monographs of the
1920s and 1930s, one would hardly know that the great majority, if not all, had as their
locale a colony of the West; yet from the initial description of society it would appear
that these societies are self-sufficient, whereas in fact they were economically, political-

ly, and culturally in a colonial situation. A rare exception which lifted the curtain was Jomo Kenyatta's *Facing Mount Kenya*.

5. The parallel with painting comes to mind. The official academies have excluded from the official *Salons* new avant-garde movements, such as the Impressionists, the Fauves, and the Cubists, who organized their own *Salons des Indépendants*.

6. This came to mind while reading the successive accounts of Marx and Spencer by Lewis A. Coser in his *Masters of Sociological Thought*. Juxtaposing the two chapters in question, one would think they belonged to quite different epochs and worlds, albeit Marx was only two years older than Spencer and both happened to be in London from 1849 to 1883 (with Spencer surviving for another twenty years). Yet what different presuppositions characterize their paradigms of the social world!

7. One is tempted to say presuppositions, which at the onset are, so to speak, the credo of the paradigm, become subject to "embourgeoisement." An illustration is Marxist sociology, which as it shifted its locale from the world of dissident émigrés living in marginal situations to its more recent level of academic respectability has muted, into near oblivion, the cardinal presupposition that only a revolutionary force can overthrow and destroy the established social order, and replace it with a revolutionary class and its agent (the party) that has a total monopoly of power.

8. The ideal type I have sought to construct has been suggested to me by my knowledge of two schools I shall discuss later, the Durkheimian School and the Parsonian School. Subsequent to my formulation, I came across the study of Yash Nandan, *L'Ecole Durkheimienne et son Opus*. Nandan (1975:4) proposes as general characteristics of what he calls a doctrinal school, such as Durkheim's, the following: (a) the master, (b) the doctrines, (c) the disciples, and (d) the means of communication and the sources of propagation of the doctrines. He also has a rather complex differentiation of the Durkheimians, which is inductively arrived at from his study of who wrote what and when in the *Année Sociologique*.

9. In support of this, Karl W. Deutsch, John Platt, and Dieter Shenghans, in their essay, "Conditions Favoring Major Advances in Social Sciences," indicate that for the period 1900-65, half of the major advances in the social sciences in the United States took place in three centers: Chicago, Cambridge (within the Boston metropolitan area), and New York. For the same period, London, Berlin, and Vienna were the locales of a total of seventeen out of thirty-one major social science advances. It would be interesting to reanalyze the authors' data to see what percentage of these advances came from persons working in the milieu or an integral part of a school.

10. The best panoramic view of the present situation and where we have come from is quite likely that presented by S. N. Eisenstadt (with M. Curelaru), *The Forms of Sociology: Paradigms and Crises*. It is as comprehensive a sociology of sociology as may be found in the literature of this decade.

11. As Terry Clark has insightfully noted in his *Prophets and Patrons*, the *Année* was in reality a research institute. Unlike the review *Année Psychologique*, which a few years before had been launched as a pilot model, Durkheim's journal was much more a collaborative effort at analyzing, sifting, and digesting scientifically interesting research and studies which needed codification for the advancement of sociology, than a medium acting as a forum for the publications of individual scholars.

12. For the best insider's account possible, see Talcott Parsons' essay "On Building Social System Theory: A Personal History"; for a crypto-Marxist account, see Alvin

Gouldner's *The Coming Crisis of Western Sociology*; and for an interesting balanced account comparing the Harvard School with the Columbia School, see John W. Heeren's unpublished dissertation, "Functional and Critical Sociology: A Study of Two Groups of Contemporary Sociologists."

13. Such informal channels of communication included, in the 1940s and 1950s, course seminars at which would be distributed mimeograph copies of papers written by core members. There were also a series of informal seminars and discussion groups, some of which formed an "inner sanctum" that provided Parsons with continuous feedback as the paradigm became more elaborated and differentiated.

14. Several of the persons cited previously became important formulators of what is broadly designated as "modernization theory." In crucial respects this comparative approach, although it by no means is reducible to structural-functional analysis, draws heavily from the paradigmatic view of social systems elaborated by Parsons, students, and associates. I should also add that at the intellectual level the internationalization of sociology at Harvard owed greatly to Sorokin, who brought to the United States in the 1920s the major intellectual currents of Europe; Sorokin, however, had little influence on the training of graduate students after the 1930s.

Gideon Sjoberg
and Ted R. Vaughan

HUMAN RIGHTS, REFLECTIVITY, AND THE SOCIOLOGY OF KNOWLEDGE

On the whole, contemporary American sociologists display little interest in matters such as ethics, social justice, and human rights. This observation is a convenient starting point for an examination of some central issues in the sociology of sociology and, more broadly, the sociology of knowledge. It has direct relevance for the kind of social theory and methodology required of sociologists who would concern themselves with the pressing problems confronting humankind today.

Most sociologists, to judge by their articles in the *American Journal of Sociology*, the *American Sociological Review*, *Social Forces*, and other "prestigious" journals, fail to analyze the impact of their particular ethical standards or orientations toward human rights[1] upon modes of theory construction and the research procedures they employ. Significantly, the theoretical or methodological perspectives of Parsons. Merton, Blalock, Duncan, and other guiding lights in sociology fail to acknowledge that human rights and moral concerns are an integral feature of social inquiry.

Herein we shall examine those aspects of the sociological enterprise which have led most sociologists to avoid fundamental issues such as ethics and human rights—issues that are not only of compelling concern to humankind but central to theory building and research.[2] This inattention to human rights and ethics is, so we contend, primarily a product of sociologists' commitment to the "natural science model" and to a special brand of positivism (cf. Ayer, 1959; Achinstein and Barker, 1969).

We challenge the disregard of ethics and human rights on practical and theoretical grounds. On the practical level, American sociologists have adopted an official code of ethics, and in a number of works on research methods we find sociologists acknowledging that researchers should be ethical and that their subjects have rights. At the same time, just how ethical decisions affect the research design, including the theoretical framework, is glossed over or ignored as an issue to be investigated.

Theoretical reasons also exist for questioning the use of the natural science model. Adherence to this orientation is at odds with a crucial feature of human nature: reflectivity (or reflexivity). Our main thesis is that employment of the natural science model leads sociologists to overlook their own role in theory building and social research. And sociologists often fail to take into account the reflectivity of the people they study. In all, the natural science model imposes a false order upon social life.

REFLECTIVITY

In *The Coming Crisis of Western Sociology*, Gouldner (1970) has performed a valuable service by calling for a "Reflexive Sociology" as the basis for understanding the nature of the sociological endeavor. His primary concern is in exposing the politically conservative infrastructure of Talcott Parsons' structural functionalism. However one may evaluate Gouldner's analysis, he does attempt to place Parsons' sociology within the context of the structural changes that have been occurring within American society. Clearly, as we look back upon the history of sociological thought, we find that the masters of the sociological tradition were products of their time even though certain aspects of their theoretical perspectives or research procedures do transcend the particular sociocultural circumstances in which they lived and worked. Likewise, there is no sociological justification for believing that Parsons, or any other sociologist, is exempt from the constraints of his/her era. In the process of criticizing Parsons, Gouldner comes to advance his own version of the sociology of knowledge.

More specifically, Gouldner (1970:490) remarks that "a Reflexive Sociology means that we sociologists must—at the very least—acquire the ingrained habit of viewing our own beliefs as we now view those held by others." He goes on to state: "A systematic and dogged insistence upon seeing ourselves as we see others would . . . transform not only our view of ourselves but also our view of others. We would increasingly recognize the depth of our kinship with those whom we study" (Gouldner, 1970:490). Although Gouldner directs our attention to the potential usefulness of reflexive sociology, or reflectivity, in theory construction and social research, his analysis is found wanting in several respects. He has, in our judgment, failed to explore the most salient implications of reflexivity for the sociological enterprise.

In developing our perspective, we draw upon—as well as reinterpret—the writings of George Herbert Mead, [3] who made reflectivity central to the definition of the social mind—of what it means to be human. Drawing upon Romanticists such as Fichte and Schelling, Mead formulated a theory of the nature of human nature which we believe is in keeping with how people can and do act. His view of the mind, in particular, differs markedly from conceptions that rely upon god-given explanations or innate features of human nature for explaining the essential nature of human nature.

We shall briefly discuss two significant dimensions of Mead's argument. First, the mind is social in nature. It is a product of the interaction of an individual with other persons. In turn, a conception of self is formed through this interaction—through "taking the role of the other." Admittedly, people are born with certain biological capabilities, but it is through interaction with others that the social mind and the social self come into existence and develop. This interaction occurs within both primary group settings and broader structural arrangements. We interpret the latter as corresponding to Mead's "generalized other."

Yet the mind does more than simply mirror social experience. Human beings are capable of reflecting back upon their own "selves" and actions and, in the process, reformulating, through various forms of reasoning, the nature of their activities, so that these come to differ from what has been conceived of as normal or habitual. In other words, human beings are capable of reflectivity. Therefore, it is possible for them to create alternative modes of action or even alternative futures. In the process of creating alternatives, actors may negate or falsify the theoretical orientations, or predictions, that are either explicit or implicit in the works of sociologists. Successful revolutionaries, for instance, those in Cuba and China, have remade social orders in ways that have not been anticipated by sociologists who typically rely upon "what is" to evaluate "what will be." Again, in Cuba and China the efforts to create new and different kinds of social and cultural arrangements have been purposive in nature. Moreover, one branch of futurology recognizes that the future is not a fact and that it does not necessarily reflect predictions based upon "what has been" or "what is." [4] Admittedly, when we deal with the future in this manner, we do not adhere to Mead in a literal sense, but we believe that such an orientation is in keeping with his conception of the mind.

Unlike theorists of human action such as Weber (1968) and Parsons (1937), Mead recognized that an essential feature of the human mind is the capacity to reflect back upon itself and make various kinds of judgments as to how to act. Some of these judgments are moral in nature. It is therefore through an understanding of reflectivity that sociologists can themselves come to terms with issues regarding ethics and human rights.

Mead's perspective is also a useful platform from which to observe theory building and social research. Sociologists employ reflectivity in their own activities, and it is essential that they recognize that the human beings they study are also capable of reflective thought and of creating alternative modes of action.

The nature of the social mind, with its capability for reflectivity, becomes the basis for our critical analysis of contemporary social theory. Our formulation of an alternative perspective also seeks to integrate ethics and human rights into the processes of theory building and social research.

THE PRESENT STATE OF SOCIOLOGICAL THEORY AND RESEARCH

Before we can discuss and critically evaluate the natural science model, in terms of the issues raised previously, we shall comment upon the present state of sociological theory and the natural science model as we see it. The field of sociology has always included competing theoretical perspectives. Much of Durkheim's early work was an attack upon the theoretical orientation of Herbert Spencer, and Weber carried on a running debate with the ghost of Karl Marx. In the period after World War II, a wide schism separated certain symbolic interactionists such as Blumer (1969) and his followers from the proponents of structural functionalism, notably Parsons and Merton.

In recent years the theoretical diversity within sociology, and social science in general, seems to have been accentuated. The field has witnessed the rise of newer forms of subjectivism, particularly various brands of phenomenology, as well as the emergence of different kinds of Marxist social science. For instance, some Marxists—for example, the followers of Althusser—align themselves with a special version of "scientific theory." We could compare this group with the existential Marxists who have in varying respects drawn upon scholars such as Sartre. Then too, certain humanist Marxists have become concerned with the inequality of power resulting from the rise of a "new class" in the Soviet sphere. In turn, Sweezy, Magdoff, and their followers have critically analyzed the political economy of capitalism and the imperialism of nations in the West. Each of these subschools of Marxism (and we have only mentioned a few) relies upon different assumptions and interprets the world in quite different ways.[5]

Also impressive is the methodological diversity within sociology. Today some mathematical model builders separate themselves from traditional statisticians, yet both of these groups tend to view the practitioners of qualitative methodology with some disdain and employ phrases such as "soft sociology" as a means of distancing themselves from the latter.

Nonetheless, even in the face of this theoretical and methodological diversity, contemporary American sociology displays a strong commitment to the natural science model. Even sociologists who would appear to be critics of "mainstream sociology" have adopted many of the tenets of "scientific theory" (e.g., Cicourel [1964] with his brand of ethnomethodology). Certainly, "official sociology"—the kind of research which is most likely to be funded, and the results published in prestigious journals—typically seeks to emulate the procedures of natural science as interpreted by philosophers of science.

The Nature of Unity in the Natural Science Model

A major feature of the natural science model is the logico-deductive format, and this has become the *ideal* toward which sociologists strive. Even Parsons and Merton,[6] whose structural functionalism is at odds with the logico-deductive orientation (in the sense that they tend to see the whole as greater than the sum of the parts), have at different times in their careers advocated logico-deductive theory as the ideal approach to scientific inquiry. Moreover, in recent years, the sociologist Peter Blau (1970) has sought to mold the study of formal organizations to make it more amenable to analysis within the logico-deductive framework. We use the term "mold," because in order to employ the logico-deductive format one must, it seems, focus upon particular kinds of problems that lend themselves to certain assumptions about reality, quantification, and so on.

Admittedly, the proponents of logico-deductive theory, whether in the philosophy of science or in sociology, hold differing views as to what constitute the basic elements of this theoretical format. In a loose sense, we follow Mary Hesse's extension (1967:404-10) of the argument of Hempel and Oppenheim.[7] There are three main aspects of logico-deductive theory. First, there are the theoretical statements or axioms in which some basic terms are nonobservable. These serve as a "bridge" to the second level of analysis—the statement of "laws." Third, we find statements about the phenomenon to be explained, such statements being derived from the laws. In Hesse's (1967:405) language, one may view "the explanation of laws by theories as analogous to the explanation of particular facts by laws."

The general format of the logico-deductive orientation is associated with a second unifying theme—quantitative empiricism. Instead of having theory emerge, through what Peirce and Hanson have termed abduction or discovery, empirical observations are employed to test hypotheses or propositions. A hypothesis is judged to be true or false according to whether or not it corresponds with the observed facts of nature. More specifically, scientific theory is designed to predict the course of events in the natural world. (To be sure, because of political and other social constraints imposed upon the use of the experimental design, sociologists tend to speak of predicting whether hypotheses are true or false, not how events will occur in the social world.)

The pervasiveness of the logico-deductive format is all the more apparent when sociologists speak of qualitative research as exploratory, for by implication the qualitative researcher has as his or her major goal the creation of testable hypotheses. Thus adherents of the natural science model do not accept the premise that descriptive, qualitative researchers can strive for a goal other than the formulation of testable propositions.

Ultimately, the advocates of the natural science model rest their case upon a set of assumptions about the nature of human nature and social reality. They assume that the social world is preexistent to, and independent of, the actor's conception and construction of it. When Homans (1961) likens humans to pigeons, he articulates the world view of the adherents of the natural science model. Such a social world is deemed orderly and governed by laws that produce regularities. In this view, actors do not engage in reflexivity, for there is the hidden assumption that if sociologists can develop sophisticated theoretical systems and rigorous research procedures, then they will be able to make predictions as natural scientists do.

The foregoing characteristics of the natural science model, particularly the assumptions it makes about social reality and human nature, are associated with the view that social scientists can and should maintain objectivity, or value neutrality, with respect to the social phenomena they study. Admittedly, the challenge to authority throughout the world has led some social scientists, including sociologists, to question this assumption. The Third and Fourth Worlds' criticism of the authority structure of industrial nations, as well as shifting power arrangements within the latter, has led some sociologists to ask: How do we define objectivity? What is objective from one person's perspective is not necessarily so from another's. Despite these problems, the leading methodologists in sociology act as though the obstacles to objectivity or value neutrality are easily overcome. They take it for granted that objective operational indicators of social phenomena can be constructed, and on this basis they proceed with their research. But all too often these indicators—with respect to crime, child abuse, and a host of other social issues—are selected by social scientists who view these problems from the vantage point of the privileged. Seldom are operational indicators constructed from the perspective of the dispossessed. For example, the more prestigious universities are typically evaluated according to criteria associated with wealth and privilege. The success or failure of the less prominent colleges and universities then comes to be judged from that perspective.

Social scientists tend to proceed on the assumption that there is a reality external to, and independent of, the observer and those persons being studied and that objectivity or value neutrality is attainable. They then assume that they are dealing with the "facts of nature" and that after developing and testing theories to explain these facts they have nothing further to contribute. There is a strong propensity to equate "what is" with fundamental natural laws. For example, Milton Friedman argues that, as scientists, economists must be careful not to tamper with the "laws of the market place." But such reasoning tends to discourage the search for alternative social and cultural arrangements. Such reasoning furthermore leads the social scientist to the view that the world "out there" can be analyzed but never substantially revised. The natural science approach does not permit sociologists, or the groups they study, to engage in reflectivity. As a result sociologists are unable to determine whether alternative sociocultural arrangements are possible or essential for improving the lot of humankind. Sociologists then have little or no role in building an alternative, and hopefully more humane, future.

The foregoing perspective on sociological thought is far from exaggerated. Earlier we observed that Homans looks upon human beings as one would pigeons. And the Duncans and Featherman (1972:31) liken the social order to a machine and view the results of properly conducted research as so many "interchangeable parts" of that machine. Significantly few sociologists, whether at Harvard, Columbia, Michigan, Wisconsin, North Carolina, or Washington (to mention some of the more prominent institutions), critically examine the nature of objectivity, the role of indicators or of operational procedures, or the possibility of alternative assumptions regarding social reality and the meaning of all of this for social inquiry. Moreover, as in the case of Diamond's criticism of Lipset's analysis of the official reaction of Harvard University to certain events of the McCarthy era, one is likely to search in vain for evidence of how social scientists and methodologists incorporate Diamond's (1977) explicit questioning of Lipset's objectivity into their own theoretical and methodological formulations.

Critique of the Natural Science Model

Thus far we have argued that despite the apparent diversity of approaches in sociology there is a dominant view concerning theory construction and social research. We need to take a closer look at some of the criticisms leveled against the orthodox view of the natural science model; both philosophers of science[8] and social scientists have questioned this perspective.

The natural science model, as reflected in the writings of the Vienna Circle, has been dissected and subjected to unrelenting attack by Karl Popper (1974), who, in the process, has disavowed any commitment to positivism or to the idea that the social sciences should emulate the natural sciences. Although Popper is admittedly difficult to classify, his world view regarding human nature and social reality places him closer to the traditional positivists than he is willing to admit. Moreover, Popper has put forth his own version of the logico-deductive method, one that stresses testability via falsification. He is furthermore committed to a stark "individualism," and such is in keeping with his dependence upon the logico-deductive orientation. Here the parts—that is, individuals—add up to the whole. This, in turn, is compatible with Popper's (1966) commitment to piecemeal planning. But because he is forced to work within existing social categories, he does not entertain the possibility of constructing alternative social and cultural arrangements.

Still other philosophers of science have questioned the orthodox natural science model. Hanson (1961; cf. Suppe, 1977), with his emphasis upon adduction, or discovery, differs in certain fundamental respects from the followers of the traditional conception of natural science inquiry. In effect, Hanson does not view the logico-deductive orientation per se as the ideal form of scientific investigation. Moreover, Kuhn's (1970) view of the nature of scientific inquiry is not in keeping with the orthodox conception of the natural science model, and, at least at one point in his intellectual development, Kuhn spoke of the preparadigmatic nature of social science—by inference the latter had not as yet achieved parity with the natural science mold. Finally, Feyerabend (1975) reasons that the scientific method is essentially "anarchistic." His approach represents a rather direct attack against the highly formalized view of natural science as it has been formulated by many philosophers of science and, more recently, by sociologists.

Sociologists have been influenced only to a limited extent by the aforementioned philosophers' criticisms of the orthodox natural science model. The major thrust of the attack upon this orientation in sociology, or the social sciences more generally, comes from other sources. At least two schools of criticism can be rather easily distinguished. The first attempts to construct "universal generalizations" about humankind, but it does so in a manner quite different from that of adherents to the natural science model. The second group attacks this model from the vantage point of historicism.

One group of social scientists—including diverse thinkers such as Jung (1964), Chomsky (1968), and Firey (1977)—has argued that the human mind is characterized by certain a priori or innate categories and by tapping these we can understand the universal features of human activity. Thus Jung posited the presence of archetypes which can be discovered, for instance, by analyzing dreams via the logic of analogy; Chomsky has argued for deeper levels of structure in language than have heretofore been glimpsed; and Firey, a phenomenologist, is searching for ideal laws that "can be seen in an object of consciousness only after that object has been divested of its factual characteristics and has been subjected to at least a limited reduction and to a process of free variation" (Firey, 1977:108). For Firey the logical procedures for establishing ideal laws do not conform to the natural science model (although the logico-deductive orientation enters into Firey's world in another guise). These scholars, and others of like mind, deserve more attention than they have received. The intellectual context in which they work must, however, be more thoroughly understood.

Within the field of sociology the foremost critics of the natural science model have been those scholars aligned with "historicism." Even in the nineteenth century German scholars such as Dilthey were contending that the natural and social worlds are distinct and that these two realities require different modes of inquiry. Where primacy is given to meaning, the social scientist must take into account the actor's own interpretation and definition of events. But because the meaning and interpretation of human action is defined within the context of a specific cultural setting, one is unable to generalize about patterned events across cultures.

In recent decades we find sociologists translating the early historicism, which focused upon broad sociocultural systems, into analysis of the actions of small groups or individuals. Although we observed that one branch of phenomenology (or subjectivism) has been searching for universals, another wing, which includes persons who label themselves as phenomenologists, ethnomethodologists, or adherents to "language analysis," has focused not on generalizations about social life, but rather upon individuals or small groups. For instance, considerable discussion has revolved around the individual's construction and interpretation of social events as the focal point of sociological investigation, and as such it has no counterpart in the study of natural phenomena. There are sociologists, too, who have not been concerned with generalizing beyond narrowly based social groups, even within a given sociocultural setting. From a sociology of knowledge perspective the intellectual focus upon individualism (i.e., self-fulfillment) is in keeping with the emphasis in American society, or more generally, the West.

We can point to still other critics of the natural science model. Although many Marxist-oriented scholars, especially in the United States, are committed to the natural science model, still others stress the role of "totality," contradictions, and the logic of the dialectic. It is their assumptions about social reality as well as their logic of inquiry which set them apart from social scientists who cling to the orthodox natural science mode of reasoning.

One of the most sophisticated and self-conscious attacks upon the natural science model was launched by those critical theorists who are loosely associated, in one manner or another, with the Frankfurt School (Jay, 1973). Relying primarily upon Marx and Freud, they sought to formulate a critical perspective toward the social world. As early as the 1930s, Horkheimer (1972:188-243), for one, explicitly set forth the differences between the natural science orientation and what he viewed as an alternative mode of theory construction. Certainly, many members and followers of the Frankfurt School have utilized some form of dialectical reasoning. This has been associated with recognition of the contradictions within social orders. More significantly, many of these scholars sought to describe the linkage between human nature and social structure. Thus their critique of a planned society based upon bureaucratic rationality, with its resultant strictures upon the human potential, was predicated upon the assumption that human beings can in some real sense reshape their social world, including its power structure.

Yet the Frankfurt School, in striving to avoid identification with the totalism that was associated with the totalitarian regimes of Hitler's Germany and Stalin's Russia, stopped short in its analyses. It did not, for example, construct or suggest alternative realities: it was oriented to the past and the present, not to the future. The strength of the School lies in its criticism of the unidimensional nature of modern industrial-urban life.

Overall, none of the theoretical perspectives that have emerged as alternatives to the natural science model are adequate for coping with issues such as ethics and human rights. For instance, we find no evidence that social scientists such as Jung or Chomsky, or phenomenologists who search for universals in other than sociocultural terms, have faced up to the basic issues of human rights and social justice—issues that arise from the power of the privileged over the dispossessed. Moreover, the historicist position leads to an extreme form of cultural relativism. Ironically, both the positivists, in practice, and the historicists, in theory and practice, are committed to a kind of cultural relativism that makes it possible to justify genocide or triage as morally right and makes it impossible for sociologists to formulate a transnational or transcultural conception of human rights.

AN ALTERNATIVE PERSPECTIVE

Here we hark back to two themes mentioned earlier in our argument. First, once sociologists recognize that ethics and human rights form an integral part of their own activities, then it is apparent that they can no longer ignore them as sociological problems. Second, we deem it clear that the natural science model—given its assumptions about human nature and social reality, as well as about the research process—is unable to come to terms with the issues of ethics and human rights. In turn, the critics of this approach seem inadequate to this task. Thus we are in dire need of an alternative perspective in sociology by which we can deal with such central issues.

Herein we shall *sketch one alternative* to the natural science model. In order to do so, we shall outline our view of theory and methodology which, up to this point, has been left largely unexplicated. For us, social theory is an overall process for interpreting, and constructing, social reality. Theory, when viewed as a process or a set of ongoing activities, rather than as an intellectual product independent of the persons who create and sustain it, has certain constituent elements. Any theory contains a set of "domain assumptions" about the nature of human nature and social reality, a logical system, and a verification procedure. The natural science model makes assumptions about human nature and social reality that emphasize stability and permanence, the actors in effect being viewed as robots. The model employs the logico-deductive mode of reasoning and uses prediction as the means for testing or verifying a theory. Significantly, the particular verification procedure one employs is closely associated with one's assumptions about human nature and social reality.

Most students of the history of social thought are aware of competing domain assumptions. However, they have been far less attuned to the fact that various logics are employed by sociologists as well as by the persons being studied. Analogy is widely used, by both actors and sociologists engaged in constructing social theories. But Mead (1934), Schutz (1962), Parsons (1937), Znaniecki (1952), and others have failed to grasp the central importance of analogy for interpreting action in everyday life. On the other hand, Goffman (1959) has used the dramaturgical analogy for analyzing human action, but he, too, has not appreciated the significance of analogy from the actor's perspective. In addition to analogy, we find a variety of dialectical logics employed by widely cited scholars such as Marx, Sorokin and Lévi-Strauss (the last mentioned also relies heavily upon analogy).[9] Moreover, a careful review of the literature confirms, we believe, the existence of a "parts-whole" reasoning or "logic" among, for instance, certain structural functionalists and those Marxists who view totality as central to their analysis. Then there is the logic for selecting the optimal means of achieving a particular end, an approach that does not seem encompassed within any of the aforementioned logics. Finally, we find phenomenologists such as Firey advocating *epoche*, limited reductions, and free variation as a means of understanding the human condition.

On a more general level, it seems possible to discover some broad relationships between the particular logics theorists employ—the logico-deductive method, analogy, and the dialectic—and the kinds of assumptions they make concerning human nature and social reality. Earlier we sought to indicate some of these relationships in our natural science model.

Our discussion so far leads to the question: What assumptions about human nature and social reality—that is, what kinds of logic and verification procedures are congruent with constructing an effective alternative to the natural science model; one that will come to terms with issues such as ethics and human rights?

We have already mentioned our conviction that sociologists must recognize that the mind is social in nature. Human beings can and do engage in reflectivity. Although many sociologists are willing to introduce this conception of human nature into introductory textbooks, they have, by and large, been unwilling to incorporate this orientation into their theory and methodology. Where such has been attempted, as in the case of Blumer (1969), the work has been sketchy and the perspective ignores the social structure that supports power differentials. Yet knowledge of these is essential for understanding human rights, justice, and ethics. Also, Blumer and other symbolic interactionists have neglected the question of how people go about creating alternative futures.

To restate our main argument and elaborate upon it further, the social nature of the mind makes it possible for actors to reflect upon themselves and their actions. Biological, technological, and power arrangements, however, set limits upon this reflexivity. Thus for the preliterate the scope and the range of reflective thought are highly circumscribed; this is not the case with many inhabitants of the modern world.

Put another way, certain kinds of regularities arise from the constraints placed upon humans by their biological and technological environments; other regularities emerge as a result of power relationships. In modern industrial-urban orders, many of the regularities in human action are responses to bureaucratic controls, and some can even be said to transcend political and ideological orientations (although it is also apparent that different kinds of political regimes lend themselves to greater and lesser reflexivity and, in turn, particular kinds of regularities).

Although we have pointed to certain regularities in social action, it is still a hazardous, and often fruitless, undertaking to formulate meaningful social laws (except in restricted areas related to the biological constraints of age and sex). There are all too many cases in which people have substantially reshaped their technological environment and even the existing power relationships. Regrettably, many modern American sociologists, socialized as they are into a particular world view (one facet being the natural science model), lack the tools for analyzing people's relationships to power structures, notably those associated with bureaucracies.

Although we see the mind as social in nature, and therefore capable of reflectivity, we also proceed under the assumption—one whose plausability is supported by considerable data—that people, as social beings, develop social structures that transcend any given person or grouping of individuals. Nonetheless, it is human beings who sustain these structures and, in certain cases involving collective effort, effect changes in them—this holds even for large-scale systems. Thus, although social structures transcend particular individuals, they do not exist apart from them. However, we must not fall into the kind of trap that Weber (1968) set for himself. Although he argued that sociologists must begin their analysis from the actor's perspective, he ignored his own advice in his analysis of bureaucratic systems. Little wonder that he came to view bureaucracy as a juggernaut, for he seems to have accepted the fact that human beings *are unable* to revise the structures that they have created.

Herein we emphasize the role of organizations—notably bureaucratic systems—for these generate the major issues associated with ethics, social justice, and human rights. These systems sustain power differentials in the modern world. More importantly, they served as vehicles for undermining human rights. The destruction of approximately six million European Jews was the work of an efficient Nazi administrative apparatus. Ordinary people who came to accept and believe in the structures of the German nation-state were instrumental in perpetuating practices involving torture and death.[10] So too, in Stalin's Russia, persons in powerful organizations of social control helped to maintain the Gulag Archipelago.

Large-scale organizations have also served, admittedly on a lesser scale, to undermine the rights of many persons in democratic orders such as the United

States. Clearly, sociologists have lacked any adequate theoretical orientation for interpreting Watergate and the many activities that were brought to light as a result of it. In large part they failed to grasp just how bureaucratic structures come to socialize their members into accepting certain activities that sustain the power group and, in turn, often violate the rights of the less privileged.

Moreover, sociologists have overlooked the hidden side of bureaucratic structures. They have left unexamined the contradictions that give rise to secrecy systems, for the very structure of organizations seems to generate a hidden, and often dark, side. Persons in power positions find it advantageous to protect themselves from being accountable to those below (as well as outsiders), whereas the underprivileged engage in a certain amount of secrecy in order to reduce the amount of control and manipulation emanating from above. Overall, the hidden side is, more often than not, employed to sustain control and privilege.

At this juncture, we shall recapitulate our argument and bind together certain loose strands of thought. Earlier, we outlined some key assumptions concerning the nature of human nature and of social reality. For us, the mind is social in nature and capable of reflexivity. Yet the amount and the kind of reflexivity that exist are to a considerable extent a product of social structure. Where does this leave us with respect to research and theory? We are committed to the view that one function of research is to examine how powerful organizations undermine human rights by stifling reflective thought, thereby making it practically impossible for actors within a system to take into account the rights of others. Although a great deal of research needs to be carried out on the aforementioned problem area, it is apparent that traditional research procedures, which rely upon "experimental designs" (and even social surveys), are not only impractical but useless for the task at hand.[11] Alternative research methods are in order. Even if we gain a sounder understanding, empirically and theoretically, of what exists, sociologists must face up to the task of creating blueprints for the construction of more humane social orders—those that will more adequately incorporate ideals concerning ethics and human rights.

We advocate the use of some mode of dialectical reasoning—more specifically "countersystem analysis"—for achieving this goal (Sjoberg and Cain, 1971). A countersystem, as we define it, is a negation of, and a logical alternative to, an existing order. A possible countersystem to the existing bureaucratic order is one wherein everyone is equal and all human beings are treated with dignity and respect.

The countersystem is a kind of utopian dream. Today most sociologists reject utopian thinking outright (a striking exception is Wilbert Moore [1966] in his presidential address to the ASA). However, a utopia can be just as "real" a standard for evaluating an ongoing system as is the system itself. Unless one

[248]   *Toward a Reflexive Sociology*

thinks in terms of some kind of countersystem, one will act, as most sociologists do, and judge "alternative" social arrangements in terms of the dominant existing social structure and typically label them as "deviant."

Again, if social scientists are to participate in the construction of more humane social organizations that advance the cause of human rights, they cannot summarily reject whatever alternative forms may arise. In addition, sociologists should set out to construct countersystems that may well serve as incentives for the world's citizenry to think and act in terms of social arrangements that will promote human rights.

Although George Herbert Mead did not actively engage in utopian thinking, his perspective is in keeping with that underlying countersystem analysis. It is through reflectivity that one is able to think in terms of alternative social arrangements, thereby contrasting "what is" with "what can be." The ongoing system can thus be judged by other than its own standards.

As for verification, the establishment of new kinds of organizations that further the cause of human rights would be a means for "testing" this kind of theorizing.

IMPLICATIONS

In this brief essay we challenge the dominant tradition within sociology—that which enjoins sociologists to be ethically neutral, or as value free as possible. From a sociology of knowledge perspective, sociologists have been unable to attain such neutrality in the past, and there is no reason to believe they can do so in the future. For one thing, how can sociologists be committed to an ethical code for themselves and yet remain unconcerned with ethics and human rights? Or would they condone Hitler's "final solution" on the grounds that morality is relative to particular sociocultural circumstances?

In point of fact, sociologists generally adhere to an ethical orientation in theorizing and in conducting research. For instance, the principles underlying utilitarianism typically inform those conceptual schemes associated with "cost-benefit analysis" or the "risk-benefit ratio."[12] Implicit here is the notion of the greatest good for the greatest number. In fact, utilitarianism is currently the dominant ethical orientation within sociology. Thus some of the champions of ethical neutrality are themselves committed to moral principles which they do not understand.

Sociologists, living as they do with a myopic world view, find it difficult to recognize the challenges to the dominant mode of thought within the discipline. Rawls (1971), although committed in some respect to utilitarianism, is a case in point. Slowly but surely his work *A Theory of Justice* is opening up a new arena of debate within the social sciences. And Dworkin's *Taking Rights Seriously* (1977) poses serious questions for sociologists. Unfortunately, most sociologists do not have the theoretical tools to come to terms with Dworkin's perspective on human rights.

If sociologists are to deal with the issues raised by Rawls and Dworkin, if they are to improve their own ethical code, and if they are to contribute to an understanding of human rights on a global scale, they must achieve a firmer grasp of the negative impact of the natural science model upon the study of human rights. Alternative theoretical and methodological orientations are mandatory if we are to come to terms with the multifaceted aspects of human rights.

Most sociologists are likely to shy away from the grand undertaking we suggest. But to the extent that they have done so, and will continue to do so, the field of ethics and human rights invariably becomes the province of other disciplines. Unlike most modern-day sociologists, we believe that sociology can make a substantial contribution to an understanding of the grave problems of the modern world and can point the way to possible solutions. But it should do so with humility. In the end, we believe that it is better to fail at such an endeavor than never to have sought to achieve a world wherein human rights serve as a basis for human conduct.

NOTES

1. The literature on human rights is becoming enormous. For example, the bibliography on *International Human Rights* (Miller, 1976), which contains only citations to English-language materials, includes over 1,000 entries for the period 1970-76. It is striking to see how few sociologists have contributed to this discussion.

2. In this essay we build upon Sjoberg and Vaughan (1977) and Vaughan and Sjoberg (forthcoming). We also have a book-length manuscript on "Ethics, Human Rights, and the Social Science Enterprise" that serves as a backdrop for this essay.

3. See Mead (1934, 1936). His views of the mind differ markedly, for example, from scholars represented in Feyerabend and Maxwell (1966) as well as philosophers such as Popper (1974). Mead's conception of the mind and its relationship to social action also differs from that advanced by sociologists such as Parsons (1937). Also compare Mead with Freud and Skinner.

4. Bell (1973) conceives of the future as a projection from the immediate past. Other futurologists see actors as having much greater control over their destiny. For a discussion of these perspectives see Miller (1974).

5. A useful, although controversial, survey of Western Marxism can be found in Anderson (1976) and Magdoff (1969). Although Althusser and Sartre are primarily philosophers and Sweezy and Magdoff are economists, they have all served to influence various sociologists in the United States and Europe.

6. Merton (1967), for example, has advocated the use of the logico-deductive orientation (chap. 4), but he has not recognized that this approach differs markedly from the logic that underlies structural-functional analysis (chap. 3).

7. Hesse, in actuality, discusses five aspects of the logico-deductive method. Be-

cause of the technical nature of the issues involved, we have only sketched the three main features of this orientation.

8. It is ironic that the logico-deductive method came to the fore in sociology after severe criticisms had been made against this perspective in the philosophy of science. In his "Introduction" Suppe (1977) discusses at some length the attacks against the "received view." However, he indicates in his "Afterword—1977" that philosophers of science are now arriving at a new synthesis in their effort to interpret the scientific enterprise.

9. Lévi-Strauss (1966) employs analogy in his analysis of the preliterate person's mode of reasoning, but he also criticizes Sartre's version of the dialectic. It is not clear to us, however, that Lévi-Strauss grasps the relationship between his use of analogy and his conception of the dialectic (see chap. 9).

10. Arendt (1963:253), in her analysis of the holocaust, spoke of the "banality of evil." She reasoned that the Germans who committed the crimes against humanity were "terribly and terrifyingly normal." Unfortunately, her discussion about the actions of ordinary people in a totalitarian setting has been obscured by the sharp criticisms of her depiction of the resistance of the Jews to the Nazi regime.

11. Blau writes: "This is the challenge of the century: to find ways to curb the power of organizations, in the face of their powerful opposition, without destroying in the process the organizations or democracy itself. Unless we can meet this challenge, the growing consolidation effected by organizations is likely to replace democratically instituted recurrent social change with alternate periods of social stagnation and revolutionary upheaval.

"The threat is serious, and the time is late. Let us remember that we are within a brief decade of 1984. And let us endeavor to prove Orwell a false prophet" (Blau, 1975:253).

In keeping with our argument Blau (1970; Blau and Schoenherr, 1971) can deal with the threat posed by 1984 by relying upon the logico-deductive framework. In fact, his approach is counterproductive. If Blau is to overcome the predicament posed by Orwell, Blau must of necessity come to terms, theoretically and empirically, with the problem of constructing new institutions or organizations, and the resultant structures will become the ultimate test of his theory.

12. Barber and his associates (1973), for example, have employed the "risk-benefit ratio" in their analysis of the ethics of medical experimentation. But Barber does not seem to understand the theoretical underpinnings of his framework. The risk-benefit ratio is an outgrowth of the utilitarian heritage. Thus within the context which Barber employs the risk-benefit ratio we find overtones of the "pleasure-pain," or in this instance the "pain-pleasure," principle. The question arises: How would Barber's data be interpreted within the framework of another ethical orientation?

POSTSCRIPT:

METASOCIOLOGICAL REFLECTIONS

The readings comprising this antholoy demonstrate that the meta-sociological choices made daily by sociologists, whether implicit or explicit, have a profound impact on the theoretical and methodological character of the discipline. It is essential, therefore, that we continually remain aware of those metasociological choices, and the assumptions under which we, as sociologists, operate. Insofar as this volume illustrates the importance of metasociology for the practice of sociology, it will have met its initial charge. In addition, however, readers may wish to utilize their newly developed metasociological acumen to interpret further the very essays which comprise this volume. As a first step in this direction, the editors would like to make some self-reflexive observations, concerning the readings in this volume, which hopefully will generate further discussion and reflection among readers.

ONTOLOGY AND EPISTEMOLOGY

An initial concern is the way in which various contributors to this volume address the issues of ontology and epistemology. As originally coined by scholastic writers of the seventeenth century, the term *ontologia* referred to questions of *being*. However, in current sociological usage the term has become a reference to those entities that sociologists study, want to study, or feel they should study. In particular, the most often asked question is whether the individual, the social group, or the society should be taken as the unit of analysis. Obviously, one is no more "concrete" or observable than the other. Each is a theoretical construct of equal complexity, if not in appearance, then certainly in fact.

From their essays, it is clear that Blau, Bealer, and Coser all wish to study society or some subset thereof (i.e., institutions). In this sense, they are convinced that the essence of sociology lies in the study of structure. Blau, of course, is deeply committed to uncovering the emergent properties arising from social interaction. Such higher-order properties of groups are not to be confused, or equated, with the characteristics of the individuals who comprise these groups. Yet it must be remembered that the decision to study emergent properties is a meta-sociological one.

Bealer also wants to study groups. What he offers is a sociohistorical explanation of how European sociologists remained realists whereas most Americans sought and found the individual as their unit of analysis. Bealer endeavors to convince us that the study of aggregate properties is more conducive to accurate predictions than is the study of individual phenomena. Yet it seems that Bealer has neglected one important element. The notion of aggregation is an analytic concept employed to refer to other concepts (e.g., atom vs. atom aggregate). As such, an aggregation has no intrinsic properties of its own. This being the case, it may be that individual behavior is predictable when examined in aggregate form. For example, let us conceive of the term "individual" in a theoretical or an aggregate sense. As so constructed, an individual could be thought of as possessing a set of descriptive constructs, for example, attitudes, dispositions, personality, behavior, and so on. Viewed in this manner it is possible to measure the various descriptive characteristics and subsequently to aggregate them. Based on those aggregated characteristics, it would be possible to predict how some individual would act under a given set of parameters. In this sense, some might question Bealer's argument for the supremacy of prediction and a realist ontology, since the same argument could be made for the individual.

Finally, Coser's realist ontological orientation is inextricably linked to a concern for studying the *relational* aspects of society. This surfaces as dismay over studies which examine individual rates of mobility to the exclusion of structural rates. Yet to associate this shortcoming with the use of sophisticated statistical analysis is to do a potential disservice to such techniques and their users. Although interested in conducting a class-based analysis, Coser appears to have overlooked the fact that, in the final analysis, it is the users of various methodological procedures and not the procedures themselves that err.

In sum, the writings of Bealer, Blau, and Coser, when analyzed meta-sociologically, are implicitly or explicitly realist in their ontology. Yet each fails to explicate an unequivocal logic for why such an orientation *ought* to be used. Some attention, it would seem, should be devoted to such questions. One possible outgrowth of such metasociological debate might be the sensitization of members of the discipline to the need for advancing arguments, for example, political, moral, scientific, or aesthetic, in favor of a particular ontological stance. By so doing, sociology might better be able to maintain its integrity as a unique mode of scientific inquiry quite apart from the biological and psychological characteristics of the individuals it studies.

The essays of Blalock and Leik are quite different, metasociologically, from any of the aforementioned articles in that both authors de-emphasize the importance of ontology. Their writings essentially transform ontological questions into epistemological ones. Given epistemology's traditional meaning as a branch of philosophy which analyzes the scope and presuppositions of knowledge, their writings show considerable interest in epistemological questions rather than ontological ones. Leik and Blalock are both concerned with theory construction, but their concern is not focused on the nature of the entities mapped by theory. Whether the individual or group is the unit of analysis is of no real moment. The question is: How does one most efficaciously study whatever it is he has chosen to examine? Both agree about the major contributions to be made by research methods, they only differ somewhat as to the best strategy for theory construction. Blalock posits an argument that is clearly out of the hypothetic-deductive model. Leik, on the other hand, explicates the need for more rigorous inductive attempts at theory construction. At a slightly different juncture it is instructive to note that although the epistemologies of Leik and Blalock are at variance at certain points, both seem to rely on a nominalist ontology.

Cicourel's work, in principle, is applicable to any data-gathering techniques. In essence, he is arguing that different levels or types of information are summarized at various stages of the research process. To account for and fully understand this hierarchical summarization Cicourel suggests that an interactive model is needed. The model would serve to illuminate the mechanisms through which information is summarized and subsequently transformed. To illustrate his argument, Cicourel draws heavily upon examples taken from dyadic relations—essentially a nominalist posture. What Cicourel leaves unexplicated is why he has chosen to focus, by and large, on the issue of data summarization. It is by no means clear that the summarization of data is the most important aspect of data gathering. What about the information given in the first place? Cicourel focuses on the summarization process, and this is a metasociological choice; yet he does not give any rationale for selecting this aspect of social interaction on which to concentrate. It is possible that such a choice once more belies the nominalist ontological bent apparent in Cicourel's discussions of the dyadic relationship?

SOCIOLOGICAL PERSPECTIVES

The first section of this book, containing essays by Martindale, Ritzer, and Wiley, attempts to order the past history and current direction of the discipline of sociology. It was noted elsewhere that their views of the discipline differ in fundamental ways. We would now like to point out some problematic metasociological issues generated by each author.

Martindale has argued that scientific theories are easily distinguishable and separable from ideologies. Theories are descriptive and explanatory whereas ideologies are prescriptive and persuasive. And although emotion or passion may help stimulate research, it should not be confused with the discovery of empirical regularities.

Upon closer inspection, it seems possible that Martindale's notion of scientific theory belies an ideal-typical notion of the social scientist, roughly corresponding to the following: a cool-headed dispassionate observer who can easily separate (because the differences are eminently clear) his/her wishes or emotions from the social world from which he/she has come, and who has the ability and desire to separate these elements. Further, it appears that this is an image of "how the social scientist ought to behave." The metasociological conception which Martindale espouses rests on a moral imperative. Left unanswered by Martindale, or perhaps unasked, are those reasons why a social scientist ought to behave in such a fashion, as well as the assets and liabilities which accompany such a stance.

It is questionable that the answer provided by traditional philosophers of science (i.e., such procedures will result in increased happiness for humankind) necesarily holds. Furthermore, those who take a position similar to Martindale's must engage in a project which will more clearly differentiate the persuasive aspects of *theory* from the persuasive aspects of *ideologies*. In short, it is not clear that sociologists can reach the ideal model sketched previously. This leads to an additional question. Given the fact that we accept the model of a scientist as a dispassionate investigator, what types of organizations will provide a suitable climate for preserving and promoting these characteristics?

George Ritzer's examination of the discipline from the perspective of multiple paradigms also raises a number of interesting metasociological questions. As Ritzer sees it, the three paradigms which dominate sociology (i.e., social factism, social definitionism, and social behaviorism) examine only selected aspects of social reality. One can only wonder how, or on what basis, Ritzer presumes to know the totality of social reality, of which each paradigm examines a part. Second, Ritzer suggests that the paradigms are in some sense irreconcilable. On what basis, then, can Ritzer presume to create an integrated paradigm? The reader will note that he *does not* maintain that his newly created integrated paradigm should replace any existing paradigm(s). What, then, is the point of creating yet another paradigm? Of what utility is it? Finally, the very manner in which Ritzer formulates the organization of sociology raises an interesting point. His formulation does not afford us a means of viewing the intellectual problems whose solution is being sought, in terms of their substantive content. Concepts like capitalism, bureaucratization, anomie, modernization, and so on, fail to appear. In their stead, the major issues addressing the discipline are reduced to questions of social order.

Norbert Wiley's essay also raises a number of metasociological concerns. Wiley tells us on the one hand that various schools, and schools of thought, have maintained their predominance, in part, by controlling the intellectual means of production. Yet, at the same time, he suggests that history is infinitely complex and cannot be known in its entirety. These two comments suggest further reflection. First, Wiley does not tell us why he chose to analyze the history of American sociology in those terms. In part, the reason may lie in Wiley's abiding belief that theory must be explained historically. Like Weber, Wiley apparently subscribes to the belief that only through use of the historical approach can important insights be gained into the rise and fall of dominant value systems. In this case the focus is on dominant ontological and epistemological orientations. Further, Wiley's use of the term "means of production," whether intellectual or economic, hints of a Marxian set of underlying metasociological assumptions. Second, the assumption of infinite complexity has profound consequences for the problem of competing explanations. For example, it is difficult to determine whether one explanation of a given "determinant event" is more adequate than another. For all practical purposes, alternative explanations may simply be seen as complementary. Furthermore, why should one make this type of assumption? What are the political, moral, or aesthetic grounds for making such an assumption?

The essays of Martindale, Ritzer, and Wiley are important for understanding the way the discipline is ordered. Moreover, the manner in which each goes about the task of ordering the discipline is also interesting. Each contributes to a better understanding of the other.

REFLEXIVE SOCIOLOGY

The final section of this anthology concerns itself with a sociology of sociology. Interestingly enough, the authors in this last section (Snizek, Sjoberg and Vaughan, and Tiryakian) examine some key issues from fundamentally different perspectives. Snizek concentrates on the problems of potential errors coincident with various theory-technique fits; Tiryakian gives us a new unit of analysis for examining the predominance of certain schools of thought; and Sjoberg and Vaughan focus on the ethics of social research.

Snizek argues that systematic covariations exist between certain theoretical orientations and adjacent analysis techniques. One rationale for the observed covariation is given in terms of the researcher's need for cognitive consistency. Does this explanation for a social phenomenon put Snizek, at least in part, in a nominalist camp? There is another question in this regard. Are Snizek's references to cognitive consistency (a nominalist ontological posture) partially responsible for his use of moderately empirical methods, in the form of chi-square and lambda, in his own essay? Admittedly, such a question raises the issue of infinite regress and the decision of when it is one ceases to "meta-sociologize." Finally, like Ritzer's writings on paradigms, Snizek's emphasis upon an "optimal fit" between theory and method runs the risk of sensitizing the discipline to exigencies of form at the expense of substance. Although obviously not an either-or proposition, the potential danger nevertheless remains if left unrecognized.

Somewhat like Wiley, Tiryakian argues that the dominance of certain schools of thought is dependent upon a founder-leader, disciples, social organization, and publication channels. Such an analysis presupposes that then, and only then, will a school of thought emerge and dominate the discipline. This framework seems to neglect a number of factors. For example, the idea that a theory is rationally persuasive to interested students is left totally unexplicated, as are those selectors (whether individual or social) that would prompt one to study under a founder-leader. Further, under what sets of conditions or circumstances can one begin a new school of thought—simply to indicate charisma as one of the elements begs the question.

Sjoberg and Vaughan's work gives us a starting point for examining the relationship among theory, research, and ethics. Their essay suggests some theories and methods are more appropriate to human research than others. However, they do not explicate their *own* position on ethics. Why should human subjects be examined from the theoretical and epistemological positions they suggest?

Further, on what do they base their own position? Again, this is not to disagree with Sjoberg and Vaughan but to alert readers to questions of a metasociological nature which they may wish to consider.

In conclusion, it should be fairly clear that metasociology often examines implicit extrascientific choices made by sociologists in the conduct of their work. At times such choices border on ethics, politics, and aesthetics. As such, metasociology does not pretend to justify one's reasons for choosing one alternative over another. Rather, its insights help to illuminate the bases of such choices and thereby extend the horizon of choice and study. Metasociology itself operates with a number of assumptions which deserve to be spelled out. First, metasociology is not an argument for utility alone, but simply for knowing oneself. Second, it can make explicit what was implicit and thereby give one the option to accept or reject such an assumption. Third, metasociology is, we *believe*, intellectually exciting—it is worth doing. And it is on this metasociological value judgment that we bring this volume to a close.

REFERENCES

Abel, Theodore F.
  1948 "The operation called *Verstehen*." American Journal of Sociology 54:211-18.
  1977 Personal interview and telephone interview, 9-5-77, 10-28-77. Chicago, Ill.
Achinstein, Peter, and Stephen F. Barker (eds.)
  1969 The Legacy of Logical Positivism. Baltimore: The Johns Hopkins Press.
Aho, James Alfred
  1975 German Realpolitik and American Sociology. Cranbury, N.J.: Associated University Presses.
Allport, Floyd H.
  1965 "Logical complexities of group activity." Pp. 27-31 in David Braybrooke (ed.), Philosophical Problems of the Social Sciences. New York: Macmillan.
American Journal of Sociology
  1930 "News and notes." 36:124-25.
  1932 "News and notes." 37:784.
American Sociological Society
  n.d. "Report of the committee to consider a plan for the control of the official journal and the other publications of the American Sociological Society." Paper presented at December 1933 meetings of the American Sociological Society.
  1936 "Report of the committee on publication of the American Sociological Society." American Sociological Review 1:122-25.
Anderson, Perry
  1976 Considerations on Western Marxism. London: New Left Books.

Arendt, Hannah
   1963   Eichmann in Jerusalem. New York: Viking Press.
Aron, Raymond
   1957   German Sociology. Glencoe, Ill.: The Free Press.
   1965   Main Currents in Sociological Thought. New York: Basic Books.
Attewell, Paul
   1974   "Ethnomethodology Since Garfinkel." Theory and Society I.
Ayer, A. J. (ed.)
   1959   Logical Positivism. New York: Free Press.
Baker, Paul J., Mary Z. Ferrell, and Susan W. Quensel
   1975   "Departmentalization of sociology in the United States 1880-1928." Paper
          presented at Annual Meetings of the American Sociological Association,
          San Francisco, California, August 1975.
Balandier, Georges
   1970   The Sociology of Black Africa. New York: Praeger.
Balandier, Georges, and Yvonne Roux
   1970   Sociologie des Mutations. Paris: Editions Anthropos.
Bales, R. F.
   1950   Interaction Process Analysis: A Method for the Study of Small Groups.
          Reading, Mass.: Addison-Wesley.
Barash, David P.
   1977   Sociobiology and Behavior. New York: Elsevier.
Barber, Bernard, et al.
   1973   Research on Human Subjects. New York: Russell Sage Foundation.
Bartholomew, D. J.
   1967   Stochastic Models for Social Processes. Second edition. New York: Wiley.
   1975   "Probability and social science." International Social Science Journal 27:
          421-36.
Bealer, Robert C.
   1963   "Theory-research: some suggestions for implementation from the work of
          Florian Znaniecki." Rural Sociology 28:342-51.
   1969   "Identity and the future of rural sociology." Rural Sociology 34:229-33.
   1970   "Conditions of action in sociological thought: whence and why?" Paper
          read at the annual meetings of the Rural Sociological Society, Washington,
          D.C.
   1975   "Theory and rural sociology." Rural Sociology 40:455-77.
Bealer, Robert C., Fern K. Willits, and Peter R. Maida
   1965   "The myth of a rebellious adolescent subculture: its detrimental effects for
          understanding rural youth." Pp. 45-61 in Lee Burchinal (ed.), Rural Youth
          in Crisis: Facts, Myths, and Social Change. Washington, D.C.: U.S.
          Government Printing Office.
Becker, Ernest
   1971   The Lost Science of Man. New York: George Braziller.
Becker, Howard S.
   1963   Outsiders. New York: Free Press.
Becker, Howard, and Harry Elmer Barnes

1961   Social Thought from Lore to Science. Third edition. Volume 3. New York: Dover.

Bell, Daniel
1973   The Coming of Post-Industrial Society. New York: Basic Books.

Ben-David, Joseph
1971   The Scientists's Role in Society. Englewood Cliffs, N.J.: Prentice-Hall.

Bender, Frederic
1975   The Betrayal of Marx. New York: Harper.

Bender, Frederic (ed.)
1970   Karl Marx: The Essential Writings. New York: Harper.

Bendix, Reinhard
1962   Max Weber, an Intellectual Portrait. Garden City, N.Y.: Doubleday Anchor.

Berelson, Bernard R., Paul F. Lazarsfeld, and William N. McPhee
1954   Voting. Chicago, Ill.: University of Chicago Press.

Berger, Joseph, Thomas L. Conner, and M. Hamit Fisek
1974   Expectation States Theory: A Theoretical Research Program. Cambridge, Mass.: Winthrop.

Berger, Peter
1963   Invitation to Sociology. Garden City, N.Y.: Anchor Books.

Berger, Peter, and Thomas Luckmann
1967   The Social Construction of Reality. Garden City, N.Y.: Anchor Books.

Bernard, Jessie
1977   "Expanding academic competence." Society 14:8-9.

Bernard, L. L., and Jessie Bernard
1943   Origins of American Sociology. New York: Thomas Y. Crowell.

Bernstein, Basil
1971   Class, Codes and Control. London: Routeledge and K. Paul.

Bielby, William T., and Robert M. Hauser
1977   "Structural equation models." Pp. 137-61 in Alex Inkeles, James Coleman, and Neil Smelser (eds.), Annual Review of Sociology. Palo Alto, Calif.: Annual Reviews, Inc.

Bierstedt, Robert
1950   "Review of Robert Merton's Social Theory and Social Structure." American Sociological Review 15:140-41.

1974   Power and Progress. New York: McGraw-Hill.

1977   Telephone interview. 10-28-77.

Bittner, Egon
1967   "The police on skid-row." American Sociological Review 32:699-715.

Black, M., and D. Metzger
1965   "Ethonographic description and the study of law." American Anthropologist 6:141-65.

Blalock, H. M.
1968   "The measurement problem: a gap between the languages of theory and research." Chapter 1 in H. M. Blalock and Ann B. Blalock (eds.), Methodology in Social Research. New York: McGraw-Hill.

1969   Theory Construction: From Verbal to Mathematical Formulations. Engle-
        wood Cliffs, N.J.: Prentice-Hall.
1971   Causal Models in the Social Sciences. Chicago, Ill.: Aldine-Atherton.
1978   "Dilemmas and strategies of theory construction." Chapter 6 in this vol-
        ume.

Blau, Peter M.
1957   "Formal organization." American Journal of Sociology 63:58-69.
1960   "Structural effects." American Sociological Review 25:178-93.
1969   "Objectives of sociology." Pp. 43-71 in Robert Bierstedt (ed.), A Design for
        Sociology: Scope, Objectives, and Method. Philadelphia, Pa.: The Ameri-
        can Academy of Political and Social Science.
1970   "A formal theory of differentiation in organizations." American Sociologi-
        cal Review 35:201-18.
1973   The Organization of Academic Work. New York: Wiley.
1975   "Parameters of social structure." Pp. 220-53 in Peter M. Blau (ed.), Ap-
        proaches to the Study of Social Structure. New York: Free Press.
1977   "A macrosociological theory of social structure." American Journal of So-
        ciology 83:26-54.

Blau, Peter M., and Otis Dudley Duncan
1967   The American Occupational Structure. New York: Wiley.

Blau, Peter, and Richard A. Schoenherr
1971   The Structure of Organizations. New York: Basic Books.

Blount, B. G.
1972   "Parental speech and language acquisition: some Luo and Samoan exam-
        ples." Anthropological Linguistics 14:119-30.

Blumer, Herbert
1937   "Social psychology." Pp. 144-98 in E. P. Schmidt (ed.), Man and Society.
        New York: Prentice-Hall.
1969   Symbolic Interactionism. Englewood Cliffs, N.J.: Prentice-Hall.
1975   "Parsons as a symbolic interactionist." Sociological Inquiry 45:59-62.
1977   Telephone interview. 10-30-77.

Bogue, Donald J.
1974   The Basic Writings of Ernest W. Burgess. Chicago, Ill.: Community and
        Family Study Center, University of Chicago.

Bosserman, Phillip
1968   Dialectical Sociology: An Analysis of the Sociology of Georges Gurvitch.
        Boston: Porter Sargent.

Bottomore, Thomas
1975   "Structure and history." Pp. 159-71 in Peter M. Blau (ed.), Approaches to
        the Study of Social Structure. New York: Free Press.

Bowers, Raymond V.
1967   "The military establishment." Pp. 234-74 in Paul F. Lazarsfeld, William
        H. Sewell, and Harold L. Wilensky (eds.), The Uses of Sociology. New
        York: Basic Books.

Box, G. M., and G. M. Jenkins
1976   Time Series Analysis: Forecasting and Control. New York: Holden-Day.

Bramson, Leon
   1971   "The rise of American sociology." Pp. 65-80 in Edward A. Tiryakian (ed.),
          The Phenomenon of Sociology. New York: Appleton-Century-Crofts.
Braude, Lee
   1970   "Park and Burgess." American Journal of Sociology 76:1-10.
Braungart, Richard
   1976   "Metatheoretical note on Max Weber's political sociology." International
          Journal of Contemporary Sociology 13:1-13.
Braybrooke, David (ed.)
   1965   "Introduction." Pp. 1-18 in Philosophical Problems of the Social Sciences.
          New York: Macmillan.
Brodbeck, May
   1968   "Methodological individualisms: definition and reduction." Pp. 280-303
          in May Brodbeck (ed.), Readings in the Philosophy of the Social Sciences.
          New York: Macmillan.
Brown, J. S., and B. G. Gilmartin
   1969   "Sociology today: lacunae, emphases and surfeits." The American Socio-
          logist 4:283-91.
Bruyn, Severyn T.
   1966   The Human Perspective in Sociology. Englewood Cliffs, N.J.: Prentice-
          Hall.
Burgess, Ernest W., and Donald J. Bogue
   1964   "Research in urban society: a long view." Pp. 1-14 in Ernest W. Burgess
          and Donald J. Bogue, Contributions to Urban Sociology. Chicago, Ill.: Uni-
          versity of Chicago Press.
Burr. Wesley R.
   1973   Theory Construction and the Sociology of the Family. New York: Wiley.
Campbell, Roy
   1955   Selected Poems. Chicago, Ill.: Regnery.
Cannon, W. H., and O. G. Jensen
   1975   "Terrestrial timekeeping and general relativity—a discovery." Science
          188:317-28.
Carey, James T.
   1975   Sociology and Public Affairs, the Chicago School. Beverly Hills, Calif.:
          Sage Publications.
Carpenter, G. Russel
   1976   "On structuralism and the sociological domain: comment on Goddard."
          American Sociologist 11:133-37.
Cartwright, Desmond S.
   1969   "Ecological variables." Pp. 155-218 in Edgar F. Bargatta (ed.), Sociologi-
          cal Methodology 1969. San Francisco: Jossey-Bass.
Cavan, Ruth S.
   1972   "Chicago and I." DeKalb, Ill.: Northern Illinois University. Mimeo.
Chapin, F. Stuart
   1934   "The present state of the profession." American Journal of Sociology 39:
          506-8.

Chirot, Daniel
    1976   Social Change in a Peripheral Society: The Creation of a Balkan Colony. New York: Academic Press.

Chomsky, Noam
    1968   Language and Mind. New York: Harcourt, Brace and World.

Cicourel, Aaron
    1964   Method and Measurement in Sociology. New York: Free Press.
    1968   The Social Organization of Juvenile Justice. New York: Wiley.
    1973   Cognitive Sociology. Middlesex, England: Penguin.
    1974a Cognitive Sociology. New York: Free Press.
    1974b "Interviewing and memory." Pp. 51-82 in C. Cherry (ed.), Pragmatic Aspects of Human Communication. Dordrecht: D. Reidel.
    1975   "Discourse and text: cognitive and linguistic processes in studies of social structure." Versus: Quaderni di Semiotici 33-84.
    1977a "Cognitive and linguistic aspects of social structure." Pp. 1-7 in The Cognitive Viewpoint. Belgium: University of Ghent.
    1977b "Language and society: cognitive, cultural, and linguistic aspects of language use." Plenary address presented at the XII International Congress of Linguists, Vienna, August 29 to September 2, 1977.
  Forth- "Interpretation and summarization: issues in the child's acquisition of
coming social structure." J. Glick and A. Clarke-Stewart (eds.), Studies in Social
    a   and Cognitive Development. New York: Gardner Press.
  Forth- "Discourse, autonomous grammars, and contextualized processing of incoming formation." Proceedings of the Institut für Kommunikationforschung and
    b   Phonetik, University of Bonn, Germany.

Clark, Terry
    1973   Prophets and Patrons. Cambridge, Mass.: Harvard University Press.

Cohen, Percy S.
    1968   Modern Social Theory. New York: Basic Books.

Coleman, James S.
    1964   Introduction to Mathematical Sociology. New York: Free Press.
    1968   Review of H. Garfinkel, Studies in Ethnomethodology. American Sociological Review 33:126-30.
    1973   The Mathematics of Collective Action. Chicago, Ill.: Aldine Publishing Co.

Collins, Randall
    1968   "A comparative approach to political sociology." Pp. 42-67 in Reinhard Bendix (ed.), State and Society. Boston: Little, Brown.
    1975   Conflict Sociology: Toward an Explanatory Science. New York: Academic Press.

Columbia University
    1931   A Bibliography of the Faculty of Political Science of Columbia University, 1880-1930. New York: Columbia.

Connerton, Paul (ed.)
    1976   Critical Sociology. New York: Penguin Books.

Cooley, Charles Horton
    1902   Human Nature and the Social Order. New York: C. Scribner's Sons.

Coombs, Clyde H.
 1964   A Theory of Data. New York: Wiley.
Corsaro, W. A.
 n.d.   Sociolinguistic Features of Adult Interaction Styles with Young Children. Unpublished manscript.
Coser, Lewis A.
 1955   "The functions of small-group research." Social Problems: 1-6.
 1956   The Functions of Social Conflict. New York: Free Press.
 1965   "Introduction." Pp. 1-26 in L. Coser (ed.), Georg Simmel. Englewood Cliffs, N.J.: Prentice-Hall.
 1967   Continuities in the Study of Social Conflict. New York: Free Press.
 [1971] Masters of Sociological Thought. New York: Harcourt Brace Jovanovich.
 1977
 1974   Greedy Organization. New York: Free Press.
 1975   "Presidential address: two methods in search of a substance." American Sociological Review 40:691-700.
 1976   "Sociological theory from the Chicago dominance to 1965." Pp. 145-60 in Alex Inkeles, James Coleman, and Neil Smelser (eds.), Annual Review of Sociology. Palo Alto, Calif.: Annual Reviews, Inc.
Costner, Herbert L.
 1969   "Theory, deduction, and rules of correspondence." American Journal of Sociology 75:245-63.
Craib, Ian
 1976   Existentialism and Sociology: A Study of Jean-Paul Sartre. Cambridge, England: Cambridge University Press.
Crane, Diana
 1972   Invisible Colleges: Diffusion of Knowledge in Scientific Communities. Chicago, Ill.: University of Chicago Press.
Dahrendorf, Ralf
 1958   "Out of Utopia: toward a reorientation of sociological analysis." American Journal of Sociology 64:115-27.
 1959   Class and Class Conflict in Industrial Society. Stanford, Calif.: Stanford University Press.
Daily Illini
 1973   "Parsons: sociology, ideology don't mix." April 5:7.
Davis, James A.
 1961   Great Books and Small Groups. New York: Free Press.
 1966   "The campus as a frog pond." American Journal of Sociology 72:17-31.
Davis, Kingsley
 1959   "The myth of functional analysis as a special method in sociology and anthropology." American Sociological Review 24:757-72.
Dean, Lois R.
 1967   Five Towns: A Comparative Community Study. New York: Random House.
de Broglie, Louis
 1953   The Revolution of Physics: A Non-mathematical Survey of Quanta. New

York: Noonday Press.

Demerath, N. J.
  1967 "Synecdoche and structural-functionalism." Pp. 501-18 in N. J. Demerath
        and R. A. Peterson (eds.), System, Change, and Conflict. New York: Free
        Press.

Demerath, N. J., and Richard A. Peterson (eds.)
  1967 System, Change, and Conflict: A Reader on Contemporary Sociological
        Theory and the Debate over Functionalism. New York: Free Press.

Demerath, N. J., III, Otto Larsen, and Karl F. Schuessler
  1975 Social Policy and Sociology. New York: Academic Press.

Denzin, Norman K.
  1970 "Symbolic interactionism and ethnomethodology." Pp. 259-84 in Jack D.
        Douglas (ed.), Understanding Everyday Life. Chicago, Ill.: Aldine.

Deutsch, Karl W., John Platt, and Dieter Shenghans
  1971 "Conditions favoring major advances in social sciences." Science 171:450-
        59.

Diamond, Sigmund
  1977 "Veritas at Harvard." (Review of Seymour Martin Lipset and David Ries-
        man. Education and Politics at Harvard.) New York Review of Books 24:
        13-17.

Dibble, Vernon K.
  1975 The Legacy of Albion Small. Chicago, Ill.: University of Chicago Press.

Diner, Steven J.
  1975 "Department and discipline: the department of sociology at the University
        of Chicago, 1892-1920." Minerva 13:514-53.

Dodd, Stuart C.
  1955 "Diffusion is predictable: testing probability models for laws of interac-
        tion." American Sociological Review 20:392-401.

Dorfman, Joseph
  1934 Thorstein Veblen and His America. New York: Viking.

Dumont, Louis
  1970 Homo Hierarchicus. Chicago, Ill.: University of Chicago Press.

Duncan, Otis Dudley
  1975 Introduction to Structural Equation Models. New York: Academic Press.

Duncan, Otis Dudley, David L. Featherman, and Beverly Duncan
  1972 Socioeconomic Background and Achievement. New York: Seminar Press.

Duncan, Otis Dudley, and Leo F. Schnore
  1959a "Cultural, behavioral, and ecological perspectives in the study of social or-
         ganization." American Journal of Sociology 65:132-46.
  1959b "Rejoinder." American Journal of Sociology 65:149-53.

Durkheim, Emile
  [1893] The Division of Labor in Society. Translated by George Simpson. New
  1964   York: Free Press.
  [1895] The Rules of Sociological Method. Translated by S. A. Solovay and J. H.
  1964   Mueller. New York: Free Press.
  [1897] Suicide. Translated by J. A. Spaulding and George Simpson. New York:

1966   Free Press.

[1912] The Elementary Forms of Religious Life. Translated by J. W. Swain. New
1947   York: Free Press.

Dworkin, Ronald
1977   Taking Rights Seriously. Cambridge, Mass.: Harvard University Press.

Edel, Abraham
1959   "The concept of levels in social theory." Pp. 167-95 in Llewellyn Gross (ed.),
Symposium on Sociological Theory. Evanston, Ill.: Row Peterson.

Effrat, Andrew
1972   "Power to the paradigms: an editorial introduction." Sociological Inquiry
42:3-33.

Ehrlich, Howard J.
1962   "Some observations on the neglect of the sociology of sociology." Philosophy of Science 29:369-76.

Eisenstadt, S. N., with M. Curelaru
1976   The Form of Sociology: Paradigms and Crises. New York: Wiley.

Ellis, Lee
1977   "The decline and fall of sociology, 1975-2000." The American Sociologist
12:56-66.

Etzioni, Amitai
1965   "Social analysis as a sociological vocation." American Journal of Sociology
70:613-22.

Fallding, Harold
1968   The Sociological Task. Englewood Cliffs, N.J.: Prentice-Hall.

Faris, Ellsworth
1953   "Review of Talcott Parsons' The Social System." American Sociological
Review 18:103-106.

Faris, Robert E. L.
1967   Chicago Sociology 1920-1932. Chicago, Ill.: University of Chicago Press.
1977   Telephone interview. 10-28-77.

Feyerabend, Paul K.
1975   Against Method. London: New Left Books.

Feyerabend, Paul K., and Grover Maxwell (eds.)
1966   Mind, Matter, and Method. Minneapolis, Minn.: University of Minnesota
Press.

Firey, Walter
1977   The Study of Possible Societies. Austin, Tex.: Privately printed.

Fleming, Donald
1967   "Attitude: the history of a concept." Perspectives in American History 1:
287-365.

Fosdick, Raymond B.
1952   The Story of the Rockefeller Foundation. New York: Harper.

Friedrichs, Robert W.
1970   A Sociology of Sociology. New York: Free Press.
1972   "Dialectical sociology: toward a resolution of the current 'crises' in western
sociology." British Journal of Sociology 13:263-74.

Furniss, W. Todd
    1973   American Universities and Colleges. Washington, D.C.: American Council
           of Education.
Garfinkel, Harold
    1964   "Studies of the routine grounds of everyday activities." Social Problems
           11:225-50.
    1967   Studies in Ethnomethodology. Englewood Cliffs, N.J.: Prentice-Hall.
Gelman, R., and M. Shatz
    n.d.   Rule-Governed Variation in Children's Conversations. Unpublished man-
           uscript. University of Pennsylvania.
Gerth, Hans, and C. Wright Mills
    1953   Character and Social Structure. New York: Harcourt, Brace and World.
Gerth, Hans, and C. Wright Mills (eds.)
    1947   From Max Weber. New York: Oxford University Press.
Goddard, David
    1976   "On structuralism and sociology." American Sociologist 11:123-33.
Goffman, Erving
    1959   Presentation of Self in Everyday Life. Garden City, N.Y.: Doubleday.
    1971   "Insanity of place." Pp. 335-90 in Erving Goffman, Relations in Public.
           New York: Basic Books.
    1975   "Replies and responses." Working Papers. Urbino: Centro Internazionale
           di Semiotica e di Linguistica 1-42.
Goldberger, Arthur S., and Otis Dudley Duncan
    1973   Structural Equation Models in the Social Sciences. New York: Seminar
           Press.
Goldman, Eric F.
    1956   Rendezvous with Destiny. New York: Vintage.
Goldthorpe, John H.
    1972   "Class, status and party in modern Britain." European Journal of Sociolo-
           gy 13:342-72.
Goode, William J.
    1969   "The theoretical limits of professionalization." Pp. 266-313 in Amitai
           Etzioni (ed.), The Semi-professions and Their Organization. New York:
           Free Press.
Goslin, David A. (ed.)
    1969   Handbook of Socialization Theory and Research. Chicago, Ill.: Rand Mc-
           Nally.
Goudsblom, Johan
    1977   Sociology in the Balance: A Critical Essay. New York: Columbia Univer-
           sity Press.
Gouldner, Alvin W.
    1970   The Coming Crisis of Western Sociology. New York: Basic Books.
    1973   "Anti-minotaur: the myth of a value-free sociology." Pp. 1-26 in Alvin W.
           Gouldner, For Sociology: Renewal and Critique in Sociology Today. New
           York: Basic Books.
Gouldner, Alvin W., and S. M. Miller (eds.)
    1965   Applied Sociology. New York: Free Press.

Grice, H. P.
  1975 "Logic and conversation." Pp. 41-58 in P. Cole and J. L. Morgan (eds.), Syntax and Semantics, Volume 3. Speech Acts. New York: Academic Press.

Gurvitch, Georges, and Wilbert E. Moore
  1945 Twentieth Century Sociology. New York: Philosophical Library.

Habermas, Jurgen
  1968 Knowledge and Human Interests. Boston: Beacon Press.

Hall, Calvin S., and Gardner Lindzey
  1957 Theories of Personality. New York: Wiley.

Hamblin, Robert L.
  1971 "Mathematical experimentation and sociological theory: a critical analysis." Sociometry 34:423-52.

Hamblin, Robert L., R. Brooke Jacobsen, and Jerry L. L. Miller
  1973 A Mathematical Theory of Social Change. New York: Wiley.

Hanson, Norwood Russell
  1958 Patterns of Discovery. London: Cambridge University Press.
  1960 "More on 'the logic of discovery.'" Journal of Philosophy 57:182-88.
  1961 "Is there a logic of discovery?" Pp. 20-35 in Herbert Feigl and Grover Maxwell (eds.), Current Issues in the Philosophy of Science. New York: Holt, Rinehart and Winston.

Hauser, Robert M., and Arthur S. Goldberger
  1971 "The treatment of unobservable variables in path analysis." Chapter 4 in Herbert L. Costner (ed.), Sociological Methodology 1971. San Francisco: Jossey-Bass.

Hawley, Amos H.
  1950a Human Ecology: A Theory of Community Structure. New York: Ronald Press.
  1950b "Some remarks on the relation of social psychology and human ecology." Paper presented at the annual meetings of the American Sociological Society, Denver, Colorado.
  1971 Urban Society: An Ecological Approach. New York: Ronald Press.

Heeren, John W.
  1975 Functional and Critical Sociology: A Study of Two Groups of Contemporary Sociologists. Unpublished doctoral dissertation. Department of Sociology. Duke University.

Heise, David R.
  1975 Causal Analysis. New York: Wiley.

Hempel, Carl G.
  1959 "The logic of functional analysis." Pp. 271-307 in Llewellyn Gross (ed.), Symposium on Sociological Theory. Evanston, Ill.: Row, Peterson.

Hempel, Carl G., and Paul Oppenheim
  1953 "The logic of explanation." Pp. 319-52 in Herbert Feigl and May Brodbeck (eds.), Readings in the Philosophy of Science. New York: Appleton-Century-Crofts.

Henle, Paul
  1951 "William James." Pp. 115-27 in Max H. Fisch (ed.), Classic American Phi-

losophers. New York: Appleton-Century-Crofts.

Herbst, Jurgen
    1959   "From moral philosophy to sociology Albion Woodbury Small." Harvard
          Educational Review 29:227-44.
    1965   The German Historical School in American Scholarship. Ithaca, N.Y.:
          Cornell University Press.

Hesse, Mary
    1967   "Laws and theories." Pp. 404-10 in Encyclopedia of Philosophy IV. New
          York: Macmillan.

Hinkle, Roscoe, and Gisela J. Hinkle
    1954   The Development of Modern Sociology: Its Nature and Growth in the
          United States. Garden City, N.Y.: Doubleday.

Hodge, Robert W., and Donald J. Treiman
    1968   "Social participation and social status." American Sociological Review
          33:722-40.

Hofstadter, Richard
    1955   Social Darwinism in America. Revised edition. Boston: Beacon.

Homans, George C.
    1941   English Villagers of the Thirteenth Century. Cambridge, Mass.: Harvard
          University Press.
    1950   The Human Group. New York: Harcourt, Brace and World.
    1961   Social Behavior: Its Elementary Forms. New York: Harcourt, Brace and
          World.
    1962   Sentiments and Activities: Essays in Social Science. Glencoe, Ill.: Free
          Press.
    1964   "Bringing men back in." American Sociological Review 29:809-18.
    1967   The Nature of Social Science. New York: Harcourt, Brace and World.
    1970   "The relevance of psychology to the explanation of social phenomenon."
          Pp. 313-29 in R. Borger and F. Cioffi (eds.), Explanation in the Behavioral
          Sciences. Cambridge, Mass.: Cambridge University Press.
    1974   Social Behavior: Its Elementary Forms. Second edition. New York: Har-
          court, Brace, Jovanovich.

Horkheimer, Max
    1972   Critical Theory. New York: Herder and Herder.

Horowitz, Irving Louis
    1962   "Consensus, conflict and cooperation." Social Forces 41:177-88.

House, Floyd Nelson
    1936   The Development of Sociology. New York: McGraw-Hill.

Hughes, R. M.
    1925   A Study of the Graduate Schools of America. Pamphlet. No publisher
          listed.

Hunt, Morton M.
    1961   "How does it come to be so? Profile of Robert K. Merton." New Yorker 36:
          39-63.

Jackman, Mary R., and Robert W. Jackman
    1973   "An interpretation of the relation between objective and subjective social
          status." American Sociological Review 38:569-82.

Janowitz, Morris (ed.)
  1966 W. I. Thomas on Social Organization and Social Personality. Chicago, Ill.: University of Chicago.
  1967 "Forward." Pp. vii-xii in Robert E. L. Faris. Chicago Sociology 1920-1932. Chicago, Ill.: University of Chicago.
  [1921] Introduction to the Science of Sociology. Chicago, Ill.: The University of
  1970 Chicago Press.
  1972 "Professionalization of Sociology." American Journal of Sociology 78:105-35.
Jay, Martin
  1973 The Dialectical Imagination. Boston, Mass.: Little, Brown.
Jessor, Clinton J.
  1975 Social Theory Revisited. Hinsdale, Ill.: Dryden Press.
Jones, Robert A.
  1972 "John Bascom 1827-1911: anti-positivism and intuitionism in American sociology." American Quarterly 24:501-22.
Jones, Robert Alan, and Robert M. Anservitz
  1975 "Saint-Simon and Saint Simonism: a Weberian view." American Journal of Sociology 80:1095-1123.
Joreskog, Karl G.
  1970 "A general method for the analysis of covariance structures." Biometrika 57:239-51.
Jung, Carl, et al.
  1964 Man and His Symbols. Garden City, N.Y.: Doubleday.
Kant, Immanuel
  [1781] Critique of Pure Reason. Translated by Norman Kemp Smith. London:
  1964 Macmillan and Co.
Kaplan, Abraham
  1964 The Conduct of Inquiry. San Francisco: Chandler.
Karl, Barry D.
  1968 "The Power of intellect and the politics of ideas." Daedalus 97:1002-35.
  1969 "Presidential planning and social science research: Mr. Hoover's experts." Perspectives in American History 3:347-409.
  1974 Charles E. Merriam and the Study of Politics. Chicago, Ill.: University of Chicago Press.
  1976 "Philanthropy, policy planning and the bureaucratization of the Democratic ideal." Daedalus 106:129-49.
Katz, Fred E.
  1976 Structuralism in Sociology: An Approach to Knowledge. Albany, N.Y.: State University of New York Press.
Kelley, Jonathan
  1973 "Causal chain models for socioeconomic career." American Sociological Review 38:481-93.
Kelman, Mark
  1974 "The social cost of inequality." Pp. 151-64 in Lewis A. Coser (ed.), The New Conservatives. New York: Quadrangle.

Kelvin, Lord (Sir William Thomson)
     1889   "Electrical units of measurement." Pp. 73-136 in Lord Kelvin, Popular
            Lectures and Addresses. Volume 1. London: Macmillan.
Kemeney, John G., and J. Laurie Snell
     1962   Mathematical Models in the Social Sciences. Boston: Ginn and Company.
Kenyatta, Jomo
     1965   Facing Mount Kenya. New York: Vintage Books.
Kneale, William
     1953   "Induction, explanation and transcendent hypotheses." Pp. 353-67 in
            Herbert Feigl and May Brodbeck (eds.), Readings in the Philosophy of Sci-
            ence. New York: Appleton-Century-Crofts.
Krantz, David H., R. Duncan Luce, Patrick Suppes, and Amos Tversky
     1971   Foundations of Measurement, Volume 1. New York: Academic Press.
Kress, Paul F.
     1970   Social Science and the Idea of Process. Urbana, Ill.: University of Illinois
            Press.
Kuhn, Thomas
     [1962] The Structure of Scientific Revolutions. First and second editions. Chicago,
     1970a   Ill.: University of Chicago Press.
     1970b   "Reflections on my critics." Pp. 231-78 in Imre Lakatos and Alan Mus-
             grave (eds.), Criticism and the Growth of Knowledge. London: Cambridge
             University Press.
Kuklick, Henrika
     1973   "A 'scientific revolution': sociological theory in the United States, 1930-
            1945." Sociological Inquiry 43:3-22.
Labovitz, Sanford
     1968   "Variation in suicide rates." Pp. 57-73 in Jack P. Gibbs (ed.), Suicide. New
            York: Harper Row.
Lakoff, R.
     1973   "The logic of politeness; or minding your P's and Q's." Papers from the
            Ninth Regional Meeting of the Chicago Linguistic Society. Chicago, Ill.:
            Linguistic Department. University of Chicago 292-305.
Langer, Susanne K.
     1967   Mind, Volume 1. Baltimore: Johns Hopkins Press.
Laumann, Edward O.
     1973   Bonds of Pluralism. New York: Wiley.
Lazarsfeld, Paul F.
     1959   "Problems in methodology." Pp. 39-78 in Robert K. Merton, Leonard
            Broom and Leonard S. Cottrell, Jr. (eds.), Sociology Today. New York:
            Basic Books.
Lazarsfeld, Paul F., W. H. Sewell, and H. L. Wilensky (eds.)
     1967   The Uses of Sociology. New York: Basic Books.
Lazarsfeld, Paul F., and Wagner Thielens, Jr.
     1958   The Academic Mind. Glencoe, Ill.: Free Press.
Leik, Robert K.
     1977   "Divorce rates: a mathematical and theoretical analysis." Unpublished
            manuscript. Minneapolis, Minn.

References [273]

Leik, Robert K., and B. F. Meeker
  1974a "An experimentalist's approach to formal theory." Paper presented at
        "Symposium: Theory Construction in Sociology." University of Minne-
        sota, Minneapolis.
  1974b Mathematical Sociology. Englewood Cliffs, N.J.: Prentice-Hall.
Lengermann, Patricia M.
  1978 "The founding of the American Sociological Review." Unpublished manu-
        script.
Leventman, Seymour
  1971 The rationalization of American sociology. Pp. 348-64 in Edward A. Tiry-
        akian (ed.), The Phenomenon of Sociology. New York: Appleton-Century-
        Crofts.
Levine, Donald M.
  1971 "Introduction." Pp. ix-lxv in Donald M. Levine (ed.), Georg Simmel on In-
        dividuality and Social Forms. Chicago, Ill.: University of Chicago.
Lévi-Strauss, Claude
  1966 The Savage Mind. Chicago, Ill.: University of Chicago Press.
  1969 The Elementary Structure of Kinship. Boston: Beacon Press.
Levy, Marion J., Jr.
  1966 Modernization and the Structure of Societies. Princeton, N.J.: Princeton
        University Press.
Lipset, S. Martin
  1955 "The department of sociology." Pp. 284-303 in R. Gordon Hoxie, et al. A
        History of the Faculty of Political Science, Columbia University. New York:
        Columbia University.
  1975 "Social structure and social change." In Peter Blau (ed.), Approaches to
        the Study of Social Structure. New York: Free Press.
Lockwood, David
  1956 "Some remarks on 'the social system.'" British Journal of Sociology 7:134-
        46.
Long, J. Scott
  1976 "Estimation and hypothesis testing in linear models containing measure-
        ment error." Sociological Methods and Research 5:157-207.
Loomis, Charles P., and Z. K. Loomis, with R. C. Bealer
  1965 "Talcott Parsons' social theory." Pp. 327-441 in C. P. Loomis and Z. K.
        Loomis, Modern Social Theories. Second edition. Princeton, N.J.: D. Van
        Nostrand.
Lovejoy, Arthur O.
  1963 The Thirteen Pragmatisms and Other Essays. Baltimore: Johns Hopkins
        Press.
Lovett, Robert Morss
  1948 All Our Years. New York: Viking.
Lukacs, Georg
  1968 History and Class Consciousness. Cambridge, Mass.: MIT Press.
Lundberg, George A.
  1956 "Some convergences in sociological theory." American Journal of Soci-
        ology 62:21-27.

Lyons, Gene M.
  1969   The Uneasy Partnership. New York: Russell Sage Foundation.
McGrath, J. E., and I. Altman
  1966   Small Group Research: A Synthesis and Critique of the Field. New York: Holt, Rinehart and Winston.
MacIver, R. M.
  1931   "Is sociology a natural science?" American Sociological Society 25:25-35.
  1968   As a Tale That Is Told: The Autobiography of R. M. MacIver. Chicago, Ill.: University of Chicago Press.
McKinney, John C.
  1957   "Methodology, procedures, and techniques." Pp. 186-235 in Howard Becker and Alvin Boskoff (eds.), Modern Sociological Theory. New York: Dryden Press.
  1966   Constructive Typology and Social Theory. New York: Appleton-Century-Crofts.
Magdoff, Harry
  1969   The Age of Imperialism. New York and London: Modern Reader Paperbacks.
Maines, David R.
  1977   "Social organization and social structure in symbolic interactionist thought." Pp. 235-59 in Alex Inkeles (ed.), Annual Review of Sociology. Palo Alto, Calif.: Annual Reviews, Inc.
Mannheim, Karl
  1949   Ideology and Utopia. Translated by Louis Wirth and Edward Shils. New York: Harcourt, Brace.
Manning, Peter
  1973   "Existential sociology." Sociological Quarterly 14:201-25.
Mansfield, Roger
  1973   "Bureaucracy and centralization." Administrative Science Quarterly 18:77-88.
Martindale, Don
  1960   The Nature and Types of Sociological Theory. Boston: Houghton Mifflin.
  1974   Sociological Theory and the Problem of Values. Columbus, Ohio: Charles E. Merrill.
  1976a "American sociology before World War II." Pp. 121-43 in Alex Inkeles, James Coleman, and Neil Smelser (eds.), Annual Review of Sociology. Palo Alto, Calif.: Annual Reviews, Inc.
  1976b The Romance of a Profession. Saint Paul, Minn.: Windflower Press.
Marx, Karl
  [1848] The Manifesto of the Communist Party. Translated by S. Moore. New
  1968   York: International Publishers.
  [1848- Capital. Translated by S. Moore and E. Aveling. London: G. Allen.
  1879]
  1949
Masterman, Margaret
  1970   "The nature of a paradigm." Pp. 59-89 in Imre Lakatos and Alan Musgrave (eds.), Criticism and the Growth of Knowledge. London: Cambridge University Press.

Matthews, Fred
   1976   The Quest for an American Sociology, Robert E. Park and the Chicago
          School. Montreal: McGill-Queen's University Press.
Mauksch, Hans O.
   1977   Personal Interview. 9-7-77. Chicago, Ill.
Mazur, Allan, and Leon S. Robertson
   1972   Biology and Social Behavior. New York: Free Press.
Mead, George H.
   [1913] "The social self." Pp. 142-49 in Andrew J. Reck (ed.), George Herbert
   1964a   Mead, Selected Writings. Indianapolis, Ind.: Bobbs-Merrill.
   [1929] "The philosophies of Royce, James and Dewey in their American set-
           ting."
   1964b   Pp. 371-91 in Andrew J. Reck (ed.), George Herbert Mead, Selected Wri-
           tings. Indianapolis, Ind.: Bobbs-Merrill.
   [1934] Mind, Self and Society. Chicago, Ill.: University of Chicago Press.
   1974
   1936   Movements of Thought in the Nineteenth Century. Chicago, Ill.: University
           of Chicago Press.
Mehan, Hugh, and Houston Wood
   1975   The Reality of Ethnomethodology. New York: Wiley.
   1976   "De-secting ethnomethodology." The American Sociologist 11:13-21.
Meroney, W. P.
   1931   "The membership and program of twenty-five years of the American Socio-
          logical Society." 25:55-67.
Merton, Robert K.
   1936   "The unanticipated consequences of social action." American Sociological
           Review 1:894-904.
   [1949] Social Theory and Social Structure. First, second, and revised editions.
   1957   Glencoe, Ill.: Free Press.
   1968
   1967   On Theoretical Sociology. New York: Free Press.
   1970   "Social conflict over styles of sociological work." Pp. 172-97 in Larry T.
           Reynolds and Janice M. Reynolds (eds.), The Sociology of Sociology. New
           York: David McKay.
   1975   "Structural analysis in sociology." In Peter Blau (ed.), Approaches to the
           Study of Social Structure. New York: Free Press.
Miller, G. A.
   1976   "Practical and lexical knowledge." Paper presented to the SSRC Confer-
          ence on the Nature and Principals of Formation of Categories.
Miller, Paula Jean
   1974   Images, Urban Middle-Class Life Styles, and the Sociology of the Future.
          Unpublished doctoral dissertation. Austin, Tex.: University of Texas.
Miller, William (ed. and compiler)
   1976   International Human Rights: A Bibliography 1970-1976. Notre Dame,
          Ind.: Center for Civil Rights, University of Notre Dame Law School.
Mills, C. Wright
   1959   The Sociological Imagination. New York: Oxford University Press.
   1966   Sociology and Pragmatism. New York: Oxford University Press.

Mitroff, Ian
    1974   "Norms and counter-norms in a select group of the Apollo moon scientists:
            a case study of the ambivalence of scientists." American Sociological Re-
            view 39:579-95.
Mitzman, Arthur
    1969   The Iron Cage. New York: The Universal Library.
Moore, Wilbert E.
    1966   "The utility of utopias." American Sociological Review 31:765-72.
Mosteller, Frederick
    1974   "The role of the Social Science Research Council in the advance of mathe-
            matics in the social sciences." Social Science Research Council Items
            28:17-24.
Moynihan, Daniel P.
    1969   Maximum Feasible Misunderstanding. New York: Free Press.
Mullins, Nicholas
    1973   Theories and Theory Groups in Contemporary American Sociology. New
            York: Harper & Row.
Munch, Peter A.
    1957   "Empirical science and Max Weber's verstehende soziologie." American
            Sociological Review 22:26-32.
Nagel, Ernest
    1956   "A formalization of functionalism." Pp. 247-83 in Ernest Nagel, Logic
            Without Metaphysics. Glencoe, Ill.: Free Press.
Nall, Frank C., II
    1962   "Role expectations: a cross-cultural study." Rural Sociology 27:28-41.
Namboodiri, N. Krishnan, Lewis F. Carter, and H. M. Blalock
    1975   Applied Multivariate Analysis and Experimental Designs. New York:
            McGraw-Hill.
Nandan, Yash
    1975   L'Ecole Durkheimienne et son Opus. Paris: Microéditions du Centre Na-
            tional de la Recherche Scientifique.
Natanson, Maurice
    1973   The Social Dynamics of George H. Mead. The Hague: Martinus Nijhoff.
Newport, E. L.
    Forth- "Motherese: the speech of mothers to young children." To appear in N. J.
    coming Castellan, D. B. Pisoni, and G. R. Potts (eds.), Cognitive Theory. Volume 2.
            Hillsdale, N. J.: Lawrence Earlbaum Associates.
Newport, E. L., H. Gleitman, and L. R. Gleitman
    Forth- "Mother, I'd rather do it myself: some effects and non-effects of maternal
    coming speech style." To appear in C. A. Ferguson and C. E. Snow (eds.), Talking
            to Children: Language Input and Acquisition. Cambridge, England: Cam-
            bridge University Press.
Nisbet, Robert A.
    1966   The Sociological Tradition. New York: Basic Books.
    1974   The Sociology of Emile Durkheim. New York: Oxford University Press.
O'Dea, Thomas
    1963   "Sociological dilemmas: five paradoxes of institutionalization." Pp. 71-

90 in Edward A. Tiryakian (ed.), Sociological Theory, Values and Sociocultural Change. Essays in Honor of Pitirim A. Sorokin. New York: Free
Press.

Odum, Howard W.
1951   American Sociology. New York: Longmans, Green.

Oksanan, Ernest H., and Byron G. Spencer
1975   "On the determinants of student performance in introductory courses in
the social sciences." The American Sociologist 10:103-9.

Ollman, Bertell
1971   Alienation. Cambridge, England: Cambridge University Press.

Olson, Mancur, Jr.
1968   "Economics, sociology, and the best of all possible worlds." The Public Interest 12:96-118.

Olson, Philip (ed.)
1963   America as a Mass Society. New York: Free Press.

O'Neill, John
1972   "How is society possible?" Pp. 167-76 in John O'Neill, Sociology as a Skin
Trade. London, England: Heinemann.

O'Neill, John (ed.)
1973   Modes of Individualism and Collectivism. New York: St. Martin's Press.

Page, Charles H.
1969   Class and American Sociology: From Ward to Ross. New York: Schocken.

Paige, Jeffrey
1975   Agrarian Revolution: Social Movements and Export Agriculture in the
Underdeveloped World. New York: Free Press.

Park, Robert E.
1918   "Review of R. M. MacIver's Community." American Journal of Sociology
23:542-44.
1952   Human Communities. New York: Free Press.

Park, Robert E., and E. W. Burgess
[1921] Introduction to the Science of Sociology. Chicago, Ill.: University of
1924   Chicago Press.

Parmalee, Maurice, et al.
1931   "Three communications from Dr. M. Parmalee." American Journal of
Sociology 37:468-70.

Parsons, Talcott
[1937] The Structure of Social Action. New York: McGraw-Hill.
1949
1951   The Social System. Glencoe, Ill.: Free Press.
1959   "An approach to psychological theory in terms of the theory of action."
Pp. 612-711 in Sigmund Koch (ed.), Psychology: A Science. New York:
McGraw-Hill.
1966   Societies: Evolutionary and Comparative Perspectives. Englewood Cliffs,
N. J.: Prentice-Hall.
1970   "On building social system theory: a personal history." Daedalus 99:826-
81.
1971   The System of Modern Societies. Englewood Cliffs, N. J.: Prentice-Hall.

1973 "Ideology and sociology." Public lecture at University of Illinois, Urbana.
Parsons, Talcott, et al.
1937 Parsons' Sociological Group: Reports of Meetings, 1936-37. Mimeo.
Parsons, Talcott, and Edward A. Shils (eds.)
1952 Toward a General Theory of Action. Cambridge, Mass.: Harvard University Press.
Parsons, Talcott, and Neil J. Smelser
1956 Economy and Society. New York: Free Press.
Patel, N.
1972 "Quantitative and collaborative trends in American sociological research." The American Sociologist 7:5-6.
Peirce, C. S.
1931- Collected Papers. Cambridge, Mass: Harvard University Press.
1935
Petrowski, William R., Evan L. Brown, and John A. Duffy
1973 "'National Universities' and the ACE ratings." Journal of Higher Education 44:495-513.
Phillips, J. R.
1973 "Syntax and vocabulary of mother's speech to young children." Child Development 44:182-85.
Pope, Whitney
1973 "Classic on classic: Parsons' interpretation of Durkheim." American Sociological Review 38:399-415.
Pope, Whitney, Jere Cohen, and Lawrence E. Hazelrigg
1975 "On the divergence of Weber and Durkheim: a critique of Parsons' convergence thesis." American Sociological Review 40:417-27.
Popper, Karl
1966 The Open Society and Its Enemies, 2 volumes. Fifth edition. Princeton, N. J.: Princeton University Press.
1974 "Autobiography of Karl Popper." Pp. 3-181 in Paul Arthur Schilpp (ed.), The Philosophy of Karl Popper. LaSalle, Ill.: Open Court.
Psathas, George
1973 Phenomenological Sociology: Issues and Applications. New York: Wiley.
Rawls, John
1971 A Theory of Justice. Cambridge, Mass.: Harvard University Press.
Reichenbach, Hans
1953 The Rise of Scientific Philosophy. Berkeley, Calif.: University of California Press.
Reill, Peter Hanns
1975 The German Enlightenment and the Rise of Historicism. Berkeley, Calif.: University of California Press.
Reissman, Leonard
1964 The Urban Process. New York: Free Press.
Reynolds, Paul D.
1971 A Primer in Theory Construction. Indianapolis, Ind.: Bobbs-Merrill.
Rischin, Moses
1965 The American Gospel of Success: Individualism and Beyond. Chicago, Ill.:

Quadrangle Books.

Ritzer, George
- 1975a Sociology: A Multiple Paradigm Science. Boston: Allyn and Bacon.
- 1975b "Sociology: a multiple paradigm science." The American Sociologist 10: 156-67.
- 1977a "On testing the paradigmatic status of sociology." The American Sociologist 12:23.
- 1977b "Reflections on the paradigmatic status of sociology." Presented at the Alpha Kappa Delta meetings, Richmond, Virginia.
- 1977c "An exemplar for an integrated sociological paradigm." Presented at the plenary session of the Midwest Sociological Society Meetings, Minneapolis, Minnesota.

Robinson, W. S.
- 1950 "Ecological correlations and the behavior of individuals." American Sociological Review 15:351-57.
- 1951 "The logical structure of analytic induction." American Sociological Review 16:812-18.

Rocher, Guy
- 1975 Talcott Parsons and American Sociology. New York: Barnes and Noble.

Roose, Kenneth D., and Charles J. Anderson
- 1970 A Rating of Graduate Programs. Washington, D. C.: American Council of Education.

Rossi, P. H.
- 1959 "Comment" on Otis Dudley Duncan and Leo F. Schnore, "Cultural, behavioral and ecological perspectives in the study of sociological organization." American Journal of Sociology 65:146-49.

Rostow, Walt Whitman
- 1963 The Stages of Economic Growth. London: Cambridge University Press.

Roth, Guenther
- 1968 "Introduction." Pp. xxvii-civ in Guenther Roth and Claus Wittich (eds.), Max Weber Economy and Society. New York: Bedminster Press.

Rucker, Darnell
- 1969 The Chicago Pragmatists. Minneapolis, Minn.: University of Minnesota Press.

Rumelhart, D. E.
- n.d. "Toward an interactive model of reading." Paper presented at Attention and Performance VI International Symposium, Stockholm, Sweden.
- Forthcoming "Understanding and summarizing brief stories." To appear in D. La Berge and J. Samuels (eds.), Basic Processes in Reading Perception and Comprehension. Hillsdale, N. J.: Lawrence Earlbaum Associates.

Sacks, H., E. A. Schegloff, and G. Jefferson
- 1974 "A simplest systematics for the organization of turn taking for conversation." Language 50:696-735.

Saint Augustine
- [401] Confessions. New York: Fathers of the Church.
  1953

Schegloff, Emmanuel
    1968   "Sequencing in conversational openings." American Anthropologist 70: 1075-95.
Schnore, Leo F.
    1965   The Urban Scene. New York: Free Press.
Schoen, R.
    1975   "California divorce rates by age at first marriage and duration of first marriage." Journal of Marriage and the Family 37:548-55.
Schuessler, Karl
    1966   "Letter." The American Sociologist 1:82.
    1971   "Continuities in social prediction." Pp. 302-29 in Herbert L. Costner (ed.), Sociological Methodology. San Francisco: Jossey-Bass.
    1975   "Prologue." Pp. 1-9 in N. J. Demerath III, Otto Larsen, and Karl F. Schuessler, Social Policy and Sociology. New York: Academic Press.
Schuman, Howard, and Michael P. Johnson
    1976   "Attitudes and behavior." Pp. 161-207 in Alex Inkeles, James Coleman, and Neil Smelser (eds.), Annual Review of Sociology. Palo Alto, Calif.: Annual Reviews, Inc.
Schutz, Alfred
    1962   Collected Papers, I. The Problem of Social Reality. The Hague: Martinus Nijhoff.
    1965   "The social world and the theory of social action." Pp. 53-67 in David Braybrooke (ed.), Philosophical Problems of the Social Sciences. New York: Macmillan.
    1967   The Phenomenology of the Social World. Chicago, Ill.: Northwestern University Press.
Scimecca, Joseph
    1976   The Sociological Theory of C. Wright Mills. Port Washington, N. Y.: Kennikat Press.
Scott, Marvin B., and Stanford M. Lyon
    1968   "Accounts." American Sociological Review 33:46-62.
Searle, J. R.
    1969   Speech Acts. New York and London: Cambridge University Press.
Selvin, Hanan C.
    1960   "Problems in the use of individual and group data." Paper presented at the annual meetings of the American Sociological Association, New York.
Shapere, Dudley
    1972   "The Paradigm Concept." Science 172:706-9.
Shatz, M., and R. Gelman
    1973   "The development of communication skills: modifications in the speech of young children as a function of listener." SRCO Monograph 38.
Shepard, Roger N., A. Kimball Romney, and Sara Beth Nerlove (eds.)
    1972   Multidimensional Scaling: Theory and Applications in the Behavioral Sciences. 2 volumes. New York: Seminar Press.
Shils, Edward
    1970   "Tradition, ecology, and the institution in the history of sociology." Daedalus 99:760-825.

Shipley, E. S., C. S. Smith, and L. R. Gleitman
    1969   "A study in the acquisition of language: free responses to commands." Language 45:322-42.

Short, James F., Jr.
    1971   "Introduction." Pp. xi-xlvi in James F. Short, Jr. (ed.), The Social Fabric of the Metropolis. Chicago, Ill.: University of Chicago Press.

Simmel, Georg
    1909   "The problem of sociology." Translated by A. Small. American Journal of Sociology 15:289-320.
    1910   "How is society possible?" Translated by A. Small. American Journal of Sociology 16:372-91.
    1950   The Sociology of Georg Simmel. Translated and edited by Kurt Wolff. Glencoe, Ill.: Free Press.

Simpson, George
    1969   August Comte: Sire of Sociology. New York: Thomas Y. Crowell.

Sjoberg, Gideon
    1959   "Operationalism and social research." Pp. 603-27 in Llewellyn Gross (ed.), Symposium on Sociological Theory. Evanston, Ill.: Row, Peterson.

Sjoberg, Gideon, and Leonard D. Cain
    1971   "Negative values, countersystem analysis, and the analysis of social systems." Pp. 212-29 in Herman Turk and Richard L. Simpson (eds.), Institutions and Social Exchange: The Sociologies of Talcott Parsons and George Homans. Indianapolis, Ind.: Bobbs-Merrill.

Sjoberg, Gideon, and Ted R. Vaughan
    1977   "The Research Process." Quarterly Journal of Ideology 1:5-12.

Small, Albion W.
    1910   The Meaning of Social Science. Chicago, Ill.: University of Chicago Press.

Snizek, William E.
    1975   "The relationship between theory and research: a study in the sociology of sociology." Sociological Quarterly 16:415-28.
    1976   "An empirical assessment of 'sociology: a multiple paradigm science.'" The American Sociologist 11:217-19.

Snow, C. E.
    1972   "Mother's speech to children learning language." Child Development 43: 549-65.

Sorokin, Pitirim A.
    1928   Contemporary Sociological Theories. New York: Harper Brothers.
    1963   A Long Journey: The Autobiography of Pitirim A. Sorokin. New Haven, Conn.: College and University Press.

Staats, Arthur W.
    1976   "Skinnerian behaviorism: social behaviorism or radical behaviorism?" The American Sociologist 11:59-60.

Stanfield, Ron
    1974   "Kuhnian scientific revolutions and the Keynesian revolution." Journal of Economic Issues 8:97-109.

Stark, Werner
    1961   "Herbert Spencer's three sociologies." American Sociological Review 26:515-21.

Stevens, S. S.
   1957   "On the psychophysical law." The Psychological Review 64:153-81.
Stinchcombe, Arthur L.
   1968   Constructing Social Theories. New York: Harcourt, Brace and World.
Stokes, C. Shannon, and Michael K. Miller
   1975   "A methodological review of research in Rural Sociology since 1965."
          Rural Sociology 40:411-34.
Stouffer, Samuel A., et al.
   1949   The American Soldier. Volume 1. Princeton, N. J.: Princeton University
          Press.
Street, David
   1976   "Applied sociology and the professionalization of reform." Paper given at
          annual meetings of the American Association for the Advancement of Sci-
          ence, Boston, Massachusetts.
Sudnow, David
   1972   "Temporal parameters of interpersonal observation." Pp. 229-58 in D.
          Sudnow (ed.), Studies in Social Interaction. New York: Free Press.
Suits, Daniel B.
   1967   "Use of dummy variables in regression equations." Journal of American
          Statistical Association 64:548-51.
Suppe, Frederick
   1977   "Introduction" and "Afterword—1977." Pp. 3-233 and 617-730 in Fred-
          erick Suppe (ed.), The Structure of Scientific Theories. Second Edition.
          Urbana, Ill.: University of Illinois Press.
Tarter, Donald
   1973   "Heeding Skinner's call: toward the development of a social technology."
          The American Sociologist 8:153-58.
Thomas, W. I.
   1973   "Life history," with an Introduction by Paul J. Baker. American Journal of
          Sociology 79:246-50.
Thomas, William I., and Dorothy Swaine Thomas
   1928   The Child in America. New York: Alfred A. Knopf.
Thomlinson, Ralph
   1965   Sociological Concepts and Research. New York: Random House.
Timasheff, Nicholas S.
   1957   Sociological Theory: Its Nature and Growth. Revised edition. New York:
          Random House.
Tiryakian, Edward A.
   1962   Sociologism and Existentialism: Two Perspectives on the Individual and
          Society. Englewood Cliffs, N. J.: Prentice-Hall.
   1971   The Phenomenon of Sociology. New York: Appleton-Century-Crofts.
   1978   "Emile Durkheim." In Tom Bottomore and Robert Nisbet (eds.), A History
          of Sociological Analysis. New York: Basic Books.
   Forth- The Durkheimian School on Sociology and Social Issues. Chicago, Ill.:
   coming University of Chicago Press.
Turner, Frederick J.
   1894   "The significance of the frontier in American history." Pp. 199-227 in the

Annual Report of the American Historical Association for the Year 1893. Washington, D.C.: Government Printing Office.

Useem, Michael
1976a "Government influence on the social science paradigm." The Sociological Quarterly 17:146-61.
1976b "State production of social knowledge." American Sociological Review 41:613-29.

Van den Berghe, Pierre
1975 Man In Society: A Biosocial View. New York: Elsevier.

Vaughan, Ted R., and Gideon Sjoberg
Forth- "Social theory." In Edward Sagarin (ed.), Sociology: The Fundamental
coming Concepts. New York: Praeger.

Volkart, E. H. (ed.)
1951 Social Behavior and Personality. New York: Social Science Research Council.

Wallace, Walter L.
1969 "Overview of contemporary sociological theory." Pp. 1-59 in W. L. Wallace (ed.), Sociological Theory. Chicago, Ill.: Aldine.

Wallerstein, Immanuel
1974 The Modern World-System: Capitalist Agriculture and the Origins of the European World-Economy in the Sixteenth Century. New York: Academic Press.

Ward, Lester F.
[1883] Dynamic Sociology. New York: D. Appleton and Company.
1910

Warner, R. Stephen
1978 "Toward a redefinition of action theory: paying the cognitive element its due." American Journal of Sociology 83:1317-49.

Warriner, Charles K.
1956 "Groups are real: a reaffirmation." American Sociological Review 21:549-54.

Watson, James D.
1968 The Double Helix. New York: New American Library.

Webb, E. J., Donald T. Campbell, R. D. Schwartz, and Lee Sechrest
1966 Unobtrusive Measures: Nonreactive Research in the Social Sciences. Chicago, Ill.: Rand McNally.

Weber, Max
[1904] The Protestant Ethic and the Spirit of Capitalism. Translated by Talcott
1930 Parsons. London: G. Allen and Unwin, Ltd.
1946 "Science as a vocation." Pp. 129-56 in H. Gerth and C. Wright Mills (tr. and eds.), From Max Weber: Essays in Sociology. New York: Oxford University Press.
1949 On the Methodology of the Social Sciences. Translated and edited by Edward A. Shils and Henry A. Finch. Glencoe, Ill.: Free Press.
1968 Economy and Society. 3 volumes. New York: Bedminster Press.

Weinstein, Deena, and Michael A. Weinstein
1974 Living Sociology. New York: David McKay Company.

Whitaker, Ian
1965 "The nature and value of functionalism in sociology." Pp. 127-43 in Don Martindale (ed.), Functionalism in Social Sciences. Philadelphia, Pa.: The American Academy of Political and Social Science.

Wiley, Norbert
1977 Review Essay: "The crises and contradictions of capitalism." Contemporary Sociology 6:416-24.

Willer, David
1967 Scientific Sociology: Theory and Method. Englewood Cliffs, N.J.: Prentice-Hall.

Willer, David, and Judith Willer
1973 Systematic Empiricism: Critique of a Pseudoscience. Englewood Cliffs, N. J.: Prentice-Hall.

Williams, Robin M., Jr.
1961 "The sociological theory of Talcott Parsons." Pp. 64-99 in Max Black (ed.), The Social Theories of Talcott Parsons. Englewood Cliffs, N. J.: Prentice-Hall.

Willits, Fern K.
1965 An Exploratory Analysis of Individual and Social Level Meanings of Rurality, Unpublished doctoral dissertation. Department of Rural Sociology. The Pennsylvania State University.

Willits, Fern K., Robert C. Bealer, and Donald M. Crider
1974 "The ecology of social traditionalism in a rural hinterland." Rural Sociology 39:334-49.

Wilson, Edward O.
1975 Sociobiology: The New Synthesis. Cambridge, Mass.: Harvard University Press.

Wirth, Louis
1939 "Review of Talcott Parsons' The Structure of Social Action." American Sociological Review 4:399-404.

Wolff, Kurt H.
1959 "The sociology of knowledge and sociological theory." Pp. 567-602 in Llewellyn Gross (ed.), Symposium on Sociological Theory. Evanston, Ill.: Row, Peterson.

Wrong, Dennis H.
1961 "The oversocialized conception of man." American Sociological Review 26:183-93.

Zetterberg, Hans
1954 On Theory and Verification in Sociology. Stockholm: Almquist and Wiksell.

Zimmerman, Donald, and Melvin Pollner
1970 "The everyday world as a phenomenon." Pp. 80-103 in J. Douglas (ed.), Understanding Everyday Life. Chicago, Ill.: Aldine.

Zimmerman, Don, and D. Lawrence Wieder
1970 "Ethnomethodology and the problem of order." Pp. 285-98 in Jack D. Douglas (ed.), Understanding Everyday Life. Chicago, Ill.: Aldine.

Znaniecki, Florian
1952 Cultural Sciences. Urbana, Ill.: University of Illinois Press.

NAME INDEX

SUBJECT INDEX

ABOUT THE
CONTRIBUTORS

ROBERT C. BEALER is Professor of Rural Sociology at The Pennsylvania State University and past editor of *Rural Sociology*. He has published in a wide variety of professional journals and has been active in exploring the general problems surrounding the use of theory in applied research. Professor Bealer is currently writing a monograph explicating the concept of rurality.

HUBERT M. BLALOCK JR. is Professor of Sociology at the University of Washington and currently President of the American Sociological Association. In addition to ongoing work in the development of methods in the social sciences, his research interests include race relations and social power. Professor Blalock has published numerous articles in major journals and authored or edited a number of books including *Theory Construction* and *Measurement in the Social Sciences*.

PETER BLAU is Quetelet Professor of Sociology at Columbia University and past President of the American Sociological Association. His research in the areas of theory, organizations, and stratification has been published in a wide variety of major journals. Professor Blau's recent books include *The Organization of Academic Work* and *Inequality and Heterogeneity: A Primitive Theory of Social Structure*.

AARON CICOUREL is Professor of Sociology at the University of California at San Diego. His most current research interest is the cognitive and linguistic aspects of social structure. He is author of *Method and Measurement in Sociology*, *Cognitive Sociology*, and *The Social Organization of Juvenile Justice*.

LEWIS COSER is Distinguished Professor of Sociology at the State University of New York at Stony Brook and past President of the American Sociological Association. His major research focuses have been in the areas of theory, conflict and violence, and the sociology of knowledge. In addition to his many journal publications, Professor Coser's list of authored or edited books includes *Masters of Sociological Thought: Ideas in Historical and Social Context* and *The Uses of Controversy in Sociology*.

ELLSWORTH R. FUHRMAN is Assistant Professor of Sociology at Virginia Polytechnic Institute and State University. His current areas of research interest include the history of sociological theory and the sociology of knowledge. He is author of a forthcoming book, *Structure and Consciousness in American Sociology*, to be published by the University Press of Virginia.

ROBERT K. LEIK is Professor of Sociology and Director of the Minnesota Family Study Center at the University of Minnesota. In addition to his work in mathematical modeling, Professor Leik has published widely in the area of family and small groups. His recent book *Mathematical Sociology* was published in 1974.

DON MARTINDALE is Professor of Sociology at the University of Minnesota. His research interests include the history of sociological theory and the sociology of knowledge. He is most well known for the volume *The Nature and Types of Sociological Theory*. More recently, he has authored *The Problems of Values in Sociological Theory*, *Prominent Sociologists Since WW II*, and *The Romance of a Profession*.

MICHAEL K. MILLER is Assistant Professor of Rural Sociology at Cornell University. His major research interests include the sociology of health, policy modeling, and community service delivery systems.

Professor Miller's publications include articles in *Health and Social Behavior, Rural Sociology*, and *Quality and Quantity*.

GEORGE RITZER is Professor of Sociology at the University of Maryland at College Park. He has written numerous articles and books in the area of work and occupations and is currently working on a book that seeks to integrate sociology's multiple paradigms. Professor Ritzer's books include *Sociology: A Multiple Paradigm Science, Working: Conflict and Change*, and *An Occupation in Conflict*.

GIDEON SJOBERG is Professor of Sociology at the University of Texas at Austin. His major areas of interest are theory, bureaucracy and planning, and methodology. Professor Sjoberg has published widely in numerous journals and contributed many outstanding chapters to edited volumes. Professor Sjoberg's books include *The Preindustrial City* and *A Methodology for Social Research*.

WILLIAM E. SNIZEK is Associate Professor of Sociology at Virginia Polytechnic Institute and State University. In addition to his long-standing interest in metasociology, he has published widely in the sociology of work and occupations. Professor Snizek's articles have appeared in such journals as the *American Sociological Review, Rural Sociology, Social Forces, Sociology of Work and Occupations, Sociological Quarterly*, and *The American Sociologist.*

EDWARD TIRYAKIAN is Professor of Sociology at Duke University. His current research interests include sociological theory and the sociology of sociology. Among numerous other works, he is author of *Sociologism and Existentialism*. He also has edited *The Margin of the Visible, The Phenomenon of Sociology,* and is a coeditor with John C. McKinney of *Theoretical Sociology*.

TED R. VAUGHAN is Professor of Sociology at the University of Missouri at Columbia. His areas of interest include the sociology of science and the sociology of knowledge. Professor Vaughan has published articles in many journals, as well as contributing chapters to numerous books. At present he is collaborating with Gideon Sjoberg on a book dealing with the issue of ethics and human rights.

NORBERT WILEY is Associate Professor of Sociology at the University of Illinois at Urbana. His past research interests have included the areas of sociological theory and political sociology. More recently, his concern has been with the linkages between micro- and macro-social structure which, in turn, has led to an interest in phenomenology and social stratification. Professor Wiley has published in such journals as the *American Sociological Review* and *Social Problems*.